'Haenni and Drevon have done the impossible: they stuck with the Syrian tragedy long after others had shifted their attention, focused on Hayat Tahrir al Sham at a time when it was not yet fashionable, and enjoyed deep familiarity with Syria's new leaders as everyone else had to play catch up. The result is a gem, a superb, edifying and eye-opening account of the evolution of the jihadist movement and a definitive response to those who wonder whether Sharaa's conversion and HTS's deradicalisation are genuine or counterfeit. If any policymaker ever questions the utility of field work, you now have your answer: just give them a copy of *Transformed by the People*. They won't regret it.'

— Robert Malley, Yale University; former Middle East adviser to Presidents Clinton, Obama, and Biden; former CEO of the International Crisis Group; and author, with Hussein Agha, of the forthcoming *Tomorrow is Yesterday: Life, Death, and the Pursuit of Peace in Israel-Palestine*

'The authors have marshalled a tremendous amount of unique field research to develop a coherent, controversial, and ultimately convincing account of the pragmatic evolution of HTS.'

— Marc Lynch, Professor of Political Science and Director of Middle East Studies, The George Washington University, and author of *America's Middle East: The Ruination of a Region*

'*Transformed by the People* looks beyond the hysterics of the War on Terror and takes a serious historical view of the forces at play. Being the first westerners to reach out and connect with Hayat Tahrir al Sham and its leadership, Haenni and Drevon—in groundbreaking fieldwork—reveal the deeper processes behind al Sharaa's moderation. This work will stand as an essential guide for any future analysts that aim at real explanation over simple polemics.'

— Martin Smith, PBS Frontline correspondent who interviewed Ahmad al-Sharaa for his documentary, 'The Jihadist'.

'Haenni and Drevon have written a timely and original book that helps illuminate a critical issue: how and why the new leaders of Syria transformed from jihadists into pragmatists.'

— Peter Bergen, author of *The Rise and Fall of Osama bin Laden*

'Those curious about Syria, its recent history, and its new transitional government will find all the necessary information and food for thought in this book. The history and transformation of HTS are presented meticulously, insightfully, and analytically. Black and white are passé; it is the shades of grey that strengthen our understanding of this enigmatic and fascinating movement and its leaders. For those who need or want to engage with the new Syria politically, this book is essential.'

— Ambassador Monika Schmutz Kirgöz, Head of Middle East and North Africa, Federal Department of Foreign Affairs, Bern

'Rather than labelling HTS in the received terms of analysis as being "liberal", "secular", or even "realist", the authors argue that it represents a new and uncharted political experiment which moves beyond such categories but has not yet established its own.'

— Faisal Devji, Beit Professor of Global and Imperial History, University of Oxford.

'An extraordinary book that dissects a complex phenomenon in a provocative and original manner. It does not dwell on paradoxes but shows concretely how a jihadist leader can evolve into a responsible national politician without denying himself. It is a rare example analysis of political sociology based on in-depth fieldwork that manages to avoid value judgments and ideological polemics.'

— Olivier Roy, Professor at the European University Institute, and author of *The Crisis of Culture: Identity Politics and the Empire of Norms*

'*Transformed by the People* is a vital resource for understanding the remarkable journey of this formerly terrorist organisation into a major, and quite possibly stabilising, force not just in Syria but the entire Middle East.'

— Ambassador James F. Jeffrey, former US Special Representative for Syria Engagement and Special Envoy to the Global Coalition to Defeat ISIS

TRANSFORMED BY THE PEOPLE

PATRICK HAENNI & JEROME DREVON

Transformed by the People

Hayat Tahrir al-Sham's Road to Power in Syria

HURST & COMPANY, LONDON

First published in the United Kingdom in 2025 by
C. Hurst & Co. (Publishers) Ltd.,
New Wing, Somerset House, Strand, London, WC2R 1LA

© Patrick Haenni and Jerome Drevon, 2025

All rights reserved.

Distributed in the United States, Canada and Latin America
by Oxford University Press, 198 Madison Avenue, New York,
NY 10016, United States of America.

The right of Patrick Haenni and Jerome Drevon to be identified
as the authors of this publication is asserted by them in accordance
with the Copyright, Designs and Patents Act, 1988.

A Cataloguing-in-Publication data record for this book
is available from the British Library.

ISBN: 9781805264101

www.hurstpublishers.com

Printed and bound in Great Britain by Bell & Bain Ltd, Glasgow

This book is dedicated to Raefa Sami'a, who perished in the earthquake that struck the Turkey–Syria border on 6 February 2023.

Raefa neither adhered to nor expressed support for HTS. However, she embodied the emerging conservative revolutionary movement in Idlib. She was a revolutionary in both spirit and the sacrifice of her fallen brothers.

As a staunch opponent of the former Syrian regime, she engaged in ongoing dialogue with the international community. More importantly, she worked within her own society, advocating for women's political rights while upholding a conservative Islamic belief system. She also championed reconciliation among the various ideological currents within the Syrian opposition.

From her political perspective, Idlib's future depended on fostering social and ideological convergence between the Islamist groups dominating the region, the broader revolutionary movement, and society at large. This convergence was not merely the vision of an inclusive activist—it was a trajectory set in motion seven years prior, one that ultimately culminated in the liberation of Damascus.

CONTENTS

Acknowledgements ix

Introduction: A Revolutionary Outlook on
Ideological Realignments 1

1. The Foundational Matrix: Jabhat Al-Nusra's Evolution in an Uneasy Jihadi Mould 17

2. The Struggle for Dominance: HTS' hegemonic Ambitions in Syria's Opposition 47

3. Dismantling the Radical Past 71

4. Exiting Jihadism 97

5. Hollowing Out Salafism 115

6. The Thermidorian Opening to Sufism 141

7. Dhimmis No More, Citizens Not Yet: Otherness Recast in Secular Minority Terms 157

8. Flirting with the Silent Majority: HTS's Mainstream Turn 173

9. The 2024 Idlib Arab Spring: Deradicalisation as Power Politics 197

10. Respect the Martyrs But Don't Kill the Market!: Moralising a Nascent Public Sphere in Idlib 219

11. HTS's Silent Revolution: Why Deradicalisation Does Not Need Moderates and Why Intentions Do Not Matter 243

12. Ideological Recentring in an Age of Illiberalism	265
Epilogue: In Search of Itself: The Ambiguous Rise of Sunni Identity Politics	281
Notes	297
Index	319

ACKNOWLEDGEMENTS

This book is the result of regular visits to the stronghold of Hayat Tahrir al-Sham (HTS), as well as continuous interaction with individuals without whom it would never have been possible.

First and foremost, we acknowledge Walid Tamer—a staunch pro-revolution activist, anything but an Islamist—who, early on, became convinced of the need to support the evolving transformation of the new rulers of Damascus. He recognised this necessity even as they were still consolidating power in Idlib, facing both international stigma and vehement opposition from abroad.

This work also stems from extensive exchanges with leaders who once shaped Idlib and are now ruling Damascus. Our discussions with them not only contributed to the theoretical foundation of this book but, in some ways, may have even influenced the transformation we explore in these pages.

The credibility of this research would have been incomplete without the perspectives of the Syrian opposition abroad and activists who remained in the country. Many prefer to remain unnamed, yet their insights were essential in verifying, refining, and contextualising the information gathered through official meetings with movement representatives.

Finally, this book owes much to countless hours of discussions, WhatsApp exchanges, and critical debates with a group of researchers who have followed its theoretical development from the outset. We extend our deepest gratitude to Obayda Amer, Jean-François Bayart, Gilles Dorronsoro, Baudouin Dupret, Agnès Favier, Jean-Noël Ferrié, Olivier Fillieule, H. A. Hellyer, Stéphane Lacroix, Felix Legrand, Thomas Pierret, Arthur Quesnay, Laila al-Refaai and Olivier Roy. Through these exchanges, the analytical framework gradually evolved—from an initial reliance on Islamic studies to a more secular perspective, one that focuses on revolutionary

ACKNOWLEDGEMENTS

dynamics and pathways out of radicalism. We also warmly acknowledge Dareen Khalifa and Noah Bonsey, our 'partners in crime' during several field visits, which regularly sparked insightful policy-making conversations.

We wrote this book alongside our work, in our personal time and outside our professional duties. The views expressed reflect our individual analysis and responsibility, and do not represent the positions of our respective organisations in any way.

INTRODUCTION

A REVOLUTIONARY OUTLOOK ON IDEOLOGICAL REALIGNMENTS

In December 2024, Ahmad al-Sharaa (formerly Abu Muhammad al-Jolani) described to us what he called a "Blitzkrieg"—a rapid and unexpected offensive that took the world by surprise. A few days before, an alliance of groups led by Hayat Tahrir al-Sham (HTS)—formerly Jabhat al-Nusra, an al-Qaeda affiliate after its split from Islamic State—launched a sweeping military campaign against the Syrian regime of Bashar al-Assad. The alliance quickly advanced on Syria's largest city, Aleppo, capturing it within days.

This was a stunning turn of events. In late 2016, the armed opposition had lost control of Aleppo's suburbs, a moment widely seen as the end of its ambitions to challenge the regime. Yet now, the country's historical economic hub was firmly in its hands—months ahead of its most optimistic expectations. Murhaf Abu Qasra—HTS's military leader at the time and now Syria's Minister of Defence—confirmed a few weeks later that, although at the outset of the operation he did not anticipate the regime's collapse, the unexpected fall of Aleppo was a clear signal: the regime's days were over. Sensing the Assad regime's crippling weakness, HTS and its allies pushed further south, seizing Hama and Homs before reaching Damascus. On 8 December, after nearly fourteen years of brutal civil war that claimed the lives of hundreds of thousands of civilians and triggered a large-scale refugee crisis—Bashar al-Assad fled to Moscow. His regime had fallen.

Another surprise followed. Unlike the global backlash that accompanied Islamic State's capture of Mosul in Iraq in 2014—prompting an international coalition to launch large-scale military hostilities against the group—this time, the reaction was strikingly different. State representatives from across the world rushed to Damascus, eager to meet with Ahmad al-Sharaa, who now resided in the presidential palace, as well as his intelligence chief, Anas Khatab, and the foreign minister Asʿad al-Shaibani—Syria was once again at the centre of international politics.

The swift victory has military explanations. Over the past few years, the armed opposition—under the leadership of HTS—had restructured its military forces, enhanced command and control, and improved discipline and training, significantly increasing its combat effectiveness. On the other side, the "Blitzkrieg" advanced against a regime that had, over the years, actively dismantled the state, reducing it to a fragmented network of militias propping up Assad's narco-state. Sustained by foreign backers, the regime had become increasingly dependent on the regional export of the amphetamine Captagon. This regime-induced state collapse severely weakened the army, leaving it incapable of mounting an effective defence in the final offensive. Ultimately, even the regime's own supporters could no longer provide effective assistance. Russia had committed nearly all its military resources to its own war in Ukraine, while Iran and its allies—chiefly Lebanese Hizbullah—faced repeated attacks in Syria itself, where Israel targeted much of their infrastructure. Hizbullah also suffered major losses in Lebanon, including the elimination of most of its top leaders. A convergence of disorganisation, low morale, operational weaknesses, lack of preparation, international disengagement, and dwindling resources ultimately facilitated the takeover of Damascus—*Fath al-Sham* in Arabic—the singular objective and political direction of Ahmad al-Sharaa for more than a decade.

However, the 8 December 2024 victory was driven by far more than military strategy alone: its foundations lay in the profound ideological transformation HTS underwent in recent years—one that enabled it to forge critical alliances, secure some local legitimacy, and cultivate essential international ties. This evolution is not merely a backdrop to the victory. It is its main enabler and the very subject of this book.

INTRODUCTION

A silent revolution: On deradicalisation and few other pivotal concepts

The transformation of HTS—a former jihadi group and once al-Qaeda's most powerful affiliate—took place in its stronghold of Idlib, a rural province in northwestern Syria, between 2016 and 2024. This development was one of *deradicalisation*, which, we argue, happened along four main axes.

First, HTS rejected jihadism—an ideological social movement composed of various groups, often affiliated with al-Qaeda and Islamic State, that reject Muslim regimes who fail to implement their interpretation of Islamic law and, often, fight the West too. HTS is the first group previously affiliated with both Islamic State and al-Qaeda that publicly renounced both global organisations before forbidding them from operating in its territory, and clamping down on their leaders and commanders. We will see that, beyond severing formal ties, HTS has also actively worked to diminish the influence of global jihadi ideologues among its own rank and file and the foreign fighters that remained in Syria.

Second, after severing ties with al-Qaeda, HTS distanced itself from Salafism—an approach to Islam that seeks to radically reshape Muslim religious practices and beliefs and govern Muslims according to its own reading of Islamic law. Instead, HTS gradually accepted a degree of *social inertia*, which we define as the tendency of social structures, cultural norms, and religious practices to resist rapid or forced change, rather than attempting to fully and coercively impose a hardline Islamist lifestyle that the population did not want.

Third, HTS strategically capitalised on the support of the silent majority, outmanoeuvring the remaining Islamist hardliners in northwest Syria. This shift enabled, for example, the reintegration of traditional Islamic jurisprudence and popular Islamic practices—including, to some extent, Sufism—into the religious and social fabric.

Fourth, the movement gradually adapted itself in response to its local social and religious environment. This process of *relocalisation* marked not only a disengagement from global jihad but also a reconnection to local dynamics and a willingness to operate within the mainstream religious views that society deems socially legitimate. In other words, the former al-Qaeda franchise allowed itself to be "transformed by the people".

As profound and, as we will see, sustainable as it was even before the takeover of Damascus, HTS's transformation remains a *silent revolution*, one absent a coherent narrative to account for its evolution: the group never formally articulated or grounded its transformation in explicit or public doctrinal revisions. HTS's deradicalisation contrasts sharply with the paths taken by other jihadis in Egypt or Libya, where former militants published public doctrinal revisions after failing to achieve their objectives, which had left them weakened, with most of their leaders and members in prison.[1] HTS's ideological shift conversely occurred without a doctrinal overhaul and from a position of strength. The group embarked on its own deradicalisation journey after solidifying its dominance over rival armed factions, all the while preserving its ambitions for a future armed takeover of Damascus.

HTS's *deradicalisation*, *ideological realignment*, or *mainstreamisation*—terms we use interchangeably throughout this book—was, in its early stage, largely unintended. Nor was it a deliberate shift that HTS had initially planned, was driven by, or was relying on. Rather, its new ideological outlook was the result of an adaptation to a set of external and internal pressures on the group. Externally, HTS has had to navigate its relationships with foreign states, particularly Turkey, as it consolidated control over northwest Syria, while also seeking to mend ties with Western countries in the context of their own opposition to Iran and Russia. Internally, too weak or uninterested to impose its will by force, HTS had to carefully balance its approach—managing a population that did not accept its ideological views while also avoiding a backlash and challenges from hardliners.

Silent but … political, irrevocable, oriented and stable

We identify four key features that underpin HTS's ideological transformation.

HTS's transformation is *politically driven*. Despite the movement's ideological roots—its jihadi genealogy, foundational ties to Salafism, and revolutionary ethos—we argue that political practice, rather than ideology, was the primary driver of transformation. HTS did

INTRODUCTION

not evolve as a result of a doctrinal shift, but rather by adapting to political realities, which in turn reshaped its ideological framework. This challenges the common assumption that jihadis—or any ideological group—blindly follow their doctrines. While ideology matters and influences political choices, it does not simply dictate them; rather, it is moulded, refined, and at times redefined through political action.

HTS's transformation seems *irrevocable*. We argue that beyond a certain threshold, a series of tactical accommodations accumulates into a deeper, strategic transformation—one that is enduring and reaches a point of no return. This 'ratchet effect,' which we will specifically identify in HTS's trajectory, renders the question of intentions largely irrelevant. Whether its shifts were motivated by pure opportunism or by genuine ideological reconsideration, the outcome remains the same: for structural reasons we will explore, HTS's transformation appeared irreversible on the eve of the takeover of Syria.

The transformation is *oriented* and has a *strategic compass*. While the prevailing narrative on HTS—emphasising the tactical nature of many of its decisions—has merit, the common framing of these choices as mere opportunism or pragmatism is analytically limiting and, at times, misleading. An opportunist navigates tactically, shifting direction at will. HTS, however, did not simply adapt on a whim. Although HTS has not authored any formal doctrinal revision, its evolution has followed a clear and consistent political trajectory rather than a directionless drift. The group did not navigate blindly or oscillate between positions; instead, its transformation unfolded along two distinct paths. The first is *relocalisation*. As previously discussed, this is not merely a process of negation, such as breaking ties with al-Qaeda or renouncing global jihad; it also represents a positive dynamic of reconnection, shaped by sustained interaction with the movement's local environment. We describe this as the *revenge of society* or the *inertia of the social* to capture how the demands, constraints, and realities of the local context reshaped HTS's nature. The second course is *deradicalisation* as a sustained adaptation to socio-religious realities, geopolitical constraints, and internal power struggles—all of which transformed the group's trajectory and political outlook.

TRANSFORMED BY THE PEOPLE

The movement had reached a state of stability—what could be considered a *doctrinal endgame* that is neither liberal, democratic or moderate before the takeover of Damascus in 2024. This endgame was framed by the opportunities and limitations of HTS's local environment in Idlib. HTS deradicalised through a transition from the ideological margins to a position of "social orthodoxy", and became *mainstream*, positioning itself within the boundaries of a broadly socially accepted religious worldview. From this perspective, radicalisation and deradicalisation are not absolute but relative. It is the conservative Sunni Muslim and revolutionary landscape of Idlib governorate in northwest Syria that defined, for HTS, the boundaries of ideological legitimacy and what is "acceptable". These views might still not be shared by Muslims elsewhere, let alone non-Muslims: shifting toward the mainstream does not equate to moderation.

Framing the change: Idlib as a Thermidorian situation

Our focus is on HTS as it is—first and foremost, a political actor. This means that when analysing the movement's relationship with religion and ideology, we avoid a text-centred or doctrine-focused approach that is common in studies of jihadi groups. We find that doctrine played a limited role throughout its transformation so our priority is to understand HTS through its social and political practices rather than through theological discourse (which is largely absent). For this reason, we also do not engage in a deep exploration of Muslim history or classical Islamic thought, whether on Salafism—modern or medieval—or its interactions with other Islamic traditions. We address these aspects only insofar as they provide analytical insight into HTS. Instead, we emphasise HTS's own actions, as perceived by a range of actors both within and outside the movement. We also include a comparative perspective, but in a "de-orientalised" manner: we look beyond the framework of political Islam to examine movements and parties outside the Muslim world that have undergone similar processes of mainstreamisation, deradicalisation or centrist ideological realignment.

Rather than anchoring this book purely in geographical context, we adopt a thematic approach, drawing insights from historical

INTRODUCTION

parallels—particularly the trajectory of the French Revolution, which serves as our methodological compass for the evolution of HTS. Our point of reference is revolutionary—in the political sense. As outlined earlier, we argue that HTS's transformation is best understood through its interactions with society and its efforts to position itself within both regional and international spheres, mostly Turkey and the West. However, this alone does not fully explain why HTS has engaged in a transactional relationship with its local social environment on the one hand, and with regional and international actors on the other. The key to this lies in HTS's *Thermidorian trajectory*—a path that is both constraining and self-transformative in the historical context of the French Revolution. Our focus, therefore, is on the moments when revolution subsides, or more precisely, when actors reposition themselves as the vision of radical transformation—the "great night"—fades from immediate relevance.

In France and in Syria, as in other revolutionary contexts, Thermidor marked the moment when the revolution confronted political reality, forced to compromise on its initial ideals and promises. It was the point at which revolutionary leaders rediscovered the inertia of society, the necessity of political negotiation, and the gap between means and ends. Yet, Thermidor was not the end of the revolution in both France and Syria. The key figures of this phase remained politically loyal to its core ambitions, and the revolution continued to shape their expectations and aspirations. As Jean-François Bayart reminds us, "Thermidor does not seek to turn the page on the revolution. It remains faithful to it, if only through war".[2] This challenges the common notion of Thermidor as a moment of moderation, arguing instead that it often manifests through military adventurism and expansionist ambitions. In the case of HTS, Ahmad al-Sharaa never abandoned the goal of either expanding towards opposition controlled areas or seizing Damascus. It was this Thermidorian resilience—a commitment to revolutionary objectives despite tactical adaptations—that ultimately drove the final, victorious assault on Bashar al-Assad's collapsing regime in December 2024.

Many concepts from the French Revolution's Thermidorian phase are applicable to HTS's transformation, not only in terms of historical parallels but also to understand the strategic approach that the group adopted. Concepts such as the *inertia of the social*—which describes how revolutionary movements must adapt their worldview to society's core beliefs—highlight the fundamental challenge of reconciling ideology with social realities. This struggle is central to the Thermidorian moment, where movements are forced to confront the limits of their transformative ambitions.

Closely related is the concept of the *revenge of society*, which underscores that society is not a passive or malleable entity easily reshaped by those in power. Instead, it often pushes back, ultimately influencing and transforming the very actors who sought to change it. This dynamic resonates with HTS's evolution, particularly given the Salafi lineage of Jabhat al-Nusra and then HTS.

However, this societal feedback on HTS's core beliefs was not simply imposed upon the group. Rather, it was a deliberate and strategic choice by its leadership. This *Thermidorian strategy* revolves around aligning with the silent majority to neutralise internal opposition from the vocal minority of hardline activists still resistant to change. By banking on broad social legitimacy, HTS was able to consolidate its transformation while marginalising those within its ranks who sought to resist it.

The reflections in this book are therefore less rooted in the studies of other jihadis and more in a historical sociology of politics. This approach examines the trajectories of revolutionary actors when revolutions follow a Thermidorian course after early ideological fervor abates. While acknowledging intellectual influences is customary, this book also owes much to our methodological experimentation. Over the years, we drew freely on the insights of colleagues and friends, as well as on their own interpretations, including the revival of concepts such as *negative solidarity*, the *identity trap*, *relocation* and *deradicalisation* dynamics. These terms are not firmly rooted in established academic or theoretical traditions but represent our attempts to interpret ongoing processes. This sense of improvisation, while unorthodox, is one we hope proves as constructive and insightful as possible.

This book presents a coherent analysis of HTS's silent revolution—its centrist ideological realignment within its stronghold in Idlib, a transformation that laid the groundwork for

INTRODUCTION

a second, far more dramatic upheaval: the conquest of Damascus. This book draws on extensive field research in Idlib during which we engaged directly with HTS itself, its affiliated government but also activists, civilians, supporters, opponents, dissidents, foreign organisations, and diplomats since 2019.

While global interest in Syria had waned by 2024, this book is now crucial, as HTS represents a unique case—a group still designated as a terrorist organisation when we wrote this book, now governing a state too strategically significant to be ignored at the heart of the Middle East. Its rule will have far-reaching consequences for both the region and the West. Understanding this development is not just an intellectual necessity—it has become a political imperative for those who, willingly or not, will have to engage with the new rulers in Damascus.

Capturing opportunities, mitigating bias and a cautious political optimism

Scepticism persists regarding HTS's transformation. Many—including in the former Syrian opposition to Assad's regime—have long believed that the group still espouses radical views and seeks to impose a strictly authoritarian form of Islamic governance. They view any apparent change or public claims as tactical manoeuvres, superficial alterations, or mere political posturing toward the West. Sceptics argue that the purported transformations may be more symbolic than substantive, with continuity in its core principles taking precedence. Diplomatic circles, constrained by their difficulty in directly assessing the situation and interacting with the group due to their own terrorist designations prior to 2025, have also long inadvertently perpetuated the prevailing narrative largely due to the absence of tangible benefits in challenging it.

For years, HTS—and previously Jabhat al-Nusra—remained a largely inaccessible political entity, before we began engaging directly with its leaders. The group initially disseminated its earliest communiqués through obscure jihadi forums. In the next few years, when Ahmad al-Sharaa started to appear on Al Jazeera and Syrian TV channels, he kept his face concealed. It was only in 2016, as the group formally broke from al-Qaeda, that al-Sharaa revealed himself publicly. The movement then began steering toward the

West, adopting a more centrist as our first interactions began. The first contacts occurred on the demand of its leadership, not from our own initiative. HTS sought intermediaries to convey its new positions to Western audiences, to shed its international terrorist designation and, for some within the group to pursue strategic alignment with the West.

The fact that our initial contacts with the movement started from above, with the leadership, at its request, brought both advantages and challenges. HTS regarded us as credible due to our academic work on jihadism (Jerome) and on political Islam (Patrick). This was crucial, as it granted access to the highest echelons of leadership—essentially the inner circle of Ahmad al-Sharaa—which included religious scholars, political figures, and key military leaders (though not the internal security leadership) and ultimately with al-Sharaa himself. Over more than five years, we developed with them a sustained, regular, in-depth dialogue on issues ranging from geostrategy to political theology, religious minorities, and military dynamics. We therefore had direct access to the way in which HTS leaders conceived and discussed their own transformation.

Without this dialogue, we could not have fully understood the evolution of their perceptions or the challenges it created, both internally and within Idlib. These interactions challenged the misconception that HTS's actions followed a preordained strategic plan from the outset, rather than a complex, winding journey also marked by ad hoc tactical political decisions. The resulting bias of this initial engagement is both subjective—stemming from the affinity that can develop through sustained engagement with a social or political actor—and objective, as it limits our understanding to what the movement has been willing to reveal.

To address this twofold bias, we complemented our engagement with HTS's leadership and the meetings approved by them—whether initiated by us or at their own suggestion—by significantly expanding our independent interactions with other actors in Idlib. These included contacts we had established during our initial visits in northwest Syria between 2012 and 2013: civil society associations, activists from the 2011 revolution, political groups, local researchers, intellectuals, dissident religious figures, businesspeople, and women activists still active on the ground. We also discussed with leaders and

INTRODUCTION

commanders of other Islamist armed groups or Free Syrian Army affiliated groups, whether allied with, opposed to, or defeated by HTS, and dissidents from HTS and its predecessor, Jabhat al-Nusra. Outside Syria, we have also maintained dialogue with representatives of the opposition, namely the Syrian Opposition Coalition and the Syrian Interim Government.

Our engagement with the opposition outside the country was nonetheless limited, primarily because their position—living abroad and in political rivalry with HTS—offered limited analytical value. Focused on competing for political representation of the opposition, some actors were also more hesitant to acknowledge changes within HTS to foreign researchers, whom they perceived as serving a legitimation agenda. While these interactions provided some insight into the dynamics of rivalry within the opposition, they contributed little to our primary objective: understanding the transformations of HTS and, through them, the emergence of a new political identity.

In the end, while we did engage with opponents of HTS—within a highly polarised Syrian context, including among the opposition, where dialogue is often equated with complicity—we undoubtedly balanced differing perspectives though blind spots remain. Key aspects, such as the functioning of the official justice system and, even more so, the role of judgments issued by the security forces—integral components of the security apparatus—remain opaque to us. The opacity surrounding the darker aspects of the movement—specifically its practices of coercion—is partly due to challenges in gaining access. It also emanates from a cognitive bias in our approach: our focus is on the movement's evolving relationship with the politico-religious sphere, given its jihadi lineage. Consequently, practices of discipline are not central to our analysis: political violence and human rights are less standalone subjects and more analytical tools we use to reveal—akin to a photographic developer—the broader transformations underway.

From this perspective, our cognitive bias can have legitimising effects in two ways: first, by not placing the movement's darker aspects at the centre of the analysis, even though we acknowledge them and dedicate two chapters to the question of authoritarianism in Idlib to illustrate how transformations in the movement's relationship with religion affect patterns of control and coercion. And second, by focusing on deradicalisation and on the tangible process of a centrist ideological realignment or "mainstreaming", our work can contribute to de-demonising a movement—or parts of it—that, at points in its recent history, embraced jihadi ideas and used violence accordingly.

This introduces an inherently political dimension to the book. At the same time, and no less politically, the very process of writing it—through our engagement with the movement—might have, in a modest manner, contributed to HTS's own reflections and its evolving understanding of the world beyond Idlib, opening new avenues for change. HTS' trajectory could chart a potential exit from global jihad. It is not a blueprint for Preventing Violent Extremism but rather a foundation for cautious, rigorous political optimism.

Navigating the book

Our analysis of HTS's evolution is not a linear historical narrative. Instead, we use the early days of its predecessor, Jabhat al-Nusra, in Chapter 1 as a reference point to better understand the movement's subsequent path. In this chapter, we highlight the persistent tensions between its pragmatic actions on the ground and its more hardline ideological convictions. We also examine how the group adapted to the evolving dynamics of the conflict, including the intervention of foreign actors—such as Western countries—interactions with other groups, including Islamic State, as well as other allies and opponents and the pressures that led Jabhat al-Nusra to renounce its ties to al-Qaeda.

The next two chapters examine how HTS leveraged governance to assert control over northwest Syria and restructure itself. Chapter 2 analyses HTS's consolidation of power over other components of the armed opposition, from more mainstream factions to the global jihadis it chose to confront in northwest Syria. Then, in Chapter 3, we argue that governance played a key role in HTS's deradicalisation by imposing an act of delegation to other actors, adapting to Turkish strategic interests including Turkey's own political process with Russia. We also argue that governance not only enabled but also

INTRODUCTION

compelled HTS to reform its internal power structures and elevate a new generation of technocrats within the organisation.

Chapters 4 and 5 explore how HTS distanced itself from both jihadism and Salafism. In Chapter 4, we demonstrate that after severing ties with al-Qaeda, HTS further marginalised its own religious hardliners through an institutionalisation process. This strategy served as a means of containing internal discourse while partially mainstreaming militant culture. In Chapter 5, we analyse how HTS moved away from Salafism and redefined the role of Islam in governance. Rather than pursuing the goal of Islamising society, it instead adopted an approach based on Shariʿa politics (or "Islamic Law-guided public policy", *al-siyasat al-sharʿiyya*) to legitimise its rule and exert control over religious edicts.

In Chapters 6 and 7, we examine HTS's relationships with the Muslim mainstream as well as its interactions with religious minorities. We argue that in both cases, HTS's pursuit of hegemony and its Thermidorian approach to the revolution—meaning a phase of consolidation and moderation following a radical period—shaped its increasing, albeit within limits, openness. In Chapter 6, we show how HTS sought to engage with Sufis, as a strategic positioning relying on silent majorities with non-threatening Muslim groups acting as a counterweight to Salafi populists. In Chapter 7, we demonstrate that, despite initial tensions with religious minorities, HTS's outreach to them ultimately served its broader ambition of positioning itself as the hegemonic force within the Syrian opposition, reinforcing its image as a nationwide state-seeking actor.

In Chapters 8, 9 and 10, we examine HTS's approach to policing morality in Idlib and its enduring authoritarianism. In Chapter 8, we analyse how HTS's authoritarianism evolved, charting its strategic re-adoption and monopolisation of the revolution. Additionally, we explore how the group gradually reduced its use of force against activists—partly as a calculated shift, but also as activists increasingly internalised HTS's dominance. Chapter 9 examines the wave of protests against HTS in 2024 and the group's response, including its strategies for managing public opposition. We analyse the reforms that HTS proposed, such as controlled elections, which echo the practices of other semi-authoritarian regimes in the region. We show in Chapter 10 that, as part of its transformation, HTS gradually abandoned the strict enforcement of religious regulations and even halted proposals from a growing populist movement—backed by influential local actors in Idlib—to impose moral policing. This decision was driven by the need to sustain a growing consumerist sector and avoid an international backlash. Instead, HTS navigated between the more rigid religious views held by various actors and the opposition of segments of the population resistant to such measures. The management of the enforcement of Islamic norms constituted a delicate balancing act, one that was not merely doctrinal but explicitly political in nature. This ebb and flow—which we define as "top-down deradicalisation" coupled with "bottom-up re-radicalisation"—only became even more pronounced following the takeover of Damascus in 2024.

Chapter 11 takes a more ontological approach, exploring the "ideological endgame" of the movement and attempting to define HTS's current identity. However, as we will see, it is easier to articulate what HTS no longer represents than to clearly define what it has become. From this perspective, we argue that examining the movement's transformation offers far greater insight than trying to determine its ultimate identity or categorise it within existing typologies of contemporary Islamic politics.

Thus, Chapter 12 offers a slightly iconoclastic conclusion, drawing bold comparative observations: unlike jihadi groups that deradicalised through ideological shifts during periods of weakness, HTS deradicalised through pragmatic actions while in a position of strength. As a result, comparing HTS to its ideological counterparts is less relevant than drawing parallels with far-right parties in the West, which have followed a similar trajectory of mainstreamisation. This chapter concludes the book by highlighting lessons learned from centrist ideological realignments and examining analogous paths taken by far-right movements in the West, particularly in France and Italy.

While HTS has significantly distanced itself from the radicalism of its early days, its centrist ideological realignment has now reached its final stage, making further shifts before the 2024 takeover of Damascus unlikely; Idlib is not an incubator for liberal, gender-sensitive, or democratic interpretations of Islam. It is

INTRODUCTION

precisely because this transformation culminated in the takeover of Damascus and now appears largely complete that documenting and understanding it in this book is both timely, analytically vital, and politically imperative.

1

THE FOUNDATIONAL MATRIX
JABHAT AL-NUSRA'S EVOLUTION IN AN UNEASY JIHADI MOULD

No transformation can be fully understood without first establishing a clear grasp of its point of origin, its foundational matrix. Jabhat al-Nusra's early matrix featured several key characteristics that shaped the group's trajectory. From its inception, the group openly embraced jihadi Salafism as its ideological foundation, which reinforced its legitimacy within domestic and international jihadi circles. It accordingly strategically aligned with al-Qaeda—not merely out of ideological affinity, but as a calculated act of radical pragmatism that allowed it to navigate a highly competitive militant landscape, particularly in response to the rise of Islamic State. Jabhat al-Nusra also developed monopolistic tendencies in response to factional competition as it strived to consolidate and expand its control over its own sphere of influence.

This chapter discusses several important developments in the history of Jabhat al-Nusra to better understand how the group started before HTS's subsequent transformation. Since Jabhat al-Nusra existed for only five years compared to HTS's eight years of existence, this analysis does not seek to cover every detail already widely documented elsewhere.[1] Instead, this retrospective overview explores the group's interactions with Islamic State in Iraq (ISI, which then became Islamic State in Iraq and Sham [ISIS] in 2013 and Islamic State [IS] in 2024; this text uses whichever acronym is relevant to the time period in question) and later al-Qaeda, other armed groups in Syria, as much as its changing tactical decisions on the ground including its involvement in governance. Understanding how Jabhat al-Nusra and later HTS engaged with civilian populations during this period is vital as they provide the context for comprehending HTS's subsequent trajectory.

Jabhat al-Nusra garnered international attention for its ties to global jihad and prominence in the Syrian conflict. The group is the only organisation that successively affiliated with ISIS and then al-Qaeda before renouncing both organisations and clamping down on their members in Syria. Throughout the entire course of the conflict, Jabhat al-Nusra's visibility also peaked due to its role as one of the most prominent actors of the Syrian armed opposition, leading many battles, factional coalitions, and attracting attention and concern from various states, including the US, European countries and Russia. The US notably targeted many of its leaders over the years in drone strikes, including leaders of so-called al-Qaeda central who had travelled to Syria, though the US never targeted its leader Ahmad al-Sharaa himself.

The transformation of Jabhat al-Nusra into HTS largely reflects the evolution of the Syrian conflict. Initially formed by a Syrian commander of ISI—the predecessor of ISIS and then IS—based in Iraq, Ahmad al-Sharaa, Jabhat al-Nusra reached prominence in the Syrian armed opposition before rejecting ISIS in 2013, publicly aligning with al-Qaeda, and later breaking ties with al-Zawahiri's organisation in 2016. HTS emerged in 2017 as an alliance of several groups active in the armed opposition to the Syrian regime, though most of them later defected. HTS, despite growing out of Jabhat al-Nusra, differed from the latter due to its new nature as an organisation governing millions of civilians in northwest Syria, which posed a unique set of challenges pertaining to how to interact with other armed groups, states, and civilians before the takeover of Damascus in 2024. This chapter's analysis of Jabhat al-Nusra's early days hence helps to better understand how much HTS transformed from its predecessor's early days, including the remaining legacy of the group's past as much as key points of rupture.

The five years of Jabhat al-Nusra's existence between 2011 and 2016 highlight persistent tensions between its pragmatic actions on the ground and its more hardline ideological convictions. Seeking to distinguish itself from its parent organisation, the Islamic State of

Iraq (ISI), Jabhat al-Nusra emphasised local engagement as it started to collaborate with other factions and adopt a more lenient approach toward civilians. Still, despite its split with then ISIS—rooted in leadership and strategic disagreements (which we will explore in greater detail later on)—Jabhat al-Nusra maintained an ambiguous stance on global jihad. While it publicly framed its fight as against the regime only and resisted any attempt to launch jihad outside Syria, it upheld ideological ties to global jihad in its propaganda—which legitimised global jihadi narratives—and in the inclusion of high level al-Qaeda commanders and leaders within its ranks.

A "front of support" that brought jihad to the Syrian revolution

Much research has been published on the formation and early years of Jabhat al-Nusra, but there are still significant misconceptions that need clarification.[2] Too much emphasis on the role of ISIS and al-Qaeda on the group's early choices undermines Jabhat al-Nusra's autonomy and cannot fully account for the group's decisions. This choice tends to overstate the group's strategic long-term planning, rather than viewing it as a political actor merely adapting to the changing necessities of the war. This is a common bias of existing research on jihadis, which consider them as long-term planners with a clear understanding of how their strategies will unfold in the future while, in reality, most of their decisions are reactive, short-term attempts to navigate immediate challenges and ensure their survival. Reviewing Jabhat al-Nusra's early roots and changing political approach is therefore essential to understand how the group adapted to new challenges during its first five years of existence, and its impact on HTS's subsequent development.

Jabhat al-Nusra's founding moment occurred during the 2011 uprisings often referred to as the Arab Spring, when a wave of popular movements destabilised several Arab countries, starting with Tunisia, Libya, and Egypt. Popular demonstrations in Tunisia and Egypt successfully provoked an immediate—though not lasting—political change while, in Libya, violent repression encouraged the militarisation of the opposition movement. As the uprising spread to Syria in 2011, the militarisation of the popular revolt that started to spread in Syria's main cities was the most likely course of action.

The Syrian regime, monopolised by the Baath Party, family and business networks, and the army and security services controlled by Alawi officers could not simply call for a new constitution followed by the election of a new leader. There was no relatively autonomous centre of power akin to the Egyptian or Tunisian army that could force the hands of the regime. Besides, the regime's allies in Iran and Russia were never going to pressure Assad to open up as Western countries ultimately did in Tunisia and Egypt. A peaceful transition of power was virtually impossible, leaving the militarisation of both the regime's response and the opposition as the most foreseeable outcomes in the absence of non-violent alternatives.

Jabhat al-Nusra was the brainchild of its leader, Ahmad al-Sharaa. Al-Sharaa, a mid-level Syrian commander of ISIS's predecessor, previously travelled to Iraq after the US invasion in 2003 before joining the Iraqi insurgency in 2005 when he was a young adult. Over the next few years, he indirectly integrated the ranks of what would become the Islamic State in Iraq (ISI) in 2006 as the local group he joined in Mosul, Sarayat al-Mujahideen, merged with the latter organisation during the insurgency.[3] Ahmad al-Sharaa was imprisoned for five years, which means that he spent most of his time in Iraq in prison rather than on the battlefield. It also means that al-Sharaa spent little to no time fighting, as he was arrested shortly after arriving in Iraq—well before the sectarian phase of the conflict began in 2006. He was held in the notorious Abu Ghraib and Bucca prisons under American control, where many ISIS leaders were detained and subsequently formed their strategies for expanding the group after 2012.

There is little detailed information about Ahmad al-Sharaa's time in prison though he and his opponents seem to agree that his views were already at odds with those of Islamic State. Al-Sharaa himself recalled in an interview that:

> In 2003 when the war in Iraq started there was strong popular sentiment in the region against the US invasion. Our thinking was simple, and we went to fight there. We weren't as aware as we are today. We were later taken by surprise by the extreme ideology that emerged in prisons in Iraq, the culture of extremism" [*ghulu*].[4]

This is not surprising, as many newcomers to the Iraqi insurgency joined as sympathisers in a fight against foreign occupation, often without fully grasping the ideological foundations of the insurgency that was taking shape. While it is convenient for him to say that now, as he is reaching out to Western countries, a letter from Abu Muhammad al-Adnani, one of the main ISIS leaders, perhaps the number three of the organisation back then, sheds similar light on some differences between Ahmad al-Sharaa and the group in prison.[5] Al-Adnani noted in a 2011 letter to the al-Qaeda leadership in Afghanistan that, though al-Sharaa had good manners, there were important disagreements with him already in the 2000s, particularly regarding the excommunication of the "supporters of the tyrants" (*ansar al-tawaghit*, which jihadis use to denounce Muslims who work for Muslim regimes not implementing their conception of Islamic law) and members of parliament. In other words, al-Sharaa already opposed the unconditional excommunication that ISI advocated while in prison. Adnani even added that three members of ISI's consultative council opposed al-Sharaa's leadership of Jabhat al-Nusra for this very reason. An article in *The Economist* mentions that a Syrian fighter who was with him in Iraq claimed that, at the time, al-Sharaa had threatened to kill anyone who endangered the Yazidi religious community—the same group that IS would later enslave following its formal split from Jabhat al-Nusra.[6] For Saleh al-Hamawi, who co-founded Jabhat al-Nusra before leaving in 2015 in opposition to some of its policies:

> Al-Sharaa held positions that diverged from ISIS even during his time in Iraq on a range of issues. Even in Syria, he supported welcoming Ash'ari [i.e. non salafi] members into Jabhat al-Nusra, though not in leadership roles—a stance I opposed at the time. He was also against targeting civilian markets and similar acts of indiscriminate violence.[7]

According to information from both al-Sharaa and his opponents in ISI, al-Sharaa played a dominant role in building Jabhat al-Nusra. Observing the escalating conflict in Syria, al-Sharaa proposed to move there and fight against the regime. Though al-Sharaa was not a high-ranking member, it's worth noting that ISI had by then become a relatively small organisation, having lost much of its leadership.

Al-Sharaa was reportedly trusted by one of the remaining leaders, which likely explains why he was chosen. As he was still a member of the group, he could not simply travel to Syria. Instead, he raised this issue internally, and ISI leaders asked him to write a report about it.[8] In retrospect, al-Sharaa argued that he presented the Syrian conflict as different from the one in Iraq; it was a revolution, not a fight against foreign occupation. This required nurturing different ties with the population and avoiding the violations that ISI committed, which had alienated many civilians but also Iraqi tribes, as ISI itself acknowledged in its own internal documents such as its 2010 *Strategic Plan*. Still, al-Sharaa and ISI later disagreed about the level of support that the Iraqi group provided. At the time of Nusra's creation, ISI was significantly weakened, with up to 90% of its leaders killed. ISI leaders later claimed that, despite these losses in Iraq, they did much to support Jabhat al-Nusra in men and weapons, which weakened their own war though al-Sharaa claimed that very little money and weapons were actually provided. Al-Sharaa rather insisted that he "asked for 100 men but only six came, in addition to 50,000$ to 60,000$ a month for six to seven months".[9]

This is crucial for understanding the group, as they suggest that, from the beginning, al-Sharaa—not ISI, let alone al-Qaeda—initiated the formation of Jabhat al-Nusra. This contradicts common arguments that al-Qaeda benefited from the Arab uprisings to expand while concealing itself to avoid scrutiny and pursue a long-term agenda while, in reality, al-Qaeda had little clue about Jabhat al-Nusra's early days, which it had to learn from a limited number of covert letters that ISI sent from Iraq. Even ISI was not fully in control from the outset. The Iraqi group merely approved the project proposed by one of their commanders without having the means to impose its views on him while he was in Syria, unwittingly granting him significant autonomy to act as he saw fit under the circumstances.

Very quickly, tensions arose between Ahmad al-Sharaa and ISI, despite Jabhat al-Nusra technically being under ISI's authority. The expansion of Jabhat al-Nusra in Syria and its early successes proved difficult for the Iraqis to control. A succession of letters from Abu Bakr al-Baghdadi, his deputy Abu Sib also known as Abu Ali al-

THE FOUNDATIONAL MATRIX

Anbari, and Abu Muhammad al-Adnani, the group's spokesperson, to al-Qaeda leaders in Afghanistan exposed escalating complaints about Ahmad al-Sharaa's behaviour.[10] Baghdadi complained to al-Qaeda central that Ahmad al-Sharaa did not adhere to their plans and made independent decisions, citing communication difficulties and Ahmad al-Sharaa's proximity to the events in Syria—the same arguments that al-Sharaa later used against al-Qaeda. ISI leaders also criticised Ahmad al-Sharaa for not being strict enough in recruitment, even accepting the allegiance of individuals who participated in political meetings in Istanbul. Worse still, perhaps for ISI, the group accused al-Sharaa of speaking about the creation of a political bureau by the group, which the Iraqi group and jihadis consider as amount to heresy since they assimilate politics and democracy. The letters revealed ISI's early fears of a split, prompting them to send al-Adnani, who would later direct IS's foreign attacks in Europe, on a scoping mission. Ahmad al-Sharaa was hesitant and unwilling to allow the Iraqis an opportunity to evaluate his leadership. He relegated al-Adnani to a subsidiary mission of welcoming foreign fighters in the north before dismissing him altogether and sending him back to Iraq, according to al-Adnani himself.

There were real strategic differences with ISI too. Initially, Jabhat al-Nusra was more lenient toward civilians, and many actors within the Syrian opposition expressed some sympathy to the group for that reason. This contrasted sharply with their views a few years later, when they blamed Jabhat al-Nusra for dismantling other armed opposition groups. Ahmad al-Sharaa mentioned that he refused specific orders from ISI, such as orchestrating suicide attacks against civilian communities reminiscent of those in Iraq, and, more importantly, he insisted that he refrained from attacking the opposition in Istanbul as ISI wanted.[11] According to Saleh al-Hamawi:

> From the outset, al-Sharaa had a strained relationship with Abu Bakr al-Baghdadi. At one point, al-Baghdadi sent six of his lieutenants to persuade al-Sharaa to adopt his approach: sectarianism and global jihad. Al-Baghdadi wanted Jabhat al-Nusra to carry out attacks against Shia populations and align with his vision of global jihad. However, al-Sharaa consistently rejected the idea of

foreign operations and attacks on civilians based on their religious affiliation, whether they were Shia or Alawite.[12]

In practice, upon al-Sharaa and his associates' arrival in Syria, they began establishing connections within an existing network of individuals already affiliated with them. In contrast to other rapidly expanding groups, especially those affiliated to the Free Syrian Army, Jabhat al-Nusra exhibited a more focused outreach and disciplined approach to recruitment focusing on selected individuals, as the group's main *modus operandi*—attacking regime targets in specific areas—did not yet require a larger mobilisation process.[13] Notably, Jabhat al-Nusra sought to select its members through recommendations (*tazkiyya*) from militants already known to the group, which was beneficial for building trust, limiting the threat of infiltrators, and avoiding incompetent recruits. This approach differed from other of Nusra's allies, such as Ahrar al-Sham, which incorporated pre-existing factions into its organisational structures. Due to the past mobilisation for Iraq, many individuals who were imprisoned in the infamous Saydnaya prison for supporting the Iraqi insurgency or sharing similar ideas were already well-known and trusted across the country. Although most of these prisoners joined other groups like Ahrar al-Sham, their widespread recognition and trustworthiness allowed Jabhat al-Nusra to mobilise some of them too and expand its influence in different areas.[14]

Numerous residents observed Jabhat al-Nusra actively recruiting within families they perceived as leaning towards the Islamists. There was a popular incubator for the group that was particularly evident in families considered Islamist dating back to the protracted conflict with the Syrian regime in the late 1970s to the early 1980s. Certain families had garnered a reputation for being sympathetic or aligned with them during that tumultuous period. In interviews, some local residents insist that it was these families who willingly extended hospitality to various jihadi factions, with Jabhat al-Nusra being one among several. A local Free Syrian Army figure opposed to the Islamists claimed that:

> There were many Islamist families linked to the events of the late 1980s [when Islamist armed groups first fought the Assad regime]. These families hated the regime. Where I lived, Jabhat al-Nusra

entered society through them, not through the big families. It empowered them to take revenge at the regime. At the same time, there were differences between them. Even in my city there were different components of Jabhat al-Nusra. Some were really convinced, and were popular locally. Others used the al-Qaeda brand to fight society and local figures opposed to them.[15]

Jabhat al-Nusra's initial *modus operandi* focused on spectacular operations rather than large-scale insurgency. In 2012, with limited territorial control, the group targeted strategic locations using precise intelligence, such as in Damascus, Aleppo, Homs and other cities. This approach, borrowed from their previous operations in Iraq, primarily targeted military objectives rather than places associated with religious minorities, as did its Iraqi counterparts, though there were civilian casualties too. This strategy meant that Nusra did not require a large cadre of militants but rather a trusted and experienced few to maintain the secrecy needed for these operations. The secrecy was so effective that even the Syrian opposition sometimes doubted whether Jabhat al-Nusra was responsible, suspecting instead that the regime might be targeting itself to vilify the opposition movement.

The population did not necessarily have a consistent view of Jabhat al-Nusra, since this largely depended on the policies of various commanders within the organisation. Until 2017, the group's organisational control remained fragmented and left much leeway to its local leaders, as later chapters discuss. Locals expressed varied opinions on the group. Some respected that Jabhat al-Nusra focused solely on combat and refrained from interfering in people's daily lives, while others viewed the group's growth as a threat to the Syrian revolution and its non-sectarian objectives.[16] They also resented the group's increasing popularity and its religious agenda, for which they often denounce Nusra's alleged external support.

Jabhat al-Nusra, along with other jihadi leaning allies like the dominant Ahrar al-Sham, began to develop a religious and sectarian narrative targeting the regime's Alawi nature, which diverged from the initial demands of the uprisings. This shift was partially informed by these groups' own religious views, and by the regime's actions and growing reliance on foreign Shia combatants, especially after Hezbollah's intervention from 2012 onwards. Jabhat al-Nusra notably advocated for the imposition of Islamic law in Syria and denounced the regime's Alawi foundations. The group was nonetheless more cautious than ISIS in its approach. While ISIS (and later IS) labelled non-Muslims and Muslims who did not adhere to its interpretation of Islam as disbelievers and apostates, Jabhat al-Nusra combined political and religious criticism of the regime. For example, in 2015, Ahmad al-Sharaa stated during an al-Jazeera interview that Alawis were outside the fold of Islam and should change their beliefs. Still, he also emphasised that the issue was their support for the regime and their significant presence in its military command, which he argued should cease.[17] Thus, Jabhat al-Nusra's opposition intertwined sectarian and political rationales against Alawis at the time.

Jabhat al-Nusra's accommodating strategy garnered some degree of acceptance within the Syrian opposition, as many appreciated its avoidance of imposing rigid control. Despite growing international scrutiny and criticism, Jabhat al-Nusra found support among those who opposed the escalating antagonism towards the group. During various Friday protests in 2013, including one named "We Are All Jabhat al-Nusra" a collective voice in the Syrian opposition sided against the international classification of the group as a terrorist organisation. Notably, the group's initial commitment to avoiding the pitfalls seen in Iraq, where the insurgency alienated civilians with stringent regulations and violence, was real in the Syrian context. The contrast suggested that Jabhat al-Nusra had adopted a more nuanced and cautious approach, steering clear of the mistakes witnessed in other conflicts especially Iraq and, previously, Algeria in the 1990s. Some analysts argue that this perspective aligns with the views of Abu Musab al-Suri, a prominent jihadi strategist who opposed certain aspects of jihadi Salafism's sectarianism. However, the leadership of HTS, including figures like Ahmad al-Sharaa and Abd al-Rahim Atun, the highest religious figure of the group, assert that this stance is their own. According to them, the Syrian uprising represented a popular revolution, distinct from the Iraqi context where insurgents fought against a foreign occupation. In this Syrian scenario, they believed it was essential to align themselves with the majority population. According to Abd al-Rahim Atun HTS's highest religious authority:

> In 2011, the situation was substantially different from Iraq in 2003. The militarisation of the conflict in Syria involved a Muslim people fighting a popular revolution. This is very different from Iraq and its foreign occupation. Our jihad was a revolution. It was not solely a reaction to occupation. Our struggle therefore had to develop according to the local context and in line with local developments. We could not be differentiated or isolated from the reality around us.[18]

Over time, an increasing number of foreign fighters became involved in the conflict, particularly at the outset when the affiliations were unclear. Many individuals joined various factions, such as those affiliated with the Free Syrian Army (FSA), Ahrar al-Sham, and other groups, without a distinct understanding or differentiation among them. The reasons often had more to do with the existence of informal networks than on a comprehensive knowledge of these groups' ideologies. For example, the Consultative Council of the Mujahideen (Majlis al-Shura al-Mujahideen) successfully recruited Europeans that came through the strategic border control of Baab al-Hawa next to Turkey, where the group settled, which triggered a self-reinforcing dynamic where new Europeans became drawn to groups where they already knew someone.[19] The fluidity of the situation allowed fighters to switch allegiances or move between groups quite easily. Often, more experienced recruits who may have received military training beforehand trained different groups without formally joining them, at least until 2013, when the fight with ISIS forced them to take a stand.[20] However, despite the ambiguity, there was a relatively effective level of cooperation, even evident in situations such as the kidnapping of journalists, where control could shift between groups seamlessly. This was notably the case of the journalist Theo Padnos, who was initially kidnapped by a local group, then transferred between various factions, ultimately ending up in southern Syria under the control of Jabhat al-Nusra's commander, Abu Maria al-Qahtani.[21]

The nature of foreign fighter recruitment changed over time. Jabhat al-Nusra was generally more discriminating compared to

ISIS, preferring to vet its recruits rather than accepting anybody. The focus for Jabhat al-Nusra was primarily on recruiting military-capable men capable of engaging in combat. In contrast, after the split with the Iraqi organisation discussed later, ISIS adopted a more inclusive recruitment strategy. ISIS welcomed individuals from various backgrounds, including women and families, as it sought to establish a state that required diverse forms of support beyond just military prowess. This marked a notable distinction in the recruitment approaches between Jabhat al-Nusra and ISIS during that period. ISIS focused on recruiting entire families to gain fighters and bolster motivation, as well as criminals who could be used for violent activities similar to the thuggery they engaged in back home. This included individuals who had previously been involved in drug use and other illicit activities.

Disruptions in the matrix: Initial points of contention between jihadis

Though Ahmad al-Sharaa showed signs of independence even without formally breaking from ISI, the group remained firmly within the jihadi milieu on several levels, first of all ideologically. Jabhat al-Nusra saw itself as part of the broader jihadi movement and adhered to broadly defined Salafi jihadi principles. This trend, championed by al-Qaeda since the war in Afghanistan against the Soviet Union in the 1980s, spread across the Muslim world, promoting the idea that regimes collaborating with the West and failing to implement Islamic law were illegitimate. Jabhat al-Nusra's founding statement first appeared on jihadi forums that had gained significant popularity during the Iraq war. In this statement, al-Sharaa emphasised his opposition to Western countries, accusing them of being complicit in crimes against Muslims despite their opposition to Assad, labelling them as "partners in crime". He also criticised Turkey, portraying it as an ally of the United States with no genuine commitment to Islam.

In the absence of prominent group ideologues, Jabhat al-Nusra's ideological views drew on the positions of al-Qaeda, particularly Atiyah Abd al-Rahman al-Libi. Al-Qaeda controlled the jihadi narrative, which shaped the group's initial thoughts. Jabhat al-Nusra generally aligned with al-Qaeda's overall views. Instead of being ideologically innovative, Jabhat al-Nusra reflected the prevailing environment of armed groups fighting Muslim regimes. The group adopted these views without much innovation, though in practice, it approached some issues differently. For example, Jabhat al-Nusra took a more nuanced approach to other groups and did not excommunicate former Egyptian president Muhammad Morsi for participating in democratic elections, a topic that sparked debates among jihadis. Paradoxically, certain al-Qaeda texts supported Jabhat al-Nusra's relatively more lenient approach according to Saleh al-Hamawi:

> Ahmad al-Sharaa did not excommunicate former Egyptian president Muhammad Morsi after the elections, nor did he broadly excommunicate supporters of the regime. He said this depended on individual circumstances. When ISI was still part of al-Qaeda, it was easier to challenge them on issues like excommunication by referencing some of these writings, such as those of Attiya al-Libi, to counter excessive excommunication practices. For example, al-Sharaa could just tell them that their own leadership had more restrained positions than theirs. Still, al-Sharaa sometimes had to conceal his true views to avoid unnecessary internal disputes.[22]

Nor did Jabhat al-Nusra release an official treaty or charter. Instead, key figures within the organisation detailed some of their positions over time in audio or written communiqués. Many were particularly critical of what happened in Iraq, and the violence perpetrated by ISI against civilians. For instance, Abu Maria al-Qahtani, the group's first mufti, was an early voice critiquing what they considered as the excesses of ISI,[23] cautioning jihadis against a recurrence of violence targeting local populations, excommunication practices, and other violations that risked alienating local communities from the jihadis—which led to a tribal alliance with US forces against them from 2005 onwards. Even Sami al-Uraydi, who assumed the role of mufti in 2014 after al-Qahtani, and who maintained close ties with prominent Jordanian jihadi scholar Abu Muhammad al-Maqdisi, asserted in a video that the group's creed (*'aqida*) adhered to Salafism and emphasised a commitment to avoid excommunication of populations and advocated collaboration with other groups.[24]

The most detailed ideological tenets of Jabhat al-Nusra exist in a series of lectures for the training camps that its latest religious mufti, Abd al-Rahim Atun, delivered, the same individual who later became a prominent critic of both al-Qaeda and IS as he justified the transformation into HTS. Al-Shami's writings initially aligned with al-Qaeda's positions. In *In the Shadow of the Tree of Jihad* (*Fi Dhilal Dawhat al-Jihad*), which was published in 2016 though it compiles texts written in previous years, Atun exposed his alignment with al-Qaeda's stances required to fight existing Muslim regimes that were not implementing Islamic law. He insisted that the legitimacy of governance is contingent upon strict adherence to Shari'a, rejecting any external influence or legislation that conflicts with Islamic principles. For the Muslim regimes not implementing Islamic law, he wrote that "we believe that fighting the tyrannical governments currently ruling in Muslim lands takes precedence and should be prioritised based on the fundamental obligation under Islamic law", the tyrants being "the apostate rulers and those similar to them, including entities and organisations that uphold disbelief, such as parliamentary councils, legislative assemblies, the United Nations, and the Security Council". Atun also firmly asserted that the local strategy of Jabhat al-Nusra aligned with al-Qaeda's overarching objectives:

> Deviating from the strategy [through localism] is for those who understand the strategy of the organisation [al-Qaeda], and not an abandonment of it. Our fight against the local tyrants is not separate from the fight against their masters [the US]. It is not a separate struggle against the interdependence and alliance between the local and international tyrants. Rather, it is a focused effort within the same framework to forcefully break their alliance and weaken their unity.

Still, Atun also distinguished Jabhat al-Nusra from ISIS with a more nuanced approach to the practice of *takfir* (excommunication) by emphasising its conditions of application to avoid excesses, especially those committed during the war in Iraq against civilian populations.

These principles were reflected in the teachings of the religious training camps, which focused on several ideological principles at the heart of jihadi Salafism. According to Saleh al-Hamawi:

Until 2016, training in Nusra included six small books as part of its curriculum. These texts covered topics such as the conditions of faith [*iman*], the rulings on those who do not govern according to what God has revealed, Abu Qatada's arguments against democracy [The Two Methods], al-Maqdissi on *al-wala wal-bara* [Loyalty—to the Muslims—and Disavowal—of the non-Muslims], the rulings of the lands from Abu Yahiya al-Libi [*Ahkam al-Diyar*], and Jurisprudential Matters of Jihad [*Masa'il Fiqh al-Jihad*] from Abu Abdallah al Muhajir. Recruits would study these materials over a one-month period in the training camp. However, all of this content was eliminated in 2016.[25]

The group's adherence to this ideological trend consolidated over the years with the influx of jihadi veterans from outside Syria. Some prominent jihadi figures came to Syria from the inception of the group, such as Abu Julaybib al-Urduni, the brother-in-law of Abu Musab al-Zarqawi, the original founder of ISI's predecessor was already in Afghanistan on the eve of 9/11. Others joined later on, such as Abu Firas al-Suri, a former Syrian army lieutenant who took part in the first uprising against Assad's father in the late 1970s before traveling to Afghanistan to join the jihad against Soviet forces. Abu Farraj al-Masri, an Egyptian longtime associate of Ayman al-Zawahiri since the late 1970s, joined after the 2013 military coup in Egypt. Later, following a 2015 prisoner exchange between Iran and al-Qaeda in Yemen, several al-Qaeda core figures were released and joined as well. Among them were Abul-Khayr al-Masri, the deputy leader of al-Qaeda, and Abul-Qasam al-Urduni, another al-Qaeda leader who had met Abu Musab al-Zarqawi in the late 1980s in Afghanistan and later became his trusted advisor.

Still, Jabhat al-Nusra was not necessarily a fully cohesive entity internally. While ISIS enforced strict ideological conformity, ruthlessly purging anyone who did not fully embrace its political and religious doctrine, Nusra exhibited greater internal diversity. A young activist from a respected family in Damascus recalls that, at the time when he joined the group during the early days of the uprising,

> In all the military units, we kept arguing about everything. Some were in favour of praying with this shaykh, others opposed it, some

> were in favor of allying with the Free Syrian Army factions, others wanted to fight them. We didn't agree on what position to take with regard to the Shiite community: some said they should be killed, others said they were Muslims. There was also no clear-cut assessment of the Muslim Brotherhood's experience in Egypt. Some saw Morsi as an infidel who had accepted democracy, while others wanted to support him. At that time, Jabhat al-Nusra was all things to all people. Yes, there was radicalism [*ghulu*] but Jabhat al-Nusra wasn't just that.[26]

The previously mentioned tensions between Jabhat al-Nusra and ISI escalated, culminating in a split in 2013. This rift can be attributed to two primary factors: struggles for control and ideological differences on violence. Jabhat al-Nusra sought to maintain autonomy in decision-making as its understanding of Syria was more nuanced than the directives from the Iraqi leadership, which often advocated large-scale violence, including against the Syrian opposition. The official split occurred when Baghdadi declared a plan to reunify the two groups, integrating Jabhat al-Nusra into ISI to become Islamic State in Iraq and Sham (ISIS) in April 2013. For al-Sharaa, this was unacceptable. Facing uncertainty, he sought to pledge allegiance to a higher authority, al-Qaeda, to maintain internal legitimacy and retain his followers. Ayman al-Zawahiri, the leader of al-Qaeda at the time, had to intervene. He was unhappy with the situation and decided to split the two groups, stating that there was "no organisational connection" between them.[27] However, the Iraqis rejected this decision. Retrospectively, Ahmad al-Sharaa argued that

> When we broke off with al-Baghdadi, we didn't have any good options. We were going to be wiped out by them so I gathered my inner circle to make a quick decision. I told them that I was considering pledging allegiance to al-Qaeda. They advised me against it, and some described it as a suicidal move. But no one was able to provide me with an alternative. We had no other option but to pledge allegiance to al-Qaeda in order not to lose everyone to ISIS.[28]

The split and its outcome were heavily influenced by differing approaches to managing foreign fighters. Al-Baghdadi and his associate Haji Bakr travelled extensively in Syria to secure pledges of allegiance, especially from the foreign fighters who were largely unaware of the internal conflicts but were easily convinced by the idea of creating a state. By integrating enough commanders and key figures, Baghdadi bolstered support for his vision. This strategy included bringing influential leaders like Abu Omar al-Shishani into the fold and empowering them, which facilitated the integration of their followers. Many Europeans also pledged their allegiance to ISIS at the time. Baghdadi's approach of continuously recruiting and empowering foreign fighters created a self-reinforcing dynamic. Over time, this made it easier for ISIS to consolidate power and grow stronger compared to other groups. The strategy of using foreign fighters and their commitment to the idea of an Islamic state was crucial in solidifying ISIS's position and influence.

While it is true that IS was an efficient fighting force, recruitment also played a crucial role. The Syrian armed opposition never had a large number of fighters, and those it did have were members of distinctive factions that operated in loose coordination in specific areas. In contrast, IS had an estimated 30,000 to 40,000 foreign fighters who, unlike local armed groups, were not bound by regional or local loyalties and could be deployed flexibly across Syria and Iraq. This ability to move fighters strategically allowed IS to capitalise on its superior manpower, giving it a significant advantage on the battlefield.

The split posed a significant challenge for Jabhat al-Nusra. The group lost at least half of its fighters and its oil resources in eastern Syria. It was severely weakened and faced the imminent risk of dissolution. Another Syrian armed group, Ahrar al-Sham, played a crucial role in helping Jabhat al-Nusra survive through financial support. Ahrar al-Sham feared that without this support, nearly all of Nusra's fighters would defect to IS while a surviving Jabhat al-Nusra could be a strong ally against the Iraqi group.[29] Despite Jabhat al-Nusra's local agenda against the regime, global jihad also played a crucial role in maintaining the group's cohesion and ensuring its survival. Most influential transnational jihadi figures sided with the group, including its ideologue Abu Muhammad al-Maqdisi, who actively encouraged their followers to join its ranks. This support was vital for maintaining internal cohesion during challenging times. According to al-Maqdisi,

> I had no contact with Jabhat al-Nusra before the split with ISIS in 2013, as I was in prison and had no means to communicate. It was only after I was released and the split had already occurred that I was able to reconnect. I threw my full support behind them, issuing a communiqué urging the youth to join their ranks. Most individuals who loved al-Qaeda sided with them. However, many younger recruits, particularly from Europe, gravitated toward ISIS, often based on personal feelings, connections, or limited understanding of the broader dynamics. Jabhat al-Nusra used jihadi Salafism as a tool to fuel the revolution. I can't say whether al-Sharaa intended to use and then reject us from the start—I can't read hearts. What's clear is the trend: people from all over joined the cause, including Europeans, Pakistanis, and people from the Gulf, many of whom willing to blow themselves up for the cause while Syrians and Iraqis were more reluctant.[30]

Al-Qaeda therefore played a symbolic role in bolstering Jabhat al-Nusra's support within Syria and enabled it to survive in a highly competitive environment where IS was aggressively attempting to poach its commanders. Without this support, Jabhat al-Nusra might have faced the risk of disintegration and eventual disappearance. Still, Ahmad al-Sharaa insisted that this did not change his "Syria-first" policy:

> I conditioned my pledge of allegiance to al-Qaeda on the idea that we will not use Syria as a launching pad for external operations, nor let others use it for that. I wrote this to Ayman Zawahiri and he agreed to it, and if you recall my response to Zawahiri after our delinking decision you will see that I never changed my position on that. Ultimately, I think that al-Qaeda's leaders are living in isolation, they are disconnected from reality. The organisation is more of a slogan rather than an umbrella organisation that offers material support. Our group, for instance, never received anything substantial from them.[31]

One of the movement's cadres recalls that, at the time:

> Only joining al-Qaeda stopped the momentum of mass desertions in favour of ISIS. In January 2014, we were haemorrhaging with sometimes close to 70 fighters a day leaving our group to join Islamic State. Al-Sharaa had no choice. Some of the decisions

taken at the time, such as the active imposition of shari'a , or the announcement of an emirate, were a way of retaining fighters, even though al-Sharaa was against the application of corporal punishment because we were in a context of war. In the end, the strategy worked as the bleeding stopped.[32]

The arrival of the so-called Khorasan network occurred independently of Jabhat al-Nusra's leadership. Rather than a structured group, this loose network includes individuals who began to arrive in Syria in 2014. Among its key members were Muhsin al-Fadhli, an associate of Osama bin Laden, and Sanafi al-Nasr. The group also included David Drugeon, a French bomb-making expert, and Abu Yusuf al-Turki, a Turkish militant involved in training and operations. Their presence heightened US fears about potential foreign attacks from Syria though many analysts and journalists affirm that the Khorasan group saw their presence in Syria more as an opportunity to consolidate and strengthen the position of Jabhat al-Nusra rather than to immediately plan foreign operations.[33] The US targeted the leaders of this group and killed them in a series of airstrikes beginning in 2014 as part of efforts to disrupt their planning of external attacks. Muhsin al-Fadhli, the informal leader, was killed in July 2015 by a US airstrike in northwest Syria while traveling in a vehicle. Sanafi al-Nasr, another senior figure, was killed in October 2015 in a US drone strike in Idlib province.

Supporting the revolution and occasionally fighting the revolutionaries

Jabhat al-Nusra was never hegemonic in the Syrian insurgency since it only became dominant after its transformation into Hay'at Tahrir al-Sham (HTS) in 2017. Prior to this, the insurgency landscape was extremely diverse, with various groups operating across Syria. Some factions aligned with the Free Syrian Army (FSA), while others had Islamist or even jihadi leanings. The main consensus within the armed opposition from 2014 onward was to fight ISIS. The opposition agreed to oppose ISIS's presence in areas under its control and to actively combat the group. However, relations between the factions themselves were far less stable. The groups frequently shifted alliances and adapted their strategic priorities.

This fluidity led to frequent accusations of double-dealing and attempts by Jabhat al-Nusra to subjugate other groups to consolidate power.

In the early days of the uprising, group affiliation was blurry and factional collaboration common. Various factions, including even ISIS before 2014, formed alliances based on immediate circumstances and priorities. These collaborations were tactical. They focused on military operations such as jointly taking over military bases, manning checkpoints, and sharing responsibilities in opposition-held areas. The lower level of institutionalisation among these groups did not prevent cross-group cooperation, which operated on an ad-hoc basis, determining contributions and dividing the spoils of war accordingly. This included coordinating checkpoints and other responsibilities to ensure efficient resource distribution and operational success.[34]

During its first two years of existence, in 2012 and 2013, Jabhat al-Nusra generally tried to accommodate the revolutionary milieu composed of local activists, FSA-affiliated armed groups, and local councils without seeking to impose its domination. The group literally defined itself as a "front of support" for the Syrian people. Jabhat al-Nusra was at the time included in local military operations rooms under FSA commanders. It did not try to insulate itself. Jabhat al-Nusra was particularly efficient in military engagements, often employing car bombs and elite troops of fighters to storm military barracks and bases. As mentioned by Abd al-Rahim Atun, "in front of what was a mass movement, we were aware that we could not impose an oath of allegiance on all revolutionaries and cram a whole people into one organisation. We would not be able to dominate, and we had to agree to make alliances."[35]

However, relations began to sour between the factions. One of the reasons was foreign intervention. Many states and private entrepreneurs started supporting the opposition, basing their aid on their own networks, pre-existing ties, and perceived efficiency. This external support influenced the dynamics of the armed opposition, as each group manoeuvred to attract resources and favour from these benefactors. A common stereotype, such as men growing beards and using Islamic terminology to name their organisations, while perhaps reductionist, hints at deeper dynamics at play in which some adopted a more consistent Islamic framing to gain more external support. This external influence started to heighten internal friction and competition, as insurgents vied for support and sought to align themselves with the preferences of their benefactors.

But not all divisions stemmed from foreign support; internal factional dynamics also played a significant role. As these started to become more clearly defined, tensions arose over resource allocation, fighter recruitment, and ideological preferences. A top leader of another jihadi-leaning group Ahrar al-Sham, which often allied with Jabhat al-Nusra in its military operations, lamented that

> We had socialised our members around key concepts such as the necessity of allegiance [*bay'a*], the revival of the Caliphate, and jihad against the regime. Jabhat al-Nusra exploited this groundwork and tried to take with our youth by affirming their belief in these shared ideals. They would also accuse us of being nationalist [*qutri*], contrasting it with their purportedly more global vision, which resonated with many. We had to develop our own identity to survive in response.[36]

These issues became even more pronounced when taking control of territory. How best to rule the newly acquired territories? Civil society actors attempted to implement their own initiatives but often lacked strong factional support—and, as a result, the weapons needed to enforce their judicial decisions. Meanwhile, various factions—Islamist and non-Islamist alike—debated governance approaches, such as imposing Islamic law or adopting other legal frameworks. Some religious scholars close to the Free Syrian Army introduced the idea of the Arab Unified Code, a model legal framework developed by the Arab League to harmonise legislation. For non-Islamists, this was useful to acknowledge the predominance of Islamic law while gaining some regional acceptance and minimising tensions with the Islamists. But the jihadis and Salafis in general, including Jabhat al-Nusra and Ahrar al-Sham, opposed the Arab Unified Code, arguing that it represented the positivisation of Islamic law—transforming divine principles into man-made statutes through codification. They viewed this process as a distortion of Shari'a, reducing its sacred and dynamic nature to a rigid legal framework that could be manipulated by human authorities.

Another divide was the growing international threat posed by IS, which seized control of significant territory in Iraq. It expanded its dominance into eastern Syria and established a brutal regime marked by oppressive governance. Where IS governed, it imposed its own harsh understanding of Islamic law enforced through violence and fear, targeting anyone who resisted or deviated from its rules. IS's actions included public executions, the killing of foreign hostages in high-profile propaganda videos, and the systematic enslavement of the Yazidi population in Iraq, which the group justified in its public publications. These measures, combined with their attempts to create a self-declared Caliphate, drew widespread condemnation for their unprecedented brutality against civilians and minority groups.

International concerns over IS pressured other Syrian Islamist groups to distance themselves from it and signal their opposition to the Iraqi organisation. They feared that IS's behaviour could feed into the regime's narrative that the opposition was entirely under the sway of this group, potentially turning global opinion against them. Syrian Islamists needed to distinguish themselves from IS to alleviate the concerns of overseas actors. To distance themselves from IS, other factions signed a public charter to articulate their principles. The Covenant of Honor (*Mithaq al-Sharaf al-Thawri*) united several groups around Ahrar al-Sham in the Islamic Front in addition to smaller organisations like Faylaq al-Sham.[37] They insisted that they were Syrian fighters striving to establish a just state that would uphold the rights of all its citizens, including religious minorities. In contrast with jihadis' views, they also legitimised collaborating with foreign states opposed to the Syrian regime.

The Covenant of Honor breached several principles and fundamentals to jihadis that justified Jabhat al-Nusra's opposition. Among these principles was the acceptance of support from foreign states, vehemently opposed by jihadis, as well as the alleged "dilution" (*tam'iya*) of the foundational principles of an Islamic state. Jabhat al-Nusra issued a communiqué in which it condemned collaboration with states perceived as enemies of Islam, the prioritisation of national citizenship over religious solidarity, and any lack of commitment to establishing a state governed by Islamic law.[38] This nonetheless created internal divisions. Abu Maria al-Qahtani, the group's religious authority back then, resigned in opposition, to be replaced by a more maximalist Jordanian, Sami al-Uraydi, a close associate of Abu Muhammad al-Maqdisi in Jordan.[39] Others, such as Abu Firas al-Suri, also vehemently attacked Ahrar al-Sham because of the Covenant.

In 2013–14, the international community began to harden its stance against Jabhat al-Nusra, a shift that started in April 2013 when the group formally pledged allegiance to al-Qaeda. Prior to this, there was still some plausible deniability regarding the group's ties to the Iraqi organisation, as these connections remained clandestine. However, once the group declared its allegiance to al-Qaeda, it started to fall under United Nations sanctions. Jabhat al-Nusra was designated under the 1267 Security Council resolution for its association with the organisation founded by Osama bin Laden. This move faced some opposition, as highlighted by Ben Rhodes, Former Deputy National Security Advisor of the United States, in his memoirs, who expressed reservations about the decision since he believed that the group was highly efficient and that sending a signal against it might have been misguided.[40]

As international pressure mounted on Jabhat al-Nusra, the group began to attack local factions that it accused of accepting Western support, alleging that such assistance was ultimately aimed at targeting the group. The most prominent factions targeted included the Syrian Revolutionary Front, the Hazm movement, and the 13th Division. Jabhat al-Nusra started in late 2014 with Jamal Ma'ruf group, the Syrian Revolutionaries Front (SRF), which it accused of corruption and profiteering. Jabhat al-Nusra launched an offensive, quickly overwhelming SRF forces, capturing key strongholds, and seizing significant amounts of weaponry and resources. Ma'ruf group, unable to match Jabhat al-Nusra's military capabilities and local influence, collapsed, forcing him and his fighters to retreat. Then, Jabhat al-Nusra dismantled the Hazm Movement, a Western-backed rebel group, which it accused of being US-supported. Hazm, already weak internally and lacking widespread local support, was unable to resist Jabhat al-Nusra's assault. According to a local FSA commander, who witnessed the clashes:

> When we saw Jabhat al-Nusra gaining strength, we tried to unite to survive but had very little chance of success. We did not have sufficient authority over our fighters, who considered Jabhat al-Nusra a very effective force. Of thousands of fighters, only fifty would fight Jabhat al-Nusra back.[41]

Jabhat al-Nusra maintained a strategic and selective approach in its attacks against other factions. It carefully targeted specific adversaries while continuing to collaborate with other armed opposition groups. Nusra hence avoided antagonising the broader opposition and refrained from asserting itself as the sole legitimate authority. Instead, it continued to actively participate in joint operations with various factions, including Ahrar al-Sham, one of the largest and most influential factions at the time, along with its local allies. There were discussions about unifying efforts under a single organisational framework at the time, such as joining the Islamic Front spearheaded by Ahrar al-Sham, but these attempts failed to materialise. In these talks, Jabhat al-Nusra expressed caution about joining other factions, particularly Jaysh al-Islam, citing concerns over its close ties to Saudi Arabia. Jabhat al-Nusra also thought that these efforts would not lead to a real organisational unity among the armed opposition, according to Abd al-Rahim Atun.[42]

Initially, armed groups did not prioritise governance, but they gradually began collaborating to address the challenges of ruling newly liberated areas. The power vacuum in opposition-held regions demanded a coordinated approach. While some civil society actors promoted new initiatives, such as the establishment of courts of justice, they often struggled due to limited resources and the lack of an enforcement mechanism. These courts occasionally relied on armed groups to implement their rulings, but this support was typically ad hoc rather than systematic. As governance efforts developed, collaboration among various factions, including Jabhat al-Nusra, became more structured. In regions like Aleppo, coalitions of armed groups established courts to replace existing civilian structures, leading to the creation of power-sharing arrangements within frameworks such as the Shari'a Commission (*al-Hay'at al-Shar'iyya*). Major factions like Ahrar al-Sham, Jabhat al-Nusra, Suqur al-Sham, and others divided authority based on the prevailing balance of power and local geography.

For Jabhat al-Nusra, governance was also driven by competition with IS. Although Jabhat al-Nusra survived the split, the idea of establishing an Islamic state remained attractive. According to Saleh al-Hamawi, this competition influenced their governance strategies significantly:

> Many people were leaving us in favour of IS in 2014, especially when it proclaimed the creation of the Caliphate. Some of them disagreed with IS, especially its excessive violence, but still believed that creating an Islamic state was important. Our only solution was to have our own governance. This started with the declaration that we created an emirate, which many groups pushed back against, up to the creation of Dar al-Qada. But we had an understanding with other groups, including Ahrar al-Sham, that we should not impose the Islamic legal penal punishments [*hudud*] because we were still at war. And in reality this helped us survive, and people stopped going to IS and remained with us.[43]

In the summer of 2015, Jabhat al-Nusra established its own courts, known as *Dar al-Qada*. Its governance efforts were primarily focused on judicial functions rather than social services, which remained minimal. While Jabhat al-Nusra insisted that it relied on Islamic law, it avoided adopting public executions as a primary method to instill fear in the population like its Iraqi counterpart, though those happened occasionally. This approach was organic to the group and not directed by external orders, though it also aligned with al-Qaeda affiliates' favoured strategies in regions as diverse as the Sahel and Yemen. In addition, Jabhat al-Nusra also provided basic services. A list of rulings by Jabhat al-Nusra's service office, though not comprehensive, suggests that most rulings were quite mundane.[44] They addressed everyday issues such as the excessive use of water by civilians, setting the price of bread, recruiting trained engineers for work, prohibiting new electric infrastructure, and regulating the prices of basic commodities. According to a local Free Syrian Army commander opposed to the group:

> We resisted Jabhat al-Nusra and opposed them locally for as long as we could. However, over time, they proved to be more astute and strategic than us. Their influence grew not through social services but by establishing courts of justice, which allowed them to deeply

penetrate and embed themselves within society. They were swift, pragmatic, and adaptive in their approach to governance, which ultimately gave them the upper hand.[45]

Although Jabhat al-Nusra was never comparable to IS, it did impose penalties and carry out killings, the *hudud* or the Islamic penal punishments, despite claims indicating agreements to suspend *hudud* punishments during wartime. A series of retrieved documents detail cases of executions for offences such as murder, extramarital relations (including prostitution), and apostasy.[46] Civilians also criticise the group for its strict local regulations, including bans on music, smoking, and gender mixing, as well as pressure on NGOs. As a result, there was also a degree of local opposition to Jabhat al-Nusra, evidenced by recordings of demonstrations and other forms of protest.[47]

Despite their collaboration, significant competition continued to exist, particularly between Jabhat al-Nusra and Ahrar al-Sham. The latter had risen as the predominant force in the region, boasting substantial resources and international connections. It aimed to garner support from abroad and advocate for a new vision, including through opinion pieces in Western publications. This drew strong opposition from more radical figures within Jabhat al-Nusra, like Abu Firas al-Suri, who openly criticised Ahrar al-Sham. Additionally, Ahrar al-Sham endeavoured to bring smaller factions under its wing to prevent them from aligning with and bolstering Jabhat al-Nusra. The most notable instance of collaboration took place in 2015 with the Jaysh al-Fath coalition. This coalition assembled foreign backers, including Saudi Arabia, Turkey and Qatar, to bolster the opposition and assist in capturing territories in northwest Syria. Ahrar al-Sham and Jabhat al-Nusra emerged as the key players within this coalition, working alongside smaller factions to gain control over the province. Subsequently, similar operation rooms were established in other regions, extending from the Qalamoun area adjacent to Lebanon to Aleppo. Some within Ahrar al-Sham criticised this, viewing it as Jabhat al-Nusra attempting to assert dominance, which they saw as contradicting Ahrar's efforts toward greater openness.[48]

THE FOUNDATIONAL MATRIX

Breaking with global jihad and the emergence of HTS

The Syrian insurgency gradually recognised the necessity of unification following a series of military setbacks subsequent to Russia's intervention in September 2015. The fall of Aleppo, pressure on other fronts across Syria, and the international perception of these events among opposition-allied states underscored the urgency of this realisation. It became clear that the armed opposition could not remain divided. Feelings hence intensified among all armed groups that a comprehensive unification of their organisational structures was becoming a military necessity for survival.

In 2016, the main impediment to this unification was the widespread fear among most opposition groups of merging with Jabhat al-Nusra due to its international designation. The United States and the European Union designated the group as a Foreign Terrorist organisation (FTO) and a Specially Designated Global Terrorist (SDGT) entity in 2012 and 2013. Jabhat al-Nusra was then designated by the Security Council in 2014 due to its affiliation with al-Qaeda under resolution 1267. This designation meant that all other states had to similarly outlaw the group. Other Syrian armed groups were therefore concerned that any new entity formed through such a union could also be similarly designated and face pressure from all states, including Turkey.

The first stage towards the unification of the opposition required severing ties with al-Qaeda. The military situation on the ground was deteriorating already prior to the loss of Aleppo in December 2016, which accelerated heated internal deliberations, which resulted in Jabhat al-Nusra's decision to sever ties with al-Qaeda that summer. Jabhat al-Nusra became Jabhat Fath al-Sham (JFS) to mark the organisation's break with the group. According to the group's highest religious figure, Abd al-Rahim Atun,

> At first, al-Qaeda told us to act according to our needs. We told them that we didn't want any external operations and they agreed. But the connection with al-Qaeda then became an obstacle to the union of the opposition. Some factions had a real problem with this connection while others used it as an excuse. But we didn't want to face the same problems as during the split with IS. Everyone feared the outcome. We wanted to avoid negative consequences.[49]

When the group split from al-Qaeda, there was considerable dissent and debate over Jabhat al-Nusra's true intentions. Some viewed the move as a strategic rebranding to gain broader support and legitimacy within Syria, in which Jabhat al-Nusra genuinely renounced the global organisation. Many analysts and foreign states alike conversely suspected it was merely a tactical manoeuvre to distance the group from al-Qaeda only in public, while remaining committed to it. Part of the reason for the confusion is that early debates revealed that Ahmad al-Sharaa had proposed to Al-Zawahiri that their allegiance remain secret. Ahmad al-Sharaa also secured an agreement from Abul Khayr al-Masri, al-Qaeda's number two. In reality, subsequent developments showed that Ahmad al-Sharaa was not attempting to deceive Western countries into believing he was severing ties with al-Qaeda. Instead, he was deceiving al-Qaeda itself. His primary intention was to obtain their approval for a public severance of ties, which would effectively force their hand but still allow him to limit internal dissidence from commanders who remained committed to al-Qaeda while, in reality, he was imposing his independence. According to Abu Muhammad al-Maqdisi, the jihadi ideologue:

> Abd al-Rahim Atun sent a message to me and Abu Qatada expressing concerns about the increasing risk of a US–Russia alliance targeting their group. He argued that they needed to change the group's name and form alliances with other factions to mitigate this threat. Atun emphasised that the change would be superficial—a mere rebranding—while maintaining a secret allegiance to al-Qaeda. Both Abu Faraj and Abul Khayr supported this as a tactical move. Atun also mentioned that if Dr Ayman [al-Zawahiri] refused the plan, they would step back but urged us to support him to prevent internal divisions. However, soon after, Saif al-Adl contacted me from Iran, expressing strong opposition to the proposal. He argued that Abul Khayr and Abu Faraj had no authority to make such a decision. Shortly after, I received a message from Dr Ayman [al-Zawahiri] himself. He explained that while he couldn't share the messages he had received from al-Sharaa, he provided the ones he had sent in response. Dr Ayman accused al-Sharaa of being deceitful.[50]

THE FOUNDATIONAL MATRIX

A retrospective of documents collected by researcher Aymenn Jawad al-Tamimi reveals extensive exchanges of opinions between commanders and leaders from both al-Qaeda and former Jabhat al-Nusra.[51] Interestingly, these discussions primarily revolved around organisational issues, decision-making prerogatives, and resource management—for example, to whom belonged Jabhat al-Nusra's weapons. A central theme from the documents confirmed Ayman al-Zawahiri's fierce rejection of the group's break from al-Qaeda. Other figures, such as Jabhat al-Nusra's former mufti Sami al-Uraydi, labelled the split an illegal rebellion, even denying claims that al-Qaeda's deputy, Abu al-Khayr al-Masri, was fully informed of the details. Critics argued that Ahmad al-Sharaa should have stepped back once Ayman al-Zawahiri opposed the separation, but he refused to do so. Zawahiri's stern message, "we will fight you until there is no *fitna* [division]", emphasised his harsh rebuttal of Ahmad al-Sharaa's decision to leave.

After Jabhat al-Nusra severed ties with al-Qaeda, the Syrian armed opposition faced a pivotal choice between two divergent paths. One side leaned toward a politically oriented approach, favouring closer ties with Turkey, their main remaining backer, which had significant strategic interests in northern Syria, and keeping a strategic depth that would both preserve the credibility of the Syrian opposition and avoid another wave of refugees into Syria. The other side prioritised a military track and resisted aligning too closely with foreign powers like Turkey. This division was especially marked within Ahrar al-Sham, which effectively splintered along these lines. Some members advocated for stronger political cooperation with Turkey, seeing it as vital for survival and strategic gains, while others focused on maintaining military independence and remained sceptical of external influence.

This divide within the Syrian armed opposition was reflected in two distinct initiatives aimed at unifying it at the end of 2016. The first aimed to consolidate factions operating under the Free Syrian Army (FSA) umbrella, while the second sought to unite Islamist factions and their allies. Jabhat Fath al-Sham (JFS), formerly Jabhat al-Nusra, joined the second initiative, which culminated in the creation of Hay'at Tahrir al-Sham (HTS) in January 2017. HTS was envisioned as an umbrella organisation to unify all groups participating in the initiative. Ahrar al-Sham featured in both initiatives. Then, the leader of Ahrar al-Sham at the time, Abu 'Ammar al-'Omar, agreed to merge with HTS, but the group's leadership council rejected the decision, citing concerns over Ahmad al-Sharaa's dominance and the potential repercussions of being associated with an internationally designated terrorist group. Ahrar al-Sham's withdrawal exacerbated divisions within the insurgency in northwest Syria, leaving HTS and Ahrar al-Sham as the two dominant factions vying for control and influence.

Meanwhile, the strongest internal opponents of Jabhat al-Nusra's decision to sever ties with al-Qaeda retreated due to the lack of viable alternatives. This included most Jordanian militants and many of the remaining foreign fighters who remained committed to al-Qaeda. Most of the remaining al-Qaeda leaders who came to Syria from abroad, including Abul-Khayr himself who initially sanctioned the split with al-Qaeda and Abu Farraj al-Masri who featured in al-Sharaa's press conference, were soon killed in US drone strikes, which inadvertently helped Ahmad al-Sharaa lower internal dissent within the group.

2

THE STRUGGLE FOR DOMINANCE
HTS' HEGEMONIC AMBITIONS IN SYRIA'S OPPOSITION

Jabhat al-Nusra did not start as a large organisation, unlike several other armed groups that quickly mobilised thousands of members between 2011 and 2012. Still, by 2019, it had become the dominant force in northwest Syria though other armed opposition groups continued to operate in the province too. How did this happen? In private interviews, HTS leaders emphasise a simple narrative: the group wasn't, paradoxically, intended to be a distinct organisation, but rather an inclusive government with a unified military. But this ambitious vision failed to materialise. Several groups, notably Ahrar al-Sham—the strongest other group in northwest Syria—along with smaller military factions, declined to unite with Jabhat al-Nusra's next brand, Jabhat Fath al-Sham. They feared al-Sharaa's control over the new group and were wary of risking designation as a terrorist organisation by most foreign countries as well as the United Nations Security Council. As negotiations faltered with other armed opposition groups, HTS made another choice. It started to seek to establish dominance, albeit through various means. This included confronting its former Islamist ally, Ahrar al-Sham, before imposing conditions on its former organisational umbrella—al-Qaeda, which it de facto dismantled, foreign-manned armed groups, and ultimately launching war against IS returnees in northwest Syria.

Striking in the centre: HTS pressures the mainstream revolutionary milieu

The creation of HTS in January 2017 exacerbated tensions within the armed opposition. The failure to unite the armed opposition meant that, in absence of unity, two dominant armed groups engaged in a zero-sum struggle for survival and domination. After the formation of HTS, the coexistence of these two large factions—HTS and Ahrar al-Sham—was untenable. Under pressure from Russia and the regime, the Idlib province could not afford to be divided between two competing armed groups; instead, it had to consolidate under a single, unified authority. Ahrar al-Sham and HTS had a shared jihadi lineage, though Ahrar al-Sham had sought to distance itself from jihadis much earlier during the conflict.[1] But they also had fundamentally different priorities and diverging views on Turkey, foreign supporters of the Syrian opposition, and internal power structures. In short, Ahrar al-Sham pursued a political strategy aligned with Turkey and foreign backers to promote an inclusive project with most other armed groups, while HTS prioritised a military-focused approach centred on its closely allied factions. Their inability to reconcile these differences meant that sharing power was almost impossible; ultimately, one faction had to prevail over the other and impose its conditions.

Between 2017 and 2019, several rounds of confrontation erupted between HTS and Ahrar al-Sham, along with their respective smaller allies. The clashes often followed the assassination of some of these groups' local commanders, which each side blamed on the other. But these incidents were more the catalysts than the root causes of the broader conflict, which was about the leadership of the province. The conflict lasted approximately two years largely because the two groups and their respective allies were of comparable strength, making it difficult for either side to secure a decisive victory.

HTS had three main rationales for confronting Ahrar al-Sham. Abu Fath al-Farghali, a former HTS religious scholar who left Ahrar al-Sham in opposition to its decision to foster closer ties with foreign countries like Turkey, argued that Ahrar al-Sham's civilian project was a threat to HTS. Second, he mentioned that HTS needed to secure the borders with Turkey, hitherto controlled by Ahrar al-Sham, which provided lucrative economic resources and political leverage internationally as the main access point to the province. Third, despite al-Farghali's own opposition to Turkey, he mentioned that HTS's internal hegemony would force Turkey to collaborate with it on its own terms.[2] Additionally, HTS generally feared that other factions might be used against it by foreign states. These fears were heightened when several factions that had joined it split in the following months, including Jaysh al-Ahrar—itself a split from Ahrar al-Sham—and the Nur al-Din al-Zinki movement.

Ahrar al-Sham, in contrast, became a counterbalance to HTS, attracting factions—including many from the Free Syrian Army—seeking protection. Ahrar al-Sham quickly brought together numerous smaller groups who were wary of HTS's ambitions. Among these were Fa-Staqim kama Umirat, Suqur al-Sham, and the northern affiliate of Jaysh al-Islam. This dynamic complicated Ahrar al-Sham's restructuring efforts. Ahrar al-Sham was recovering from a two-year internal quarrel between two contending factions—from which would form Jaysh al-Ahrar in December 2016 before joining HTS in January—which had largely impeded internal reforms. Ahrar al-Sham was therefore not ready to confront HTS. According to an Ahrar al-Sham leader,

> Jabhat al-Nusra used our refusal to join them and our relations with foreign countries to attack us. Our organisation had been blocked for two years by internal quarrels. We were only starting to prepare a central military force, but we were not yet ready to defend ourselves. We should have delayed the confrontation with them.[3]

Between 2017 and 2019, Ahrar al-Sham and HTS engaged in a series of clashes, in which HTS ultimately prevailed. HTS initially gained the upper hand in July 2017 due to its centralised military force and successful isolation of Ahrar al-Sham's strongholds.[4] HTS established small sub-groups within localities where Ahrar al-Sham operated, since the group continued to rely primarily on geographically-based military forces rather than centralised units detached from specific areas. By forming these sub-groups, HTS was able to prevent the involvement of Ahrar al-Sham's stronger military units. HTS achieved this by encouraging local agreements stipulating that all military groups within these localities would abstain from participating in the factional fighting. In response, Ahrar al-Sham formed the Syrian Liberation Front with the Zinki Movement in 2018 to regain strength, before joining the National Front for Liberation in August 2018 under the lead of Faylaq al-Sham, a faction aligned with Turkey. The alliance temporarily stabilised the conflict through a series of skirmishes and tactical engagements, which allowed the counter HTS alliance to regain some lost ground.

The decisive phase happened in January 2019, when HTS took control of the province. HTS launched a comprehensive offensive that overwhelmed the Syrian Liberation Front, focusing on the Zinki Movement in the north of Idlib, and then going after Suqur al-Sham and Ahrar al-Sham in the Zawiya mountains. In a matter of days, HTS secured critical locations, including western Aleppo and southern Idlib, expelling al-Zinki from strategic points in northern Aleppo such as Darat Izza. The decisive factors were military support from the Turkistan Islamic Party (TIP) and the neutral stance adopted by Faylaq al-Sham, the Turkish-supported faction, despite its affiliation with the National Liberation Front that Ahrar al-Sham had joined beforehand.[5] These gave HTS a critical advantage in a brief but conclusive battle in which HTS imposed its terms on other factions, including their acceptance of the authority of the Salvation Government aligned with HTS, which we explore in the next chapter. The conflict between HTS and Ahrar al-Sham reflected their fundamental differences. HTS, which grew out of Jabhat al-Nusra, was more ideologically committed and cohesive than Ahrar al-Sham, which had become a coalition of various factions struggling with internal cohesion and decision-making divergences.

However, the first paradox of HTS's victory is that, despite its success, it still needed to collaborate with former adversaries on the military front. HTS established dominance over Ahrar al-Sham and its allies, but it had to allow them to remain in the province as long as they dismantled their civilian structures that the Salvation Government replaced. The sole exception was the Zinki Movement, which HTS expelled to areas under more direct Turkish control. HTS could not simply dismantle other factions, such as Ahrar al-Sham, as this would have undermined the province's overall military defence. Forcibly integrating them into HTS was equally unfeasible, as these factions were unwilling to join the very group that had recently defeated them, as Murhaf Abu Qasra, HTS's military leader, recognised in an interview.[6]

This marks the first clear instance of the "social inertia" that HTS repeatedly faced in its governance experience between 2019 and 2024. By this, we mean that society is not infinitely malleable and cannot be shaped in any direction at will. Despite its strength, HTS had to contend with the reality that armed factions are also social phenomena. They emerged from specific segments of society, carrying their own identities, histories, and local ties. HTS could not simply sideline them and impose its authority on the communities they represent without significantly undermining the province's overall capacity to resist the regime's onslaught.

HTS's victory coincided with the near-collapse of the opposition by spring 2020. The latter faced a severe military setback due to the regime's offensives, bolstered by intense Russian bombardment, which caused the loss of almost 40% of the territories controlled by HTS and its allies on the eve of the offensive. At the time, many feared that the regime and Russia did not necessarily aim to conquer all of Idlib but sought to secure control over the two strategic highways connecting Aleppo to the Syrian coastline, while confining the opposition to a narrow strip of land of 10 to 15 km along the Turkish border that would not even include Idlib city. Only a decisive Turkish military intervention in early 2020, combining the deployment of substantial ground troops with the destruction of significant regime forces through extensive drone strikes around Aleppo, prevented this outcome. This intervention culminated in a de facto ceasefire reached between Russia and Turkey in Moscow in March 2020 that we cover in other chapters.

HTS's victory over its rivals, coupled with the latest military setbacks, compelled the armed opposition as a whole to start a significant reconfiguration. The prevailing idea was that the opposition could no longer function as a loose coalition of factions, each with its own internal structures and objectives. The lack of genuine military institutionalisation created a fragmented landscape: some factions were rooted in local villages, while others operated as more professional, centralised forces capable of redeployment based on operational needs. Training also remained inconsistent, ad-hoc, and lacked a cohesive strategic framework aligned with the development of specific operational capabilities. Furthermore, competition between factions often hindered their effectiveness. Many were reluctant to commit their full strength to the frontlines, fearing that heavy losses in battle could leave them vulnerable to rival factions seizing power in their absence.

The armed opposition therefore collectively agreed to coordinate its efforts and formalise their military operations in a new command structure, al-Fath al-Mubin (the Clear Victory). The concept behind al-Fath al-Mubin, a military operation room, was to reorganise all factions into a unified structure of a number of brigades (*liwa*), each based in a specific geographic area and encompassing all necessary military specialisations, from snipers and infantry to tanks and artillery. There would also be specialised brigades resembling elite forces, which would be centrally organised rather than tied to any specific area, allowing them to be deployed flexibly based on operational needs. This new military operation room was initially made up of 40 brigades of 600 men each, which were all affiliated to one of the existing armed groups.[7] They initially agreed to cooperate, but preferred to stay apart because of HTS's continued international listing. As an FSA leader in Idlib mentioned at the time,

> For now, we are all keeping our structures. And our training is still separate. HTS insists on establishing a military council but it is difficult for us to engage in some fully integrated project with an organisation classified internationally as terrorist. It will be hard to go beyond the operations room.[8]

HTS and Turkey both advocated for this approach to the centralisation of military structures in Idlib though their visions differed. The reorganisation of the military forces posed a key dilemma: it could either dilute HTS's dominance, which was Turkey's vision, or consolidate it, which was HTS's objective. HTS had advocated for the unification of armed forces for the past two years, but it faced resistance from other factions that perceived it as seeking a monopolistic grip on power.[9] They believed they had already dismantled their civilian structures, so if their military structures also fell under HTS control, nothing would remain of them as independent armed groups. For Turkey, on the other hand, the goal was to fundamentally transform HTS and, paradoxically, to unify the military in Idlib under a structure resembling the Syrian Democratic Force (SDF) model in the east. The SDF operated as a unified military council under the ultimate control of the Kurdish YPG; similarly, Idlib's military structure would function as a unified council led by HTS. According to a Turkish official back then:

> The recent battles humbled HTS and broke its previous hubris. HTS fighters are not inherently better than others; HTS is simply better organised. In the past, they thought they could stand alone. Now [in 2020], HTS realises they aren't as strong as they believed and are more open to compromise. On the other hand, factions that had previously harbored strong hostility toward HTS and even fought against it were also more inclined toward compromise. We see that these groups, despite their differences, are now united by a shared enemy, which creates an opportunity for cooperation.[10]

The process of military institutionalisation therefore had to account for the enduring influence of factionalism while simultaneously working to gradually diminish it over time. HTS military leader Murhaf Abu Qasra articulated the ultimate goal of transforming Fath al-Mubin into a military council despite practical difficulties:

> If we manage to unite all the military forces in a military council, we do not believe that we can mix the military brigades of different groups. That would create tensions and weaken us. It is better instead that each group [HTS, Ahrar al-Sham, Faylaq al-Sham, and other smaller groups] creates a certain number of brigades [*liwa*] that perform all the military functions. Each brigade is responsible for a specific geographic area, which helps to cover all the frontlines and increase accountability. In addition, we think that this helps to create a healthy competition between the brigades, which will help them get better over time.

However, Ankara feared unintentionally strengthening HTS. Centralising the opposition's military forces without undertaking meaningful structural reforms could reinforce the dominance of the leading faction, HTS, rather than address factionalism. Turkey also worried that the newly unified structure could be internationally designated as a terrorist organisation, which would undermine Turkey's efforts to normalise it, and feared, according to a Turkish official, that "challenging factionalism means shaking a precarious equilibrium that is fragile but currently under control. The transformation of factionalism might change the balance in the field and disrupt the current order."[11] Despite Turkey's urgent need to streamline the military capacities of the armed opposition groups it supported, it remained cautious and minimally interventionist. For example, salaries continued to be distributed through the existing factional structures. While Turkey closely monitored military operations rooms, its direct involvement was limited. Moreover, the factions still conducted their military training independently, maintaining a degree of autonomy from the leadership of the operations room.[12]

The centralisation of military efforts within the Fath al-Mubin Operations Room also created new challenges for other groups, notably Ahrar al-Sham. The latter's leaders found themselves in a contentious situation, torn between two factions with differing stances. The historical leadership of Ahrar al-Sham, while initially open to the idea of transforming the military forces into new brigades with specialised roles, sought to maintain control by appointing military leaders who remained loyal to them. They were particularly concerned about figures like Abu Mundhar, their own military leader, and a former Ahrar leader, Hassan Sufan, whom they perceived as being too closely aligned with HTS.[13] This disagreement eventually led to a split within the group that marginalised the historical leadership. As a result, the leadership council under their control was dissolved, and a new leadership aligned with the second faction, which had stronger ties to HTS, assumed control.

Breaking the truce with radicals: The all-out war on al-Qaeda

It is reasonable to question why HTS prioritised targeting more mainstream groups over al-Qaeda supporters if it was genuinely committed to transforming and renouncing global jihad. The answer is actually quite straightforward: HTS viewed mainstream groups as a more immediate threat. These groups were its strongest competitors, with the potential to attract external support and establish themselves as a viable alternative to HTS—something al-

Qaeda supporters, lacking broad appeal and external backing, could never achieve. This was not an indication of increased radicalism on HTS's part but rather a strategic prioritisation. However, once this threat was neutralised, HTS had more leeway to clamp down on more radical factions too.

Former Jabhat al-Nusra commanders who refused to align with HTS's new direction had three primary grievances with al-Sharaa's group. Their chief concern was HTS's decision to sever ties with al-Qaeda in the summer of 2016, which they saw as a betrayal of the global jihadi movement. Many of these commanders, veterans of previous jihadi campaigns abroad, rejected the shift toward a Syrian-focused agenda, which they believed would lead to unacceptable concessions.[14] The two other issues appeared later on. First, in late 2017, HTS permitted the entry of Turkish troops into Idlib province, a move these commanders denounced as collaboration with an "apostate" NATO member state. Even more contentious was HTS's acceptance of the 2020 Russian-Turkish truce ratified in Moscow, which followed HTS's acceptance of joint patrols by Turkey and Russia on the M4 highway connecting Aleppo to the coast that the next chapter explores.

The threat to HTS intensified when its adversaries exploited the conflict with Ahrar al-Sham to establish Hurras al-Din, a new al-Qaeda-affiliated group, in February 2018. Unlike Ahrar al-Sham, Hurras al-Din was not a fully developed organisation but rather an unstructured coalition of approximately 1,200 to 1,500 fighters.[15] Despite its relatively small size and weak organisational structures, the group garnered significant international attention, particularly from foreign states concerned about its potential to orchestrate attacks abroad. Hurras al-Din included most former Jabhat al-Nusra commanders who united around their refusal to sever ties with al-Qaeda. The group included a mix of Syrian fighters, Jordanians closely linked to al-Qaeda, and other foreign fighters. Some of its leaders maintained strong connections to al-Qaeda's central leadership, such as Abu 'Abd al-Karim al-Masri, further cementing its ideological alignment with the global jihadi movement. Others, like Sami al-Uraydi, were close to Abu Muhammad al-Maqdisi—the jihadi ideologue—in Jordan.

When Hurras al-Din appeared, HTS initially avoided a direct confrontation. HTS was willing to collaborate militarily with all factions opposing the regime.[16] The head of HTS's military Murhaf Abu Qasra emphasised this policy at the time, stating that "our stance is to accept all groups that engage in combat, provided they refrain from involvement in destabilising activities."[17] One unspoken reason was that HTS was wary of the sympathies some of its commanders and sub-factions held toward Hurras al-Din, fearing that a direct confrontation could undermine its own internal cohesion. There were clear indications of this vulnerability. For instance, incidents involving the arrest of Hurras al-Din members had previously led to the suspension of HTS membership for certain sub-factions and group leaders, highlighting divisions within the organisation.[18]

The neutralisation of Ahrar al-Sham and its allies in January 2019 allowed HTS to shift its focus to Hurras al-Din, after eliminating the most immediate and significant threat to its dominance. By March 2019, HTS established strict terms for coexistence with Hurras al-Din.[19] These required the group to renounce external operations—jihad outside Syria—disband its courts of justice, detention centres, and checkpoints, and submit to the jurisdiction of HTS's military courts. Essentially, Hurras al-Din had to adhere to HTS's rules and refrain from involvement in civilian affairs.[20] This containment strategy extended to military and economic domains. HTS exerted control over weapon supplies and pressured financial intermediaries with Hurras al-Din to weaken it. It also controlled the group's military activity. For instance, HTS prevented Hurras al-Din from launching a diversionary campaign in Aleppo in May 2019 during heavy fighting in southern Idlib, partly due to concerns over potential Iranian intervention.[21] HTS finally prevented Hurras al-Din from nurturing new local alliances. After the formation of the Harid al-Mu'mineen ("Incite the Believers") operations room in October 2018, which included Jabhat Ansar al-Din and Ansar al-Islam, HTS aligned another group, Ansar al-Tawhid, with its political agenda.[22] By increasing material support to Ansar al-Tawhid in May 2020, HTS encouraged the group's gradual distancing from Hurras al-Din and alignment with its own objectives.[23]

The agreement with Hurras al-Din remained intact for nearly thirteen months, before Turkey's significant military intervention in Idlib in February 2020 disrupted the fragile balance between the two groups. Prior to that, Ahmad al-Sharaa recognised that "the relationship with Hurras al-Din has always been strained. Issues occasionally arise, requiring our intervention, but so far, they have always been resolved."[24] However, the Turkish intervention disrupted the fragile equilibrium between the two organisations. After approximately two months of hesitation, HTS chose to align itself with the newly established Russian-Turkish agreement. In doing so, it effectively accepted the periodic presence of Russian forces through joint Turkish-Russian patrols in rebel-controlled areas. An analyst close to HTS remarked that

> the Putin-Erdogan deal on the patrols immediately reshaped the ideological narrative within Hurras al-Din. This transformation coincided with the gradual deterioration of the situation in Idlib, where Hurras al-Din, facing financial difficulties, increasingly resorted to abductions, pillaging, and theft.[25]

Taking the initiative, Hurras al-Din launched a spectacular assault on regime forces in the village of Tanjara in the Ghab plain, briefly seizing control on 9 May 2020. In hindsight, the HTS military leader Murhaf Abu Qasra regarded this as the opening move in the ensuing escalation. He explained, "this large-scale operation was not directed against the regime; it was a political maneuver intended to rally all groups opposed to HTS's policies and possibly sow the seeds of desertion within our ranks."[26]

The security crackdown began in the summer of 2020, following the end of HTS's containment policy toward Hurras al-Din. This shift occurred in a context where, according to the HTS leadership, the outcome of the conflict was no longer in question. HTS now saw Hurras al-Din as a security threat rather than a direct military one. Still, although it no longer posed a direct threat to HTS's dominance, Hurras al-Din retained the ability to inflict significant damage. This included attacks on checkpoints, operations against Turkish patrols, provocations against Russian positions aimed at breaking the ceasefire, and potential external operations.[27]

The confrontation between HTS and Hurras al-Din started with the alignment with Turkey's sanctuary policy in parallel with internal power dynamics within HTS. The clashes commenced following the defection of a prominent HTS leader, Abu Malik al-Tally,[28] who joined forces with Abu Abd Ashida, a former HTS commander responsible for establishing a group called "Tansiqiyyat al-Jihad" (the coordination of jihad), and Abu Salah al-Uzbeki, a former leader of the Katiba al-Tawhid wa al-Jihad group.[29] These three leaders played a pivotal role in the formation of the "Fa-Ithibitu" (Be Steadfast) operations room in collaboration with Hurras al-Din. Its establishment underscored the growing divide prompted by the significant deployment of Turkish military forces earlier in the year. As one analyst close to the HTS leadership pointed out, "this marked the first front of dissent against al-Sharaa's leadership."[30] Abu Malik al-Tally's association with Fa-Ithibitu led to his arrest, even though Fa-Ithibitu was not a substantial military threat to HTS. As the analyst noted, "out of the 320 frontline positions we have, only 10 to 15 were held by Fa-Ithbitu."[31] The conflict rapidly escalated into public view. Hurras al-Din set up checkpoints to protect its positions, although some HTS leaders believed their purpose was to apprehend activists from the organisation for potential negotiations. For the HTS military leader, this was tantamount to "a declaration of war."[32] In response to the threat, HTS prohibited any defections that were not pre-approved by the leadership and mobilised its own international supporters.[33]

HTS adopted a deliberate approach by choosing not to target Hurras al-Din's official leaders—including its leader Abu Humam al-Shami, whom they deemed weak and internally contested—but instead focusing on the military commanders who posed the most significant threat. Al-Sharaa, in explaining this strategy, emphasised that HTS's intention was "to afford them some room to manoeuvre. Arresting the leaders would likely trigger media reactions. It was more prudent to keep them concealed and under surveillance rather than elevate them as potential victims that could garner sympathy."[34] Furthermore, HTS implemented a systematic policy of engaging in negotiations with local commanders, leading to a de facto series of local agreements. According to the same analyst:

> The crucial point to remember is that Hurras al-Din represented a front of opposition to HTS's efforts to sever ties with al-Qaeda, rather than a well-structured organisation. Its leadership was

THE STRUGGLE FOR DOMINANCE

particularly weak, and HTS declined to engage with their senior leaders when they offered to negotiate.[35]

This strategy entailed a combination of co-optation, promises of amnesty for combatants, and the initiation of security proceedings against select commanders. These measures were effective, as within the last week of June, HTS only needed a few days to silence Hurras al-Din and prevent it from maintaining a visible presence in its strongholds, including Armanaz, Darkouch, Jisr al-Shughur, and Arab Sa'id.[36] Ultimately, HTS chose not to arrest all Hurras al-Din members, including its leader Abu Humam al-Shami and its religious authority Sami al-Uraydi. According to an HTS security official, the group became defunct, with a debilitated leadership incapable of engaging in armed activities. Arresting these figures could inadvertently have led to their replacement by more capable leaders, posing a greater risk than their weakened state.[37]

The polarisation caused by the large influx of Turkish military personnel and the subsequent factional conflicts marked a crucial turning point in the Syrian armed conflict. For the first time in nine years, al-Qaeda no longer had an active military presence in Syria. The organisation retreated into hiding, relinquishing its frontline positions and military bases. Al-Qaeda's once-substantial organisational and financial resources diminished significantly, with Hurras al-Din barely operating after 2020. Lacking access to the spoils of war and foreign support for jihad, its operational capacity had been severely compromised. HTS, intent on maintaining control, became resolute in preventing any potential resurgence of al-Qaeda-related networks in the region. An incident in Raqqa province in January 2021, far removed from northwest Syria, suggests that group commanders may have decided to shift their focus to other battlefields.[38] Additionally, the remaining foreign fighters, including the Turkistan Islamic Party and the Chechens, aligned themselves with HTS's new stance. Al-Qaeda would ultimately dissolve its Syria branch after the downfall of Assad, in early 2025.

In contrast to HTS leaders' early concerns, the confrontation with al-Qaeda and the group's acceptance of the new Turkish dynamics did not result in any significant internal schisms or widespread desertions. While HTS's strategic adjustments were met with some internal reluctance, the number of individuals leaving for more radical groups remained limited. The HTS leadership emerged from this conflict strengthened, with its political stance facing increasingly fewer challenges and a notable absence of radical alternatives. In the meantime, HTS developed new specialised units dedicated to tracking down non-aligned jihadis still present in Idlib up to the 2024 takeover of Damascus. This transformation occurred primarily through the construction of the General Security *(jihaz al-amn al-'am)*, which grew out of Jabhat al-Nusra's own internal security or intelligence services, which built two units focused on "counter-terrorism", one dedicated to tracking al-Qaeda and the other to tracking IS.

An even more violent war against Islamic State

In early 2014, ISIS's attacks on other Syrian armed groups in northwest Syria prompted a strong response from various armed opposition groups, which led to its expulsion from the region. A coordinated offensive in January 2014, involving the Islamic Front spearheaded by Ahrar al-Sham, local Free Syrian Army groups, and Jabhat al-Nusra, targeted key ISIS positions in areas such as Atarib, al-Dana, and Azaz. This offensive resulted in the recapture of several strategic towns, which weakened ISIS's hold in the region. By February 2014, the combined resistance forced ISIS to retreat from key strongholds in the Aleppo and Idlib provinces, with local support and superior knowledge of the terrain playing a significant role.

The expulsion was a result of strategic military actions and broad local backing, with different factions putting aside internal differences to unite against a common enemy. For instance, the Jaysh al-Mujahideen alliance in Aleppo formed explicitly to fight ISIS, a first in the Syrian conflict. By March 2014, ISIS had largely withdrawn to its strongholds in Raqqa and Deir Ezzor. The only group that remained in the northwest with an ambiguous stance toward ISIS was Jund al-Aqsa, which preferred to be neutral between al-Qaeda and ISIS.

THE STRUGGLE FOR DOMINANCE

IS then staged a comeback in several waves. Some sympathisers remained in Idlib after their expulsion in 2014, taking shelter with relatives and friends, particularly around Sarmin, Kafr Hind and Jisr al-Shughur. A first significant influx occurred in October 2017, when IS fighters moved into south-eastern Idlib while besieged by regime forces in northern Hama. The regime gave safe passage to hundreds of IS militants with their weapons, knowing full well that they would soon attack other armed groups in the region. All the armed opposition groups, including HTS, had to confront this new IS surge. They successfully quelled its presence, though they did not capture all the IS fighters. The last wave of IS infiltration occurred in March 2019 when Russian airstrikes on an HTS prison in Idlib allowed many ISIS members to escape and form new cells. In the meantime, IS fighters and commanders entered Idlib individually from central and north-eastern Syria after the fall of Baghouz in 2019, though this happened in a more limited fashion through the areas north of Aleppo.

HTS's response was severe and relatively efficient. The group launched a counter-insurgency campaign to dismantle IS networks in a series of raids and arrests. Some of these operations culminated in the public execution of many IS militants to deter others from joining their ranks when HTS felt that the province was under threat, according to an HTS security official.[39] A good understanding of jihadi networks rooted in shared organisational frameworks, close connections in the past, and common military and security expertise, enabled relatively effective tracking of the group. HTS arrested six "governors" (*wali*) or leaders of IS in Idlib after 2018 as well as the former leader of Raqqa in 2021. The operational lifespan of an IS militant in Idlib did not exceed a few months before 2024, which effectively prevented the group's rebirth. Instead, the only IS cells that managed to form consisted of small groups of three to fifteen individuals who were self-sufficient in funding and therefore resource-limited, making it difficult for them to carry out large-scale operations in the governorate.[40] HTS also thwarted major operations, such as the attempted car bomb attack in Biksraya in 2020 against a gathering of HTS-allied factions. HTS also dismantled several large networks, with the most noteworthy being "*maktab al-Hijra*" (the office of migration), a group of approximately twenty individuals preparing for attacks in Europe and Turkey. IS has not carried out any significant actions in the region since then.

IS ultimately sought to forge alliances with dissidents from Hurras al-Din, particularly those who formed groups like Saraya Abu Bakr al-Sadiq and Saraya Abdullah bin Unais, according to HTS security officials.[41] One of the leaders of these factions released a document accusing HTS of apostasy for an array of reasons including forming alliances with Turkey and other "apostate" armed groups, failing to fully implement Islamic law and its prescribed penal punishments, imposing non-Islamic taxes, permitting secular education, and supporting the UN-backed political process. According to HTS security officials, IS offered financial support to these groups in exchange for the right to claim responsibility for their armed attacks but these efforts yielded no significant operational results.

The remaining question, then, is: if HTS's counter-insurgency campaign was truly efficient, why were two IS caliphs found—and eventually killed—in the region under its control? While HTS demonstrated effective tracking of active IS networks, monitoring dormant cells demands more than just intelligence. It requires robust population control, which hinges on a well-established local bureaucracy that was lacking at the time. The General Security organisation focused its efforts on major cities and refugee camps. A comprehensive census was underway, but the priority was urban areas and camps. The Salvation Government prioritised cities for security purposes, as census efforts are easier there due to the presence of local administrations. It also focused on the refugee camps due to their administrative structures and the fact that the census aimed to gather crucial data for distributing UN and NGO aid.[42]

In other words, outside the cities and the refugee camps, the limited institutionalisation of bureaucratic population control and the high mobility of these populations created "gray areas" for non-active militants. These spaces could harbor dormant cells, even as active cells were quickly identified and neutralised elsewhere. Unlike active militants, dormant cells were less detectable through intelligence networks and required robust population monitoring to be traced effectively. This monitoring, in turn, depended on the presence of a well-established administrative framework—

something HTS had yet to fully develop at the time. For instance, in urban areas like the city of Idlib, where a comprehensive census and house-numbering initiative were implemented, HTS made numerous arrests, which contributed significantly to urban security. In contrast, rural areas—often populated by newcomers and marked by frequent population mixing—remained largely beyond administrative oversight. This lack of control complicates efforts to identify dormant cells. As one source noted, "we lack population records in rural and remote areas. Our focus has been on camps and major cities due to limited resources and the need to prioritise. These rural areas escape our oversight. We have no statistics, no names; property transactions are entirely informal, and populations are highly mobile."[43]

This largely explained the presence of Abdullah Qardash, IS's second Caliph, in Idlib. His hideout was a rented house owned by his guard, a low-key merchant from Aleppo, with no direct affiliation to the organisation.[44] The rental was arranged through a real estate transaction office in the village of Atmeh, which did not report property transactions to any authority.[45] Qardash went to great lengths to hide, with only one armed accomplice serving as both a courier and a guard, using only a rifle as a weapon. He even avoided surveillance cameras around the house, which he had previously installed in his former residences.[46] "He was under the radar, which was his strength, precisely because security, to this day, cannot rely on an effective administrative framework," according to an HTS security official.[47] One of the movement's leaders pointed out, "it is obvious that we have weaknesses in our security apparatus. We cannot compare security structures that are barely five years old with those of existing states".[48] Al-Sharaa, not necessarily incorrectly, also noted, "the first time I saw [Abu Bakr] al-Baghdadi was north of Baghdad when it was a place with American presence. Leaders are alone and mobile. Qardash was here, but he could have been elsewhere".[49]

The factional conflict against IS, initially driven by internal power struggles and some ideological differences, then evolved into a counterinsurgency effort that also involved elements of deradicalisation. HTS recognised the need to combat the appeal of IS's ideology, not solely because HTS is less radical (which it is), but also as a means of preserving control. By addressing the ideological appeal of IS, HTS sought to maintain its dominance and prevent the erosion of its authority. For example, Ahmad al-Sharaa stated that:

> Now [in 2022], in Idlib, IS has a very low recruitment capacity. To reduce the appeal it might still have, we need an alternative project. We shouldn't be seeking a pro-American Islam but an attractive Islamic project that can prevent young people from being drawn towards this group. It is important that the West allows us to develop an Islamic project without hindrance.[50]

HTS also sought to diminish IS's appeal by actively shaping religious discourse, closely monitoring mosque sermons, and implementing its own religious programs. HTS's senior religious figure, Abd al-Rahim Atun, along with the judges he trained, claimed to have delivered hundreds of lectures and courses since the conflict with IS began in 2013. These efforts relied on pragmatic arguments rooted in Islamic jurisprudence while highlighting the excesses (*ghulu*) of IS leaders to denounce the Iraqi group and weaken its appeal. The aim was twofold: to win over low-level IS followers and to fortify HTS members against its rhetoric. These initiatives were part of HTS's broader strategy to control religious discourse. Additionally, the group banned practices such as excommunicating other Muslims (*takfir*) and prohibited incitement against non-Muslim minorities. While HTS acknowledged the difficulty of changing the mindset of IS hardliners, it believed it had successfully disseminated its interpretations of Islam within its own ranks. These interpretations include a greater acceptance of non-Salafi Muslims and a renewed emphasis on the traditional schools of Islamic jurisprudence, which HTS claimed have found resonance among its base.[51]

HTS created the al-Jamiliyya camp as a hybrid facility as a detention centre, a refugee camp, and a space for reintegration for IS returnees. The camp housed approximately 250 families, primarily composed of foreign women and children, mostly Arabs and Muslims from Central Asia. Due to limited resources, it operated more as an internment camp than a structured reintegration facility. There were no formal reeducation programs; instead, authorities focused on monitoring behavior. Families' release from the camp was contingent upon meeting specific conditions, such as accepting the education provided by the Salvation Government, recognising its courts for marriages, and agreeing to assistance from NGOs linked to HTS's governance structures.[52] Released families were allowed to rent homes but remained under surveillance. Authorities generally favored integrating these families into broader society despite the risks, as isolation could deepen their radicalisation. However, this approach carried challenges: some families reportedly maintained allegiance to IS through online networks, which the authorities monitor but tolerate to some extent.[53]

Imposing a tight grip on the remaining foreign fighters

In northwest Syria, a small number of foreign fighters remained before the 2024 takeover of Damascus, who neither joined IS nor aligned themselves with al-Qaeda. These individuals were often loosely affiliated with smaller, independent factions or integrated local groups that focused primarily on the Syrian conflict rather than a global jihadi agenda. Many of them were veterans of earlier phases of the conflict and chose to distance themselves from IS and al-Qaeda, preferring to support Syrian objectives over transnational ambitions.

The groups varied significantly in size and influence. The largest among them, the Turkestan Islamic Party or TIP, was predominantly composed of Uyghur fighters from western China. This group was militarily potent and operated as a tight-knit community in Syria during the conflict while maintaining some connections with its counterparts in Afghanistan, which were much smaller in size and under Taliban control. The group's stance is clear, according to several of its military commanders: while each faction—whether in Afghanistan or Syria—remains theoretically committed to its long-term objectives in China, in practice, they respect local authorities, HTS in Syria and the Taliban in Afghanistan, and comply with their demands. Consequently, if local authorities instruct them to refrain from attacking Chinese targets, they follow these orders. In the meantime, their primary objective is to ensure the survival of their community while preserving its Uyghur identity, including their language, schools, and military infrastructure.[54]

In contrast, other groups were much smaller and less consequential. These included small clusters of Albanian trainers offering support to opposition forces and the remnants of Chechen fighters who chose not to align with ISIS. Despite their presence, these smaller factions held minimal strategic relevance compared to the more organised and cohesive TIP.

After consolidating its control over the province and neutralising al-Qaeda and IS, HTS imposed strict constraints on the remaining foreign fighters who did not fully align with its agenda. The crackdown on Hurras al-Din in June 2020 notably became a blueprint for dealing with other smaller factions that resisted aligning with the new military direction in the province.

After dismantling Hurras al-Din, HTS moved against two other groups: Junud al-Sham and Jund Allah at the end of 2020. These factions were led by Abu Muslim al-Shishani, a veteran Chechen militant who had fought in both Chechen wars, and Abu Hanifa al-Adhari, a Tajik militant. HTS accused al-Adhari of engaging in excommunication (*takfir*) and held al-Shishani responsible for sheltering him. Although HTS reached an initial agreement with them, negotiations quickly collapsed. The confrontation was swift. HTS captured most of the militants, though it did not stop at military action alone. As part of its strategy, HTS introduced a deradicalisation initiative targeting approximately seventy detained fighters. For the first time, it implemented ideological training and refutation courses within prisons. These sessions, known as Shari'a courses (*dawrat shar'iyya*), spanned over thirty days and focused on intensive lectures and "refutations of misconceptions" aimed at dismantling hardline ideological views. However, the programme encountered strong resistance, particularly from converts, including individuals from Russia, Turkey, and Azerbaijan. Of the seventy participants, twenty were eventually released under a guarantor system, where local notables took responsibility for their oversight and reintegration into the community.[55]

HTS's policy towards other foreign fighters followed a similar approach of containment without direct confrontation. The central principle was that HTS sought to manage and control these groups, provided they respected the general order in the province. This strategy applied to a variety of foreign factions, including Uzbeks, Caucasians, and groups with membership ranging from 50 to 150 individuals. HTS prohibited them from recruiting, creating civilian media outlets, planning operations abroad, independently confronting the regime, establishing governance structures, or engaging in judicial matters. As Ahmad al-Sharaa stated,

> Our principle of accepting these groups is based on respect for the law. We judge them solely by this criterion. The key is their acceptance of our institutionalisation efforts. Those who respect the law are tolerated. Operations abroad, for example, are strictly prohibited. We do not think in terms of radicalism [*ghulu*], but in terms of adherence to the law. From this perspective, the issue lies with illegal organisations.[56]

Firqat al-Ghuraba (the Group of the Strangers), a group led by Omar Omsen—whose real name is Omar Diaby—offers further insight into HTS's approach to foreign fighters.[57] HTS arrested Omsen, a Franco-Senegalese national and a prominent recruiter of French jihadis, in 2020 on suspicion of abducting the daughter of a French fighter who had died in combat. After lengthy negotiations regarding the return of the four-year-old girl to France, HTS released Omsen at the end of January 2022, under the condition that he disclosed the girl's whereabouts. HTS also accused him of operating his own courts, which handled matters such as marriage and divorce. Upon his release, HTS allowed Omsen to rejoin his small brigade—which by then operated under the group Ansar al-Tawheed—but under strict conditions. He could not make media appearances, recruit new members, or engage with French families in their camp, and he remained under constant security surveillance. More importantly, HTS explicitly forbade him from administering any form of justice independently, requiring him to defer to the authority of the Salvation Government—a restriction it similarly imposed on other groups of both foreign fighters and Syrians.

Ultimately, all armed groups, including those with foreign fighters, had to comply with the directives of the Fath al-Mubin operations room and were strictly prohibited from acting independently. HTS used this system to assert control over the small number of foreign-led brigades through two options: either integrate into HTS's own military forces by joining newly formed specialised brigades or, at a minimum, adhere to the orders issued by the shared operations room. Over the next two years, HTS restructured most groups of foreign fighters, which had to join HTS's new military brigades. This restructuring imposed new military regulations and organisational changes that allowed HTS to exert control over them while aligning them with the broader military strategy of the province. This indicates that HTS did not have to confront all foreign fighters. HTS confronted the most defiant and antagonistic foreign fighters aligned with al-Qaeda before offering a non-confrontational alternative to the others. The price of this reprieve for them was twofold: adherence to HTS's agenda and a complete renunciation of any role in governance. In essence, the survival of these groups depended on their depoliticisation.

HTS's dominance ultimately brought the foreign fighters—once a powerful force within the armed opposition—under its control though HTS had been one of the Syrian groups most closely aligned with them. For HTS, this was above all a matter of political control: it could not allow these factions an independent military voice that might challenge its authority or undermine its strategic priorities in the province. Over time, however, this effort also took on a deradicalisation dimension, as HTS came to view some of these groups' ideological positions as a threat in themselves.

The only problematic group that HTS never fully controlled—or struggled to keep under control—was Ansar al-Islam. Ansar al-Islam originated as a jihadi group in Iraq in 2001, composed mainly of Kurdish Islamists. It was known for its strict Salafi jihadi views and opposition to both secular Kurdish factions and Western forces. After the US-led invasion of Iraq in 2003, the group was largely dismantled but remained active in insurgent activities. Over time, remnants of Ansar al-Islam reemerged in Syria, where it operated independently and resisted full integration into HTS. This resistance made them a persistent challenge for HTS, as they maintained a degree of autonomy and ideological rigidity that often clashed with HTS's broader strategic goals.

Overall, the foreign fighter groups consisted of, at most, a few hundred members each before the takeover of Damascus, up to a few thousand in total. Despite their limited numbers, they proved to be highly effective on the frontlines. However, even before 2025, they posed international challenges for HTS, as many were independently designated by the UN Security Council (in addition to HTS's own listing). The proscribed groups include Jaysh al-Muhajirin wal-Ansar, primarily composed of Chechens; Harakat Sham al-Islam, mainly consisting of Moroccans; Jund al-Aqsa (now Ansar al-Tawheed); Katiba Imam al-Bukhari; and Katiba al-Tawhid wal-Jihad, both largely made up of Uzbeks. While keeping these factions might seem unnecessary—given that they each numbered only a few hundred fighters compared to the tens of thousands of Syrians in HTS, which was leading an armed force of 30,000 fighters by the time of Aleppo's takeover in 2024—their continued existence was primarily about control. HTS security officials emphasised that:

> We established clear boundaries, and as long as the remaining foreign fighters respect them, we allow them to continue operating within our ranks. Keeping their organisational structures intact—now under our forces—helps us maintain control over them. For example, if a group has fifty fighters, we know their commander, and we make him responsible for them to ensure that they follow our directives and do not violate our rules. If we were to dismantle these groups, those fifty fighters would scatter, making it difficult to track them or monitor their activities. Some could even be recruited by IS and end up fighting against us. It is far better to keep them under our supervision.[58]

Still, some foreign diplomats and individuals close to various armed groups take a different view of the remaining foreign fighters.[59] While they acknowledge that most of these cadres unequivocally reject IS and, to a large extent, al-Qaeda, they also see them as a kind of Praetorian Guard for Ahmad al-Sharaa and his inner circle—highly committed fighters who are fiercely loyal to him yet unable to challenge his power because they are foreigners, not Syrians. For instance, they view the appointment of Abu al-Hussein al-Urduni, a prominent Jordanian HTS military commander, as head of the new Syrian Republican Guard in 2025 as a strategic move to safeguard the new government against a potential coup.

3

DISMANTLING THE RADICAL PAST

Governance within the uniquely constrained context of Idlib—shaped by both local and international factors—played a pivotal role in the transformation of Jabhat al-Nusra into HTS. Jabhat al-Nusra's predominantly military structure, centred on minimal governance primarily enforced through ad-hoc Islamic courts, was incompatible with the establishment of a centralised structure under the Salvation Government. The institutionalisation of a new governance framework not only served the objective of stabilising and unifying the province under the Turkish Russian strategic play over Idlib, it also unwittingly facilitated the emergence of a new militant ethos in the group. It ultimately contributed to the growth of a conservative political stratum that produced a new generation of technocrats whose importance became more visible after the takeover of Damascus in 2024.

HTS territorialisation: A neo-liberal hegemon

HTS used its military dominance over rival factions to impose its own governance through the establishment of the Salvation Government in November 2017, which consolidated through three key mechanisms: the centralisation of all governance structures including those previously held by other armed groups, the partial delegation of authority to an educated urban elite, and the outsourcing of select public services to independent third parties outside the existing administrative framework.

The initiative that gave rise to the Salvation Government was the final attempt to present a civilian governance project in north west Syria—a success made possible by HTS's dominance. Before 2017, Idlib's educated and conservative urban elite made multiple attempts to establish unified governance in the region. However, the dominant influence and competing agendas of local armed groups repeatedly undermined these efforts and prevented the consolidation of an independent administrative structure.[1] HTS's dominance over its competitors paradoxically created space for this urban elite to operate, albeit under control. Syrian academics spearheaded the final attempt, the Civil Administration Initiative, which culminated in the establishment of the Salvation Government as a centralised governance structure for Idlib in 2017.[2] This elite comprised a diverse array of profiles, including urban, educated, and conservative non-militant Islamists such as Bassam Sihiouni, Farouq Kishkich, and Mujahid Na'iss; academics like Taher Samaq, director of the University of Idlib, and Muhammad Bakour, an economics professor from Aleppo; as well as individuals actively involved in local initiatives. They were united by their activist experience after 2011 but did not have factional affiliation. On the contrary, they harboured:

> A feeling of exclusion from the Syrian Interim Government (SIG), mostly located abroad, and other factions. What unites them is the confiscation of representation by the Syrian National Coalition (SNC) and the deception of opposition entities operating abroad. HTS sensed very well the existence of this excluded elite and was able to offer them a place.[3]

The leaders of the academics' initiative were joined by businessmen, who participated in the institutional building efforts that were taking place within the framework of the Salvation Government. Businessmen were more interested in rebuilding order and security than driven by ideological affinities. They believed that unifying governance would improve security and limit factional intrusions in their work. The chamber of commerce sponsored and covered the full costs of the second constituent body, which in February 2019 appointed the first legislative assembly in charge of reforming the Salvation Government and was attended by fifty or so participants.[4]

The Salvation Government formed in a top-down logic. The first government created a limited number of ministries, which began to codify internal regulations to impose their authority on the armed groups and the local councils. As HTS took over the province gradually, the Salvation Government seized the governance functions formerly exercised by the factions. In the field of justice, the first step was to take over factional courts by force or through negotiations. The Salvation Government kept the detainees in detention with sentences handed down, unless families requested it,[5] and transferred the archives to the Ministry of Justice. It also generally maintained the court staff. Similarly, the Idlib Chamber of Commerce committed to the creation of the Salvation Government and transferred several prerogatives to the Ministry of the Economy of the new government. The trade register was also transferred despite having been kept during the days of domination by the fragmented factions. Finally, HTS handed over the directorates of the camps and displaced persons to the Ministry of Humanitarian Affairs.

HTS's push for centralisation intensified tensions with the local councils, which had previously functioned either autonomously or in coordination with other factions. Rather than a uniform strategy, HTS adopted a tailored approach based on the specific local balance of power. This balance was influenced by factors such as the level of civilian resistance and the councils' existing relationships with other armed groups. HTS employed a combination of co-optation, local agreements, and repression, as negotiations between the Salvation Government and local councils were handled on a case-by-case basis. Following HTS's military takeover in January 2019, all local councils had to formally recognise the authority of the Salvation Government, though they were not immediately integrated into the new central structures. The integration process varied. In areas historically dominated by Jabhat al-Nusra, such as Harem, local councils were often quickly brought under the direct control of the Salvation Government. In other instances, the Salvation Government oversaw elections through its Ministry of Local Administration, sometimes appointing the electoral bodies responsible for selecting local councils.[6]

For example, when HTS seized military control of Maarat al-Nu'man in January 2019, a delegation from the Salvation Government came to negotiate with the heads of local power structures. They sought recognition of the Salvation Government's authority and moved to take control of the police station and the court. They struck a deal; HTS dismantled its checkpoints in exchange for control over the courts and a pledge not to target civil society activists. Within a month, the Salvation Government began consolidating power by seizing local revenue sources, including the town's bread oven and the civil and land registries, followed by the strategic office of control and statistics. Although the local council remained in place, the new authorities changed its composition—female representation, which had reached 20% under the previous administration, ceased. Over time, authority in the city increasingly shifted towards HTS and the Salvation Government.[7]

In regions where revolutionary Islamist groups were more influential—such as Suqur al-Sham in Jabal al-Zawiya and Faylaq al-Sham in Kafr Takharim—local councils managed to resist the grip of the Salvation Government for longer. The stronger the local faction, the greater the council's ability to maintain a degree of autonomy. Prominent revolutionary councils supported by former Free Syrian Army groups in areas with strong civil activism displayed prolonged resistance. They opposed Jabhat al-Nusra's attempts to assert control and later resisted the expanding influence of HTS and the Salvation Government's governance structures. This was particularly evident in Atareb, Saraqib, Maarat al-Nu'man, Ariha, and Sarmada. However, the Salvation Government's institutional penetration gradually extended across all areas. One key mechanism was the provision of electricity, which enabled the government to impose taxes even in territories where former local councils continued to operate. Over time, these fiscal and administrative strategies eroded the remaining autonomy of resistant councils.[8] Police functions were transferred to HTS and judicial matters to the Ministry of Justice. In the end, the local councils of Saraqib, Maarat al-Nu'man and Kafranbel fell with the regime's military reconquest of these villages in early 2020.

The Salvation Government garnered some support from segments of the remaining local elite, including urban professionals, entrepreneurs, and tribal figures who participated in its governance structures.[9] However, this alignment faced significant opposition from civil activists and journalists, who criticised the government for its ties to HTS, corruption, and suppression of independent civil structures. HTS initially adopted a coercive approach toward civil society organisations though over time it evolved into a more ambivalent strategy that blended permissiveness with new mechanisms of social control. The former revolutionary civil society was gradually supplanted by depoliticised bureaucrats with a strictly managerial approach to governance. Members of this new civil society often identified themselves as "technocrats" as they distanced their roles from the political ideals of the past.[10]

The inclusion of the urban elite in the Salvation Government's hegemonic project was not solely an authoritarian co-optation. The project also had structuring effects as it enabled certain actors to assert themselves independently—such as professionals and businessmen—while others, like tribal groups, were co-opted and placed under indirect HTS control. The alignment of various actors with the project had different rationales: ideological affinities, particularly among academics; corporatist interests, such as those of businessmen and doctors; and the strength of social bonds, particularly evident among southern tribes. This nuanced dynamic reflects a combination of voluntary engagement and strategic co-optation, shaped by overlapping social, ideological, and economic motivations.[11]

While HTS played a leading role in the establishment of the Salvation Government, unlike the Kurdish movement in the northeast the organisation did not embrace a logic of micro-management and daily control.[12] Aware of its limits in terms of governance and in the absence of a real commitment to directly rule the population, HTS agreed to delegate authority to segments of the educated urban elite. While this delegation was less an ideological choice than a practical reality informed by the scarcity of resources, it allowed the group to incorporate a more technocratic elite alongside parts of the previous revolutionary elite.

In addition to the centralisation of governance and the delegation of some authority to a 'technocratic' elite, HTS outsourced important public services. The Salvation Government did not have the financial resources to provide full government services to an estimated population of around 3.2 million,[13] which would have been useful to bolster local popular support. Unlike the oil-rich northeast, the Salvation Government was sorely under-resourced. It could rely on fewer than 10,000 civil servants.[14] In the field of justice, tribes were therefore asked to administer the law, including the use of tribal standards in murder cases.[15] Entire sectors of governance were also subcontracted to private actors, mostly local organisations supported by donor states. In the health sector, international NGOs and their local partners took over a largely deficient health ministry. 1,600 employees in the sector thus benefited from the assistance of Western donors. However, it ceased in 2019 since "Idlib was becoming an increasingly toxic environment," as a European expert familiar with the Syrian file noted.[16] In the education sector, the trend was to hand it over to third parties. The Salvation Government Ministry of Education existed, but only paid salaries to the administrative staff. It did not have teachers on its payroll. The Ministry relied on a list of 4,000 volunteers while ensuring the maintenance of school buildings and coordinating with circa twenty educational organisations. Private religious institutes, often controlled by members of the Sufi orders, were still involved in education.[17] Moreover, foreign organisations maintained their assistance to primary education, although they dropped their contribution to other programmes in 2018.[18] The Qatar Foundation financed the distribution of UN-endorsed school curricula for the preparatory and secondary levels while, at the end, the Syrian Interim Government issued schooling certificates.[19]

In the absence of resources, HTS and the Salvation Government had to make concessions. They had to compromise for a period of time with some revolutionary councils. They had to rely on tribes and negotiate with (local and international) NGOs and the Syrian Interim Government while giving up organising public service sectors to preserve foreign support. The institutionalisation of the revolution that the ex-jihadis promoted therefore remained a strongly transactional project in which space for autonomy remained. It also opened up new opportunities for foreign support for a population always in need. As an example of concessions, attempts by the Salvation Government to impose taxes on international aid convoys at the Bab al-Hawa crossing point sparked enough resistance for officials to back down. Likewise, on two occasions HTS renounced reopening crossing points to regime-held areas following opposition from the population, which took to the streets several times,[20] though the crossing points were a major source of revenue for the Salvation Government.

In the end, the Salvation Government was the product of an encounter between a revolutionary Islamist movement forced to engage in the field of governance while lacking expertise and a pious middle class which benefited from a partial delegation of authority to be involved in local governance. The Salvation Government more or less independently managed all administrative issues, yet security operatives continued to process cases related to alleged regime collaborators, IS cells, and organised crime including kidnapping and extortion. Unwittingly neo-liberal, the hegemonic project was therefore not an intrusive one-party model since it functioned through multiple acts of delegation and outsourcing. The Salvation Government contributed to HTS's power strategy but could not be considered an offshoot of the management of HTS or its civil branch. This reality results from the absence of means rather than specific ideological choices.

HTS's adjustment to the Turkish strategic game

The consolidation of governance under the Salvation Government forced HTS to adapt to a new international context. No longer merely one armed group among many, HTS had to shift from its own organisational interests and ideological preferences to a more state-like logic. As the primary authority responsible for civilian administration in the province, HTS had to navigate external pressures and geopolitical dynamics. This shift was particularly evident in how the group adjusted to the strategic maneuvering between Turkey and Russia over Idlib.

Turkey's military presence in Idlib deepened between 2017 and 2020. The Turkish presence in Idlib began with the establishment of observation posts under the Astana Process and the 2017 Sochi agreement with Russia. Turkey established these observation posts to officially monitor the military de-escalation throughout the country but also prevent a large-scale regime offensive on opposition-held Idlib, which would have resulted in a massive flow of refugees into Turkey. Additionally, these posts were a means for

Ankara to maintain influence in northwest Syria, develop leverage in negotiations over Syria's future, and counter Kurdish-led groups it viewed as a security threat for their ties with the PKK. Despite HTS's previous opposition to other armed groups' ties to Turkey, this relatively benign Turkish presence was not initially problematic for the group.

In early 2020, Turkey deployed substantial reinforcements to Idlib, sending an estimated 10,000–12,000 troops to deter a looming regime offensive. This move significantly reshaped Ankara's role in the province. The joint Syrian regime and Russian offensives of 2019–20 had left numerous Turkish observation posts isolated behind regime lines, rendering Turkey unable to defend them. As tensions escalated, concerns grew that a full-scale assault on Idlib in January–February 2020 could trigger a massive refugee influx into Turkey that would be very destabilising domestically. In response, Turkey deployed large-scale reinforcements to defend Idlib and launched devastating drone strikes against regime forces stationed around Aleppo. Western diplomats later suggested that Turkey could have effectively annihilated regime troops in the area had it chosen to press further.[21] Russia then agreed to a ceasefire.

The map on the following page depicts the Turkish observation points by 2020, located between regime-held areas and the territory controlled by HTS.[22]

The unprecedented influx of Turkish troops, which HTS recognised as necessary to protect the province, fundamentally reshaped their bilateral relationship and created an asymmetrical power relationship between them. Turkey, whose role was previously indirect, became the dominant actor responsible for the protection of the province, which relegated HTS as the subordinate actor forced to adapt to a new strategic reality. The transition to a patronage-based relationship was aptly captured by Yahya al-Farghali, an Egyptian religious scholar affiliated for a few years with HTS, whose perspective, while unofficial, reflected perceptions of these shifting dynamics. Farghali observed that the large-scale Turkish military presence shifted HTS from a position of relative autonomy—where it held "*al-dhuhur*," or mastery of the game and dominance over the balance of power—to an asymmetrical

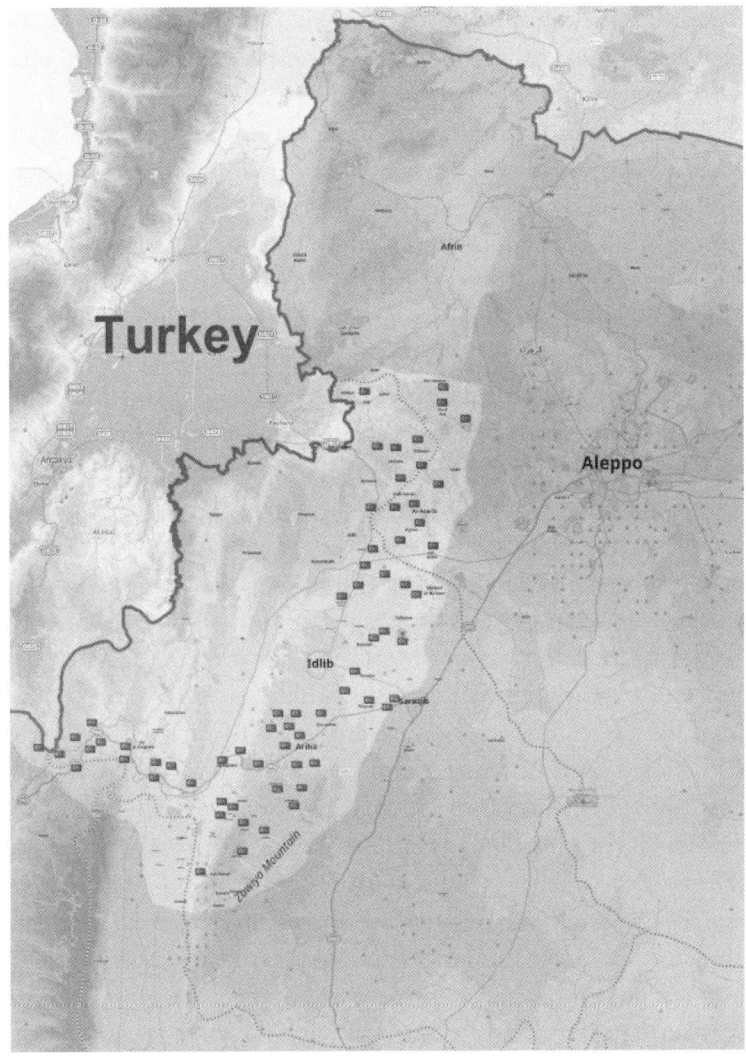

relationship that limited its control over strategic decisions regarding the territories it governs.[23]

The patronage relationship between HTS and Turkey was not inherently problematic politically, as both shared key strategic interests. HTS's strategy of resilience aligned closely with Turkey's objectives. Al-Sharaa sought to maintain control on the ground, preserve his authority, protect and organise the population, and outlast the regime through a long-term war of attrition.

Meanwhile, Turkey aimed to maintain a stable strategic depth, preventing spillovers into its borders while delegating governance and pacification of the territory to HTS in the northwest.

The situation in Idlib province differed significantly from northern Aleppo, where Turkey played a more direct role amid competition between various factions under the Syrian National Army for influence and local control. While HTS was less susceptible to Turkish demands—having the ability to interpret them as it saw fit and even reject certain requests—it still presented a more manageable dynamic for Turkey. Unlike in northern Aleppo, where Ankara had to navigate a fragmented landscape of rival factions, in Idlib, it only had to engage with a single quasi-hegemon.

The next map, from 2024, depicts Syria's territorial divisions by that year. HTS controlled the white area, while the two green areas in the north were in the hands of the Syrian National Army with the support of Turkey. The yellow area was under the control of the Syrian Democratic Forces with the support of the US.[24] Considering that the regime heavily relied on Iranian and Russian support, the map clearly illustrates how each local actor needed a foreign backer to maintain control over parts of Syria. This makes the armed opposition's victory in December 2024—achieved largely on its own—even more striking.

For HTS, the problem was that Turkey's sanctuary strategy in Idlib was deeply intertwined with its relationship with Moscow. While HTS and Turkey may have shared overlapping interests in maintaining a revolutionary sanctuary and strategic depth, the patronage relationship introduced significant complications for the group. Adhering to a Turkish-sponsored sanctuary strategy imposed difficult political choices that challenged HTS's leadership and tested its ability to adapt. These choices also forced HTS to transform and balance its ideological imperatives with pragmatic considerations pertaining to its relationship with Turkey.

Three key points of friction quickly became apparent between HTS and Turkey: the geography of strategic depth that Turkey sought to secure in northwest Syria, the issue of international "terrorism", and the mixed Turkish-Russian patrols along the M4 highway. While these bilateral differences were initially stark, they gradually diminished as both sides aligned around a common goal:

DISMANTLING THE RADICAL PAST

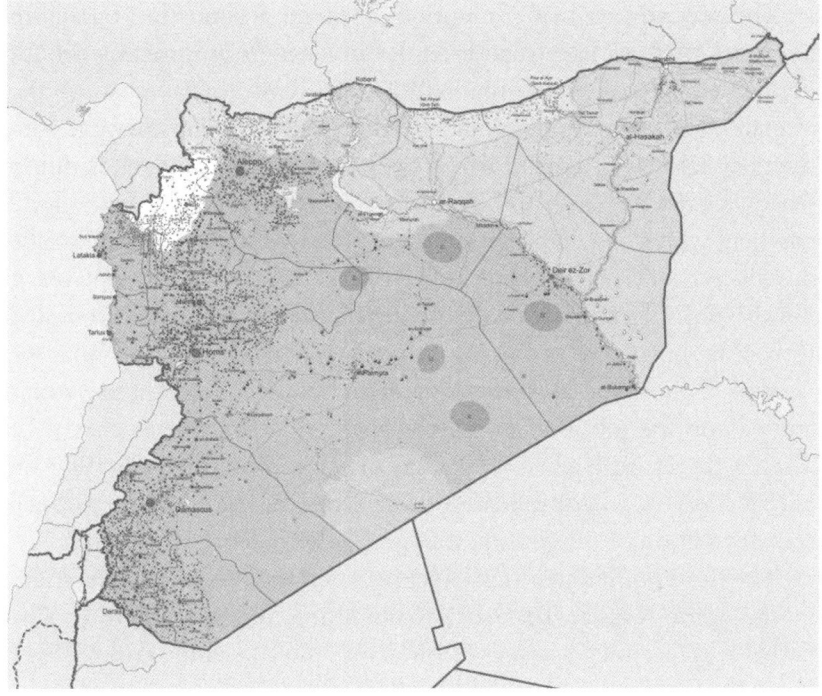

securing the Idlib sanctuary during a time of mutual vulnerability and relative weakness.

The first point of contention concerned the strategic depth Turkey aimed to secure. The March 2020 agreement with Russia defined the truce's frontlines, but there was still significant ambiguity regarding areas south of the M4 highway, which connects Aleppo to the coastal regions. Turkish infantry primarily positioned itself north of the highway and along Idlib's eastern flank, which left the southern frontlines relatively exposed. This deployment strategy did not reflect a consensus with Russia but rather Turkey's logistical constraints, as securing the entire perimeter would have required substantial resources.[25] The issue was partially addressed in November 2020, when Moscow and Ankara reached an understanding on the redeployment of Turkish observation posts besieged by regime forces in southern Idlib. This agreement helped consolidate the fragile truce in the region, stabilising the situation while reflecting Turkey's pragmatic prioritisation of its military commitments.[26]

The second point of contention revolved around the "terrorism question." Ankara had to address the presence of numerous groups designated as terrorist organisations by Russia and most of the international community, while avoiding a direct confrontation with them or taking on a hands-on governance role in Idlib, as it did in Afrin and northern Aleppo. Turkey's approach needed a strong local partner, which inevitably positioned HTS—despite being officially designated a terrorist organisation by Turkey itself—as a key player. A Turkish official summarised this pragmatic stance: "we need to combat terrorists, but we're not going to wage war against them. What we need is a local force to weaken them. HTS knows these groups and can do the job. But ultimately, HTS will also have to change."[27] Turkey therefore backed al-Sharaa's hegemonic project, betting on HTS's capacity to consolidate power while envisioning its eventual transformation or integration into a broader defence framework.

The third point of contention concerned the Russian involvement in the joint Russian-Turkish patrols along the M4 highway. The patrol was intended as a test of Turkey's ability to assert control over the armed opposition, reflecting Russia's desire to assess whether joint military patrols along key highways were feasible. Turkey emphasised that failure to implement the patrols would jeopardise the truce, while HTS appeared to bank on popular resistance to disrupt their operation and eventually force their cancellation.[28]

Shortly after the Moscow agreement, a grassroots movement called the "Sit-in of Dignity" started, which hindered the patrols. While HTS officially denied involvement, evidence suggested that the group and the Salvation Government played instrumental roles in orchestrating the resistance. HTS constructed trenches along key routes, and subsequent clashes erupted between Turkish forces attempting to clear the road and demonstrators mobilised by HTS.[29] The confrontations revealed the depth of polarisation within HTS, with Turkish officials quickly concluding that the group was deeply divided over its strategy concerning the patrols.

The HTS leadership around al-Sharaa accepted the idea of a truce, but intermediate commanders found it difficult to follow: "our patrols face very different views in HTS. On the one hand, they sent us patrols to protect our men, and, on the other hand, others opposed it. Al-Sharaa has to find a balancing act and it is difficult," remarked a Turkish official.[30] A local journalist added that

> The dignity sit-in must be understood as an instrument of regulation by the HTS leadership of the internal opposition raised to the Moscow agreement. It was not possible to let the patrols pass without resistance. On the one hand, because of Turkey, HTS was forced to accept but, on the other, because of internal opposition the leadership of the organisation was forced to refuse them. Therefore, HTS chose to make an act of resistance while giving in, but simply in small steps.[31]

Gradually, HTS's vision became clearer and more politically realistic. In July 2020, the military leader of the organisation recognised that:

> Of course we consider that accepting the passage of the patrols is morally problematic. The entry of the Russians is seen as a betrayal by the majority of the population. But for us, as leaders, we are well aware that this is the best way to consolidate the truce. We authorised a sit-in for fifty days but as soon as the situation drifted we intervened to explain the logic to the people and to convince the Turks to implement the patrols in a progressive way in order to save time and prepare our bases.[32]

More broadly, Abu Maria al-Qahtani—who was Jabhat al-Nusra's first religious leader—acknowledged how the international system—including Turkey's role—significantly shaped the group's choices and forced it to make concessions and adapt its religious views in response:

> The international system does not favour the strongest but rather those who can adapt to it. As the former legal authority for Jabhat al-Nusra, I strive to develop a methodology that aligns with the modern era, as every time and place has its own jurisprudence. Shari'a is not a rigid mathematical formula; it is far broader than our narrow interpretations. You cannot reconcile jihadi rhetoric, which provokes the West, with the task of nation-building.[33]

The issue is that HTS's *de facto* support for the Moscow agreement went well beyond merely accepting a new reality. HTS had to play an active role in the protection of the patrols that some of its men had fought against a few weeks before. In fact, it was in late July

2020, after the eradication of al-Qaeda, that the last patrol first crossed the M4 without a hitch. The patrol ceased afterward, as its primary objective was not routine surveillance but rather for Russia to assess Turkey's ability to maintain control over the situation in Idlib.[34]

If we step back and consider the broader context, why did HTS choose to align with Turkey, despite its previous strong reservations towards other factions advocating for precisely that? The most evident reason was that HTS had little choice, considering Turkey's critical role in preserving the province. But HTS also had other objectives. First, HTS sought to restructure and strengthen its military apparatus and improve its defence capabilities in the face of external threats. Second, the group's security forces needed a truce to stabilise the region and regain control of the territory, especially with the looming threat of remaining al-Qaeda-aligned groups shifting to clandestine operations against HTS. Last, the Salvation Government recognised the need for a breathing space for the population to recover and solidify its relationship with Turkey, which meant that the agreement was an essential step in preserving both internal stability and external alliances. Summarising the new consensus, the military commander of HTS Murhaf Abu Qasra considered that:

> The longer the truce, the more useful it is to us. The people need to breathe while we, the military, support the truce because we need to reorganise. Time is useful to us because we have more time to catch up in terms of training and recruitment after losing nearly 1,000 martyrs and 2,000 wounded during the last campaign by the regime and Russia against us.[35]

Retrospectively, Abu Qasra's words, when read in 2025, are remarkable, as they eerily mirror the course of events of the following four years. While the regime faltered, HTS used the truce to strategically prepare for the final battle, in which it emerged victorious.

In practice, Turkey favoured a military reconfiguration in the region. With more than 12,000 men, including special forces and observation posts, Turkey started to coordinate with an operating room with other armed groups, the Fath al-Mubin operation room that the previous chapter discussed, which formalised the patronage relationship. According to a Turkish official, "the current context offers new opportunities when it comes to dealing with radicalism. With our military surge and cooperation with the factions, we now have much more leverage on them. Not only on military issues but also on political affairs."[36] In general, a patronage relationship is an asymmetric dynamic in which the sponsor holds leverage over its client. However, in this case, the relationship resulted less in a power imbalance between the sponsor and client and more in an internal rift within HTS. This division was particularly evident between the inner circle around Ahmad al-Sharaa and the resistance from some mid-level commanders. From this perspective, the patronage relationship had a unifying effect within HTS that helped to consolidate the movement's achievements in its confrontation with al-Qaeda. Still, Turkish pressure on HTS remained constant.

When institutionalisation serves a containment of radicalism policy

Some former radicals, often following their expulsion from the movement, transitioned from political or military roles to focusing on *da'wa* or religious preaching by establishing religious institutes, which were to became controversial in their own right. While independent, they became new arenas for cognitive dissonance, as their political and religious views aligned more closely with Jabhat al-Nusra's earlier positions than with HTS's new strategy. HTS's response was, once more, a strategy of institutionalisation to manage and contain these religious scholars within a formalised framework.

Regulations over religious education intensified after 2020, as the Salvation Government consolidated its dominance and the active war with the regime paused. As the government integrated control over secular education, it targeted private Shari'a institutes, particularly during heightened confrontations with hardliners. This marked a shift toward centralisation, where the pursuit of institutionalisation and authority reinforced each other. By institutionalising religious education, the government aimed to reinforce its political authority, marginalise rival ideologies, and ensure alignment with its vision of governance as it standardised religious education and brought it under its direct oversight.

Regulations introduced significant reforms to the institutes. For instance, the regulations mandated the integration of both religious and secular curricula to ensure that students attending these institutes were not confined to limited career paths. This dual approach sought to provide graduates with broader opportunities, including access to higher education, particularly at institutions like the Faculty of Shari'a. Ideologically, the Faculty of Shari'a played a central role in shaping the religious direction, and its approach aligns with broader policies. According to the Dean:

> The Faculty of Shari'a imposes the teaching of the religious creed ['aqida]. But on what basis? For the Faculty, it doesn't matter. Teaching the creed can be done with or without reference to the teachings of the Shafi'i school. The essential thing is to avoid major deviations. Besides that, we are open to any approach, whether it stems from the Ash'ari school or the Ahl al-Hadith [which largely aligns with Salafism] for instance. All of this falls within an acceptable centrist line [khat 'am]. Within this framework, the institutes can do what they deem appropriate. This centrist line defines our religious orientation. Its primary aim is to prevent divisions because we do not want to engage in theological disputes, and, most importantly, we want to avoid ideological polarisation. We do not want to impose anything on people but simply follow a religious policy that can bring everyone together.[37]

The government's institutionalisation efforts led to the closure of many Shari'a institutes. According to Abd al-Rahim Atun, "before the Salvation Government, everyone opened institutes as they pleased. We tried to bring order, and the institutes resisted. Many were closed due to their violations of internal regulations".[38] Only twelve Shari'a institutes successfully navigated the new regulatory constraints. Additionally, a small number, such as the Nawawi Institute and the Abd al-Huzafa al-Shami Secondary School of Shari'a, remain unregistered but operated within a margin of tolerance. This exception was largely due to their unambiguous religious orientation, firmly anchored in the Shafi'i school of jurisprudence with some Sufi leanings, which aligned with HTS's framework for religious education.[39]

DISMANTLING THE RADICAL PAST

Ideological, administrative, and security pressures have significantly diminished the influence of the institute scene, which, according to somebody close to HTS, can no longer be seen as a breeding ground for radicalism. This shift also marks the decline of Salafism's central role, as the environment has moved away from its previous dominance. The transformation reflects broader efforts to control and moderate the ideological direction within the region.

Controlling the religious sphere: The mainstream strategy

HTS's approach to other religious institutions also revealed a real transformation. Initially, the group actively sought to assert control over these institutions and to suppress dissent while enforcing its own ideological views. However, faced with growing resistance, practical limitations, and resource constraints, HTS gradually loosened its grip. The group had to recognise that complete domination was unfeasible. Instead, its priorities shifted away from curbing religious diversity within the Muslim community toward focusing more heavily on suppressing political dissent.

HTS initially sought to assert control over local religious leaders by strategically installing its own members where the balance of power tilted in its favor. This strategy included removing critical imams from key positions in regions under HTS's influence. However, the organisation encountered resistance in various localities. One notable case of resistance was in Maarat al-Nu'man, a city historically opposed to Jabhat al-Nusra and, later, HTS. HTS's attempts to effect changes, including the removal of imams, muezzins, and well-known preachers, faced resistance primarily due to the influence of prominent local families like the al-Alwan family. Over time, HTS had to acknowledge its limitations. Although the group claimed it only dismissed clerics who opposed the revolution or supported the regime, some observers have noted a discernible shift in its approach. A former judge recalled that:

> At first, HTS tried to change the clerics who opposed its views and replace them with young people who had come out of their ideological training camps. Then, it had to reinstate the old ones for two reasons: to compensate for the lack of its cadres and their weakness, and to manage popular anger.[40]

Acknowledging the impracticality of consistently confronting local populations to assert control over mosques, HTS adopted a pragmatic strategy for managing the lower clergy, commonly known as the "community shaykhs" (*shuyukh al-hara*). This approach blended elements of co-optation, tolerance, and coercion, with the emphasis on each component varying according to the local balance of power. Essentially, in a classic patronage policy, according to an influential religious scholar of the region:

> The known shaykh, recognised by local notables and appreciated by the people will be approached by the Ministry of Religious Affairs [of the Salvation Government], which will try to influence them. At worst, if they oppose his directives, they run the risk of being dismissed.[41]

Ibrahim Shasho, a former Minister of Religious Affairs of the Salvation Government, acknowledged that

> We run over 1,200 mosques. And each mosque has a staff of around five people. It is simply impossible for us to replace them. We are not trying to push for a specific ideological orientation or to change the staff. We do not reject any person with the necessary knowledge [*talib al-'ilm*] and we do not categorise between Salafis and Asharis or Sufis.[42]

As a result, HTS's interference in the religious landscape diminished and it stopped imposing the sermons from above. While local preachers might have been encouraged to relay certain positions on specific events, they were not pressured to conform to specific religious views. In Idlib City, for instance, the forty-six major mosques were still managed by the same staff who were in place before the establishment of the Salvation Government.[43]

Likewise, the theological teaching circles (*halaqat al-ta'lim*) within mosques continued to operate without HTS attempting to impose its religious doctrines though these circles were officially supervised by the Ministry of Religious Affairs. The organisations overseeing theological teaching circles were diverse and largely reflected the region's complex religious landscape. They included the Turkish Ministry of Religious Affairs (*Diyanet Waqf*), the Syrian Islamic Council aligned with the opposition in exile, and the Institute of Imam al-Nawawi, which follows Sufi traditions and teachings. Together, these entities contributed to shaping the theological discourse and practices within the area.[44]

Within the Shari'a institutes, HTS adopted a relatively hands-off approach, primarily due to an unfavorable balance of power. One former teacher from the Shari'a Institute of Imam al-Nawawi, now in Turkey, recalled the situation:

> As of 2015, we established more than thirty branches in the liberated territories. Three years ago [in 2017], HTS attempted to exert control by intervening in the curricula. Their desire for dominance was evident. HTS's security officials involved in education sought to censor our textbooks and pushed for alterations in the content. In response, we resisted and leveraged media attention. Eventually, they relented. They are responsive to media pressure, and their focus shifts to individuals with occasional arrests.[45]

It's noteworthy that HTS stopped operating its own Shari'a institutes in 2017. A cleric closely associated with HTS explained that religious training did not undergo the same institutionalisation efforts as other areas:

> HTS previously ran Shari'a Institutes for the religious training of its militants, especially in historical Jabhat al-Nusra strongholds like Harem and Salqeen. However, they closed these institutes in 2017 when HTS began relying on more informal methods, such as ideological training during military camps and conferences conducted by clerics associated with the organisation in mosques.[46]

With the exception of some independent initiatives led by former religious leaders from factions defeated by HTS, the training of imams remained the responsibility of traditionalist institutions like the Institute of Imam al-Nawawi, which played a central role in training local clergy.

A similar non-coercive policy applied to education. One contentious matter was the attempt to impose the Salafi approach to the religious curriculum at the al-Khasnawiyya School and the al-Imam al-Nawawi Institute. Ultimately, both parties reached a mutual agreement. A teacher at one of these institutions emphasised that "institutes have the freedom to teach as they see fit.

All schools of jurisprudence are accepted, as long as Sufism is not overtly promoted, and institutions refrain from teaching positions antagonistic to Salafism or the stances upheld by HTS."[47] Even the Faculty of Shari'a at the University of Idlib, despite the incorporation of Salafi references into its curriculum, continued to rely on the teachings of the Faculty of Shari'a at the University of Damascus. Moreover, it retained Ash'ari Sufi scholars in its leadership.

HTS also lifted pressure on public schools. The group initially tried to reform religious education and introduce the logo of the Salvation Government alongside that of the Syrian Interim Government recognised by the international community. For instance, the government distributed the manual authored by Abu Fath al-Farghali, mentioned earlier, to supervisors although its usage was left to their discretion.[48] But there were no substantial changes to the curriculum in secular schools, including religious education.[49] The primary reason for this was the lack of resources. Up until September 2019, education was primarily funded by international donors and mainly Westerners. Taking control of this sector would have necessitated significant human and financial resources that the movement was not prepared to allocate. The Ministry of Education played a limited role, functioning primarily in a supervisory capacity and maintaining a small number of civil servants without taking full responsibility for school management. As one local analyst aptly put it, "assuming control of the education sector would have simply been too complex."[50] Educational advisers (*muwajih al-tarbawi*) tried to introduce certain Islamic concepts through support courses and specific religious training for teachers. However, these initiatives were generally well-received and not perceived as overly intrusive by the teaching staff.[51] There was nonetheless still some push back, including the introduction of religious clothing in schools in summer 2023.

HTS's involvement in the religious sphere was therefore more pragmatic than ideological before the takeover of Damascus. The organisation prioritised a strategy centred on political control over a zealous pursuit of religious transformation within society. HTS shifted its focus away from actively attempting to reshape society through religious guidance in mosques, instead opting to accommodate and tolerate religious diversity. Furthermore, HTS initiated institutionalisation efforts in the production of fatwas, a move that ultimately sidelines the creation of new religious norms. Additionally, the lower clergy had become less subjected to replacement and more subject to engagement due to limitations in human resources and the influence of local dynamics. The primary objective here was political compliance rather than full religious alignment.[52] To date, there have been no consistent efforts to promote a specific world view as required by a Salafi-type posture.

Replacing Emirs and Shari'ins: How to dismantle Jabhat al-Nusra's organisational legacy

The transfer of governance to the Salvation Government helped HTS restructure itself. In 2018, HTS decided to dismantle its decentralised structure in which local sections or power structures (*qati'a* or *qawati'a* in plural) had a high level of autonomy in the management of local affairs. The local *amir*—military commander—backed by a shari'—religious leader—were in charge and had a great deal of leeway to administer justice. The decision to dismantle the system of local sections, which HTS took in 2018, was maybe the most important move in the policy of internal transformation endorsed by the movement since 2016. According to a former HTS-allied leader, "the real turn towards transformation and deradicalisation happened in 2018 when HTS restructured itself, not in 2016 with the delinking with al-Qaeda, or in 2017 with the creation of the Salvation Government".[53]

If HTS's overarching narrative was one of centralisation and institutionalisation, the objective was both broader and more political. It sought to dismantle the decentralised power previously held by local emirs and militant clerics (*shari'in*) and replace it with a new generation of Islamist technocrats. These individuals, influenced by the ethos of the Syrian revolution, were directly connected to Ahmad al-Sharaa himself. This connection provided them with the authority necessary to manage local affairs and ensure a more centralised and coordinated approach to governance. According to an advisor of al-Sharaa:

> In the past, the management of the local level was left to the emirs of the local sections [*qawati'a*]. We were used to govern in a decentralised way, but this was giving all the authority and power to the emirs. Therefore, we were keen to disempower the sections and give the authority to a new profile of individuals that would be deprived of any means of direct coercion on the population. We wanted individuals able to speak with authority, but without a pistol on the table.[54]

To which Ahmad al-Sharaa added that

> The dismantling of the local sections occurred alongside a gradual process of centralisation within Jabhat al-Nusra. Initially, the centralisation was internal, with the consolidation of the courts, which were no longer left in the hands of local shari'a judges. Only after we completed the internal process of centralisation we moved toward external centralisation, culminating in the establishment of the Salvation Government.[55]

One key reason, beyond the institutional narrative, directly pertained to internal power dynamics. The Salvation Government struggled to assert its authority over the local sections within Jabhat al-Nusra. According to the leader of a faction allied to HTS: "after the establishment of the Salvation Government, there was a gap between the government and the regions, particularly between the central government and the local sections, which were not always responsive to the demands of the government".[56]

According to a close associate of al-Sharaa, dismantling the local sections was a gradual and deliberate process that began in urban centres. The first step was removing the military presence from these areas, followed by establishing tribunals. Security forces remained in place for a longer period, especially as the old local sections system continued operating in the provinces. Once the decision was made to centralise authority and establish a civilian administration, the process accelerated.[57] According to the commander of a faction allied to HTS:

> Tensions arose with the local sections, which were initially military in nature and resistant to the authority of the newly formed Salvation Government. The local sections struggled to accept decisions

from civilian leaders, especially those with no affiliation to HTS. Following the creation of the Salvation Government, repeated clashes erupted with the local sections, which only recognised al-Sharaa as their supreme authority. To address this, we created the Administration of the liberated areas [*idarat al-manatiq al-muharara*] in 2018 within the Ministry of Local Administration. This new structure de facto aligned with al-Sharaa and HTS. In parallel, we dismantled the local sections and reintegrated their leaders into the movement. Some took up security positions, others military roles, and some remained local, joining the administration of the regime. However, former local sections members now no longer hold positions within the Administration of the liberated areas.[58]

The elimination of factional religious courts of law and the institutionalisation of justice also deprived armed commanders, often at the head of local Islamic courts, of their control over the population. The unified rules of law applied in the province are administered by the courts and not by men of religion.

The dismantling of Jabhat al-Nusra's local sections and the reassignment of their local leaders and religious scholars into the new civilian and military structures encountered little resistance. A former member of the movement mentioned that, "there was no resistance. We were in a situation of a highly disciplined movement with total allegiance to the leader. The new cadres of the Administration of the liberated areas are all newcomers, trained for their new roles".[59] This is primarily "because al-Sharaa commanded genuine moral authority over these individuals, and the principle of 'listening and obeying' [*al-sama' wa al-ta'a*] was firmly upheld within the movement. Without this moral authority, sidelining the religious scholars could never have worked so smoothly".[60] Some of the religious scholars had to attend the Faculty of Shari'a at the University of Idlib or the Shari'a Institute affiliated with HTS, under Abd al-Rahim Atun and Mazhar al-Weis, another HTS leadership council member.

The local head of the Administration of the liberated areas took charge of the police station and local administrations. They acted as a link between the Syrian Salvation Government and the population. "The Salvation Government arrived, but de facto, at the beginning, it was the Administration of the liberated areas which supervised the schools, the bakeries, and the police stations. Then, gradually, everything was transferred to the ministries."[61]

The Administration of the liberated areas: An incubator for a post-jihadi political generation

The Administration of the liberated areas (*Idarat al-Manatiq al-Muharara*) was one of the most important institutions in local power politics in Idlib since HTS centralised its structures. It was a political body consisting of 350 individuals divided into local sections of 25 to 40 people across the seven "regions" (*manatiq*) of Idlib. Formally established in 2018 based on a decision by the Shura Council to address the weaknesses and dysfunctions of the Salvation Government, the Administration of the liberated areas drew its authority from its very strong informal ties to the leadership of HTS. The latter created this structure to address the deficiencies of the Salvation Government, which it established a year earlier though it struggled to assert its authority locally, where communities contested its legitimacy. Its authority was also challenged by the emirs and religious clerics in charge of the former sections. From this perspective, this new structure had become one of the key instruments in the transformation and deradicalisation policy, as it is fundamental to the centralisation efforts led by al-Sharaa's inner circle and their policy of dismantling Jabhat al-Nusra's old local structures, which it replaced.

The Administration of the liberated areas started with a dilemma. Al-Sharaa understood the significance of governance but was reluctant to directly oversee it. As a result, he advocated for the delegation of the civil responsibilities of Jabhat al-Nusra, including the management of institutions such as the courts of justice, to others. As one HTS source noted, "because nothing makes you unpopular like a court of justice".[62] But al-Sharaa also recognised that the Syrian Salvation Government alone could not effectively address the challenges of governance. The question was therefore how to delegate responsibilities without losing control or unintentionally reverting to the principle of *mubay'a*, in which what matters is the pledge of allegiance to the group like in the past.[63] HTS chose to create a "second stratum," defined as "an influential class that permits the rulers to rule, without being elite themselves".⁶⁴ According to an HTS leader:

> The Administration of the liberated areas was created during the summer of 2018 [one and a half year after the establishment of the Salvation Government]. The Salvation Government faced a serious problem of authority in the beginning. Factions or local councils were still in charge and were often reluctant to accept its authority, including people from our group. We had to bring a class of people empowered by their connection with HTS to convince the forces on the ground to accept the authority of the Salvation Government.⁶⁵

HTS's "second stratum" was not a distinct social class but rather a group of political personnel with relatively homogeneous social profiles. While they differed in their places of origin and factional backgrounds—some recruited from Jabhat al-Nusra, others from the Free Syrian Army, and some with no prior involvement in armed groups—they shared key characteristics.⁶⁶ They were well-educated, with most holding university degrees, and were relatively young, predominantly in their thirties. Crucially, they identified with the Syrian revolution as their political reference point, rather than global jihad or even Salafism. Their discourse was state-centred, legalistic, and technocratic. They eschewed ideological rhetoric, focusing instead on pragmatic solutions to challenges of governance and authority. The Administration of the liberated areas played an active role in mediating local conflicts and implementing governance initiatives. It intervened in disputes between the Turkish military and local populations and supported tribal notables in enforcing arbitration decisions, particularly in cases of tribal vendettas.⁶⁷ In Idlib, it addressed issues such as street vendors obstructing traffic in the city centre.⁶⁸ Each project carried out by the Salvation Government went through a formal validation process through the Administration of the liberated areas that culminated in a memorandum of understanding between this institution and the Salvation Government.

The Administration of the liberated areas was a partial expression of a one party state logic, but it should not be mistaken for a reconfiguration of the Baath Party. Its origins lie in a genuine, though flawed, act of delegation to the Salvation Government, which conferred it administrative responsibilities but without real authority. As a result, the Salvation Government faced a significant challenge in asserting effective authority—a challenge that became central to the formation and function of the Administration of the liberated areas.

Fundamentally, the Administration of the liberated areas operated as an authority provider within a fragile institutional framework. Its purpose was to bridge the gap between the central leadership and the peripheries of society, fostering a connection between the core and the margins while attempting to address the structural weaknesses in governance.

The influence of the Administration of the liberated areas stemmed largely from its close association with the HTS leadership. As one cadre in Idlib explained, "we possess moral influence because the people are aware of our identity." While elements of vanguardism were evident, the power structure in Idlib did not conform to a traditional one-party model, where the party predates institutional frameworks and imbues them with ideological significance. Instead, vanguardism in Idlib operated as a pragmatic, non-ideological corrective mechanism. Initially, HTS relied on a network of allies to take on limited administrative responsibilities. However, these entities lacked the necessary authority and delivered subpar performance. Many qualified individuals either left the region or joined non-governmental organisations (NGOs), exacerbating the governance gap. Approximately a year and a half later, Ahmad al-Sharaa made a strategic move to reassert control and rebuild the system. In this context, vanguardism in Idlib was a reinvention, developed retroactively by a dominant force that lacked a preexisting party structure to depend on—unlike the PYD in northeastern Syria. Forced into governance, HTS had to create a new "second stratum" of power at the local level, filling the void left by the dismantling of prior alternatives, such as autonomous factions, former Jabhat al-Nusra local sections, and independent local councils.

4

EXITING JIHADISM

HTS, which started as Jabhat al-Nusra as an ideological vanguard aligned with IS and later al-Qaeda, could not impose a new strategic direction at odds with the past without internal resistance. Without essentialising armed groups' ideology, mobilising and socialising militants around certain ideological principles means that those beliefs matter—at least for a number of commanders and foot soldiers who may be genuinely convinced by them and unwilling to abandon them when convenient. To successfully transition, HTS had to persuade its own soldiers and commanders that the new strategy was not a betrayal driven by opportunism but also to isolate and marginalise—if not expel—those who refused to abide by the new direction. Before the conquest of Damascus in 2025, HTS had not articulated a clear narrative for its emerging post-jihadi identity, as its ultimate goals remained ambiguous amidst ongoing uncertainty. Nevertheless, it managed to distance itself from global jihad, marginalise hardliners opposed to its new strategic direction, and initiate the development of a militant culture distinct from its past.

Severing the ideological ties with global jihad

A key feature of global jihad is its internal fragmentation. Historically, al-Qaeda emerged as a vanguard organisation that boasted only a few hundred followers at the time of the 9/11 attacks. Rather than seeking to be the sole legitimate jihadi legitimate group, as IS later attempted, al-Qaeda engaged with several other groups, forging alliances in some cases while encountering disagreements in others. Over time, Osama bin Laden's organisation transitioned into a network of affiliates, a structure that persists to this day. Global jihad therefore extends far beyond al-Qaeda itself. It encompasses a loose, diffuse movement of sympathisers and supporters who lack formal affiliations, allegiance, or a unified command and control system. The emancipation of IS from al-Qaeda in 2013 further deepened divisions within the jihadi movement and effectively ended al-Qaeda's monopoly. The main difference between the two is that, unlike al-Qaeda, which frames itself as a vanguard for global jihad, IS claims to be the sole legitimate Muslim authority worldwide and rejects all other groups and ideologues.

Al-Qaeda lacks a formal religious authority capable of issuing unequivocal religious edicts. While it did have an internal religious committee headed by Abu Hafs al-Mauritani—who resigned shortly before 9/11 in opposition to the forthcoming attacks—the organisation has historically sought legitimacy and support from external figures rather than from within. After the early demise of the Palestinian Abdullah Azzam—who never embraced al-Qaeda as a project—a key figure in the Afghan jihad, the group turned to independent religious scholars in the 1990s. Two of its most visible figures over the past decades have been Abu Muhammad al-Maqdisi and Abu Qatada al-Falastini. Although they never officially joined al-Qaeda, they have often published statements and issued religious edicts in its support. This reliance on external figures has both strengths and weaknesses: it has broadened al-Qaeda's legitimacy without necessitating formal ties, but it also means that these figures might not always share the same organisational interests. In particular, Abu Muhammad al-Maqdisi has often emphasised maintaining doctrinal purity over political considerations, occasionally siding against al-Qaeda in doing so.

The significance of these ideologues was evident throughout the Syrian conflict when jihadis clashed. Abu Muhammad al-Maqdisi and Abu Qatada, among others, repeatedly participated in cross-factional conflict resolution due to their legitimacy in the eyes of many foot soldiers, who socialised in the religious camps through their writing. For HTS, their centrality was also clear following the split with al-Qaeda. As tensions escalated regarding the stance to adopt toward Hurras al-Din before 2020, as discussed in previous chapters, some HTS commanders opposed their leadership's attempts to discipline the al-Qaeda-aligned group. They announced that they would temporarily freeze their membership in HTS and threatened to split from the group if HTS refused to accept an independent judgement of Abu Muhammad al-Maqdisi, Abu Qatada, and others.

Before the creation of HTS in 2017, Jabhat al-Nusra was therefore partly transnational despite its prioritisation of a Syria-first policy. The earlier chapters mentioned that the group had included, over the years, a number of militants of global jihad, including individuals closely linked to al-Qaeda's leadership such as Abu Julaybib al-Urduni, Abu Firas al-Suri, Abu Farraj al-Masri, and later Abul-Khayr al-Masri—who did not formally join Nusra or its successors—and Abul-Qassam al-Urduni. While many of these leaders and commanders were killed over the years in combat or US drone strikes, their influence shaped the group's global narrative on violence, as reflected in much of its propaganda. More importantly, their presence lent Jabhat al-Nusra legitimacy and authority through associations with renowned jihadi scholars and ideologues, including Abu Qatada and Abu Muhammad al-Maqdisi, which proved crucial in helping the group weather its 2013 split with IS.

But Jabhat al-Nusra's transnationalism also presented distinct challenges. The group's reliance on external networks and ideologues occasionally clashed with its local objectives and priorities. Unlike other local groups that primarily depend on domestic constituencies, global jihadis rely—albeit to varying degrees—on transnational ideologues and organised networks to legitimise their actions, mobilise resources, and endure periods of difficulty. This dynamic proved advantageous during the 2013 split with IS, as prominent transnational jihadi ideologues sided with Jabhat al-Nusra and helped it retain fighters and maintain its legitimacy. Yet, this relative reliance on global jihadis also imposed constraints. Global supporters and ideologues could set boundaries on what groups like Jabhat al-Nusra could pursue politically, particularly when it involved significant strategic shifts. According to jihadi ideologue Abu Muhammad al-Maqdisi,

> You should not view al-Qaeda as a hierarchical organisation. Instead, it functions as a network of groups, where allegiance plays a

crucial role. For example, I believe the concept of allegiance [*bay'a*] is both valuable and beneficial, as it helps maintain ideological orientation and the method [*manhaj*]. It ensures that decisions are made collectively through consultation within the network of affiliates. This structure preserves the ideological orientation and reinforces our commitment to the ultimate objective: the creation of Islamic states and the establishment of monotheism [*iqamat al-tawhid*]. Without this unity, there are no boundaries. Look at figures like Abd Rab al-Rasul Sayyaf and Gulbuddin Hekmatyar in Afghanistan: although they also sought to establish an Islamic state there, they ultimately embraced a democratic framework. HTS is doing the same after it rejected the allegiance to al-Qaeda.[1]

When Jabhat al-Nusra officially split from al-Qaeda in the summer of 2016, it was first of all an organisational rupture. Ahmad al-Sharaa's first public address emphasised that the newly rebranded group, Jabhat Fath al-Sham, no longer maintained any foreign ties. In essence, he formally renounced his allegiance (*bay'a*) to al-Qaeda's leader Ayman al-Zawahiri. Although al-Qaeda never imposed its decisions on Jabhat al-Nusra and communication with Ayman al-Zawahiri had ceased for three years, the break was significant. It signaled that all future strategic decisions would be made unilaterally, in Syria, without the need for consultation with al-Qaeda figures, as was already—paradoxically—the case when the split occurred. This move also sent a clear message to other armed groups that the group was now fully focused on the Syrian conflict. It also conveyed to foreign states that the group's international ambitions were effectively over, though Nusra never directly threatened them previously.

However, for jihadi ideologues, it was evident that an ideological shift also began to coalesce. Renouncing al-Qaeda signaled that the group was gradually moving away from some of the core principles of jihadi Salafism. This development did not go unnoticed—ideologues of global jihad perceived it as a significant threat and reacted accordingly. Their responses serve as a valuable political barometer for assessing the movement's trajectory; there is perhaps no better way to understand the process of deradicalisation than by examining how radicals themselves narrate and criticise such transformations. This was evident in public debates between them, as well as in our own private discussions with them. Though much of this has been analysed before, we will briefly recap the main features of this ideological divergence.

A key difference between the tenets of global jihadism and HTS lies in their relationship with the revolution. Global jihadis adopt a vanguardist approach and emphasise an exclusivist distinction between jihadis and revolutionaries, rooted in the religious principle of Loyalty—to the Muslims—and Disavowal—of the non-Muslims (*al-Wala wa al-Bara*) that states that Muslims should be loyal to one another, and oppose non-Muslims. They denounce HTS's "integrated" approach to the revolution. Abu Muhammad al-Maqdisi notably lamented that:

> HTS instrumentalises jihadism. They are the opportunists [*mutasaliqeen*] of jihad. They have no problem sacrificing other committed jihadis for the sake of the revolution. They used the jihadis as the fuel of the revolution, before betraying them later on. For us it is clear. HTS pushes the trend toward dilution [*tamiya*] and compromise [*talawun*] while ISIS drives it toward extremism [*ghulu*].[2]

In their early debates, the highest religious scholar of HTS, Abd al-Rahim Atun, engaged with jihadi ideologues and insisted that not only al-Qaeda fighters but all those who took up arms against the Syrian regime should be considered *mujahideen* or engaged in jihad. This position was completely unacceptable to Abu Muhammad al-Maqdisi. Reflecting on these discussions, Maqdisi claimed,

> I emphasised that the establishment of Islam can only be achieved through the actions of committed jihadis. [Abd al-Rahim] Atun, however, believes that fighting Bashar al-Assad alone is enough to classify someone as a *mujahid*. This perspective reflects a revolutionary mindset rather than a genuine jihadi commitment, as it disregards the principle of loyalty and disavowal [*al-Wala wa al-Bara*]. This is not merely a tactical adjustment to the Syrian context to survive international scrutiny, contrary to what they initially claimed. It represents a profound ideological and political shift.[3]

HTS's rejection of al-Qaeda was therefore not only organisational. It was also an ideological rupture. Global jihadis took the affiliation seriously as it is a tool to ensure ideological cohesion and avoid the dilution of the creed (*ta'miya*):

> As revolutions tend to manipulate jihadis and exploit them for their own purposes, pledging allegiance to al-Qaeda serves to safeguard certain fundamentals [thawabit]. You can see that when they severed themselves from the allegiance, they started to operate without any guiding framework [dawabit] to prevent deviation. Without this structure, their actions lost their direction and have become purely based on their short term interests. HTS leaders once drew from our vocabulary, emphasising concepts like "fighting in the path of God" [fi sabilillah] and monotheism (tawhid). A mujahid, for instance, was someone striving to elevate the word of God. Now, however, they label anyone fighting against Bashar al-Assad as a mujahid. This is a clear rejection of what we stand for.[4]

What is particularly interesting is that HTS's decisions divided global jihadi ideologues. Not all of them adopted the same stance on HTS. In fact, two of the most prominent and symbolic figures in the jihadi ideological sphere, Abu Muhammad al-Maqdisi and Abu Qatada al-Filistini, diverged significantly due to their opposing views on HTS. A Jordanian expert on jihadism underscored the depth of the ideological rift caused by HTS's choices:

> For Abu Muhammad al-Maqdisi, the paramount concern is preserving the purity of jihadism, ensuring it remains distinct from other revolutionary movements. In contrast, Abu Qatada adopts a more pragmatic approach, prioritising political considerations and the interests [maslaha] of the broader community of believers. Rather than judging HTS solely by its alliances, Abu Qatada evaluates it within the broader framework of adhering to essential principles of Islamic governance [al-siyasat al-shar'iyya]. From this perspective, HTS does not present a significant issue for him.[5]

Nature abhors a vacuum, so when HTS severed ties with global jihadi ideologues, it had to replace them with new figures embedded in the Syrian context. This shift was a deliberate strategy to diminish the influence of global jihadi scholars over mid-level commanders and ordinary members. HTS notably reoriented its religious framework by returning to traditional schools of Islamic jurisprudence (madhhab), particularly adopting the Shafi'i school, as we argue in our chapter on Salafism. HTS additionally transferred the responsibility for issuing fatwas to an expanded and inclusive council designed to marginalise hardliners without completely excluding them. As Abd al-Rahim Atun explained, "to avoid transnational fatwas, we decided to link our religious education to the schools of jurisprudence [*madhhab*]."[6] In the same spirit, HTS localised its teachings for rank-and-file members, shifting focus away from the various places of jihad abroad to prioritise the local Syrian context and the revolution. As a close advisor to Ahmad al-Sharaa explained, "we absolutely wanted to avoid fighters being dragged into debates and disputes about differing global jihadi views. Instead, we aimed to focus on the real enemy: the regime."[7] To further reduce the potential influence of global jihadi scholars and the risk of their fighters defecting to more hardline movements like in 2014, HTS incorporated a specific section in its ideological training programme titled "Warning against Extremism" (*tahdhirat did al-ghulu*), emphasising the dangers of radicalism and steering members toward a more localised and pragmatic approach.

Relocalisation against global jihadi influence: The jurisprudential shift

In its quest for social acceptability, HTS deviated from the conventional paradigm of jihadi Salafism by embracing the classical schools of jurisprudence (*madhhab*). These schools dominate Sunni Islam and serve as legal traditions that provide guidance on interpreting Islamic law. The four main Sunni schools are the Hanafi, Maliki, Shafi'i, and Hanbali schools. Each school has its own distinct methodology for deriving legal rulings from the Quran and Hadith (sayings and actions of the Prophet Muhammad). These schools address various aspects of daily life, including matters of worship, family law, business transactions, and more. While there are differences in interpretation and emphasis among the schools, they share the common goal of seeking to understand and apply Islamic principles in accordance with their respective methodologies. Muslims often follow one of these schools in their personal and communal religious practices, but there is also flexibility for individual interpretation and choice within the bounds of Islamic jurisprudence.

HTS's renewed emphasis on the schools of jurisprudence had two primary motives. First and foremost, HTS aimed to establish deep local roots in its local community. The adoption of the schools of jurisprudence had been a subject of debate within the ranks of Jabhat al-Nusra for several years. However, the transition to a governance role solidified this stance. According to Abd al-Rahim Atun, who leads HTS's religious council, "we are always trying to anchor in the movement the idea of relying on the schools of jurisprudence because it is a way of getting closer to people".[8]

The emphasis on jurisprudence schools was instrumental in drawing the movement closer to the local population. These schools are an integral part of the curriculum in HTS's internal training programs.[9] HTS opted for the Shafi'i school over the Hanbali school, despite the latter's historical proximity to Saudi Salafism and alignment with the Salafi teachings. This choice was driven not by doctrinal considerations but rather practical ones. As a member of HTS's political bureau explained, "we chose Shafi'ism because it corresponds to the majority of the local population."[10] Clearly, it is not the intrinsic qualities of the reference that are invoked but its social effect. It is a political rationale justified by the group's reliance on Shari'a politics (al-siyasat al-shari'yya).

The second rationale for rehabilitating the schools of jurisprudence was control. This strategic move was part of a broader effort to diminish the influence of competing sources of authority. The objective was to regulate public religious discourse through institutionalisation. According to Bassam Sihiouni, a prominent member of the High Council of Fatwa and former prime minister of the Salvation Government:

> The schools of jurisprudence provide a secure framework for preserving a correct and innovative intellectual orientation while upholding the laws, ethics, and morals of Islam. Abandoning these schools, on the other hand, would lead to a decline in jurisprudence based on just and righteous thinking.[11]

The revival of the schools of jurisprudence served as a means to manage and temper radicalism within HTS's own ranks. It facilitated the institutionalisation of religious discourse, sidelining the influence of global jihadi figures and silencing dissenting voices within the organisation. This institutionalisation of religious authority was further bolstered by the consolidation of governance structures under the Syrian Salvation Government.

Marginalising the internal hardliners

The second main challenge for HTS was to manage its own internal divisions. While the most radical figures chose not to join the group—either splitting off to align with the al-Qaeda-affiliated Hurras al-Din or, in some cases, having left Jabhat al-Nusra as early as 2013 to join Islamic State—HTS still remained a heterogeneous movement. This diversity included older, long-standing members of the organisation as well as more recent recruits, particularly independent religious preachers who joined HTS without previously being part of Jabhat al-Nusra. Many of these new entrants brought their own distinct political and religious views, which increasingly were at odds with HTS's new strategic choices.

HTS imposed a new ideological line while minimising the risks of internal fragmentation or polarisation through its incorporation of many religious scholars that were not previously in Jabhat al-Nusra. These individuals, despite their divergent views, were occasionally useful in legitimising unity around HTS on various issues at critical junctures. However, managing them was always a delicate task. As a close associate of al-Sharaa once remarked, "we needed to deal with the legacy of the early days pragmatically."[12] Part of this effort involved integrating these figures into the group's authority structures, such as its own Shari'a Council or either the Fatwa Council or the Shura Council of the Salvation Government. This containment strategy allowed HTS to monitor and influence them directly. But the group was dissatisfied when these individuals continued to act independently, engaging with the media, issuing statements, or delivering Friday sermons—activities that often revealed significant cognitive dissonance between their worldview and HTS's evolving political and theological orientation. This strategy, for the most part, proved effective. According to a former cadre of the movement, now a vocal critic, "over time, the current leadership managed to silence any significant opposition within the movement. Today [in 2022], there is no real force capable of contesting the decisions made by the leadership."[13]

After breaking away from jihadi ideologues outside Syria, HTS undertook a strategic effort to marginalise the hardliners within its own ranks—those who resisted the organisation's transformation and new strategic choices, which marked a significant departure from traditional jihadi stances and reflected HTS's move towards a more pragmatic, locally-focused strategy that prioritised political and territorial stability over ideological purity.

The first priority was to isolate HTS members who opposed the group's evolving ideological and political choices. According to a former Jabhat al-Nusra leader, this concerned an estimated 1,700 individuals:[14]

> At the beginning, resistance was strong. In 2017, when HTS decided to accept the deployment of the Turkish army in the territories under their control, the choice was difficult to make. It was backed by al-Sharaa but there were strong objections to this choice when he consulted the Shura Council of the movement.[15]

The more difficult the choices, the more polarised the organisation became and, as a result, "three years ago [in 2019], the decision was taken to marginalise the voices of those who could express dissent", according to an HTS ally.[16]

HTS established a new policy to impose internal control over its ranks while maintaining internal cohesion. HTS's policy toward radical elements was pragmatic and straightforward: it accepted everybody, regardless of their past, as long as they aligned with the group's new political direction or, at the very least, refrained from openly opposing it. To prevent the formation of competing groups or alliances among ideological adversaries, HTS leadership tried to maintain cooperative relationships or, at least, ensure that individuals or groups could part ways on amicable terms when conflicts arose. However, when dissent threatened to jeopardise the movement's cohesion or challenge its new trajectory, HTS acted decisively, resorting to exclusion or repression to maintain control. Over the following years, the group notably excluded two Egyptian scholars who had previously been part of Ahrar al-Sham before joining HTS—Abu Yaqthan al-Masri and Abu Shu'ib al-Masri— who, HTS claimed, had violated internal regulations with their public opposition to the group's new policies.[17]

Another prominent figure, Abu al-Fath al-Farghali, remained within the organisation for an extended period despite increasingly opposing some of HTS's new strategic choices. HTS's transformation had long been a point of contention for Farghali. He publicly voiced his disagreements over the group's military partnership with Turkey, became known for his systematic obstructionism during Shura Council discussions, and often held political positions that deviated from HTS's official line. Then, he had also raised concerns about the new training manuals introduced for militants. According to an HTS leader,

> The tensions with him—such as his recurring, unwelcome comments on democracy—is something we can tolerate for now, as we prefer to keep him within the fold rather than risk him going underground. While we maintain a margin of tolerance, it is important to note that his statements do not reflect the views of our leadership. The relationship between him and the HTS leadership remains strained, with only a fine line separating the current situation from his potential expulsion from the organisation.[18]

In this context, a logic of amicable separation came into play:

> Managing tensions with people like al-Farghali is always challenging. He was with us for years, and while his public statements were often problematic, we gave him some leeway. However, within the organisation, he consistently obstructed discussions, and his divergences from our political direction were significant. After several discussions, he ultimately decided to resign from the Shura Council. We do not wish to exclude him from our ranks or the region, so he remains with us, but without any official roles or responsibilities.[19]

HTS consistently maintained a strategy of partial distancing from controversial figures who struggled to align with the movement's evolution. The case of Abdullah al-Muhaysani illustrates this strategy well. Al-Muhaysani, a young Saudi cleric, served as an independent mediator and religious authority before joining HTS in 2017.[20] Tensions between him and the HTS leadership grew over the next few months. These were less about ideological radicalism and more about differing strategic priorities. During the period of conflict between HTS and Ahrar al-Sham, al-Muhaysani, known for his conciliatory stance among revolutionaries, advocated for unity between the factions. At the time, he was a member of HTS Shari'a council but was disavowed when a vote opposed such unification. In 2018, the rift deepened further. When HTS's Shari'a council narrowly voted—5 to 6—in favor of combating Ahrar al-Sham, sparking a battle between the two groups, Al-Muhaysani resigned. Despite his resignation, he found a *modus operandi* with HTS. Al-Muhaysani was a particularly difficult figure to manage. His controversial background—being designated by the US for financing al-Qaeda and recruiting minors—along with his foreign nationality (as a Saudi), his critical stance on HTS's human rights record, and his opposition to arbitrary justice, made him an unpredictable and challenging public figure. An implicit arrangement was eventually reached: Al-Muhaysani would be permitted to visit Idlib but was prohibited from public speaking, particularly delivering Friday sermons, to avoid further complications.

Some former public figures, once regarded as hardliners, also had to step down as their radicalism no longer served a functional purpose. Osama Qasem is a notable example. Qasem, a former leader of the Egyptian Islamic Jihad, spent decades imprisoned in Egypt before relocating to Syria following the 2013 military coup. His background explains his role in justifying the disassociation from al-Qaeda by discrediting Ayman al-Zawahiri's leadership, portraying him as disconnected from the realities on the ground (referring to him as the "imam of the cave"). This critique carried particular weight given that al-Zawahiri had once led Qasem's former group, Egyptian Islamic Jihad. Qasem later provided theological justifications for internal conflicts, such as the war against rival factions like Nur al-Din al-Zinki and Ahrar al-Sham, which he framed as a fight against disbelief as he denounced these groups as infidels (*kuffar*). However, Qasem eventually became a liability for the group as his positions increasingly clashed with HTS's new strategic direction, and he had to step down.

While HTS had to differentiate itself from more radical contenders and marginalised its own hardliners, it has refrained from openly engaging in formal ideological revisions. Instead, the group's evolving strategic views are shaped by new practices—

pragmatic adaptations made by the leadership to maintain the movement's internal cohesion. These shifts indicate a trajectory toward deradicalisation or mainstreaming, not as the product of a newly formulated ideology, but rather as the cumulative effect of a series of pragmatic adaptations over time.

"Diluting" jihadism: The reality check of militant training

The final dimension of HTS's deradicalisation policy involved a complete overhaul of the ideological training provided to the fighters. This transformation ensured that the new direction and strategy of its leadership were clearly communicated to rank-and-file members, helping them understand and internalise the shift. This approach mitigated potential resistance from foot soldiers who might otherwise have struggled to reconcile turning away from key ideological tenets only a few years earlier.

In 2016, Jabhat al-Nusra ceased the ideological training it had previously conducted, which included the teaching of key texts authored by figures like Abu Muhammad al-Maqdisi and Abu Qatada. The group went even further by banning the production and dissemination of Maqdisi's works entirely.[21] This came after online clashes with Maqdisi, during which HTS religious scholars actively participated in debates to refute and denounce his criticisms. Al-Maqdisi, in turn, condemned HTS for what he perceived as leniency and a betrayal of jihadi principles, particularly their break from al-Qaeda, describing their actions as a "dilution" (*ta'miya*). He also indirectly excommunicated HTS by referencing arguments that accused the group of becoming nullifiers of Islam through their collaboration with states like Turkey, even against other jihadis. HTS responded by claiming that, despite his differences with IS, Maqdisi remains an ideological figurehead for radicals. They accused him of being out of touch with the complexities of the Syrian conflict and incapable of grasping its unique dynamics.

HTS shifted its focus from religious creed (*'aqida*) to jurisprudential issues as part of its new strategy. A former Jabhat al-Nusra commander confirmed this transition, stating that "progressively, we saw the movement diminishing the focus of its teachings on the creed and replacing it with an increased emphasis on *fiqh* [jurisprudence]."²² Religious creed lies at the core of Salafism, as the next chapter elaborates. This primarily involves defining the attributes and characteristics of God (*al-Asma wal-Sifat*)—for example, questions such as whether God has a hand or where He is. These theological specifics distinguish Salafis from other traditions, such as Ash'arism, a school followed by most Muslims worldwide. The new focus on jurisprudence not only avoided the divisive nature of theological absolutes but also equipped HTS with tools to interpret religion in a way that adapts to contemporary contexts. Reliance on jurisprudence, as the next chapter develops, also facilitated the development of new tools, such as the jurisprudence of contemporary contexts, enabling the justification of strategic choices that deviate from past practices. This approach, which draws on Shafi'i jurisprudence, proved advantageous in supporting the group's emphasis on localism and its control over religious edicts.

HTS also established the Preaching Preparation Institute (*Ma'had 'Idad al-Du'at*) to train its preachers. The institute operated under the supervision of the Shari'a Faculty of the University of Idlib, which provided the curricula of the institute. Upon completing their training, the preachers had the opportunity to join the Faculty of Shari'a for further education.²³

What remained of the study of the religious creed reflected a simplification of the curriculum that deliberately avoided contentious issues. Instead, HTS emphasised the collection of forty hadiths of al-Imam al-Nawawi that are very mainstream among Muslims. The lessons presented the religious creed in a concise book, *Mithaq: An Introduction to the Jurisprudence of the Pillars of Faith* by Abdullah Hamad Al-Rukf, which provided a simplified yet comprehensive exploration of Islam's foundational beliefs for a broad audience in an easy-to-digest format. The new teachings also placed greater emphasis on Islamic history, shifting away from the previous focus on the various contemporary jihadi contexts where al-Qaeda is active. According to Abd al-Rahim Atun:

> Due to the changing characteristics of the fighters, we had to adapt and modify the training programmes [*manahij*]. The previous generation of fighters was more politicised, ideologically driven, and somewhat educated, with many being students of Islamic

knowledge [*tulab al-'ilm*] who had a certain level of understanding. Now, the recruits are much younger, typically aged 18 to 20, with little to no formal education and no Islamist background. Today's recruits are not influenced by radical ideas, which gives us greater flexibility. As a result, we had to significantly simplify the training programmes.[24]

The neutralisation of radicalism aligned the militant culture with the leadership's new political orientation. This shift represented an adaptive move to ensure coherence between the teachings provided to the rank and file and the evolving political context. In this new phase, where understandings and interactions with Turkey, the UN, foreign media, and think tanks have become commonplace, the ideological stance softened. According to Abd al-Rahim Atun,

> In the beginning, we saw the UN as part of a global conspiracy against us. Now, that is no longer the case. Similarly, we abandoned the outright rejection of the 'other'. We are in a new political experience, and we needed the teachings to align with the new perspectives we have adopted.[25]

The training programs also sought to clarify these political choices to the militants. "We facilitated the opening of churches, engaged with minorities, and developed relations with states. It was necessary to craft a narrative that explained and justified these new realities."[26] It is therefore no surprise that the very inner circle of al-Sharaa that initiated the transformation since its very beginning in 2019 wrote the new curriculums. According to Abd al-Rahim Atun, "We could not stay in 2022 like we were in 2012. Over the past decade, we had the rise of extremism—*al-ghulu*—and all these battles we waged against them. As a result, we had to differentiate ourselves from *al-ghulu*."[27]

A former court judge close to the organisation observed that the religious education curriculum had shifted away from a focus on jihad jurisprudence and condemning esoteric Sufi tendencies toward addressing contemporary contexts and challenges in a pragmatic political manner. He insisted that, even five years ago, "their leaders previously talked a lot about the issue of Islamic sovereignty [*hakimiyya*]. It's no longer the case now. They limit themselves to saying that what the movement wants is Bashar's downfall, without delving too deeply into the nature of the alternative."[28] He considered that:

> Religious education curricula changed. It was previously embedded in the jurisprudence of jihad in addition to condemnation of esoteric tendencies present in Sufi Islam, confrontation with the Shia and the purification of beliefs. But they have changed recently [in 2020]. They teach the jurisprudence of the contemporary context [*fiqh al-nawazil wa al-azamaat*], instead of focusing on jurisprudence of jihad like in the past. New horizons have opened up.[29]

Abd al-Rahim Atun justified the change by referring to the changing sociology of the movement. He argued that:

> Shari'a remains our reference. I am still convinced by these concepts in my heart. But there are conditions for their application. This is not necessarily understood by foot soldiers. I can only debate these issues with people who reach a certain level of understanding. Many foot soldiers cannot understand *al-wala wal-bara* [Loyalty—to the Muslims—and Disavowal—of the non-Muslims] for instance. And they do not need these levels of detail.[30]

However, HTS never grounded this redirection in a new theology. According to a foreign researcher closely tracking HTS, "HTS religious leaders spent more time justifying policies like agreeing to bring the Turks in or supporting ceasefires without really offering a new ideological vision to their fighters."[31]

The leadership's new policy direction did face internal resistance, especially among middle-ranking commanders. Some members found it challenging to accept the changes, which largely diluted previously held principles. According to a former judge close to the movement:

> There are clear signs that we have come to a point when it is becoming necessary to purify the curricula. But some people reject the new orientations of HTS and the Salvation Government because of the acceptance of conduct previously prohibited. It is seen as diluting old principles. What was prohibited yesterday becomes lawful today.[32]

Two other graduates from Shariʿa institutes close to HTS argue that resistance was particularly prominent among early recruits from the time of Jabhat al-Nusra, who were socialised by its militant ideological training. The deputy to the dean of the Shariʿa Faculty acknowledged that some students, especially those who underwent military and ideological training during the Jabhat al-Nusra era, initially held hardline views. He emphasised that "they needed this training. Less than a year ago [in 2019] we were fighting the worst enemy so in order to fight you need to have an iron will that gets strengthened with those ideas. Now it is time to carefully correct them."[33]

According to one of the leaders of the movement, deradicalisation, ultimately, was also the result of a key objective: differentiation:

> The military confrontations with ISIS and later with al-Qaeda compelled us to clarify our positions. Engaging in war against these groups necessitated a clear articulation of our differences. Initially, during the conflict with ISIS, we realised that without defining a stance on them, we risked losing the loyalty of our fighters. Similarly, when we turned against al-Qaeda, it again forced us to refine and assert our own identity. The primary catalyst for these shifts was the series of internal shocks that disrupted the jihadi landscape, driving us to adapt and differentiate ourselves from our adversaries.[34]

For them, governing northwest Syria is not only about administration but also a means of combating radical elements. Abd al-Rahim Atun added that fighting radicals meant it was essential to:

> Create a Sunni model different from the radicals [*ghulu*]. It is fundamental. During the years of revolution, IS had a concrete model to promote. They mobilised around major slogans with a strong appeal such as the caliphate or an Islamic state. And in front of them there was nothing truly established capable of capturing the enthusiasm of the youth. ISIS was de facto the only existing Islamic project. This is exactly what we want today: an existing, concrete political project, capable of proposing an alternative. Because it is in our strategic interest to eliminate IS. IS is no less threatening than [the Russian military base in] Hmeimim or the regime.[35]

5

HOLLOWING OUT SALAFISM

HTS's early ideological and theological views were anchored in Salafism, which is a theological approach to Islam that describes how to understand God and worship him as much as a religious-political framework on how to organise society, the daily life of Muslims, and apply Islamic law. Over time, however, and without formally renouncing Salafism, HTS has progressively hollowed out its doctrinal core. This transformation was informed by the constraints inherent with Syria's international landscape, the resilience of local civil society, and the group's own internal evolution. As a result, while certain Salafi elements remain embedded in its militant culture, they no longer define HTS's political outlook or its engagement with society.

Salafism: A struggle for purity over tradition

Salafism is an approach to Islam's religious creed that helps Muslims understand God and how to worship him. The name Salafism refers to the *Salaf al-Salih* (the pious predecessors), who are the first three generations of Muslims that followed prophet Muhammad. Salafis insist that they understand the fundamental attributes of God similarly to the early Muslim generations, in contrast with other Muslims—especially the dominant Ash'ari tradition—whose religious creed was swayed by Muslim involvement with other intellectual traditions, especially Greek philosophy. Salafis differentiate themselves by their emphasis on strict monotheism and their rejection of what they perceive as unlawful innovations in Islam which, they argue, lack direct grounding in the Quran and Prophetic tradition (Sunna). Nearly all Salafis criticise and distance themselves from other Muslim approaches, which they either fully reject as un-Islamic and worthy of excommunication or consider at best deviant.

But Salafism is more than just a religious creed. It is also a social movement that seeks—in very different ways—to purify what it perceives as unorthodox innovations in Islam, striving to return to the foundational sources of Islam. Salafism is a modern reformist movement rooted in medieval historical debates, which was initially largely inspired by the successful efforts of Muhammad bin Abd al-Wahhab and his successors in Saudi Arabia, who believed that the path toward the empowerment of the Muslim world lay in the purification of Islam rather than in embracing non-Islamic "innovations". Abd al-Wahhab is the namesake of "Wahhabism", a term usually rejected by its proponents, which embraces a strict interpretation of monotheism through its rejection of a range of practices like visiting tombs and venerating saints. Wahhabism is a branch of Salafism rooted in Saudi Hanbali jurisprudence, which rose to prominence through the alliance between Muhammad ibn Abd al-Wahhab and the Al Saud family that laid the foundation for the establishment of Saudi Arabia.

Salafism does not prescribe any clear political stance. Salafis range from unwavering obedience to Muslim rulers to advocating for violent opposition against them. This is because Salafis found themselves compelled to engage with the changing world around them for the past century and had to formulate responses accordingly. A major turning point occurred during the First Gulf War in 1990 when Saudi Arabia aligned itself with the US-led coalition to combat Iraq and welcomed US troops on its soil. Salafis' responses divided them. Prominent scholars within the Salafi movement—especially the Saudi clergy—legitimised the presence of US troops in Saudi Arabia, which gave rise to the Sahwa or Awakening movement, which not only opposed the US troop presence but also called for more comprehensive reforms within Saudi Arabia itself. Other Salafis chose to follow Saudi Arabia's lead in spreading the Salafi approach globally, prioritising religious teaching and outreach over political engagement. Only some Salafis, as in Kuwait, started to engage in political participation as early as the 1990s when their own political context became favourable to it. They were followed two decades later by their Egyptian counterparts who also created Salafi political parties.

The advocates of violence within the Salafi movement, from which HTS emerged, are a distinct subgroup, rather than the entire Salafi community. The proponents of violence saw the weakening of the Arab world after the 1967 war against Israel and believed in the necessity of restoring its strength. In Egypt and Syria, they believed that seizing control of the state and establishing an Islamic state were the only viable paths forward. These Egyptian and Syrian militants gravitated towards Afghanistan by the mid-1980s, where they joined forces with other Arab fighters that congregated to fight the Soviet Union and its local allies. Among these fighters was Osama bin Laden from Saudi Arabia. Bin Laden fell under the sway of Abdullah Azzam, a prominent Palestinian Muslim Brotherhood preacher renowned in the 1980s for his advocating that Muslims bore a personal responsibility to engage in the struggle to liberate Muslim territories from foreign occupation. His powerful message spurred the mobilisation of thousands of recruits who journeyed to Pakistan and Afghanistan to support the indigenous mujahideen fighters in their cause. These debates and interactions in Afghanistan would ultimately culminate in the establishment of al-Qaeda by the late 1980s. Although al-Qaeda was just one among many jihadi groups in the 1990s, the failure of other jihadis fighting their home regimes (especially in North Africa), combined with the global impact of 9/11, elevated bin Laden's organisation to the forefront of the jihadi movement in the 2000s. This facilitated the development of a global network of affiliate groups, including HTS's predecessor, Jabhat al-Nusra.

Taming Salafi core principles

Salafism remains key to HTS's religious views, though its leadership has gradually sought to deprive it of its political implications. HTS's predecessor Jabhat al-Nusra was formed by individuals who had either adopted Salafism prior to endorsing violence, including many of its leaders in the 2000s following the US invasion of Iraq, or individuals who embraced Salafism concurrently with their involvement in violence. The group's leadership continues to uphold some key tenets of the Salafi religious creed (*'aqida*), though Salafism's core principles do not guide its political strategies or its relation to society.

Within the religious landscape of Idlib, Salafi teachings left their mark on prominent organisations such as the Faculty of Shari'a at the University of Idlib, the High Council of Fatwa, the Ministry of Education, and the Judicial Training Institute. For instance, the Faculty of Shari'a at the university continued to impart teachings from the *Book of the Foundations of Faith* (*Kitab Usul al-Iman*) by Muhammad Ibn Abd al-Wahhab, a seminal text for modern Salafis. A former student insisted shortly after HTS's takeover of the province in 2019 that Salafism wielded influence within the faculty and among the student body: "HTS has henchmen in the faculty and among the students. They are the ones who bring the religious figures in the movement to the university and the rector of the university cannot oppose it".[1]

Salafism initially influenced HTS's militant culture, though it was already enmeshed with political considerations. An illustrative example of this perspective is in a book, *The Student's Provision* (*Zad al-Talib*), authored by a religious scholar formerly affiliated with HTS, Abu Yahiyya al-Farghali. This publication did not officially represent HTS's stance, but provides insights into a prevalent perception of the conflict a few years ago, after HTS took control of Idlib province. At its core, *The Student's Provision* upheld Salafi religious doctrine and its opposition to "blameworthy innovations" (*bid'a*) within religion, the remnants of polytheism (*shirk*), and the promotion of the Salafi creed (*'aqida*).

However, political considerations also informed HTS's religious views at the time. *The Student's Provision* classified theological hostilities based on the political positions of various religious groups in Syria. For instance, the book did not stress religious differences with groups aligned with traditional Islam, as HTS sought to establish alliances with them, particularly the lower-ranking clergy. Therefore, Ash'ari Muslims and Sufis were not direct targets of theological attacks; instead, the book underlined the legitimacy of collaborating with them against common adversaries. Conversely, the book was unwavering in its religious opposition to Shia Muslims, Alawites, and instead criticised Shia Muslims and Alawites for their perceived support for the regime while denouncing IS with the term *khawarij* (heretic) inherited from Islam's early days. The book finally promoted the traditional Salafi stance against democracy, which it viewed as fundamentally incompatible with the implementation of God's legislation. However, it also took a relatively mainstream approach to what an Islamic state should look like, which it grounded in the highest principles of Islamic law (*maqasid al-shar'ia*), which promotes the preservation of universal principles like justice, public welfare, and the preservation of life, over a rigid application of the law.

HTS nonetheless gradually evolved toward a more inclusive religious approach while maintaining its theological opposition to democracy and secularism associated with Salafism. This transformation involved the development of a public discourse grounded in the concept of "Shari'a Politics" or "Islamic Law-Guided Public Policy" (*al-siyasat al-shar'iyya*), a concept associated with the most influential medieval scholar among Salafis, Ibn Taymiyya. Shari'a politics helped HTS legitimise pragmatic political positions within the framework of the Islamic tradition. HTS justified its prioritisation of specific adversaries by framing the conflict as a matter of survival that necessitates certain compromises. While these compromises were not explicitly detailed, they encompassed alliances with a state like Turkey and tacit acceptance of agreements like the Sochi Accords co-sponsored by Russia. HTS also limited the application of the concept of excommunication (*takfir*) to prevent its excessive use by individual members. Instead, HTS scholars stressed that Muslims might lack knowledge in certain religious matters and thus should be "excused" for their "ignorance". Salafis often use the "excuse of ignorance'" (*al-'udhr bil-jahl*) to avoid excessive application of their religious views. In Syria, it served as both a strategy to foster rapport with the local population and a mechanism to facilitate the coexistence of diverse religious perspectives within their overarching project. The Shari'a Faculty of Idlib, which teaches the Salafi religious creed, also emphasised the importance of various schools of jurisprudence, with particular attention given to the Shafi'i school due to its prevalence in Idlib. The deputy dean of the Faculty of Shari'a acknowledged this approach, stating that: "We are actively seeking common ground that allows for comprehensive teaching. Among us, we reject the use of the concept of takfir; no one can declare others as outside of Islam".[2]

HTS shifted its approach by actively establishing a more structured and institutionalised internal religious authority to further control Salafi religious discourse. The group implemented clearer norms and procedures to regulate the release of new religious edicts by shifting towards procedural rather than theological considerations. Essentially, HTS sought to channel dissenting voices within the organisation by imposing institutional and administrative norms. Ahmad al-Sharaa stressed that "there is now a general order that everyone must accept".[3] According to Abd al-Rahim Atun, "we were forced at the beginning to accept dissident voices. But, gradually, we stabilised internal order by putting rules in place."[4] One other prominent HTS religious leader and *shura* member added that now "you can judge the violation of the law and not necessarily the idea itself. We have established a framework for discussions."[5]

This transformation toward controlling what the HTS leadership saw as Salafi "excesses" unfolded incrementally. The first step was to prohibit the use of excommunication (*takfir*) outside the jurisdiction of the fatwa committee of its Shari'a Council, effectively putting an end to its widespread application by group members, and to ban "the publication of fatwas and rulings before their revision by the general Shari'a Council".[6] These rules helped to silence dissident voices, including former HTS Egyptian clerics who had previously disassociated themselves from Ahrar al-Sham when it began to engage with Turkey. For instance, Abu Shu'ib al-Masri was expelled for "not respecting the policies of the group repeatedly", and Abu Yaqthan al-Masri for not abiding "publicly by the framework set by HTS through its leadership and Shari'a council."[7] These measures contributed to the Syrianification of the Shari'a Council. They were followed by a ban on the publications of Abu Muhammad al-Maqdissi in the group's training camps, along with explicit denunciations of him.[8]

The ideological training provided to HTS members similarly shifted direction years prior the conquest of Damascus, as it became less about inculcating religious norms and more about fostering determination in combat along a specific political line still articulated in sectarian lines. HTS continued to frame, a few years ago, the conflict in terms of '*nusayriyya*' and '*rawafid*,' derogatory terms for Alawites and Shia Muslims that are fighting "the Muslim and Sunni presence in the countries of the Levant" in a "battle between the infidels and the followers of the Prophets"[9] in which "the lost ones—*ahl al-batil*—cannot bear the presence of the bearers of the truth among them and they must therefore be expelled."[10] However, the group no longer insisted on core Salafi jihadi concepts such as the Loyalty—to the Muslims—and Disavowal—of the non-Muslims (*al-wala' wal-bara'*) and the "prohibition of seeking assistance from non-Muslims" (*'adam al-isti'ana bil-kuffar*), apostasy of Muslim leaders (*takfir*) and the supreme authority of Islamic law (*hakimiyya*).[11]

The confrontation with IS exerted internal pressure on radical voices within the ranks of HTS. When radicalism persisted, it was increasingly confined to certain fighters who found themselves positioned between al-Qaeda and IS. However, these radicals faced constraints due to HTS's security policies, which targeted individuals suspected of IS membership. A former professor at the Faculty of Shari'a in Idlib noted that

> The conflict with IS moved from the battlefield to the battle of ideas. They used to call themselves *ikhwat al-minhaj* [the brothers adhering to the same religious approach] but, after the confrontation, the crisis was transferred to the field of religious conceptions. Ideas began to transform. Leaders that are too hard-line are now accused of IS-isation [*da'ashana*].[12]

These dynamics created a disconnect between HTS's new political approach and its religious doctrine, which remained largely untouched at its core. Political postures changed more rapidly than militant culture. Militant cultures are the primary platform for the expression of ideological identities, and they display greater inertia. An activist from a family closely associated with HTS expressed concern, a few years ago, that excessively altering the internal religious discourse could have pushed militants toward more radical groups like the al-Qaeda affiliate Hurras al-Din or even IS at the time: "by reducing too much the religious discourse internally, the risk is that the militants could slip away among more radical groups like Hurras al-Din or IS cells. Religious discourse cannot change too quickly with the risk of losing their social bases."[13]

The suspension of the normative project

Considering HTS's previous ideological leanings, why, after taking full control of Idlib, did the group gradually stop pursuing an ideological project for society? Its predecessor Jabhat al-Nusra explicitly sought to establish an Islamic state in Syria. However, in the context that preceded the takeover of Damascus in 2024, the management of the religious domain no longer served as the foundation for a normative project aimed at imposing a specific set of religious values and principles on society—values that were not previously embraced by the broader population.[14]

While many question HTS's willingness to renounce its ideological views, in practice, the group maintained its theological orthodoxy but deliberately refrained from enforcing it. This was not simply a paradox but a calculated strategic decision: the Islamisation of society was no longer a primary objective for the group. Responding to al-Qaeda, which accused the movement of preventing other organisations from fighting, Abd al-Rahim Atun, HTS's senior religious authority, explained the renunciation of the normative project:

> HTS never claimed that it represents the Muslim community as a whole [*jama'at al-muslimin*], which, as such, would have the right to the establishment of the Islamic order. We are simply an organisation of Muslims [*jama'at min al-muslimin*]. Yes, indeed there is no comprehensive application of Islamic law at the present time and no religious order is possible since we are not in a phase of empowerment [*tamkin*]. On the other hand, there is a unified administration organising public affairs in the liberated territories of the north at all social, security and economic levels and striving to develop its performance to the extent of its means.[15]

Clearly, for the religious scholar, the implementation of an Islamist normative project would require conditions that were not met in Idlib and that Atun, preserving his room for manoeuvre, was careful not to define too precisely. This regime of conditionality allowed multiple compromises with the normative project: a suspension

HOLLOWING OUT SALAFISM

of corporal punishment due to the ongoing war, a marginalisation of divisive Salafi concepts, alignment with local references—the Shafi'i school of jurisprudence—and acceptance of Sunni religious diversity—Sufism.

The hegemonic ambition also disrupted the normative project in another way: the consolidation of the hegemon in a context of strategic weakness compelled it to adapt to the expectations and demands of the population. Therefore, for Abd al-Rahim Atun,

> Our philosophy is not to transform society to align it with our point of view. Even when Islam was in a strong position in the days of the early caliphs, they did not impose their ideas by force. It is against our religious creed to impose our ideas. This is IS's problem. They are against the Sunna from that point of view. The problem with IS is not just the use of excommunication [*takfir*] but the approach itself.[16]

Taking stock in particular of the Iraqi experience, he considered that "to force society to abide with our views is not a strategic objective. Every time you try to align the views of society with those of the organisation that controls it, it is a failure."[17] In other words, the religious domain is becoming a space for transaction with society instead of domination, where the latter's views tend to prevail over those of the organisation. For Anas Ayrout, former dean of the Faculty of Shari'a at the University of Idlib and one of the influential religious figures in the High Council of Shari'a,

> It all started with a spontaneous revolution. After that, one cannot impose the idea of one faction on the others. You can't lead the boat alone. Factionalism has been overtaken by the establishment of a civilian government. We are moving from a revolution by one faction to a large collective revolution. We then have to deal with society. Sufism is the religious orientation with which most preachers and the general public identify. We are not going to go to war with them when people really have other concerns.[18]

Beyond the collateral consequences of institutionalisation and the lessons learned from IS in Iraq, a calculation of acceptability defused the normative project. According to an HTS leader, "The most important thing is to emphasise conflict management in our region. We don't want religion to create problems. We accept the difference to avoid conflicts in the areas under our control."[19] This calculation of social acceptance is central to the relationship of the dominant group to the populations it leads. According to researcher Elizabeth Tsurkov, who interviewed a range of HTS members,

> The attentiveness of HTS to public opinion manifests in issues pertaining to governance and policies vis-à-vis the Assad regime and the international system. When it comes to governance, for example, HTS banned smoking, but is not enforcing the ban due to its unpopularity. On multiple occasions, HTS released popular revolutionary activists who have criticised it due to public pressure. HTS also attempted to avoid levying heavy taxes on the population, and when forced to do so in 2019, allowed protests to take place with a relatively minimal resort to violence. Public statements and internal communications of HTS leaders and fighters attest to a great deal of awareness of public sentiment.[20]

HTS sacrificed—without outright abandoning all of its core principles—the imposition of a Salafi normative project on the population and prioritised political pragmatism driven by the imperatives of survival and consolidation. Sceptics might argue that this suspension was easily reversible given the absence of a formal ideological revision. Their argument holds some weight, as the core objective of Salafism is to transform society and "purify" its beliefs. However, the constraints imposed by Idlib's strategic environment at the time, coupled with HTS's evolving priorities, made the imposition of such a normative project increasingly unlikely already before the takeover of Damascus, as later chapters argue. It also meant that the suspension of the normative project was not merely temporary but sustainable. In other words, HTS abandoned Salafism in practice despite not condemning its religious tenets.

Codifying Shari'a: A deradicalisation policy

After establishing an administration, HTS had to address the challenge of governing the population of Idlib through the Salvation Government. The group emerged from the Salafi tradition, which generally rejects the codification of Islamic law since it compares this process to positivist man-made legislation. Instead, Salafism emphasises its reliance on authoritative sources such as the Quran and Sunna, as well as established jurisprudence. Still, once in power, HTS recognised the need for a more balanced approach. Its leaders understood that a clear administrative structure was essential to avoid granting judges too much flexibility, which could lead to excessive autonomy and the implementation of radical rulings that its leaders wished to avoid. The group hence aimed to establish a predictable and relatively consistent system of governance. This shift had significant implications for the ongoing religious debate surrounding governance.

On 16 June 2021, the Faculty of Shari'a and Law at the University of Idlib organised a conference on the codification of Shari'a.[21] Anas Ayrout, the dean of the Faculty of Shari'a and a member of the Fatwa Council, hosted the event, with the presence of religious clerics from the Fatwa Council, officials from the Ministry of Justice of the Salvation Government, as well as several foreign dignitaries and clerics. The event was more than just scholarly; it was a direct implementation of the mainstreaming policy pursued by the movement in recent years. The objective, according to Husam Hajj Hussein, the Minister of Awqafs in 2022, was to "settle once and for all the scholastic debate on the issue of codifying Shari'a and legitimise the principle of codification."[22] According to the Minister, there was indeed a lively debate between two schools of thought. On one hand, the school of individual interpretation (or *ijtihad*) advocated for allowing judges to decide based on their knowledge of Shari'a. On the other hand, another school aimed to formalise Shari'a into a canonical text of established laws, thus reducing the scriptural ambiguity of Shari'a and, by extension, the discretion of judges. "We lean towards this approach because we do not have enough interpretive [*mujtahid*] scholars. We wanted a single reference point because we had clearly observed that judges sometimes contradicted each other," he explained. According to Abd al-Rahim Atun, "codification is now a necessity on which there is consensus. This conference has come in support of the overall direction pursued from the beginning and has encountered very little resistance."[23]

The conference highlighted that codification, despite its advantages and disadvantages, remains a subject of interpretation (*ijtihad*) and Islamic public policy (*al-siyasat al-shar'iyya*), which had proponents and opponents in HTS and its allies. However, the conference cautiously insisted that "the codification of Shari'a is, in our time, a religious duty that is incumbent upon rulers if they consider it beneficial for the public interest." Despite objections from some Salafis who believed that codification removes any direct connection with transcendence from the resulting text and falls under a certain form of positive law or even under "*jahiliyya*" (pre-Islamic ignorance), the conference settled the need to codify Islamic law.

The idea of codifying Shari'a is not a new one; it dates back to the late nineteenth century during the Ottoman Empire. In the 1860s and 1870s, the Ottomans began codifying Shari'a into a comprehensive body of written law known as the *Journal of Judicial Rulings (Majalla al-Ahkam al-'Adliyya)*. By doing so, they transformed Shari'a into a fixed, self-referential legal text. This codification eliminated the need for religious scholars in legal interpretation, as the *Journal* was designed to be comprehensive and self-sufficient. The text gave rise to legal specialists who were trained specifically in the *Journal*, which sidelined traditional Islamic scholars in the process. From this perspective, the Ottoman model of codification marked the disappearance of transcendence in the legal framework. This shift is precisely what renders the concept of codification problematic in the eyes of Islamists, particularly Salafis, who, like many ulémas in the late nineteenth century view it with suspicion.

By taking a clear stance, the conference, and with it, the leadership of HTS, positioned themselves in the decade-old debate between conservative revolutionaries advocating for the codification of Shari'a and the Salafi Islamist camp that called for Shari'a without the mediation of a specific legal framework. After initially rejecting codification during the era of Jabhat al-Nusra, HTS gradually came to openly embrace it. This shift was not just a legal or administrative decision but also carried implications for HTS's own identity. The push for codification aligned HTS more closely with the broader Syrian revolutionary camp—one they had previously opposed. Atun retrospectively sees that:

Our previous reluctance towards codification, back in 2012–13, was related to the fact that this project had become politicised. The jurists [*fuqaha*] were divided, with some considering it forbidden [*haram*], while others deemed it permissible, but subject to certain conditions that align with Shari'a. These former divisions are now outdated.

The call for codification also carried political implications in another way, as it is part of a deradicalisation policy. Codifying Shari'a, from an instrumental perspective, aims to constrain or limit the interpretation of the jurists in the realm of law. According to a leading member of the Fatwa council:

> *Tahkim al-Shari'a* (i.e., relying solely on Shari'a) is too vague a term. Shari'a itself is ambiguous and allows too much discretion for judges; religious matters often become points of contention. We don't want a multitude of viewpoints; and nor do we want to leave justice in the hands of judges' interpretations was one perspective.[24]

A similar approach to restricting independent legal reasoning (*ijtihad*) emerged as part of a broader bureaucratic rationalisation effort and a reduction in the scope of religious education. Following the establishment of the Salvation Government in 2017, it introduced a new requirement mandating authorisation from the Ministry of Awqaf (Religious Endowments) for religious education institutes. This regulatory framework extended to both personnel—requiring staff to hold university degrees—and curriculum, enforcing the standardisation of educational materials and the adoption of the Shafi'i school of jurisprudence across all institutions. Additionally, the Ministry imposed internal regulations on these institutes. As a result, many were forced to close, leaving only twelve still operational as of October 2021.[25] In a similar vein, Abd al-Salam Qassem, from the Shura Council, argued that without codification,

> We would open the door for extremists [*mutashadideen*] to impose their judgments. We need a clear standard, which is why we want to codify Shari'a. And because there was significant resistance from individuals influenced by Saudi thought, there was a wooden wall of opposition—people who oppose positive laws. We are managing

an area that has experienced IS and all forms of extremism. We must manage this to prevent a ticking time bomb.²⁶

In this strategy to counter radicalism, codification and a renewed commitment to the schools of jurisprudence work synergistically within a unified framework. The objective of codification, beyond its identity-driven aspect that aligned HTS with the revolutionary camp against the jihadis and committed Salafis, was to restrict the interpretive authority of religious clerics. Achieving this goal necessitated a legal framework under its control, which HTS grounded in the Shafi'i school of jurisprudence. It is no coincidence that the decision to implement codification and the formal recognition of the Shafi'i school occurred within months of each other. This dual move aimed at limiting interpretive flexibility and constraining judges' discretion in applying the law, thereby reinforcing the authority of the institutional order HTS sought to establish.

The processes of containing radicalism and promoting institutionalisation reinforced one another though this did not necessarily lead to individual deradicalisation. HTS allowed former hardliners to retain their beliefs, provided that they complied with the newly established framework and new norms. While they may not transform into moderates, this new configuration effectively contained their capacity and authority to impose more hardline judicial rulings.

HTS's priority was not to create a new legal corpus but to ensure that new regulations aligned with Islamic principles. The movement fell short of systematically translating Islamic law into a unified and coherent legal corpus—a task HTS was neither equipped to undertake, due to its lack of international standing religious scholars, nor prioritising given its focus lies elsewhere. Instead, the emphasis was on transforming the Ministry of Justice's old circulars into formal laws while ensuring their compliance with Islamic law. In other words, the movement did not aspire to achieve some religious standardisation through the codification of a comprehensive Shari'a-based legal corpus, but through a logic of Shari'a compliance, at the heart of Shari'a politics (*al-siyasat al-shari'iyya*). According to a member of the Fatwa Council:

We now require laws so codification has become a necessity. We seek a unified legal framework that applies to everyone. In matters of discretionary punishment [*ta'zir*], there is significant room for interpretation. However, when it comes to the laws governing penal punishments [*hudud*], they are explicit and leave no room for debate. Our goal is to finalise a comprehensive legal framework, and we estimate that completing this project will take two to three years.[27]

Unlike codification, which embeds Shari'a into formal texts but simultaneously secularises the process by sidelining religious scholars in favor of legal professionals, Islamic-guided public policy offers a degree of political autonomy. This approach enables policymakers to incorporate Islamic principles while retaining significant control over legal and policy decisions, rather than fully ceding authority to religious scholars. Religion serves as a regulatory guide for legal production but no longer functions as the foundational organising principle of the law, as envisioned in the philosophy of codification. However, Islamic-guided public policy remains inherently ambiguous in balancing its dual components. It can either support a trend toward extending political authority over religion, fostering secularisation, or conversely, facilitate the "religionisation" of politics, intertwining the two more deeply.

Fatwas and Shari'a politics: Another shift away from Salafism

The Salvation Government relied on the High Council of Fatwa (*majlis al-'ala lil-ifta*), an institution that HTS established in early March 2019 to oversee and regulate public religious opinions (*fatwa*). The fatwas were the outcome of collective deliberation. While diverse voices existed in the deliberative process, ultimate control of the High Council of Fatwa rested with close advisers to al-Sharaa. This institutionalisation of religious leadership aimed to further erode the authority of global Salafi jihadi thinkers and mitigate the influence of remaining hardliners within the organisation.

The creation of the High Council of Fatwa was a deliberate move to invite a broad spectrum of scholars, including Sufis, Ash'aris, and clerics associated with other factions. Its primary goal was not to monopolise fatwa issuance but to establish a body with strong legitimacy, capable of asserting itself as an undisputed reference point. For Abd al-Rahim Atun, incorporating a diverse range of voices perceived as legitimate was crucial to demonstrate that decisions reflected a broad spectrum of perspectives and to contain the hardliners' voices.

> We made sure we invited everyone: sufis, ash'ari, shaykhs linked to other factions. Our objective was not to monopolise the fatwa but to set up a body with a legitimacy able to impose itself as an indisputable reference. The opinions of the High Council are rare but strong; they also aim to prevent people from following fatwas that come from abroad. Especially Abu Muhammad al-Maqdisi, Hani al-Siba'i and others.[28]

The council served as a mechanism to contain dissenting voices, the inclusion of which allowed religious scholars, including a mix of local and moderate clerics, to express their views within the council. However, their views no longer carried public authoritative weight, as the council ultimately remained under the influence of al-Sharaa's close associates. This regulation of religious discourse through institutionalisation was invaluable to the group's leadership, particularly in promoting the acceptance of Turkey's presence and garnering support for the fighting forces in Idlib—a stance previously rejected by the organisation.

Before the takeover of Damascus in 2024, the High Council of Fatwa primarily focused on issuing traditional fatwas on topics such as Zakat and Ramadan.[29] HTS did not try to use the council as a platform for advancing a particular worldview, preaching moderation, or promoting Salafism. Since its establishment, the High Council of Fatwa only generated a relatively few opinions, primarily on consensus-based ritual matters.[30] An exception was a fatwa addressing the Charlie Hebdo caricatures.[31]

The Higher Council of Fatwa effectively functioned as a Shari'a board. This body of individuals, acting in the name of Islamic compliance, ensured that the legislative process or any decision emanating from the authority aligns with their understanding of Islamic principles. Indeed, as Abd al-Rahim Atun pointed out regarding the Fatwa Council, "the goal is to establish a religious reference body in opposition-held territories that operates in synergy with other relevant institutions, such as the Faculty of Shari'a or the Judicial Council."[32]

The fatwas are authoritative but not mandatory opinions given based on requests from the Higher Council of Fatwa by various government bodies, either when facing a political decision or before submitting laws to the Shura Council. As in other Arab states, fatwas, though ultimately non-binding legal opinions, have increasingly become embedded in the fabric of their institutions, influencing lawmaking through a range of structures such as state muftis, councils of senior scholars, and Fatwa Councils. HTS mirrored the practices of modern states by initiating processes of bureaucratic rationalisation. Its fatwas, issued by the High Council of Fatwa, carried binding authority not through formal legal obligation but through the group's dominant influence. Notably, no fatwa issued by the Higher Council of Fatwa was openly debated, questioned, or rejected, underscoring the group's control over religious and legal discourse. While in principle, a fatwa serves as a means of invoking the transcendent, in practice, in many cases, it is the inner circle of al-Sharaa, the political leadership, that ensured compliance with Islamic teachings, rather than an autonomous clerical body guided by its own corporate logic. They often played a more significant role in political counsel than in theological opinions and were frequently involved in guiding the political and legislative actions of an emerging and relatively inexperienced power structure.

We managed to access most of the fatwas issued before 2025 by the Higher Council to various executive and legislative bodies, including ministries, the Council of Ministers, and the Shura Council. These fatwas were particularly valuable as they reflected the internal formulation of religious and political norms by the movement's leadership. They offer insight distinct from the public-facing positions crafted for external audiences.

Fatwas were highly diverse and addressed a wide range of religious issues, sometimes with political implications. For instance, the fatwa that the Presidency of the Council of Ministers requested concerning the traffic law promptly affirmed that the draft submitted to the Higher Council of Fatwa did not conflict with Shari'a. However, the fatwa went further with the issuance of a series of recommendations, some of which were notably political in nature. These recommendations covered various aspects, including the wording of different points of the law, the suggestion to use the dollar or its equivalent in Turkish lira for fines to avoid constant adjustments due to the collapse of the Syrian pound. The fatwa also called for minimising the use of already overloaded courts and limiting cases of preventive detention as much as possible. To achieve this, it advocated for the establishment of a specific section of the law for offenses requiring the arrest and transfer of individuals to the courts. The objective was, once again, to minimise resorting to the courts by clearly delineating their scope of jurisdiction.

Other fatwas were more mundane, such as one requested by the Ministry of Economy regarding certain bakeries mixing wheat and barley in their bread production. The response was that not informing the consumer amounts to deception and fraud, while specifying that the principle of mixing, if the consumer is informed, does not pose any problem. The Higher Council of Fatwa referred to a saying of the Prophet, stating that transactions of freely consented goods based on transparency are blessed.[33]

The mobilisation of religious references in the fatwas was grounded in broad, general principles. For example, there were fundamental reservations about allowing authorities to impose restrictions on the freedom of commerce. However, discretion was often left to competent authorities, who were encouraged to make decisions based on their potential impact on the common good. In other words, fatwas urged policymakers to act without rigid adherence to specific religious norms, such as restricting the issuance of pharmacy licenses, and sometimes advised them to establish expert commissions. This was evident in the response to an inquiry from the Presidency of the Council of Ministers, which sought the Higher Council of Fatwa's opinion on the principle of price capping for essential goods. The Higher Council of Fatwa did not oppose the idea. It viewed it as consistent with the general welfare of Muslims and a means to stabilise markets by preventing price manipulation and the misappropriation of funds. It stressed the importance of fairness in setting prices to ensure the interests of both sellers and buyers.

Many requests for fatwas concerned commercial transactions and market regulations, including price definitions, the imposition of operating licenses, and the adoption of anti-monopoly policies. The concerns of various ministries reflected those of an emerging administration that was less in search of religious guidance on the exercise of power and more focused on delineating its scope of intervention in social life. The responses from the Fatwa Council, while framed in terms of what is permissible and impermissible, were based on a broad mobilisation of religious references. They effectively constituted more of a reflection on the intervention of public policies than a tightly calibrated adjustment of the authorities' actions to a binding set of religious norms. Overall, from this perspective, the Fatwa Council's relationship with the exercise of power leant more towards "leading from behind" than towards a theocratic order.

The recommendations proposed by the Higher Council of Fatwa to various requesting authorities are noteworthy.[34] On occasion, they may reaffirm religious norms, as in the case of a real estate rental law. When the Shura Council sought to cap rents, the Fatwa Council reminded them of the principle of property rights while acknowledging the merit of the Shura Council's approach to protecting tenants in times of crisis. The Fatwa Council suggested extending contract durations to reduce opportunities for rent hikes without undermining market freedom. In a similar vein, defending the freedom of commerce, the Fatwa Council opposed the Ministry of Supply's attempt to regulate and cap profit margins on certain essential commodities. Not surprisingly, in numerous inquiries related to private property or consumer protection, the Fatwa Council adopted an orientation that could be described elsewhere as right-leaning conservatism.

Elsewhere, as in the case of the labor union law, the focus was on the taxation and income systems—not to comply with a religious norm, but for the sake of consistency, ensuring that unions adhere to the "final ruling on collections". In such instances, as in many other inquiries to the Fatwa Council, the recommendations pertained not to Islamic-guided public policy (*al-siyasat al-shari'yya*), but to politics (*siyasa*) in general. For example, when discussing the law on rental contracts for humanitarian organisations, the Fatwa

Council defended NGOs by prohibiting tenants from subletting. This issue arose because some radical Muslims argued that these NGOs were "unbelieving" (*kufriyya*) and that their assets could be used or sold. The Fatwa Council countered that these organisations possess assets that serve the public good, making it impermissible to deprive them of these assets. They also addressed currency depreciation (the law of currency collapse), which involves comparing the original value of the currency with its value at the end of the contract, using the midpoint value to calculate the difference. This practice dates back to the time of the followers of Imam Abu Hanifa. Overall, the Fatwa Council's recommendations often extended beyond religious considerations, addressing broader political and economic issues, as demonstrated in their discussions of these laws and regulations.

According to these religious authorities, every law should have an Islamic foundation. However, purely positive laws are accepted as they are—such as traffic laws, for example—"if they do not contradict a specific religious norm and if it serves the public interest for the law to be enacted" according to a member of the Fatwa council.[35] But their advice goes far beyond a mere consideration of compliance with Shari'a principles and is indeed part of a comprehensive top-down process of political decision-making and legislation.

In reality, among the available corpus, the only fatwa strongly grounded in religious justification was the fatwa on the coronavirus. The question, submitted to the Higher Council of Fatwa by the Council of Ministers in September 2021, was whether mandatory vaccination should be considered. The Higher Council of Fatwa answered in the affirmative but presented a comprehensive religious argument. The fatwa first acknowledged the commonplace occurrence of viruses, sent by God as a test for humanity. However, it emphasised that no disease is sent without a corresponding treatment. The fatwa then drew on a rule of *fiqh* (Islamic jurisprudence) to explain that authority (*al-Imam* or *al-Hakim*) may legitimately act on its subjects based on considerations of the common good. It reiterated that the argument of necessity (*darura*), applies, which means that public necessity takes precedence over individual needs. In addition to

Islamic jurisprudence, the authors also invoked Islamic history with the example of one of the Prophet's companions, Abu Ubaida ibn al-Jarrah, who ordered people to disperse into the mountains to contain the spread of a plague. Another argument involved referencing the views of global Islamic institutions, specifically the International Academy of Islamic Jurisprudence (*Mujama'a al-Fiqh al-Islami al-Duwali*), based in Jeddah and affiliated with the Organisation of Islamic Cooperation. Furthermore, they included a practical argument that international organisations validated the vaccines, and major states had promoted their use. Finally, if any doubt remained, they invoked a Shari'a rule stating that in cases of doubt between two evils, one should choose the lesser evil if it can protect against a greater harm. The conclusion was framed by the teachings of Ibn Tamiyya, quoting his general statement that Shari'a came to collect and enhance benefits while preventing or containing corruption.

The strong religious and non-religious underpinnings of the fatwa on the coronavirus stemmed from the opposition of many religious figures in northwest Syria and abroad to some of the proposed measures. Some preachers had argued that collective prayer in mosques on Fridays was compulsory, with some even insisting on the requirement to pray all five daily prayers in mosques. Additionally, doubts about the coronavirus and its origins—both in Western and Muslim countries—resonated with certain preachers and segments of the population. Some believed the virus was either not significant or, in more extreme views, that it was a conspiracy aimed at harming Muslims.

The process of codification, which involves converting circulars (*ta'amim*) into legal texts and aligning the law with Shari'a, primarily focused on administrative law. This is because administrative matters address the most immediate and practical needs, even if they are often mundane. HTS did not cover more controversial aspects, such as criminal law. One reason for this is that criminal law would require the introduction of Islamic penal punishments (*hudud*), which are explicitly mentioned in the Quran. These punishments—such as executions by stoning and flogging—are highly controversial, as they would provoke both popular and international backlash. HTS was reluctant to implement them, partly due to the political consequences, but the group could not openly reject them, especially in the eyes of other Islamists, Salafis, and even jihadis, for whom these penalties are seen as obligatory due to their explicit mention in the Quran.

> To date, we do not have criminal law [qanun al-'uqubat]. We rely on a few circulars and the jurisprudence of judges. There are two reasons for this. First, we have a sequencing issue. We want to address procedural law [qanun al ijra'at] first. Second, the application of criminal law must be based on a currently absent context. We believe that criminal law cannot be enforced without stability, sovereignty, and empowerment.[36]

The name "Council of Fatwa", despite of its literal meaning, should not be read as a strictly religious driven body. While it carries religious connotations, governance in Idlib was not based on "divine decree" in the same way as the Assembly of Experts in Iran. Unlike in Iran, where the conformity of laws is assessed by a clerical hierarchy with some autonomy from political power, Idlib had no clerical government. Instead, a small group of decision-makers closely aligned with al-Sharaa oversaw the political and legislative process and ensured compliance with Islamic teachings, rather than an autonomous clerical body operating according to its own institutional logic. In the legislative realm, the Council of Fatwa served as the counterpart to the management of the region at the local level. Both were instruments of support and structures of control for emerging institutions that remained too embryonic and inexperienced to function independently. From this perspective, the focus was more on power than religion, although power strategies may occasionally involve reliance on religious principles.

Over the years, HTS's decisions were driven primarily by political considerations, while only a limited number reflected clear references to religious transcendence. However, HTS avoided the potentially most contentious area of legal development—criminal law—both for political reasons and due to the significant social and international ramifications its implementation could provoke. This cautious approach relies on a calculated balancing act, where HTS applied religious principles selectively, but left unsolved the complexities of certain legal domains, particularly those with severe penalties or controversial implications. This strategic ambiguity allowed HTS to navigate the delicate intersection of religious authority and political pragmatism, while maintaining flexibility in the face of evolving dynamics within both their own ranks and the broader international community.

A quiet break from Salafism: Shifting tides in doctrine and power

HTS is the first (ex-)Salafi organisation to fully take charge of governance, marking a sharp break from past Salafi political experiences. This is also distinct from the century-old Saudi model, where power has always remained in the hands of the Al Saud family, with the Salafi clergy, religious institutions, and religious police playing important but subordinate roles within the state.

Political practices have profoundly reshaped HTS's Salafism, not through direct rejection or ideological refutation, but by gradually hollowing out its core principles. Rather than openly confronting foundational tenets, the movement has pragmatically sidelined them, adapting its doctrine to the constraints of governance, local realities, and strategic imperatives. This transformation has not led to an outright renunciation of Salafism, but rather to its dilution, as political necessities have taken precedence over rigid doctrinal purity.

This shift stems from the leadership's deliberate effort to prevent ideological excesses and engage with society pragmatically. The impact of this transformation was evident in several key areas: the role of religion in society, the approach to education and governance, and HTS's interactions with non-Salafis. Unlike traditional Salafi movements that often impose rigid interpretations of Islam, HTS adapted its religious stance to accommodate political realities, shaping a governance model that is far more flexible than Salafis elsewhere.

The first divergence from Salafism concerns its approach to education and the comprehensive reform of society through the purification of beliefs and religious practices. This shift is particularly evident in education. While HTS maintained religious instruction, it remained a minority and deliberately capped, whereas secular education dominated—a stark contrast to classical Salafi approaches.

Moreover, HTS exerted little control over teachers or textbooks, further distancing itself from traditional Salafi models that prioritise religious oversight in education By delegating education to external actors and restricting private religious schooling—ensuring that it does not compete with public education but instead functions as a secondary "religious alternative" akin to the Islamic Secondary School (*Thanawiyya al-Shar'iyya*) model in other contexts—HTS demonstrated a non-Salafi approach to education.

This ideological shift was also evident in the movement's approach to religious education. As we previously discussed, the book chosen to teach dogma at the Faculty of Shari'a, *Mithaq: An Introduction to the Jurisprudence of the Pillars of Faith*, presented a broad and adaptable theological framework. Similarly, ideological training manuals for fighters reflected a decline in the influence of strictly Salafi concepts such as Loyalty—to the Muslims—and Disavowal—of the non-Muslims (*al-Wala wa al-Bara*). At the university level, the *Book of the Foundations of Faith* (*Kitab Usul al-Iman*) by Muhammad Ibn Abd al-Wahhab was no longer a core subject (*mada asasiyya*) across faculties and was taught exclusively within the Shari'a department. It was replaced by *The Islamic Creed* (*al-'aqida al-Islamiyya*) by Muhammad Hassan al-Habanaka, an Ash'ari scholar from Damascus—further signaling a move away from rigid Salafi doctrine and the adoption of a centric ideological realignment.

Pressure on personal lifestyles also eased. Women, for instance, noted the disappearance of the moral police or *hisba* units that once enforced moral codes in markets, and the push for the full veil was lifted. In a discussion with local journalists at the end of Ramadan, Ahmad al-Sharaa stated that the only norms subject to enforcement are those with broad consensus among Muslims—essentially aligning with the definition of the mainstream. Politically, this reflected a strategic shift: he prioritised the referential framework of the moderate majority over that of radical factions. His emphasis on customs as a positive reference point reinforced this approach. However, by granting authority to majority practices, he challenged a core Salafi principle, which sees prevailing traditions not as guiding norms but as subjects of reform under the imperative of the purification of doctrine (*tanqiyya al-mu'taqad*).

With limited emphasis on education, and fewer pressures on lifestyles, HTS also moved away from the second pillar of the Salafi approach to society: the purification of dogma (*tathir al-mu'taqad*) and the rejection of blameworthy innovations (*nahi 'an al-munkar*). This shift was particularly evident in the resurgence of popular Islamic traditions that blend local culture, religion, and elements of mystical Islam.

The statements of the movement's leader aligned with its broader religious policy. Moving away from the traditional Salafi suspicion of mainstream religiosity, Abd al-Rahim Atun advocated for a more inclusive definition of legitimate religious practices, accepting "everything, except *khawarij* on the one hand and *turuqiyya* on the other".[37] However, as we will elaborate in the next chapter, even *turuqiyya* practices—such as visiting tombs—are no longer sanctioned and have even experienced a revival.

6

THE THERMIDORIAN OPENING TO SUFISM

The hollowing out of the former Salafi worldview was not merely an ideological turn; it was also a calculated political move—a "Thermidorian bet"—on the so-called "silent majority," or what is often referred to as "popular Islam". This strategic repositioning reflects an effort to align with broader, more socially rooted religious currents rather than rigid ideological frameworks. Nowhere was this shift more evident than in the group's evolving relationship with Sufism. Once viewed with suspicion or even hostility, HTS then started to engage, tolerate and even leverage Sufism as a counterweight to political Salafism. This transformation underscores a broader realignment: an attempt to consolidate legitimacy by appealing to mainstream religious sentiments while simultaneously neutralising potential ideological challengers.

The management of Sufism—Islamic mysticism—provides a valuable lens for understanding HTS's local engagement. It is a testing ground for a three step process of relocalisation: reliance on silent majorities, the inertia of the social, and the resurgence of society. To grasp how HTS managed Sufism, it is essential to analyse the trajectory of Sufism—its key figures, *murids* (Sufi disciples), and rituals—throughout the entire revolutionary period since 2011. This chapter therefore focuses on Sufi transformation as HTS entered a Thermidorian phase, particularly from 2017 onward, as it abandoned its Salafi and revolutionary aspirations to an ideological tabula rasa and shifted instead toward a pragmatic engagement with its social environment.

First, this shift was part of HTS's broader relocalisation and reflected a significant acceptance of social inertia: a religious orientation that HTS's former leanings condemned and marginalised ideologically for years gradually regained a degree of legitimacy with the authorities, which expanded the range of accepted rituals. Second, this opening also constituted a calculated political strategy aimed at leveraging silent majorities—an approach that aligns with Sufism both as an intuitive form of religiosity and as a current forced to go underground. This strategic turn occurred in opposition to a wave of radical populism seeking to reassert itself by capitalising on an unprecedented wave of contestation against the movement's leadership in 2024.

Before the revolution: Sufism as intuitive religiosity

Sufism alone cannot encapsulate popular Islam, yet it has historically played a profoundly structuring role within it. Before the 1980s, Idlib was known as the "Little Azhar"—in reference to the Egyptian university and mosque—due to the many scholars from the governorate who pursued religious studies in institutions in Aleppo and Damascus. According to a Sufi shaykh, "before 2011, Sufism was at the heart of the intuitive religiosity [*tadayyun wijdani*] of the majority of Idlib's society."[1]

Nevertheless, while Aleppo had long been a major centre of Sufi brotherhoods, which flourished during the Ottoman era and remained deeply rooted through figures such as shaykh al-Hut and others, Idlib lacked prominent Sufi figures who were associated with specific sites of devotion, *zawiyas* or *tekkes* (Sufi lodges) within the governorate. With the exception of the *zawiya* of shaykh Khalaf Abu Hamoud, there were no significant Sufi personalities in Idlib who had such centres. According to Thomas Pierret, this can be explained by aspiration, whereby religious families such as the Hassouns and the Salems—both disciples of Nabahani—were drawn toward Aleppo as they rose in stature.[2]

As a result, the devotional aspects of Sufi practice—such as the sanctification of shaykhs by their *murīds* and the seeking of their blessing (*baraka*) at the tombs of saints—appear to have been less prevalent in Idlib than in Aleppo. This is corroborated by interviews with clerics and scholars from Idlib.[3] Shaykh Abdallah Barakat confirmed this distinction, stating, "Sufism was much stronger in

THE THERMIDORIAN OPENING TO SUFISM

Aleppo than in Idlib. It was also more traditional. In Aleppo, *murids* [spiritual seekers] would kiss their shaykhs, seek blessing [*baraka*] from their touch, and even kiss their hands. Such practices were inconceivable in Idlib"[4].

However, the confrontation between the regime and the Muslim Brotherhood in the early 1980s led to a significant decline in religious vocations. As one murid recounts, "after the massacre of the Brotherhood and the raids on Jabal al-Zawiyya, a real fear emerged regarding the public expression of religiosity. Becoming a shaykh became risky—even attending the mosque was dangerous".[5]

During the 1990s, state-imposed restrictions on religious actors gradually eased. With Bashar al-Assad's rise to power, there were official visits from the Minister of Awqaf, and the government gave greater latitude to religious figures, particularly Sufis. This decade witnessed a proliferation of religious gatherings and the expansion of *zawiya*s. The celebration of the Prophet's birthday (*Mawlid al-Nabawi*) was reinstated in most mosques, and Sufi shaykhs were increasingly invited to give blessings to newborns. Shaykh Abdallah Barakat argues that:

> At that time, everyone participated in collective celebrations [*hadra*], and people would invite Sufi shaykhs to bring blessings to their newborns. There was a popular religiosity deeply infused with Sufi rites, even if few explicitly identified as Sufis. Conversely, apart from a handful of intellectuals and shaykhs' disciples, no one spoke of reprehensible innovations [*bida'*] or made distinctions between Sufis and Salafis—such classifications were simply not relevant.[6]

The dominant Sufi brotherhoods during this period were the Rifa'iyya, Qadiriyya-Naqshbandiyya, and Shadhiliyya. However, this resurgence of Sufism took on a largely reformist character. "The regime granted them considerable space because they did not engage in politics", explained shaykh Abdallah Barakat. "Many scholars associated with Sufism adhered to a reformist tradition that either ignored or openly opposed the more esoteric dimensions of traditional Sufi practice. Shaykh Nafia al-Shami, for instance, rejected the sanctification of clerics, a hallmark of certain Sufi traditions".[7] Similarly, shaykh Muhammad al-Sandal, a disciple of Muhammad al-Nabahani, sought to propagate a form of religious knowledge purged of superstitious elements associated with popular Islam. As one of his grandsons, himself a Sufi, explained,

> He traveled to rural areas to spread a version of religious knowledge that was stripped of practices he deemed un-Islamic. His goal was to reform shirk and traditional customs that he considered non-religious. He adopted a reformist approach, aiming to purify doctrine. His Sufi orientation completely distanced itself from associationist tendencies, relying exclusively on the Sunna and the Quran rather than on jurisprudential schools.[8]

One shaykh argued that due to the activism of influential clerics such as shaykh Muhammad al-Sandal and shaykh Khalaf Abu Hamud, the reformist current in Idlib significantly weakened the esoteric tendencies within the local Sufi landscape.

In the shadow of revolutionary radicalism: The occultation of Sufism in Idlib

The revolution abruptly ended the modest resurgence of Sufism that had begun in the 1990s, leading to renewed suppression in three key ways. First, public figures known for their Sufi orientation faced heightened pressure. Second, Sufi disciples fragmented—some were forced into silence, while others, under duress, joined the armed resistance, often at the expense of their ideological principles. Third, Sufi rituals largely vanished from public life.

While the revolution was not initially driven by a specific ideological agenda, its militarisation quickly reinforced Salafi dominance. Unlike anti-colonial jihads or the early stages of the Afghan resistance, the shift to armed struggle marginalised Sufis. Sufism did not serve as a reference point for any of the factions, with the exception of two groups: in Hama, Liwa Abu al-'Alamein—a Sufi faction that later relocated to western Aleppo province and rebranded itself as al-Haraka al-Sufiyya—and Tajamu' Ahrar al-Sufiyya, led by Omar Rahmoun, who later defected to the regime and became an ardent counter-revolutionary propagandist.

Jihadis—who embrace the Salafi approach to Islam—played a decisive role in this renewed suppression of Sufism. Their growing influence was not only evident on the battlefield but also in the social sphere. Jihadis condemned the *quburiyyun*—those who venerate saints' mausoleums—as well as Sufi rituals such as *hadra*, which involve spiritual immersion and communion with the divine. These groups significantly influenced young local fighters through their ideological training programs (*dawrat shar'iyya*). Jihadis rejected Sufism along two lines: they framed Sufism as a doctrinal deviation from Islam and as a political liability due to its perceived association with the regime. As shaykh Abdallah Barakat explains:

> Over time, as Salafis gradually asserted their dominance over Free Syrian Army factions, Salafism hardened. Its leaders regarded any pre-2011 student of religion, even those involved in armed struggle, as inherently Sufi—someone who sought blessing [*baraka*] from saints' tombs, was sympathetic to the regime, and therefore suspected of theological deviation.[9]

Sufi esoteric practices also raised suspicions of ideological proximity to Shiism. According to the son of Muhammad al-Sandal, "factions viewed Sufis as *quburiyyun* who were closer to Shiism. This was because of their devotion to saints' tombs. Many esoteric groups were killed—especially by ISIS. Jabhat al-Nusra also executed some, but mainly in Aleppo"[10].

For Hassan Dugheim, a religious scholar initially close to the Free Syrian Army, the war strengthened Salafism:

> During the war, states provided support to Salafis, while Sufis sought stability and were largely uninvolved in armed struggle. As a result, Salafism gained strength through the conflict. It quickly occupied the political space, dominated the media, and imposed itself on armed factions.[11]

According to one of the grandsons of shaykh Muhammad al-Sandal, "most of those who once identified as Sufis withdrew. Since 2012, there has been no visible Sufism in Idlib. No one dares to publicly declare themselves a Sufi, fearing reprisals from all factions, as every group, in one way or another, was influenced by Salafism".[12]

This occultation of Sufism took three main forms. First, Sufi clerical figures (*ulama'*) withdrew from public life. Some were summoned by the regime to leave opposition-held areas. Others, who were sympathetic to the opposition but still remembered the massacres of the 1980s, feared another wave of state repression against religious figures. Some chose to remain but opted for silence. At best, figures like shaykh Muhammad al-Sandal were consulted by factions, but any association with Sufism—or even with Ash'arism, the dominant non-Salafi understanding of the religious creed—inevitably led to a severance of ties.

Second, the suppression manifested through the ideological adaptation or silence of *murids*. They became deeply divided between two responses: either retreating into apolitical silence or embracing the revolutionary struggle at the cost of theological and doctrinal concessions. Age played a crucial role in this divide. As the son of shaykh al-Sandal explained:

> The elderly withdrew into silence and secluded themselves in their homes. Meanwhile, many young murids made compromises with armed groups. Some joined as religious advisers [*shar'iyyin*], while others became fighters. Some were motivated by a desire for vengeance, particularly those whose families had suffered during the anti-Muslim Brotherhood massacres of the 1980s. However, once these murids entered armed factions—where Salafism was overwhelmingly dominant—they abandoned their original ideology and instead conformed to a kind of mainstream Salafism.[13]

Finally, the suppression of Sufism resulted in the disappearance of its rituals. The practice of *dhikr* in mosques vanished. The celebration of births with Sufi rituals continued sporadically but only in the privacy of homes. All saints' mausoleums were destroyed, and visits to the tombs of ancestors ceased entirely.

Social inertia: After a decade of occultation, the return of Sufism

Despite its repression and marginalisation during the war, Sufism has resurged through two key mechanisms. First, it reemerged through social inertia—the tendency of existing cultural and religious traditions to persist despite periods of suppression. As Salafi influence waned with the rise of HTS, Sufism found increased tolerance, enabling it to gradually re-establish itself at the grassroots level. Second, HTS actively facilitated its resurgence as a strategic

THE THERMIDORIAN OPENING TO SUFISM

move to appeal to the silent majority, paving the way for its return through political channels, or from the top down.

The reaffirmation of Sufism did not happen immediately with the emergence of the Salvation Government in 2019. Rather, much like the development of the consumerist public sphere we analyse in Chapter 8, it was shaped by the ceasefire and the end of active armed conflict. The COVID-19 pandemic further delayed this revival, which only became fully evident between 2021 and 2022—initially manifesting within the realm of ritual practices.

One shaykh, for instance, observed a renewed demand for the presence of Sufi shaykhs at *aqiqa* ceremonies—religious and musical celebrations held to mark the birth of a child, weddings, or other festive occasions. Unlike traditional musical performances, these ceremonies feature religious chants and praises, rhythmically accompanied by a frame drum (*mazhar*). The presence of a Sufi shaykh is believed to bring blessings to the gathering and its participants, in addition to contributing to the performance of these religious chants.

Others noted the revival of collective ritual recitations (*majalis al-dhikr*) and various devotional gatherings, such as the communal recitation of divine names and religious hymns. These events have drawn dozens of disciples and students of Islamic knowledge (*tullab al-'ilm*), with reports of gatherings ranging from 80 to 150 participants in private settings. However, these meetings were neither clandestine nor hidden; rather, they were publicly announced and marked a cautious revival of Sufi brotherhoods, particularly the Rifa'iyya, Naqshbandiyya, and Khaznawiyya orders. In the region of Ma'arrat al-Nu'man, which was less influenced by Salafism, Sufi spiritual gatherings (*hadral*) also made a return.

On a more public level, the celebration of the Prophet's birthday (*'Aid Mawlid al-Nabawi*), which had completely disappeared since 2011, reemerged over the two years before the 2024 victory. Online and in-person teaching of the Sufi tradition resumed, with renewed discussions of classical texts such as those by shaykh Serajeddine, the *Book of Healing* (*Kitab al-Shifa'*) by Ibn Sina or Avicenna and the *Revival of the Religious Sciences* (*Ihya' 'Ulum al-Din*) by al-Ghazali. This revival of collective ritual practices was accompanied by the continued operation of Sufi-oriented religious institutions, such as the Imam al-Nawawi Institute and the Shaykh Hussari Institute, which had remained active throughout the years.

The resurgence of Sufi rituals was not without resistance. Some conservative religious scholars (*ulama'*) criticised this revival, and, as one shaykh noted, "any shaykh with a significant social base and a reputation for spiritual insight [*mutabasir*] is under surveillance".[14] This observation underscores the continued caution surrounding Sufism's return, which remained largely private and restrained.

A second aspect of this return through social inertia was the increasing presence of Sufis within religious institutions. This is particularly evident in the growing influence of Sufi scholars within governance structures in Idlib. The Religious Guidance Council (*al-majlis al-shar'i*), for instance, had become increasingly open to Sufi perspectives according to a local cleric.[15] Additionally, close relationships existed at the leadership level—for example, the director of the Imam al-Nawawi schools is reportedly close to HTS leadership.

Students graduating from Sufi-affiliated institutions also steadily integrated the broader religious landscape. The Imam al-Nawawi Institute alone had fifty-five branches across opposition-controlled territories, producing a significant number of students who go on to pursue advanced studies in faculties of Shari'a at universities in Idlib and Aleppo. Many of these graduates had since become mosque imams and, according to some local clerics, recently began organising *dhikr* gatherings.[16] Estimates suggested that approximately 40% of Friday preachers in these areas adhered to a Sufi orientation.[17]

One shaykh summarised this phenomenon as follows:

> At its core, people are naturally inclined toward Sufism. They enjoy celebrations—when a man marries and a shaykh comes to lead *dhikr* and chant *anāshīd*, this is part of the cultural fabric. The population is imbued with this tradition; they are Muslim by default and therefore, in a sense, Sufi.[18]

Figures such as the *misaharati*—responsible for waking people for dawn prayers during Ramadan—the *hakawati*, a storyteller who narrates legendary epics like *Antar Ibn Shaddad* or *Beni Hilal*, and the *munshideen*, singers of religious psalms who perform at weddings,

THE THERMIDORIAN OPENING TO SUFISM

circumcisions, and the end of Ramadan, have experienced a remarkable revival in the past two years.[19] Previously, during the years of open conflict, many factions—including Jabhat al-Nusra—largely suppressed these cultural traditions for practising *bida'a* (blameworthy religious innovations). Forced into silence for over a decade, these traditions reemerged in line with HTS's power consolidation, growing control over the religious sphere since 2019–20, and the marginalisation of the movement's own radicals. As one *misaharati* from Idlib explains:

> In the beginning, we were also accused of *bida'a* [unlawful innovation in Islam]. Many radicals were hunting us down, some claiming to be from Islamic State, others from Jabhat al-Nusra. But now that these factions have been disbanded, there is order and we have new room to manoeuvre. But we have had meetings with those in charge. We explain to them that this has been our job for a long time and that we want to do this, and they understand and gradually accept us.[20]

In the same vein, this *munshid* recounts an experience of engagement with the new power structure set up by HTS:

> We engaged the authorities. These authorities say they represent the people. But the people want our *anashid*. Everyone has martyrs and wants to live again. We have had discussions with the Ministry of Religious Affairs. At the beginning, three years ago, I was arrested by the security guards for a few hours. But since then things have calmed down and *mushideen* are tolerated again.[21]

Other areas of religious practice previously challenged by Salafi dogma also made a quiet but significant comeback. Visiting graves, which had been completely prohibited until 2021, gradually resumed—initially in a discreet manner but then with increasing visibility. In 2024, for the first time in years, women participated in large numbers, something unimaginable only in 2022.[22] Similarly, *fan hadif*—or "committed music," a genre of modern music with moral and conservative themes—also re-emerged.[23] Recording studios, once forced into the shadows, were officially registered again, signaling a broader shift in the religious and cultural landscape. HTS not only accepted but also actively regulated traditional Islam.

149

For instance, in the case of the *misaharati*, authorities registered individuals, allocated territories, and oversaw ritual details. Similarly, with the *mushideen*, the ministry approved the *anashid* they performed. In other words, while HTS once fought against many popular Islamic practices in the name of unlawful innovation in Islam (*bida'a*), it then not only tolerated them but also intervened in their content, framing and institutionalising these traditions. No longer operating outside of popular Islam, HTS had become an active participant in shaping it—integrating itself into the very religious landscape it once sought to control. According to Abu Abduh, an old Misaharati from Idlib:

> Last year I decided to bring out the *tabla*, the *tartoura* and the Arab folk costumes. I took my cart, a horse and a child with me to gradually bring out the traditions. I had to get permission from the Ministry of Religious Affairs for what I was going to say, and for the use of the horse and cart, but it went off without a hitch. It's clear that HTS now encourages tradition and rituals to get closer to people.[24]

According to Hassan Dugheim, "this resurgence of Sufism is not a planned or orchestrated effort. It is happening organically, without a deliberate policy to promote Sufism. Rather, Sufism is naturally reintegrating into the various institutions that are taking shape in HTS-controlled territories".[25]

If Hassan Dugheim is right to claim that there is a strong organic dimension in this resurgence of Sufi Islam, not everything is spontaneous. It is also a consequence of the thermidorian policy of reliance on silent majorities.

A Thermidorian bet on the silent majority

This resurgence of Sufism was therefore not merely society's attempt to reclaim space after nearly a decade of suppression by a revolutionary and militant dynamic; it was also a deliberate policy pursued by the new HTS-led authorities in Idlib. This policy operated on two levels before the 2024 takeover of Damascus: first, by broadening the boundaries of acceptable religious expression, and second, by leveraging Sufism as a counterforce against militant anti-HTS Salafism.

The broadening of these boundaries was evident in several ways. For instance, the preacher training institute, which was previously reluctant to engage with Sufis, was increasingly relying on them through shaykh Mohi al-Din. Another clear example is the case of the director of al-Ansar Bookstore, who adheres to Sufism. In 2024, to his great surprise, the Idlib Book Fair allowed his bookstore to promote 3,000 traditionalist books, including iconic works on Sufism, such as *Sufism Between the People of Hadith and the People of Fiqh (Al-Tasawwuf Bayna Ahl al-Hadith wa Ahl al-Fiqh)*, which explores the relationship between Sufism, traditional Islamic scholarship, and jurisprudence to defend Sufism as an integral part of Islamic tradition. According to a Sufi shaykh,

> The establishment of the Salvation Government has significantly changed our situation. The leadership of the new government wanted to appear open. The Minister of Religious Affairs has been meeting frequently with Sufi-oriented preachers and students of religion. They were able to voice their grievances—mentioning past accusations of murder simply for being Sufi, or the conflation of Sufi affiliation with support for the regime. Since the arrival of the Salvation Government we do not see true openness, but we do see an expanding margin of tolerance. They want to give people some breathing room, and they are now allowing certain rituals that they previously rejected.[26]

However, this shift was not merely about increased tolerance; it also reflected a calculated political strategy to mobilise the silent majority against more vocal radical and dissenting factions. In late summer 2024, following months of anti-HTS popular unrest, the authorities—reportedly at the request of the highest cleric in the movement—ordered all unregistered Sufi institutes to formalise their status. Initially, the directors of these institutes saw this as a form of pressure, fearing it was driven by conservative factions seeking to exert control. However, they were later surprised to find that this administrative regularisation came without doctrinal restrictions. For a prominent Sufi religious figure,

> We expressed our willingness to comply, but feared governmental interference in our teaching methods. However, this did not happen. No ideological conditions were imposed on the registration of our institutes, and we were able to maintain our teachings unchanged. Our stance has always been to avoid divisions over doctrinal differences, prayer methods, or accusations of *shirk* or apostasy. We emphasised the need to focus on what unites us—namely, the revolution—and to avoid fragmentation over religious issues.[27]

Although the authorities did not officially confirm this, those involved viewed this doctrinal openness as a political calculation. As one shaykh put it:

> The authorities appreciated the fact that Sufis did not take part in the protests against them. Most young people within Sufi networks sought to ease tensions and, unlike the Salafis, avoided provocation or calls for street demonstrations. Instead, they consistently emphasised that unity against the regime must take precedence over everything else.

Openness does not imply that doctrinal disputes were resolved. HTS dismissed some preachers due to their association with Sufism, only to be reinstated later under pressure from institutions such as the League of Ulema in Idlib. Sufi religious students (*tullab al-'ilm*) faced pressure to abandon devotional dances, with sanctions imposed for non-compliance. In Ariha, authorities attempted to mandate official authorisation for the religious students to engage in public preaching, but once again, pressure from Sufi circles on the Ministry of Religious Affairs led to the decision's reversal. As for tomb visits, they continued but in a "de-Sufised" manner—for instance, the traditional practice of tying a thread (*rabt khutt*) on a grave did not resurface.

Ultimately, the policy on Sufism was mixed, granting limited flexibility while still imposing restrictions. Religious authorities in Idlib also issued warnings and called to restrict Sufi brotherhood practices, particularly when conducted in large gatherings. The ability of the religious students from Sufi-affiliated institutes to obtain official positions within the Ministry of Awqaf depended on the degree of their engagement in esoteric religious practices.

THE THERMIDORIAN OPENING TO SUFISM

As one shaykh explained, "If they are known for practicing certain things, like the Sufism of al-Junayd, the Sufism of al-Jilani or seeking intercession from saints [*istighatha*], then they will not be granted official employment." From the perspective of Sufi shaykhs, the overall assessment of this openness remains mixed. According to another shaykh,

> Pressure on Sufism has decreased but still persists, mainly because the revolution is fundamentally rooted in the principles of Shari'a politics [*al-siyasat al-shari'a*]. What we are witnessing is not really an opening, but rather a policy of turning a blind eye. And this varies significantly from one region to another.[28]

One of the grandsons of the reformist Sufi shaykh Muhammad al-Sandal holds an even more pessimistic view:

> Sufism is not making a comeback. Today, no one can openly say they are Sufi. If a greater margin of tolerance emerges, then perhaps Sufi thought could return to Idlib. But for now, Salafism has left a strong imprint, particularly among young people born after 1985. For them, Sufism remains associated with a form of idolatry—'*āda shirkiyya quburiyya* [grave-worshiping polytheistic customs].[29]

In conclusion, Sufism was tolerated, but only in its reformist version. Anything that fell under deep esotericism (or *turuqiyya*, the traditional Sufi brotherhood system) remained prohibited. In reality, if HTS moved away from its Salafi roots, it was only to embrace an authoritarian and reformist form of Islamic modernism—one that is partially anti-traditionalist and institutionally punishes religious "deviance." This shift was driven by both social inertia and a strategic bet on the silent majority. As shaykh Mohi al-Din explains,

> Until 2019, Sufism was subjected to a policy of maximum pressure. Then, the adoption of the Shafi'i school of jurisprudence provided some stability. The authorities came to realise that they could not change people by force and that they had to accept the people's intuitive religiosity [*wijdaniyya*]. They did this to gain popular support and to prevent the population from becoming susceptible to foreign ideological agendas.[30]

The return of Sufism in the toolbox of HTS's political strategy

Sufi practices gradually resurfaced at the grassroots level through a cautious and limited reopening of rites between 2021 and 2022. By 2024, however, the relationship with Sufism became partly politicised due to the Sufis' silence during the anti-HTS social movement. While Salafis sought to capitalise on the *hirak* in a populist manner, as we cover in chapter 10, Sufis remained quiet, aligning with HTS under the pretext of "avoiding discord." In response, HTS pursued a careful strategy of co-optation, granting Sufi institutes official accreditation while refraining from interfering in their curricula.

HTS adopted a pragmatic approach to religious ideology, making concessions where they were politically beneficial and came at minimal ideological cost. For example, its openness toward Christians and, to a lesser extent, Druze was driven by strategic considerations—enhancing its image of tolerance to the West while broadening its appeal within the Syrian population. In contrast, fully recognising Sufism carried a higher ideological cost, as it risked alienating radical factions within HTS without offering substantial political gain, given that Sufis posed neither a direct threat nor a significant strategic advantage.

HTS's authoritarianism, therefore, varied depending on the religious group in question, exerting strong pressure on fellow Muslims who competed with HTS religiously too. Unlike Christians and Druze, whom it reframed as minorities and integrated into a nationalist positioning strategy, as we examine in the next chapter, Sufis were a competing and "deviant" current within Islam. Rather than fully recognising Sufism, HTS merely tolerated it while keeping it under pressure and forcing it to maintain a low profile. However, Sufism continued to reaffirm itself at the grassroots level through social inertia while also being politically courted from above when it demonstrated loyalty—most notably in the summer of 2024, at the height of anti-HTS protests that we examine in chapter 10.

By doing so, HTS normalisd itself and, in a regional context, appeared strikingly at the centre of the ideological spectrum. Like many Arab rulers, it instrumentalised Sufism as a counterbalance to political Salafism. This Thermidorian centrist realignment was part of its authoritarian strategy, where mainstream repositioning and selective religious openness serve both to regulate the religious sphere and to delegitimise faith-based opposition.

This was not only about authoritarianism and control but also about modernisation. This process was part of a broader sociological transformation in which Sufism, despite its historical influence on local Islam, was gradually being erased by the combined forces of religious modernisation and HTS's reformulation of mainstream orthodoxy—thereby reinforcing its own ideological repositioning.

Ultimately, HTS's management of Sufism revealed its threefold trajectory of 'normalisation.' First, it demonstrates a form of 'localist normalisation,' in which the group gradually adopted popular religious practices rather than opposing them.

Second, this relocalisation did not constitute a return to tradition; rather, HTS framed it within a reformist mindset shared by the most prominent Sufi ulama in Idlib. This return aligned with a long-term trajectory of doctrinal modernisation that began in the second half of the nineteenth century, which we examined in the previous chapter.

Third, it reflected an 'authoritarian normalisation,' where the controlled integration of Sufi institutions primarily served to weaken oppositional Salafis. This phenomenon, characteristic of Arab authoritarian regimes, illustrated HTS's departure from radical Salafism as it repositioned itself as a pragmatic politico-religious actor—one willing to instrumentalise Sufism to consolidate power while subtly broadening its social base.

7

DHIMMIS NO MORE, CITIZENS NOT YET

OTHERNESS RECAST IN SECULAR MINORITY TERMS

Syrian religious minorities captured major international attention during the conflict, primarily because of how the regime and its supporters insturmentalised their safety against the threat of the armed opposition. Supporters of the regime notably propagated a narrative that Christians and Druze were under threat of extinction from the Syrian armed opposition because of its radicalism. This claim was bolstered by a wave of armed attacks from opposition groups which still occasionally targeted religious minorities. This was particularly the case for the jihadis or groups close to them. Though many factions within the Free Syrian Army (FSA) were by no means immune to episodes of sectarian violence, as observed during fieldwork conducted in 2012 and 2013.[1]

The transformation of HTS relations with Christian and Druze communities reflected a significant shift in how to deal with the non-Muslim "Other". Under the influence of a less ideologically driven governance structure coupled with HTS leadership's interest in presenting itself as a nationalist and revolutionary actor, these communities came to be perceived less through the lens of religious categories and recast in political terms as minorities.

Coping with sectarian Sunni radicalism

Syria is a multicultural society. Before 2011, the country was home to a diverse array of religious and ethnic minorities. Christians made up about 10% of the population, with significant communities living in cities such as Damascus, Aleppo, Homs, and Latakia. The Druze, constituting around 3% of the population, primarily resided in the southern region of the country, particularly in the Jabal al-Druze area in As-Suwayda Governorate. Other notable minorities included Alawites (10 to 15% of the population), who are concentrated in the coastal regions, Kurds predominantly in the northeastern regions, and smaller groups such as Ismailis, Armenians, and Assyrians spread across various parts of the country.

In the northwest, particularly in Idlib province, many religious communities had to live under the rule of armed opposition groups. Initially, Christians and Druze in this region chose a political stance of non-alignment, not aligning with any faction while providing shelter to displaced civilians passing through their villages. Then, starting from late 2012, the gradual Islamisation of the armed opposition forced the Druze to flee or massively adapt. Jebel al-Samaq, a traditional place of immigration, became coveted due to the significant departures of resident Druze. The situation also worsened for them according to a Druze notable:

> The mountain is poor and has long been a land of emigration, leaving many houses abandoned. Some residents left at the onset of the conflict, while waves of newcomers from elsewhere in Syria took their place. They treated us as if we were responsible for their displacement, becoming new oppressors, no different from Bashar in their eyes. The situation brought many problems. I was threatened, and religious pressure increased. They even issued death threats, accused people of not praying or fasting, and condemned our clothing choices.[2]

Christians also went through a period marked by frequent land expropriations, kidnappings, and assassinations. "Other Syrians occupied our churches, our lands, and our houses," recalled one of the local notables who remained.[3] Counter-intuitively, the initial arrival of ISIS in the village of Yaqubia brought some temporary stability, albeit at a significant cost. While the community suffered from real insecurity caused by the existence of many local armed groups engaged in threats and violence, two ISIS commanders, including—surprisingly—a Frenchman, imposed strict conditions on the community. In exchange for security, the residents had to cease public displays of Christian religious symbols and submit to the new group. ISIS called this the pact of Omar. But this stability was short-lived, as ISIS soon escalated its violence when pressure on the group increased in the province.

There were individual and collective conversions to Islam. Many Druzes defensively converted to Islam, initially in an individual manner, gradually incorporating more Sunni Muslim rituals into their practices, a process some had already undergone while living in Aleppo when acculturating to a conservative Sunni urban environment. Local adjustments became more substantial as pressure for Druze conversion grew insistent. In 2013, there was a shift from the incorporation of religious practices to a collective and public conversion, led by around thirty notables from various Druze villages and spearheaded by Shaykh Rabeh Sabunji, on behalf of the entire Druze community. According to one of the signatories of the conversion document, "since the possession of religious knowledge is voluntary, and only the wise eldest [*uqal*] can consider themselves initiated, the choice of belief, the return to the Muslim faith, and the incorporation of Islamic practices do not pose a problem, especially among the laymen who are not keepers of religious dogma."[4]

In November 2013, under pressure from ISIS, the Druze community officially converted to Islam through a handwritten document signed by a group of notables on behalf of the "most guided and educated individuals" from Druze villages in Idlib Governorate. This phrasing appears to echo the traditional Druze division between ʿ*uqal* (the initiated, knowledgeable in religious matters) and *juhal* (the uninitiated). The document itself reflected this adaptation to a radical milieu in several ways. First, it signaled a categorical renunciation of Druze beliefs, explicitly rejecting the doctrine of reincarnation and condemning Muhammad Ibn Isma'il al-Darazi, the sect's historical figure, as a cursed proponent of esoteric heresy (*kufr*). Second, it entailed the community's adherence to Sunni Islam, but in a manner tailored to the expectations of the dominant forces in Idlib at the time—namely, by aligning with the Shafi'i school of jurisprudence, the region's historically prevalent school. Beyond this, the document carried a jihadi dimension as it emphasised jihad as a core obligation of Islam. It was also overtly anti-Shiite in two ways. First, it adopted the Sunni stance on the caliphate, listing

Ali as the fourth and final rightly guided caliph, thereby rejecting the Shiite belief that his predecessors were illegitimate usurpers. Second, it invoked the excommunication of those who criticise Aisha, one of the Prophet Muhammad's wives—a stance commonly associated with Shiism.

After a brief period of control by the Syrian Revolutionary Front, which was later defeated by Jabhat al-Nusra, the Jabal al-Sammaq region, including Qalb Lozeh, came under the control of Jabhat al-Nusra. Under their rule, religious tensions escalated as the group's foreign commander, Abu Abd al-Rahman al-Tunisi, questioned the sincerity of the Druze community's official profession of Sunni Islam. He pointed to the continued presence of shrines as evidence of lingering heterodox beliefs. In response to this scrutiny and pressure, the local Druze reaffirmed their conversion to Islam and even went as far as destroying their remaining shrines to prove their adherence.[5]

Despite these efforts to conform, distrust persisted, culminating in the brutal massacre of twenty-three Druze villagers in Qalb Lozeh in June 2015. The attack started with a dispute over property confiscations between al-Tunisi and the al-Shabali family. Tensions reached a breaking point when al-Tunisi attempted to confiscate the home of a family member who was living in regime-held Syria, on the grounds that he was a soldier in the Syrian army. However, the property was within the larger estate of the man's relatives, who confronted Jabhat al-Nusra fighters. The situation escalated quickly, with heated arguments turning into violence as the militants opened fire on the residents. In the ensuing massacre, two dozen Druze villagers were killed. Jabhat al-Nusra publicly denounced Abu Abd al-Rahman al-Tunisi's attack on the Druze villagers of Qalb Lozeh and sought to distance itself from the killing. In response, the group formed a committee to investigate and judge al-Tunisi, whom they jailed for a few months. Abd al-Rahim Atun later claimed that he had personally requested al-Tunisi's execution for his role in the atrocity.[6] However, the committee ultimately ruled that there was no evidence directly linking al-Tunisi himself to the killings—only his subordinates were found responsible. Many Druze viewed this decision as insufficient, as it failed to hold the commander accountable for the actions of his men.

DHIMMIS NO MORE, CITIZENS NOT YET

The journey of the Druze community through the revolutionary period also transformed their environment and, to some extent, led to substantial changes in religiosity, especially among the laymen. Fasting and practising home and mosque prayers became common. As pressure increased, the Lebanese Druze leader Walid Jumblatt also offered them sanctuary in Lebanon, but without success. The defensive adaptation through formal practice of the Druze, known as *taqiyya*, seems though to have, over time, produced profound socio-religious transformations. "One guy said my son is eight years old and he doesn't know what it means to be Druze, and he learned part of the Quran and he prays and fasts. To be a Druze is a risk. There is a new generation raised in a new situation, and it's not *taqiyya*; it's all they know."[7]

In all Syrian villages there is a mosque, and an important part of society has become Sunni Muslim. But society is divided. Women stay at home, so they are less under pressure and more inclined to keep the old faith while men change. The construction of the mosque of Qalb Lozeh, for instance, was started in 2021 as a result of an initiative by Druze from the village but they were unable to complete it. The Turkish Awqaf, touring the areas, decided to support them, under the supervision of the Salvation Government. A similar process took place in Maaret Ikhwan and other villages.[8] These transformations sometimes run deep but are often marked by pain and division. For example, a Druze professor from the mountain testified,

> Many individuals transition from a state of non-religion to a situation of forced religiosity, especially after the massacre of Qalb Luza, creating situations of schizophrenia. Children, in particular, have been affected by religious teachings and education. They have become more devout than ordinary adults. As for the latter, they live in seclusion. However, some families truly convert to Islam to the extent that not even Ibn Taymiyyah witnessed in his time.[9]

The approach of HTS's predecessor toward minority communities reflected broader ideological and strategic transformations over time. Initially viewed through the rigid lens of Salafi religious doctrine—or, more broadly, subject to social marginalisation—Christians and Druze in Syria found themselves among the many victims of the revolution's upheaval. Today, these communities are largely dispersed across three cantons and eighteen villages, with approximately 600 Christians from various denominations and around 6,000 Druze. Politically, the Druze tend to align more closely with Walid Jumblatt's Progressive Socialist Party, maintaining a degree of communal identity despite ongoing challenges under the rule of the factions.[10] Tensions with religious minorities exacerbated and religious pressure increased when Jaysh al-Fath took over the whole of Idlib province in 2015. Jaysh al-Fath was an alliance of various Syrian armed opposition groups led by Ahrar al-Sham and Jabhat al-Nusra (before its transformation into HTS). The alliance was supported by regional backers with the goal of capturing the remaining areas held by the Syrian regime inside the province of Idlib.

In practice life became very difficult initially. Confiscations of houses, threats, petty humiliations, desecrations of mausoleums and graves accelerated the exodus and demographic transformation of the Druze mountain. For example, in Kaftin, 60% of the population left. There were 3,000 people before, and now there are 1,500. A local Druze affirmed that

> The majority are not leaving because they don't want Islam or because they support the regime. Instead, they are leaving because they can no longer afford to survive. Regarding the social structure in the fifteen villages. Initially, Jabhat al-Nusra took over houses and gave them to Uzbeks and Turkistanis. They are accommodated in two schools. There was some chaos at the beginning, but since 2015, Jabhat al-Nusra has gradually taken control and redistributed properties. They claim to only take vacant houses. They also empty some internally displaced persons (IDP) camps and replace them with Uzbeks and Turkistanis. HTS initially followed a policy that prioritised the families of jihadis. There are now almost more non-Syrian Arabs.[11]

As a result, some villages were completely emptied of their original inhabitants and repopulated by Central Asian Muslim communities, primarily Uzbeks and Uighurs, with no significant presence of Arab foreign fighters. Over time, Uighurs have established themselves as a distinct local community in the same areas where the Druze have faced increasing pressures to Islamise. Initially, relations between the local population and the Central Asians were tense. The presence of armed factions led to a period of strict control, with checkpoints, courts, and *hisba* (religious police) enforcing rigid social norms. Women, in particular, faced heavy restrictions on their dress and behavior, while men were subjected to humiliating rules regarding their appearance and daily conduct. However, as power became more institutionalised under the governance of the Salvation Government and the Administration of the liberated areas (*Idarat al-Manatiq*), the situation gradually stabilised. The formalisation of authority helped ease some of the more arbitrary pressures, fostering a more predictable—albeit still repressive—environment for the remaining minorities.

Since then, the primary point of contention has been the Druze community's refusal to marry their daughters outside the group. The Druze defended this stance by asserting, "We are acting like a tribe"[12] while some Sunni muslim newcomers to the area commented that, "they are not true converts if they do not give their girls in marriage."[13] This tension underscored deeper questions about the sincerity of their forced or strategic conversions. Nevertheless, the interplay of *taqiyya* (religious dissimulation), demographic shifts, and the emergence of a post-conversion generation profoundly altered their social fabric. Over time, Druze society has undergone partial Islamisation, with *juhhal* (non-initiated Druze) initially serving as the most vulnerable entry point for this transformation. The rise of a new generation, coupled with religious education under the new governance, has further solidified these changes. As a result, Druze society now finds itself integrated into an evolving, mixed social landscape, where Central Asian Muslims—particularly Uighurs—have come to play a significant role.

The twofold minority coming-out of Ahmad al-Sharaa

On 10 June 2022, Ahmad al-Sharaa made a surprise visit to the Druze community during the inauguration of a well in the village of Qalb Lozeh, the site of the 2015 massacre. The presence of Al-Sharaa himself was intended to send a strong and deliberate signal—not only to the Druze community but to Idlib as a whole—

that the dynamics of their relationship were shifting. His appearance underscored an effort to redefine the status of the Druze under the new order, signaling a move away from the previous tensions toward coexistence. According to a close associate of al-Sharaa:

> Why go through the media this time rather than working discreetly with them? There were several reasons. Keeping a rapprochement and a *musalaha* [reconciliation] secret is not good for trust building. We wanted to reassure them and show we are able now to endorse our choices publicly. But we also wanted to send a message inside our movement and impose the dynamics of change within HTS. This is why we decided to go public and to go public through a visit done by al-Sharaa himself. Decisions coming from the leader himself have a strong credibility; decisions coming from the other levels can be contested.[14]

In stark contrast to his stance seven years earlier—when he declared in an interview with Al Jazeera that Alawites should renounce both their beliefs and their support for Assad—al-Sharaa now found himself addressing a small group of Druze dignitaries seeking religious recognition.[15] As they reaffirmed their pride in being Muslims, in order to build trust, he responded by emphasising that "there should be no compulsion in religion." In doing so, he cast doubt on the legitimacy of their collective conversion, implying that it had been imposed by force rather than genuine conviction. He was also implicitly acknowledging the right to retract a conversion, at least when it was undertaken under coercion. This stance was interpreted by some as an implicit acceptance of apostasy, as it directly challenged the prevailing doctrinal position that considers conversion—particularly to Islam—as an irreversible commitment. By suggesting that a coerced conversion could be nullified, he undermined the rigid theological view that equates leaving the faith with apostasy, which, in many interpretations of Islamic jurisprudence, is considered a grave offense, often punishable by severe legal and social consequences. By implying that conversion under duress could be reversed, he was challenging this deeply entrenched doctrinal position, which regards religious commitment as irrevocable.

After the initial surprise had passed, the Druze dignitaries present at the meeting took al-Sharaa's gesture seriously. They saw his visit to Qalb Lozeh as a step toward reconciliation and acknowledged a shift in the HTS leadership's vision. However, they approached the HTS leader's rejection of religious compulsion with caution, fearing that the new direction might not be followed or could even be contested by the movement's grassroots. One of the dignitaries remarked, "goodwill from the leadership alone is not enough. We are in a hostile environment. Al-Sharaa came once, but the local commanders have been here for ten years."[16] Another pointed out that they had decided to build a mosque to avoid being labeled as infidels by the groups in their surroundings.[17] That's why they focused their demands on tangible rights on the ground, such as the restitution of confiscated homes and lands, as well as requests for development assistance, rather than addressing issues related to freedom of belief or political rights at this stage.

Similarly, a month later, on 19 July 2022, Ahmad al-Sharaa paid a visit to a group of local Christian religious dignitaries. Unlike the Druze community, HTS had established contact with the Christians through the management of the region since late 2019, which reinforced their cooperation on various matters such as the restitution of homes, agreements on sharing profits from absentee-owned agricultural lands, the reduction of hate speeches, and the return of Christians from Idlib into internally displaced territories controlled by the regime. The Christian dignitaries acknowledged these improvements and commended the work of the management of the region. In response, al-Sharaa suggested not dwelling on the past, including the historical context of the Crusades and the regime's manipulation of minorities. He also pointed out the abuses committed during the era of various factions and highlighted the current difference, saying:

> When you say things have been improving since 2018 or 2019, it's because there is an authority being established. We are in the process of rectifying everything that has happened. We want justice to prevail under the rule of law and also Shari'a, but in a fair way. For example, we are working on land restitution. We are building

a new Syria, a Syria with many coexistences. We are preparing the Syria of the future, and at the core of it is the principle of justice.[18]

With the Christian community, al-Sharaa maintained a relatively conventional Muslim jurisprudence. He reminded Christians of their rights to security and the practice of their faith, placing these rights within a dual normative framework: the law and Shari'a. However, what is noteworthy is that this was the first time an opposition leader has systematically and consistently taken a series of concrete actions aligned with their new discourse. Among both the Druze and the Christians, the first noticeable improvement was primarily in the security situation. This included the expulsion or distancing of aggressive militants—often Uzbeks and groups associated with Hurras al-Din—who sought to seize land, the deployment of new police stations, security cooperation with locally established community guards,[19] increased use of courts by Druze and Christians,[20] house restitutions for Christians,[21] sanctions against imams or militants for hate speech,[22] and facilitating the return of the last families from the three villages of Qniyye, Jdeide, and Yaqoubiyya, who were still residing in regime-controlled areas, to their homes.[23] The Salvation Government also facilitated the restitution of properties belonging to both residents and absentees, followed by the return of lands to the people, including Christian awqafs.[24] Four churches were also returned, except for the Idlib church due to a lack of resources for its restoration. The local clergy decided to temporarily place it under the protection of HTS.[25] The population upheaval caused by internal migrations and the forced settlement of armed groups and their families became a focal point for tensions with minority communities. In the Druze mountain of Jebel al-Samaq, most displaced individuals were Uighurs and Uzbeks.

> They are religiously radical and closed off. There were problems in the past. Radical leaders incited them against us. But now, it's much less the case because the radicals have disappeared. And for the past year, the situation has been calming down, either through HTS intervention, amicable solutions [*sulh*] directly in real estate transaction offices, or through the courts.[26]

HTS also facilitated the reopening of a church in Idlib, allowing, for the first time in ten years, the celebration of Saint Anne's feast day on 28 August 2022, in the church bearing the same name, albeit under heavy surveillance by the General Security Directorate.[27] Among Christians, caution initially prevailed. Some acknowledged that:

> Now the security situation is good, the periods of theft and looting are over. Security measures have intensified, and unlike a year or two ago, HTS now proactively manages crimes committed on our lands: investigations, security measures, arrests, cooperation with our village guards.

On the other hand, the political translation of this observation was still in its infancy: "there are still many individuals linked to the new authorities who are making money from our lands. But the Salvation Government is now a reality, and we must participate, or else we will be excluded. In this context, our policy is to take what they give us and gradually express our demands. We don't want to open a front against al-Sharaa."[28] Among the Druze community as well, they took note and engaged in dialogue with HTS while being cautious not to commit too deeply. The offer from Ahmad al-Sharaa,[29] stating that there should be no compulsion in religion, was not an opportunity they were ready to seize at this stage:

> Al-Sharaa talks about "no compulsion in religion." But what about the ruling on apostasy [*hukm al-rida*]? We need clarifications before we engage with this question. So far, we are afraid that this progress may lead to backlashes. We have oral commitments for now, but we need written commitments. al-Sharaa seems to be telling us that our faith is not a problem. But we need to see.[30]

Seizing the opportunity of HTS's "speaking openly" while maintaining a hostile environment carries significant risks. Thus, to regain possession of their homes, the pursuit of informal deals remains the top priority because "if we go through the court, the risk of making enemies is too great."[31]

However, the situation was far from perfect, and challenges persisted. While there was a real improvement in security, especially among Christians, aggressive actions, although significantly reduced, did not cease, primarily against the Druze community. Hate speech, stone-throwing attacks, and even murders followed al-Sharaa's visit, prompting HTS and the Turkistan Islamic Party to intervene multiple times to de-escalate tensions. For instance, a Druze dignitary, informing a close associate about the situation in the mountainous region following the visit of HTS leader, said,

> After Sheikh al-Julani's visit to the mountain villages, we noticed resentment from the majority of our neighbors towards us. Some of them started working to sow discord between the mountain people and the Uzbek and Uighur foreign fighters who live in the mountains, to undermine HTS for the work they've done. The discovery of trash in a mosque in Qalb Lozeh led the imam to mobilise against us, provoking the Uighurs. They fired shots in the air, forcing HTS to intervene and resolve the issue. Another incident occurred in the village of Hilla, where an elderly villager allegedly called for the departure of the foreign fighters [*muhajireen*] from the mountains. They felt provoked, and HTS had to intervene again to calm the situation, this time by asking the elderly man to leave.[32]

Regarding House and Land Property, property restitution was nearly complete before 2024 among Christians but still has a long way to go among the Druze. When it comes to agricultural lands, the issue was more complex. The agricultural lands of families in exile were seized and distributed to members of the various factions and their families, including HTS. Deals existed between HTS and local farmers, but agreements on the distribution percentages of the income generated from land exploitation was contested and adjusted over time, often to the detriment of legal landowners or their families. These agreements were agreed upon orally with the Directorate of Agriculture, which was under the Ministry of Agriculture of the Salvation Government. Therefore, they were highly dependent on the individuals in charge. A personnel change could easily lead to a disadvantageous redefinition of the percentages. A Druze villager from Jebel al-Samaq testified,

> In the past two years, we've sensed a new direction from HTS, and they say they are protecting us. But the houses are still occupied,

and local councils have taken the agricultural lands of emigrated individuals. They initially gave them to Uzbeks and Turkistanis, then to government officials and security personnel. The deal is that HTS and the new farmers share the revenue. Initially, it was a 50/50 split, and now it's 73% for HTS and 27% for us. Currently, they are giving the lands to individuals closest to the legal owners. We have probably regained 30% of the agricultural lands, but 70% are still pending.[33]

Threats, incitement to hatred, and acts of violence—ranging from stone-throwing to armed attacks and even murder—persisted despite a decline in frequency and the imposition of sanctions. For instance, in April 2023, a Christian woman was attacked, which triggered an intervention of the local staff from the (*Idarat al-Manatiq*) Administration of the liberated areas which expelled the attacker from the area. According to the Druze community, mosque preachers struggled to align with HTS's new political stance, prompting repeated interventions by HTS. They intensified after al-Sharaa's visit, which forced the HTS leadership to take action. Some non-Syrian jihadis remained a source of tension for locals.[34] Additionally, attacks and two assassinations took place in the villages of Qalb al-Lozeh and Kaftin. According to one of the Druze dignitaries,

> There are clearly people inciting discord [*fitna*]. Even today, the mosque preachers talk about the Turks and criticise the Turkish-Regime rapprochement. The provocations continue and increase. It's as if Jebel Samaq has become a stage for settling scores. We are really afraid. It is clear to us that there is a group of radicals who reject HTS's openness towards us. But HTS has been very concerned about avoiding trouble in the mountain: investigations have always taken place immediately, followed by arrests and an intensification of security measures. Now the region is closed off, with patrols in the villages and at the mountain's entrance. HTS's responses show that the group is serious about its promises of redressing grievances and equality between religions. The foreign fighters are under intense pressure. For example, to facilitate security control, HTS no longer allows foreign fighters to wear masks, and arrested many of them.[35]

Minority politics and implicit secularisation: When politics prevail, religious views pay the price

This new approach to religious minorities also revealed what HTS was becoming, both politically and religiously before the 2024 victory. The organisation had two possible ways to position itself regarding minority groups. The first was to engage in a complex modernist *ijtihad* (legal reasoning), requiring a full reinterpretation of religious sources to develop a contemporary understanding. However, this posed significant challenges for a movement that was military and elitist, as it lacked the necessary scholarly expertise and risked provoking internal resistance.

HTS, therefore, adopted a more political approach. The second option was to redefine these groups using non-religious categories, leading to the mobilisation of minority rhetoric. This shift represents a process of secularisation, as HTS started to classify these groups based on categories detached from a theological framework. Notably, HTS did not invoke traditional Islamic references such as *Ahl al-Kitab* (People of the Book), *Ahl al-Dhimma* (protected non-Muslims), or *Firaq Batiniyya* (esoteric sects, often used pejoratively) for the Druze. This redefinition allowed HTS to sidestep policies traditionally associated with these classifications. The issue was particularly significant for the Druze, as Christians hold a recognised status in Islam—even among Salafis—whereas the Druze do not enjoy the same religious legitimacy. For Abd al-Rahim Atun:

> When I look at the Druze, I evaluate their actions in relation to the revolution. Did they take up arms against us? Did they side with the regime? No. They did not fight us; in fact, they even sheltered refugees in their homes. So, I judge the situation accordingly. Now, when you ask whether I, as a religious preacher, should attempt to convert them, my answer is simple: I believe in Islam and in preaching. However, if I were to go into the Druze community and preach Islam, they wouldn't see just a preacher—they would see someone backed by authority and armed force. In the end, that would amount to coercion, which is not the Islamic approach.[36]

HTS's shift reshaped its discourse and identity. The group's political rhetoric gradually moved away from the Salafi framework that once shaped—or justified—its policies toward these groups. Instead, it started to align with a secular, modern narrative of minorities,[37] where the focus is on their relationship with the state rather than religious transcendence, occasionally emphasising equality under the law.[38] This discourse, which had become systematic within the group's leadership, represented a highly strategic and political transformation. As Ahmad al-Sharaa explained:

> The regime had built its governance principle on the idea of intimidating minorities. It wants to hold onto power by involving the Alawites, pushing them into a war against the Sunnis to position itself as the sole protector of minorities. Our approach to the Druze and Christians is a message to the people in regime-controlled areas and even to the Alawites themselves. We are proposing a social contract for Syria's future, regardless of the dominant force, founded on coexistence [ta'ayush]. And for that, we need to think in terms of "minority rights".[39]

This shift also had a significant impact on radicals in the region. Growing grassroots pressure revealed a clear resistance to normalisation, prompting local radicals to respond in increasingly extreme ways. This, in turn, forced HTS to intervene through legal measures, including arrests, investigations, bans on hate speech, and expulsions—sometimes affecting minority individuals as well. At the same time, this evolving landscape encouraged certain ideologically aligned armed groups, such as the Turkistan Islamic Party and Jaysh al-Ahrar, to adopt a more politically open stance toward minorities.

It also meant that HTS had not adopted a religious stance on the issue. According to al-Sharaa:

> Are the Christians Ahl al-Dhima [protected minorities in Islam] or not? For us, the main thing is that these people are under the authority of the Salvation Government, and they must be treated with the same rights as other individuals. We do not intervene in Shari'a matters.[40]

According to one of his advisors, along the same lines:

> Rather than adapting our ideological positions regarding the issue of the Druze and Christians, we prefer to build trust through political action. Ideological positions will come later. It is not

essential to take a religious stance on the issue of minorities. The Fatwa Council has not taken a position on this issue to date.[41]

If we view secularisation as the process of prioritising political considerations over religious worldviews, then HTS was secularising at least *vis-à-vis* other religious communities, since religion continued to play a role in governance. This secularisation was nonetheless ad hoc, implicit, and tied to a specific issue; it was not an overt or ideological stance. As al-Sharaa's advisor pointed out, it is revealing that the Fatwa Council consistently refrained from taking a stance on the issue. De facto, HTS's policy created a distinction between the exercise of power (*al-sulta*) and what al-Sharaa refers to as religious injunctions (*al-masa'il al-shar'iyya*). This deliberate separation was a means to avoid engaging with theological questions that could lead to internal conflicts. HTS's discourse hence bypassed theological issues and instead employed political concepts historically associated with the construction of the modern state.

Paradoxically, the preservation of religious doctrine occurred through the secularisation of political practices and representations toward Christians and Druze. Why, then, all these efforts? Because the question of Christians and Druze extends far beyond managing local communities in Idlib. What was at stake is HTS's broader national ambitions. In this sense, the openness to minorities was deeply woven into the movement's hegemonic project.

8

FLIRTING WITH THE SILENT MAJORITY
HTS'S MAINSTREAM TURN

Although the rejection of jihadism and the containment of Salafi influence had become discernible by 2024, the nexus between religious de-radicalisation and the reality of authoritarian political structures remained a subject of debate. The case of Muhammad bin Salman underscores a key dynamic in the region: that religious liberalisation, often framed as part of broader modernisation agendas, does not inherently catalyse political openings. In the context of Idlib, we similarly posit that the ideological repositioning of HTS and its disavowal of jihadism did not translate into a substantive modification of the structure of power and control.

The Thermidorian dynamics of the Syrian conflict influenced the rejection of jihadism and authoritarianism in distinct ways. "Thermidorian" here refers to a period of reaction against radicalism following a revolutionary phase, as in the later phase of the French revolution. The de facto ceasefire in northwest Syria, which featured only limited skirmishes across frontlines without high-intensity fighting, changed HTS. In an hegemonic position, HTS understood that it could cautiously open towards the revolutionary centre while distancing itself from its own former radical fringes. Although the group continued to rely on force, pressure on the revolutionary centre eased, as reflected in a decline in arrests of critical voices in political and media circles. Paradoxically, this shift towards the centre, while pacifying Idlib province internally, also motivated a resurgence of military adventurism and ventures outside Idlib, as

HTS started to nurture ambitions of broader representation of the revolutionary centre in opposition to the regime.

Revolution rediscovered

HTS's revolutionary realignment began with its embrace of revolutionary symbols—such as the flag and its public celebration—marking a stark shift from its earlier opposition as Jabhat al-Nusra. This shift was accompanied by a gradual rapprochement with other revolutionary actors. At this stage, this rapprochement contributed to the depolarisation of northwest Syria, albeit without fully integrating non-HTS elites or posing any real challenge to the new power structures. This shift reflected a significant evolution in HTS's relationship with the local political landscape, which had remained largely resistant to its rule.

HTS's recognition of the revolutionary symbols occurred step by step. The first contacts with the revolutionary milieu occurred in 2018, one year after the establishment of the Salvation Government. Several individuals with revolutionary backgrounds, including former Free Syrian Army fighters and members of local councils, urged al-Sharaa to raise the flag of the revolution. According to them, al-Sharaa expressed his initial acceptance but believed that a gradual approach was necessary due to the ideological resistance of some of his fighters. Leaders of the Administration of the liberated areas across northwest Syria also called on the mobilisation of local councils. According to one participant,

> We find ourselves, with HTS, sharing the same goal, the celebration of the revolution. For HTS, it's a way to show that they have become members of society. They helped us with logistics and security, though we faced a dilemma: cooperating could lead to a takeover and a one-party logic, even though the initiative for the celebration was originally ours, but refusing the extended hand could lead to a clash with what is, in practice, the one party.[1]

The celebrations expanded gradually. In 2020, it was limited to Bab al-Hawa, the border control with Turkey. One year later, in March 2021, HTS committed to sponsor and protect the celebrations of the start of the 2011 revolution more proactively. HTS set up stages in certain cities, raised the flag of the revolution on the highest flagpole in the governorate at Dawar al-Mihrab in central Idlib, and the Salvation Government ministries provided logistical support. In 2022, the government called on administrations and schools to participate and, in some places, they distributed the long-proscribed flags of the revolution. Officials from the Salvation Government and members of the Shura Council participated and delivered speeches,[2] though the organisers remained mostly the activists who were present in the coordination committees of the 2011 demonstrations. The dynamics between HTS and revolutionary activists varied from place to place. In some areas, HTS participated without intervening in the content of speeches and the identity of the speakers, while in others, it imposed stricter access controls to the stages and checked speakers' speech drafts.[3]

The relationship between HTS and the revolutionary elites evolved in the lead-up to the 2024 takeover of Damascus, though persistent criticism of HTS's governance cautions against overstating the extent of this shift. Their rapprochement was not merely symbolic; the embrace of revolutionary celebrations created new political openings while simultaneously deepening divisions within the revolutionary landscape. According to one participant,

> We are divided between those who refuse and those who, more pragmatically, say that participating with HTS is also a way to protect and strengthen the revolutionary reference. By participating, I acknowledge that my participation serves them. If I don't participate, I weaken my own position. The dominant position leans towards participation to avoid a clash with HTS.[4]

The first formal contacts between the revolutionary milieu and HTS emerged through an initiative by a group of revolutionaries and the public relations officer of the HTS Shura Council in late 2019. This followed HTS's decisive victory over Ahrar al-Sham in January 2019, which cemented its dominance over Idlib. The initiative led to several meetings with the HTS leadership, yet both sides remained cautious. Lingering tensions from past confrontations, the forced alignment of the local councils, and the departure of many revolutionary elites to opposition-controlled areas in northern Aleppo created obstacles on one side. On the other, HTS feared losing control or provoking backlash from its hardline factions. These factors ultimately prevented any formal agreement at the time.

Between 2019 to 2024, HTS also sought to co-opt segments of the revolutionary elite into its administrative structures. Rather than engaging in dialogue with established political bodies—which could have led to more meaningful political concessions—HTS focused on integrating individual actors to appease the local revolutionary milieu, which had long felt marginalised by outsiders.[5] However, these efforts were met with scepticism from parts of the revolutionary community. As one woman, whose family endured multiple arrests despite having martyrs from Jabhat al-Nusra in their ranks, recalled: "On one hand, the revolutionaries were interested, but on the other, many people were still in prison. In these circles, it was common to say that there was no difference between HTS and the regime."[6] A new, somewhat bitter, realism took hold among the revolutionary elite:

> Yes, gradually, local elites are drawing closer to HTS—not out of alignment, but out of necessity. We are from here, we existed before HTS, and we continue to hold our positions. We want democracy and citizenship, and we want it here. What has changed is that HTS is now engaging in dialogue with us. We are in direct contact with its leadership, making it clear that they will not change us. In return, they no longer seek to eliminate us outright but instead apply pressure to bring us under their influence. It is a familiar authoritarian strategy—one that relies less on physical coercion and more on controlled accommodation.[7]

Another cadre from the revolutionary political bodies, originally from Maarat Nu'man and a former minister in the opposition's interim government in exile, noted that:

> The security pressure on the revolutionaries has decreased. Some are now thinking about creating a party to rejoin the game inside. The mindset is changing. A few years ago, we rejected invitations to participate made by HTS during the establishment of the Salvation Government in 2017. They had offered us ministries, but we refused them. First, because we demanded a clear separation of military action from civilian commitments. Second, it was difficult for us to join an administration controlled by a designated

terrorist group. Now we meet with them cautiously because it is still inconceivable for us to join an administration as long as it is controlled by a military organisation.[8]

Another cadre, while acknowledging that governance remains under the control of an armed group classified as a terrorist organisation, also conceded: "To HTS's credit, they have eliminated the radicals, and today, Ahmad al-Sharaa is the best available choice."[9]

HTS's policy toward the revolutionary milieu followed a multi-pronged approach: appropriation of symbols, co-optation, and coercion. The group adopted the flag and revolutionary imagery it once opposed as Jabhat al-Nusra, gradually embracing revolutionary celebrations through orchestrated demonstrations under the Salvation Government's umbrella. Over time, this symbolic alignment deepened and allowed HTS to position itself as part of the revolutionary movement. All the while, HTS employed selective coercion, though with limited intensity, using targeted arrests of activists under the guise of non-political justifications. Notably, this strategy bears striking similarities to that of the Syrian Democratic Forces (SDF), the Kurdish-led movement in northeast Syria, which also blends political appropriation, individual co-optation, and controlled repression to maintain its authority.

Politicised women's empowerment constrained by HTS's and Western ambiguities

Warming relations between HTS and the revolutionary milieu also extended to women in Idlib. Over the past decade, Syrian women launched their own revolution within the broader revolutionary struggle as they politicised along two main axes. First, women sought to integrate into the new power structures that emerged from the revolution, a process primarily driven by local actors. Second, there was a distinct feminist mobilisation aimed at the empowerment of individuals—*tamkin*—through general political training, often without immediate, tangible objectives. This second strand of empowerment received significant support from Western aid. Initially, Western-funded programs contributed to the first objective as well, but after the rise of HTS, these gender-based initiatives had the unintended effect of depoliticising and limiting the political participation of what are often referred to as "empowered women" (*al-nisa' al-mutamakinat*). These programs, once a catalyst for engagement, had become a barrier to full political inclusion under HTS's governance.

Revolutionary politicisation in Syria began with the formation of the first local administrative entities, a process that was entirely driven by domestic actors and independent of foreign support programs. One candidate for election within the ranks of the Coalition of Opposition Forces, a member of the pharmacists' union, recalled that:

> We participated in the protests from the beginning of the revolution. It is from revolutionary activism that we derive legitimacy. We then managed to enter the political bodies of the revolution through elections. In 2012, 7 women and 40 men ran for the municipal council of Idlib in exile in Reyhanli, and 5 women were elected to a council of 25 people. When the governorate council was created, the presence of women was ensured, supported by some prominent figures, sometimes even religious leaders like Shaykh Ayman Mohsen, though there were reservations from others.[10]

This candidate also remembered that:

> The key factor influencing women's participation was not the opposition between Islamists or religious figures and others, but rather the urban–rural divide. Islamists, including the Muslim Brotherhood and Sufis, did not oppose women's involvement at the time.[11]

However, the presence of women in local councils remained low, rarely exceeding two or three individuals, as was the case in the councils of Salkin, Harem, and Binish.[12]

The participation of women was an entirely internal dynamic from 2011 to 2013, that is until Western NGOs provided the first training sessions and workshops for women. Women's initiatives began to form around these training programmes. The most significant and enduring of these initiatives, Barikat Amal (a Glance of Hope), created a network of approximately seventy women across opposition-held territories and operated as a pro-political participation lobby. Several other initiatives, such as the Makers of

Change (*Sani'at al-Taghir*) and Spaces of Hope (*Masahat Amal*), also emerged. These initiatives achieved undeniable successes inspiring women to enter the public sphere. Through the combined effect of training abroad and the endogenous drive for revolutionary representation, women established a presence, albeit modest, in professional unions, student unions, the Civil Defence, and other bodies representing the ongoing revolution.[13] For instance, there were three women among the fifteen members of the executive board of the political commission (*al-hayat al-siyasiya*) in Idlib, the most significant existing political entity there. In general, women's presence in NGOs faced a constant struggle between donor pressure for participation and local patriarchal resistance.[14]

The path toward political engagement for women set in motion but soon met the reality of HTS. Over time, much like their male counterparts, women came to recognise HTS as both a lasting force and one capable of adaptation. As a result, resistance to involvement gave way to a more complex outlook—where ongoing objections coexisted with a pragmatic willingness to engage. As one activist put it:

> Just two years ago, I would have refused to participate because we clearly saw HTS's total control over the Salvation Government. But now, it's more complex, and we can see that this control is diminishing, and the Salvation Government is becoming more civilian and less military than before.[15]

The primary obstacle, perhaps paradoxically, stemmed from the depoliticisation driven by NGOs and the United Nations system. By prioritising private goals—such as individual protection—over public ones, like women's participation in political structures, these organisations inadvertently hindered women's access to power. Despite their stated commitment to women's empowerment, international NGOs, in particular, promoted a depoliticised agenda that limited meaningful political engagement. As one high school teacher observed:

> Unfortunately, donors consult us very little on defining objectives and fund things that are secondary to us, redirecting priorities. They push us towards protection and raising awareness about gender-based violence when we would like support for our

> political action. We wish that international NGOs would more directly support women's participation in existing governance structures, but unfortunately, UN aid does not deal with politics.[16]

The emphasis on protection and gender-based violence redirected women's focus from direct political engagement to the private sphere. NGO interventions often discouraged political participation by offering salaried positions, creating a depoliticising effect within civil society—a dynamic that similarly impacted men: "With salary disparities sometimes reaching 1 to 20, I will leave my public commitment—in education—to concentrate on issues I consider less important but allow me to support my family."[17] This woman described the power dynamic between politicised women and foreign donors:

> Idlib is a conservative society, and on that basis, we can only reject what we see as opposed to our culture. The egalitarian spirit underlying some projects on forced sexual relations within marriage is problematic. What interests us is the development of skills that we can then use against the authorities and allow us to enter positions of power in Idlib.

Second, the empowerment of supported women fostered their individual interests, including their participation in conferences, foreign travel, and access to Western officials that could be jeopardised by engaging with structures close to HTS, including the Salvation Government. In these circumstances, any form of political engagement was a risk. According to Raefa Sami'a, who used to be one of the most dynamic women in the UN Women's Advisory Board:

> Two women were approached for positions within the Salvation Government. One of them accepted and later withdrew due to the issue of the terrorist listing, which is a real obstacle for women. Two years ago, I was advocating for women to be present in the local council of Idlib. I spoke to three women to encourage them to run for the local council. However, they were afraid of the consequences in terms of continuing their training abroad. And rightly so. One of them was elected and now heads the Women's Council of the local council of Idlib. I wanted to bring her to an

International conference in Turkey, but she was rejected by the organisers due to her affiliation with the Salvation Government.[18]

Still, HTS itself was also an obstacle to women's political empowerment. Despite the opening of public space, the political system remained largely closed.[19] There were no women in the Shura Council, the equivalent of Parliament, or in the ministries of the Syrian Salvation Government. The group's reluctance towards political participation was a matter of general principle, although HTS leaders did not make a final decision on the matter and remained open to change. According to Abd al-Rahim Atun, HTS's higher religious authority,

> It is too early to take a stance on women's representation. We must first agree on the very nature of the political bodies where they would be present, such as the Shura Council or local councils. If these local councils professionalise, then it might be possible to consider their presence in sectors such as education, health, child-related issues, or women themselves. Everything needs to be carefully considered.[20]

Thus the situation could evolve as politicised women, like other revolutionary cadres, evinced increasing interest in participating within existing power structures though this was met only with hesitant overtures from the leadership in Idlib. Consequently, joint projects with certain ministries, such as the Ministry of Agriculture in 2022, could potentially include women. Notably, the possibility of women holding positions was no longer taboo. This included roles in local councils as well as higher-ranking positions, such as the vice-presidency of the Ministry of Education. The Bureau of Administrative Affairs proposed the offer to a woman who was the school principal affiliated with the ministry who initially accepted, but later declined out of concern for the potential repercussions of HTS's designation as a terrorist organisation.[21] A woman involved in negotiations with the Salvation Government recounted her experience:[22]

> I was the only woman among twelve agricultural engineers when we met with the Salvation Government's agriculture committee to present our project, "Qamah" [Wheat]. In our first meeting,

they were visibly surprised to see a woman in our delegation. We explained that many men had disappeared—lost in combat, imprisoned, or killed—and that my presence would help us better engage with female members of the community. It took four months of persistent effort to gain their acceptance, but now cooperation with the ministry is strong. The initial resistance was real, but persuasion was possible, and today, it works.[23]

Over the three years leading up to the takeover of Damascus, similarly to what we saw with minorities, the "women's question" underwent a significant shift in meaning. What was once framed as a moral and religious issue—implicitly regulated by the *hisba* (moral police) until 2016—gradually evolved into a political matter, as reflected in the changing ways it was policed. Security institutions affiliated with HTS or administrative bodies under the Salvation Government replaced the now-defunct morality police. As a result, while women still faced pressure, this pressure was no longer primarily religious or ideological; rather, it was shaped by a political logic that mirrored the broader constraints imposed on the wider revolutionary milieu.

HTS's leadership did not adopt a clear or consistent doctrine on women's political participation. Instead, ambiguity prevailed: persistent security pressures coexisted with a hesitant openness toward politically engaged women. However, tensions remained—particularly regarding the compatibility of politicised women's values with the social and religious conservatism upheld by HTS leadership. Ultimately, the women's question had become increasingly intertwined with the broader revolutionary question—that is, the organisation's management of political opposition. While HTS's authoritarianism had not disappeared, it secularised in the sense that it became driven by political considerations of control more than by a normative religious project. As a result, it operated with relatively less intensity, relying on subtler forms of control.

Softening the edge: Shifting attitudes towards the ideological centre

HTS's revolutionary realignment led to a relative relaxation of its authoritarian grip. While such control persisted, its intensity diminished. This shift was driven by two key factors. First, HTS's uncontested dominance paradoxically reduced its reliance on coercion. The revolutionary landscape had become smaller and less assertive, with many viewing HTS not as an irreconcilable enemy but as a potential—if uneasy—partner. As a result, maintaining control required less overt repression.[24] Second, HTS's political strategy played a crucial role. HTS started to appeal to the soft majority—a loosely organised and less confrontational revolutionary centre with broad legitimacy—and only intensified its repression of hardline minorities, both within and outside the movement. This approach mirrored the Thermidorians' strategy in post-revolutionary France, where consolidating power involved rescuing the nation from the excesses of the Terror while sidelining radical factions.[25]

While the Syrian opposition abroad remained opaque to the ongoing transformations, human rights organisations monitoring the situation on the ground took note of the change. Bassam al-Ahmad noted that:

> HTS's policy towards the revolutionary milieu is evolving. The number of arrests is decreasing, and the intensity of torture in prisons is diminishing. This can be attributed to several reasons. First, due to emigration or internal displacement, this milieu is much smaller. Additionally, the revolutionaries on the ground understand their limits and the red lines. The situation remains problematic, particularly due to the lack of transparency in trials and the absence of defence lawyers. However, overall, there are fewer arrests than in opposition-held areas controlled by factions of the Free Syrian Army.[26]

Sarah Kayali, based on her monitoring of the situation for Human Rights Watch, also observed that political pressure decreased at a noticeably slower pace as HTS's hegemony solidified:

> They were much more oppressive, both religiously and politically. The goal was to weaken existing competing structures. Once they established their hegemony, a second phase of oppression aimed at restricting the space for civil society to operate. Activists and journalists were the main targets during that period. It was designed to isolate these individuals from the outside world and send a message to people inside Idlib: any connections with external donors are viewed with suspicion. However, over the

course of 2019, arrests of journalists and activists decreased due to concerted campaigns by activists, combining internal protests and external media coverage.[27]

On the ground, young activists attested that social media remained a tightly monitored space, where posting overly critical or acerbic content about HTS could result in consequences such as press card revocations and official warnings. While authoritarian control loosened, this relaxation remained partial, leading to differing opinions on the extent of political space now available for activism and critical discourse. Young revolutionaries, accustomed to street mobilisation, held varying perspectives on HTS's approach to public political expression. Some saw a cautious opening, while others remained sceptical of the group's willingness to tolerate dissent. A young activist from Harem, for instance, observed that:

> It is now possible to protest. Against the rapprochement between Ankara and Damascus, in support of the revolution, etc. But we know that there are also red lines, such as the power structure in Idlib, economic matters, and foreign relations. When we express ourselves in the media, I receive calls and warnings but no longer arrests.[28]

Another activist mentioned that

> Spontaneous protests organised by activists are mostly against Ankara's opening to Damascus, the use of chemical weapons, the regime's starvation policies. There have also been several protests about the local situation, calling for the release of prisoners held by HTS or protesting against rising prices. HTS tolerates these protests and has not made arrests unless the protesters turn to provocation and insults.[29]

For a third activist, the pressure was not directed toward the centre, and the use of street protests was not necessarily the work of the centrist activists from the early days of the revolution. The persistence of authoritarianism affected—and perhaps primarily—the former strongholds of Jabhat al-Nusra. For instance, in 2022, the village of Kili, near Dana, saw radical youths being arrested, leading to protest demonstrations and increased security monitoring of this sector. "The young people in the village are known for their radicalism, and HTS really wants to neutralise them. Hence, this cycle of arbitrary arrests and protests. But it's slow because these circles were the striking force that allowed al-Sharaa to liberate Idlib in 2015."[30]

Local revolutionary elites—the influential figures such as political activists, intellectuals, and community leaders who played pivotal roles in the uprising—also noted the relaxation of authoritarianism. For instance, a member of the Political Committee (*al-Hay'at al-Siyasiyya*) in the Idlib governorate based in Salqin, a political body, pointed out that the relaxation of authoritarianism, the rediscovery of "social inertia"—that Francois Furet theorised in the French revolution—and internal transformations go hand in hand:

> At the beginning, Jabhat al-Nusra didn't have the skills and were obsessed with changing us: banning shisha, pressuring the face veil on women [*niqab*], and enforcing moral policing. When they got rid of other factions, they opened up to society. They sought points of convergence with society. Yes, I was arrested, but they treated me well, released me, apologised, and asked me to work with them. I refused. At first, they built their legitimacy on jihad, then on Islam, then on administration, and finally on social acceptance. So they gradually changed, abandoned criticism of the revolutionary flag, gave up on their divisive religious concepts like loyalty—to the Muslims—and Disavowal—of the non-Muslims [*al-wala wal-bara'*], accepted public celebrations, etc. They no longer want to change people, and start criticising their radicals. In fact, it's them more than society that is now changing.[31]

HTS started to lead a model of low-intensity authoritarianism that increasingly relied on the internalisation of constraint rather than on direct enforcement. A member of one of the political bodies still present in Idlib today, the Union of Syrian Democrats, confirmed that

> After all the confrontations, we are in a logic of self-restraint that we regret. We self-limit, hesitate to mobilise. When you see that media activists are constantly threatened, sometimes arrested if they take a critical stance against HTS, in the end, we don't dare to be very active. At the Union of Syrian Democrats, we just maintain our network, hesitating to expose ourselves for fear of reprisals.[32]

The same observation of a relaxation of authoritarianism was true on women's issues. An activist woman noted:

> Until three to four years ago, there was a women's section of the morality police that would intervene and apply pressure, mainly through foreign women, mostly Tunisians and Egyptians. This caused an outcry in civil society organisations. Once, these women were physically assaulted in the market. Even then, HTS backed down. The moral police no longer exist. There was the Centre of Devotional Prosperity [*Markaz al-Falah*], which monitored the activities of our women's group, but even their actions were increasingly restrained. They were present, with their cars, but no longer intervened. They came to our organisation, we discussed, clarified what we could do, and they left. They gave us the impression that they were more interested in gathering information than promoting virtue. They were in the market but no longer intervened. On a broader scale, we observe a return of conservative mixing, the appearance of makeup, and so on.[33]

However, the reduction in moral pressure in public spaces did entail a relaxation of political and security pressure on organisations of politicised women. Security harassment was constant, including investigations, summons, administrative hassles, close scrutiny of activities, requests for reports, threats of non-renewal of permits granted to the organisations these women lead, often practised by the development bureau (*Maktab al-Tanmiyya*). Like the men, due to this relatively calibrated pressure, women internalised the constraints and self-limited their actions. As one activist put it,

> We are still afraid that HTS's changes are only cosmetic. We undergo interrogations even if they tell us it's just to know what we are doing. But we know that activities related to citizenship, for example, are sensitive, so we publish little and limit our actions.[34]

In fact, according to another activist,

> Investigations have significantly intensified over the past year. All female activists have been subjected to investigations, and some of their organisations have had their permits revoked. I was investigated following a series of online conferences. We feel that these practices originate from lower levels of the movement, and

there is a diffuse fear within it that we receive foreign aid and disseminate values that are potentially contradictory to our own values. Therefore, it would be crucial for us to engage in dialogue with the leadership of the movement.[35]

Still, activists were also killed. Raed Fares and Hamoud Jeneid were prominent Syrian activists and journalists known for their outspoken criticism of a range of groups, including HTS. Based in Kafranbel, they used media, particularly independent radio broadcasts, to advocate for democracy, civil rights, and the original ideals of the Syrian revolution. Fares, in particular, gained international recognition for his creative protest banners and campaigns promoting freedom of expression. Both faced repeated threats due to their activism and were ultimately assassinated in November 2018 by unidentified gunmen, which many activists blamed on some HTS commanders.

How flirting with the silent majority nurtured warlordism

Amid cautious overtures toward the revolutionary milieu—and just as al-Sharaa sought to publicly reconcile with Druze and Christian groups—HTS launched a surprise offensive on territories controlled by other armed opposition groups in the north of Idlib, towards Afrin, on 20 June 2022. Leaving their stronghold in Idlib, HTS forces crossed the Ghazawiyya crossing point and swiftly seized control of Jendiris, a small town along the Turkish border. Caught off guard by the sudden arrival of hundreds of fighters, Turkey swiftly intervened, insisting that HTS respect existing zones of influence and withdraw to Idlib. The standoff lasted three days, during which HTS partially retreated while consolidating its positions along the separation line. Eventually, under Turkish pressure, HTS fully withdrew from Syrian National Army-controlled areas by the end of June 2022.

HTS framed the incursion as a preemptive measure and sought to reassure Turkey by portraying it as a necessary response to the growing expansionist ambitions of its longtime rival, al-Jabhat al-Shamiyya. According to Ahmad al-Sharaa,

> Tensions among our neighbours mean tensions within our own ranks. Seven IS leaders were arrested in Idlib, all of whom

came from there, where IS operates officially with its members integrated into certain factions. We also want to maintain a balance in the power dynamics among the factions. We fear the expansionist ambitions of al-Jabhat al-Shamiyya, which seeks to dominate the North. Every time they try to expand, we restore the balance. The regime can take advantage of these tensions. We must prevent anyone from opening the doors of evil. Our ambition is to maintain equilibrium without causing chaos.[36]

HTS's main issue was the growing alliance between al-Jabhat al-Shamiyya and Jaysh al-Islam, a Salafi faction historically hostile to Jabhat al-Nusra. Both were reinforced by significant defections of groups defeated by the regime in the Damascus Ghouta, which was a stronghold of Jaysh al-Islam before its relocation to the North. But this explanation did not convince the Turks. According to a Turkish analyst close to the military:

> For a while, HTS has wanted to expand its influence in the North, but we oppose it. Our position is that we have a deal with them in Idlib that grants them some power but not in Afrin. Elsewhere, we are in charge. They always have this idea of going North to control the other groups. HTS's leadership wants to go North to impose order and reduce chaos. Turkey recognises their organisational skills but will not accept this.[37]

The first incursion slightly strained relations with Turkey.[38] In Western diplomatic circles, the attack on opposition factions cast further doubt on the credibility of HTS's supposed transformation. It appeared to contradict the group's claimed efforts to distance itself from Salafism, pursue internal deradicalisation, realign politically around revolutionary ideals, and engage in outreach to minority communities.[39]

Despite the high political costs, HTS pressed forward. In the summer of 2022, the group launched an intensive campaign to court various armed factions willing to align with its expanding influence. This "northern push" ignited intense internal debate within HTS. Some leaders advocated for an aggressive expansion to unify all liberated territories, while others prioritised maintaining stable relations with Turkey. Known for his risk-taking approach, Ahmad al-Sharaa ultimately leaned toward the expansionist strategy, though with calculated caution.[40] This outreach targeted groups in conflict with al-Jabhat al-Shamiyya, former demobilised units from factions previously defeated by HTS—such as certain elements of Nour al-Din al-Zinki—and even factions within al-Jabhat al-Shamiyya itself. Through strategic alliances and co-optation, HTS sought to consolidate its hold over northern Syria, despite ongoing tensions with Turkey and skepticism from Western actors.[41]

On 12 and 13 October 2022, HTS once again took up arms against factions of the former Free Syrian Army (FSA). Justifying its offensive with familiar rhetoric about the threat posed by al-Jabhat al-Shamiyya, HTS framed it internally as a necessary step to defend the North against a potential regime attack, which it labeled the "weakest link of the revolution".[42] Under the banner of unifying opposition ranks, HTS launched a second blitzkrieg, catching Turkey off guard. In less than two days, its fighters seized full control of the Kurdish region of Afrin, halting only at the outskirts of key FSA strongholds in northern Aleppo following a ceasefire brokered by Turkey on 13 October coupled with direct threats of military retaliation from the Turkish army.[43] Unlike the first incursion in June, this northern offensive triggered real combat, primarily against Jaysh al-Islam and the core of al-Jabhat al-Shamiyya, resulting in approximately ten casualties. While most HTS forces withdrew to Idlib after several days, reports indicated they maintained a covert presence in Afrin, blending in with allied factions and ensuring continued influence in the region.

The movement triggered anger among Turkish military officials who considered Afrin a territory that they had taken over themselves. Although HTS units carefully avoided direct confrontations with Turkish forces, the Turkish military drew a clear distinction between HTS-held territories and former SDF strongholds in Afrin and the north of Aleppo.[44] Firmly opposed to HTS's northern expansion, Turkey viewed the incursion as a direct challenge to its strategic control over the region. The United States also condemned HTS's adventurism and reiterated its classification as a terrorist organisation. However, on the ground, the second northern push was far from a failure. It exposed the weakness and lack of popularity of the factions present in the region and highlighted the success of

HTS's cooptation campaigns within the world of factions north of Aleppo and in Afrin.

Faced with two primary rivals in the region—al-Jabhat al-Shamiyya, an Islamist faction from Aleppo, and Jaysh al-Islam, a Salafi group originally from Damascus's Ghouta region—HTS successfully built a network of alliances with various factions, including Firqat al-Hamzat, Sultan Suleiman Shah Division (also known as al-Amshat), Ahrar al-Sham, Tajamu al-Shahba, Sultan Murad Division, Tha'irun, al-Mu'tasim Division, Firqa 50, and several hundred defectors from al-Jabhat al-Shamiyya. These agreements provide mutual benefits, including HTS's protection of these groups, security cooperation, and economic arrangements, particularly in securing trade routes. HTS was particularly frustrated with al-Jabhat al-Shamiyya's taxation on its oil imports from northeast Syria, which added further economic and political tensions to their rivalry.[45]

An armed group commander based in Azaz, who is somewhat critical of HTS and a former leader of a local council, admitted, "due to the ineffectiveness of the armed groups, people do not necessarily view HTS negatively." A civil society activist also recounted a meeting of revolutionary coordinations against HTS, where a woman asked,

> I no longer know who to align with as a revolutionary? Wouldn't al-Sharaa be better than Abu Amsha [a local armed group leader] if he were not classified? Is the Salvation Government not better than SIG? There are real divisions within the revolutionary camp. The factions are unified in their mediocrity.[46]

HTS's push encountered little military resistance. According to an observer:

> The military council of Tal Rifaat suspended its membership in the third division after the fighting and did not engage in combat. Liwa Samarcande also refused to fight. Some factions from Jarablus, originally from Manbij, did not participate. Many local leaders of al-Jabhat al-Shamiyya have good relations with al-Sharaa. It is mainly Jaysh al-Islam and Firqa al-Majd that are at the forefront against HTS.[47]

Armed groups largely drove local reactions. Multiple witnesses assert that local factions initiated the protests. In Azaz, Jabhat al-Shamiyya and its affiliates led the demonstrations, while in Al-Bab, Jaysh al-Islam played a central role.[48]

These new developments significantly undermined HTS's recent diplomatic positioning with both the West and Turkey. Despite the group's efforts to distance itself from global jihad and its gradual shift in Western perceptions—where HTS was increasingly seen as less of a threat and, in some circles, even as a potential ally for managing the presence of foreign fighters in areas under their control, or as a necessary compromise for humanitarian actors—these actions served as a wake-up call for many Western states.[49] They raised concerns that these more favorable perceptions might not fully reflect the group's intentions.

While HTS generally avoided direct clashes with Turkish forces in their deployment zones, these actions nonetheless forced Turkey to intervene. Turkey required HTS to dismantle certain checkpoints and closed off the road to block their advance in Kafr Janna.[50] This escalation had a more direct and adverse impact on HTS's relationship with Turkey. According to a Turkish official,

> In entering Afrin, they are creating immense pressure on our system. Afrin is not Idlib. We cooperate in Idlib because our military entered Idlib to support them. In Afrin, it is different. It is our area of influence. By entering Afrin without our agreement, they must realise that, for our military, it means they are fighting the Turkish army.[51]

In an October 2022 discussion a Turkish observer closely linked to the military noted that

> For the army, HTS is neither a friend nor an enemy, but its track record speaks for itself. Since the March 2020 truce, several Turkish soldiers have been killed within Idlib—by IEDs, ATGMs, RPGs, and small weapons. For the army, HTS is at best incapable of protecting them or, at worst complicit in these attacks.[52]

This ambivalence underscored the fragility of Turkey's engagement with HTS and the underlying tensions shaping their interactions.

Following the October confrontation, HTS temporarily paused its military offensives, but the devastating earthquake in February 2023 provided an opportunity to advance its influence through soft power rather than direct territorial control. Responding to a request from the White Helmets, HTS deployed search and rescue teams to assist in relief efforts in the area, where aid was scarce and casualties exceeded 1,000. This allowed the movement to embed a military unit on the ground, which reinforced its presence under the guise of humanitarian assistance. A month later, on 20 March 2023, the armed group Ahrar al-Sharqiyya killed four Kurds during the Newroz celebration, prompting outrage among locals who had long suffered abuses from armed groups. Seeking protection, some Kurds turned to HTS, appealing to its leadership to restore order in Afrin. When the victims' bodies were transferred to a hospital in Atmeh, within HTS's sphere of influence, their families met with al-Sharaa, who had increasingly engaged with local communities. Expressing their frustration and rejection of the chaotic factional system, they provided al-Sharaa an opportunity to present HTS as a stabilising force. This reinforced HTS's legitimacy in the North while further undermining the credibility of rival factions.

HTS's northern push unfolded in four distinct phases: symbolic advances in June 2022, an outreach campaign targeting armed factions over the summer, full-scale military confrontations and territorial gains in October, and finally, a strategic soft-power initiative following the March 2023 earthquake. This sequence underscored HTS's unwavering pursuit of hegemony through a combination of co-optation, confrontation, and opportunism, despite Turkey's presence and its explicit restrictions. Turkey had sought to contain HTS within Idlib, maintaining a strategy of "indirect rule" while exercising tighter control over areas east of the Ghazawiyya crossing. However, HTS repeatedly defied these constraints, leveraging both military force and political maneuvering to expand its influence beyond its designated stronghold.

HTS's northern push forced Turkey to reassess its approach to managing territories where the group had gained influence, leading to increased Turkish control over the other armed factions and discussions about bolstering its military presence.[53] Additionally, Turkey worked to reduce the presence of armed groups, easing their burden on local populations by decreasing checkpoints and deploying military police in their place. Efforts to unify and place prisons under military police control were also underway before 2024. Meanwhile, military forces withdrew from cities, and the security apparatus of various factions started to be dismantled. Crucially, factions contemplating an alliance with HTS were warned that doing so would result in losing their salaries, further underscoring Turkey's strategic recalibration in response to HTS's territorial ambitions.

A strategic game of cat and mouse emerged between HTS and its Turkish overseers in Idlib, as Turkey remained convinced that al-Sharaa was relentlessly pursuing a multifaceted northern expansion. While Turkey attempted to counter or contain HTS, the group has repeatedly adapted—retreating temporarily under pressure, only to reassert itself later through confrontation, discreet alliances, and opportunistic soft-power initiatives, such as its humanitarian response to the earthquake. A Turkish official acknowledged the challenge, stating,

> We are not going to accept this trend, but al-Sharaa continues. For him, it means more money, more territories, more control. Al-Sharaa initially focused on achieving international legitimacy through delisting, but then he pivoted back to expansionism by increasingly relying on economic ventures and strategic partnerships to consolidate influence in the North as military options become more constrained.[54]

Why did al-Sharaa gamble on military adventurism within the territory of his Turkish protector and risk direct military retaliation? And why did he persist despite his diminishing political credit in Ankara? Once again, the Thermidorian reference is instructive. As HTS moved toward a more pragmatic, less overtly religious posture, it paradoxically fuelled new political ambitions and military assertiveness.

Let us recall the quote from Jean-François Bayart mentioned earlier in the introduction: "Thermidor does not seek to turn the page on the revolution. It remains faithful to it, if only through war".[55] The ideological softening coincided with a reinforced drive for hegemony. Feeling constrained by the current status quo, al-

Sharaa saw two paths forward. Resuming hostilities against the regime was a non-starter at the time due to Turkey's firm red lines. Instead, territorial expansion to the North offered a way out—both to break free from his micro-state in Idlib and to position himself as the legitimate political representative of the revolution. To achieve this, he sought to reinvent himself as a nationalist leader, reaching out to Druze and Christian communities while opening to the Sufis, and strategically celebrating the revolution to broaden his appeal.

From this perspective, the military offensives against opposition factions in the North in June and October 2022 and the simultaneous policy of revolutionary and religious re-centring and outreach to minorities were not contradictory but rather two complementary aspects of the same overarching strategy. Both efforts served a dual purpose: consolidating HTS's dominance by weakening rival factions while simultaneously broadening its legitimacy beyond its traditional Islamist base.[56] By expanding militarily, HTS asserted its authority and territorial control; by engaging with minorities and embracing revolutionary symbols, it repositioned itself as a nationalist force rather than a sectarian movement, ultimately aiming for greater political influence.

HTS sought to promote a governance model that appealed to all Syrians, with a particular focus on those living under regime control, whom its leadership—rightly or wrongly—perceived as holding the greatest revolutionary potential today.[57] One of al-Sharaa's advisors believed that

> Since 2017, the revolution has undergone a genuine process of institutionalisation, with all communities engaged and seeking mutual recognition. Idlib, as a diverse microcosm of Syria, is a potential model for the country's future. HTS envisions an Islamic yet nationalist project that extends beyond Idlib, distinct from groups like the Muslim Brotherhood by emphasising Sunni identity over a strictly ideological Islamist framework. While minority outreach is not the central priority, it serves as a strategic tool to clarify and legitimise HTS's broader political vision, positioning it as a unifying force rather than a factional entity.[58]

HTS's ultimate ambition was to position the group as the sole political force capable of embodying the revolutionary narrative in Syria. This strategy involved systematically undermining rival factions, such as Jabhat al-Shamiyya, while gradually co-opting groups excluded from alliances in northern Syria under Turkish control. Ahmad al-Sharaa's former associate, Abu Maria al-Qahtani, encapsulated this vision in a statement on Twitter, framing HTS as the inevitable hegemon and the only viable alternative to the fragmented opposition. He presented HTS as "the spearhead of an integrated project that has proven itself in all liberated regions," contrasting it with "the reality of those who question the credibility of the Idlib model and those who bet on its disappearance," where there is nothing but "confusion and disunity."[59]

Contrary to many analyses, al-Sharaa was not flirting with the West but instead positioned HTS within the existing Syrian landscape, engaged in different ways against both the regime and rival opposition factions in the North. His goal was to establish HTS as the most viable alternative—whether or not it was realistic—while discrediting competitors. From this perspective, HTS's rhetorical shift on minority rights, its internal deradicalisation efforts and its militaristic power plays all served a single overarching objective: asserting dominance within Syria's opposition itself, which remains (at the time of writing) the leadership's primary arena of competition. Beyond this Northern expansion, it is Damascus that was already—and always—in the sights of the Islamist leader.

9

THE 2024 IDLIB ARAB SPRING
DERADICALISATION AS POWER POLITICS

HTS's governance faced a critical challenge when a significant wave of protests openly contested the group between March and August 2024. A range of local actors began to openly denounce HTS and its governance, particularly in terms of human rights and political freedom. While the demands varied, the protests were fundamentally anti-authoritarian. They targeted HTS's monopolisation of power and control of the economy of the Idlib province, as well as arbitrary arrests and numerous cases of torture by its General Security apparatus. More importantly, they called for greater political participation. This protest movement, often echoing the anti-Assad rhetoric of 2011, offers deeper insights into the relationship between religious de-radicalisation and the reality of authoritarian political structures.

A scent of déjà vu: Idlib's 2024 Arab Spring and the return of the people

Just over a decade after the popular protests of 2011–12 and ten years of armed conflict, Syrian society once again mobilised throughout the country. This new mobilisation defied the widespread notion that the conflict had become "frozen." Simultaneously, or almost, the street was once again becoming a space for the expression of political grievances and demands. In Suweida, Druze had increasingly radicalised their opposition to the regime and started to militarise since August 2023. In the northeast, tribal revolts and demonstrations against the high cost of living had similarly spread since summer 2023. In spring 2024, demonstrations in the north of Aleppo, which is under the domination of Turkey and local armed groups, contested the local rule of several of the latter that had settled in the region.

Idlib followed suit on 25 February 2024. That evening, a few dozen people gathered in the square of the small border town of Sarmada to protest arbitrary arrests and ill-treatment in the jails of the General Security, HTS's own internal security. The new mobilisation was part of an anti-authoritarian "*hirak*" or protest movement that had already taken to the streets in 2017 and 2018 to demand reforms. But in 2024, the *hirak* was bigger, longer-lasting, and also more radical. Very quickly, the wave of protest spread across all the territories controlled by HTS. Its demands were becoming increasingly political, with a new, diverse, audience. It was also enduring. The protest lasted more than six months. Over this period, approximately 30,000 people participated in various forms of demonstrations, expressing anger and discontent.[1]

The shadow of 2011 was evident in the methods employed in the new protests. They drew on the mobilisation techniques spearheaded by activist networks from 2011–12 and marked a return to the local coordination committees (*tansiqiyyat*) and grassroots cooperative structures. The practice of *faza'a*—militant solidarity between villages in response to repression—also reemerged, alongside the revival of old anti-regime slogans, now with al-Sharaa's name replacing that of Bashar al-Assad. These included "the people want the fall of al-Jolani", "let the General Security fall", "we want the return of prisoners", "neither al-Jolani nor al-Assad, we want to build the country", "by God, get al-Jolani out of the way", to name but a few.[2] For HTS critics, the conclusion was clear: HTS was nothing more than a local remake of the regime's authoritarianism. As a leader of a faction allied to HTS remarked:

> Al-Sharaa listens superficially, acknowledges some mistakes, promises reforms, attempts to co-opt or corrupt local leaders, and even shifts blame onto the Islamists. He then seeks to silence dissent by invoking the primacy of a higher cause—jihad against the regime for HTS, or resistance against Israel for the Assad regime. Ultimately, what emerges is, quite plainly, a police state.[3]

THE 2024 IDLIB ARAB SPRING

This sense of *déjà vu* cast a shadow over the rebranding efforts of the former al-Qaeda affiliate. While al-Sharaa had renounced radical religious views and contained Salafism, he remained firmly entrenched within the framework of Middle Eastern authoritarianism. At first sight, much like Muhammad bin Salman (MBS) in Saudi Arabia, he appeared to pair the loosening of religious radicalism with a tightening grip on authoritarian rule. However, a closer examination actually revealed a different dynamic in Idlib: the easing of religious radicalism seemed to coincide with a slight relaxation of authoritarianism.

To explore this, it is important to review the dynamics of the protests and how they were managed by the Islamist organisation. Then, we will examine the darker side of HTS—its enduring relationship with political authoritarianism.

The people's Thermidorian's fatigue and its instrumentalisations

Paradoxically, after several years of HTS governance, a profound sense of fatigue was taking hold among the population, just as the major confrontations were winding down. On one hand, the truce had opened the door to new demands; on the other, a society that had survived for years on its limited reserves was reaching breaking point.[4] War no longer served as a smokescreen, and holding forces in all zones now had to be held to account on the question of governance. Thermidor reminds us that the end of a revolution or war is always a moment of risk.[5] Politically, the return to calm is the most dangerous phase of a revolution. As this senior HTS executive well understood:

> The years go by, we have become a governing force, and at some point, people start holding you accountable. We moved out from the full-fledged confrontation and demands are rising, building on a legacy of animosities with HTS that accumulated over the years. We are paying the price of stabilisation.[6]

In Idlib, the prevailing sentiment among the population was that the return to order—while broadly welcomed—had come at the cost of excessive control over nearly every aspect of life. "Why does Security interfere with trade?" deplored one of the *hirak* leaders.

"Why does any trader have to take on a security guard, almost always a former Jabhat al-Nusra member, as a partner? Security is too present in civil affairs. I submitted my papers to the Ministry of Education and was refused."[7]

Fatigue with HTS's excessive control, compounded by its authoritarian practices, further intensified after revelations of torture in General Security detention centres were made public. These revelations came out in late 2023 when the HTS leadership became suspicious that certain cadres were collaborating with the US-led Coalition against Islamic State. Major purges led to over 135 arrests of members and senior executives. They provoked multiple desertions to other opposition-controlled territory or even to the regime.[8] Internal divisions within HTS were less about ideological differences between pragmatists and hardliners and more about internal factional rivalries, often informed by regional affiliations. Tensions reportedly stemmed from competition between leaders from Binish and those from eastern Syria. Over the years, Ahmad al-Sharaa had worked to curb the influence of HTS's radical wing. However, the crackdown that followed the belief in an internal conspiracy was spearheaded by Anas Khattab, the head of the movement's security wing and minister of the interior after March 2025, whom many regarded as a hardliner at the time. Meanwhile, figures involved in the alleged coup, such as Abu Maria al-Qahtani, were critical of al-Sharaa but positioned themselves on the more "moderate" end of the spectrum, effectively outflanking him from that direction. The arrests led to widespread mistreatment of the former HTS cadres.

HTS's crackdown on its own cadres sparked uproar, both internally and among its wider support base. Ahmad al-Sharaa publicly acknowledged the abuses and personally visited the families to apologise and offer financial compensation. However, as survivors of torture began to speak out, their families also raised their voices. This sparked a wave of public dissent, further fuelled by political and military forces. Among them were Hizb al-Tahrir, an unarmed Islamist group whose objective is to restore the Islamic Caliphate, which demanded the release of its detained members. Jaysh al-Ahrar, the group that previously split from Ahrar al-Sham before integrating HTS for a few months, was also outraged by the torture of its members. Protests erupted, particularly in Binish and across various refugee camps, amplifying calls for accountability and justice. According to one of the mobilisation leaders,

> We were being economically strangled, and HTS refused to tolerate anyone outside their inner circles. On top of this, there was constant pressure on freedom of expression—even gatherings of former revolutionaries were banned. All of this fostered a deep sense of frustration. When the purges began and the security forces started detaining members of HTS's own military, it ignited a fresh wave of protests against al-Sharaa. General popular discontent then merged with the specific frustration of military members targeted by the crackdown, further fueling the unrest.[9]

The demands then escalated. In the early days, the demands focused primarily on ending arbitrary practices and securing the release of detainees. However, by mid-March, the almost daily demonstrations had begun to embrace the revolutionary spirit, spreading rapidly to towns across HTS-controlled territory. Binish, Armanaz, Tawun, Foua, Sarmada and Dana. Very quickly, according to a local organiser, "the wall of fear came down. After the first demonstrations, the city of Idlib followed. Just like in 2011, because now we see a group that has tortured and killed. It's just not as bad as the regime because it has fewer resources".[10]

The veteran revolutionaries and their seasoned activist networks became central to the *hirak*. 15 March, the anniversary of the revolution, marked the peak of their involvement. However, the revolutionaries of 2011 also faced significant challenges. The organised revolutionary groups largely abstained from mobilising; many had become institutionalised, losing the drive to take to the streets. The broader revolutionnary milieu was also divided: some adhered to a maximalist stance, demanding sweeping changes, while others adopted a more pragmatic approach, advocating for reforms to make the system more inclusive. This latter group maintained that reforms were the only viable path forward, given the absence of a realistic alternative. As this leader, who was imprisoned during the *hirak*, explained: "The problem is that we have to be realistic: the only alternative to HTS is the regime. We can coexist with HTS, but not with the regime."[11] Poorly organised and often overshadowed, the revolutionaries struggled to take leadership of the movement. They faced challenges not only from former HTS members who joined the protests to renegotiate their positions of power or to facilitate the return of their factions to influence but also from some who were wary that pushing HTS too hard could either lead to their own annihilation or inadvertently strengthen the regime.

By late March, attempts by HTS to co-opt the movement had slowed its momentum. Social media pages shifted tone, adopting a more subdued and even mocking stance toward former HTS leaders. Mobilisation waned temporarily, only to be reignited by the factions later that month. Small demonstrations rotated from one place to another, led by different groups: Hizb al-Tahrir, Faylaq al-Sham, Ahrar al-Sham. An observer noted: "I've seen demonstrations starting in Binish at 7.30pm. There are 150 of them and they go to Sarmada. Then from Sarmada to Idlib."[12]

Internal divisions and competing agendas also divided the movement. Differences arose between realists, who favored pragmatic demands and dialogue with HTS, and maximalists, who rejected any negotiation. Former political bodies representing the 2011 revolution remained silent, leaving a leadership vacuum. Religious populist groups, such as Hizb al-Tahrir, called for the strict application of Shari'a, while Islamist populists like Judge Abu Humama al-Halabi blamed the lack of Shari'a implementation for abuses in prison. Others criticised HTS from a more hardline perspective, accusing it of systematically opposing the establishment of a religious police force.

Factional interests further complicated the movement, including demands for the release of hardliners like Abu Shu'ib al-Masri—a former HTS cleric who was expelled from the movement—and continued demonstrations led by Hizb al-Tahrir, often involving prisoners' wives. Opportunistic former outcasts sought to use the protests to negotiate their return to political relevance, while corporatist demands also surfaced, such as protests by the teachers' union demanding overdue salaries. These competing narratives and agendas fragmented the movement, diluting its focus and cohesion.

In this fragmented landscape, a 2011 activist observed:

> Protesters are deeply polarised. Some want to turn back the clock, while others reject terms like 'Shura Council' simply because it sounds religious. In discussions among twenty revolutionaries, some criticise HTS, while others admit they couldn't have imagined, even a year ago, that elections would be possible.

The movement's leaders often lacked the leverage needed to unify its representation and demands. As one activist candidly puts it:

> Let's be clear: revolutionaries are weak. We can't ask influential figures like Abu Malik al-Tally [a former HTS hardliner expelled from the movement], Abd al-Razzaq al-Mahdi [a populist cleric], or others to step aside. Sometimes they impose themselves or their vision because, in the end, those who control the microphones control the agendas. We don't want to alienate key figures who at least respect the basic rules of the game.

Ultimately, only Hizb al-Tahrir was excluded from the movement and forced to organise its own demonstrations at separate times and locations, further highlighting the fractured nature of the *hirak*.

Strategic patience and beyond: HTS's multilayered response to the hirak

Widely accepted in principle but feared for its excesses and susceptibility to manipulation, HTS addressed the *hirak* with a set of guidelines. According to an advisor to al-Sharaa: "Our response to the *hirak* is strategic patience, intense dialogue, and drawing clear red lines—particularly when it comes to sovereign ministries."[13] HTS quickly recognised the fragmented nature of the movement and deployed a multi-faceted strategy to manage it. This included applying security pressure, issuing threats, employing occasionally forceful crowd control tactics,[14] and organising counter-demonstrations that often leveraged tribal leaders co-opted into HTS-established representation structures. The group also engaged local notables to reason with protesters and supported third-party initiatives like the "Reform Initiative" to present a façade of compromise. Simultaneously, HTS made strategic concessions to address specific grievances, such as releasing prisoners,[15] adjusting taxes,¹⁶ and lowering the prices of essential goods like bread, electricity, and sugar. In the longer term, it sought to mitigate unrest by proposing a package of political and institutional reforms aimed at addressing popular demands while maintaining its authority.

However, confronted with the factional exploitation of the *hirak*, HTS reaffirmed its hardline stance against radical factions:

> Political and military organisations have attempted to push their agendas through the *hirak*. However, we quickly reach red lines because these groups view their relationship with us as a zero-sum game. In some cases, particularly with groups aligned with Huras al-Din [the al-Qaeda affiliate], we have had to take firm action, as seen in Jisr al-Shughur. You invite them to dialogue, and they respond by labeling you apostates or infidels, or even resort to violence, such as bomb attacks. With extremists [*ghulat*], containment alone is insufficient.¹⁷

HTS adopted a more nuanced stance toward the protests overall. "The *hirak* is not pure evil," said Abd al-Rahim Atun. "It also forced us to address issues we had been neglecting. In its initial phase, the *hirak* was civilian and popular, with acceptable demands that did not threaten our institutions."¹⁸ Al-Sharaa echoed this sentiment, acknowledging the unexpected nature of the protests: "The demonstrations came as a complete surprise to us. Many of the demands are legitimate, and we believe it's better to adapt to them rather than confront them."¹⁹

Starting on 12 March 2024, HTS initiated meetings with local notables and *hirak* activists to discuss a substantial reform project aimed at defusing the growing protest movement. As part of this effort, HTS announced a package of institutional reforms. Four of these reforms are particularly significant in assessing HTS's authoritarian tendencies in managing the protests. The first reform involved the creation of a consultative council, designed to provide HTS-allied factions with a platform to voice their opinions on strategic and military issues. However, this council would be entirely appointed and limited to an advisory role, signaling no real shift in decision-making power. The second reform concerned the Legislative Assembly (Shura Council), which was set to expand from 90 to 160 members. The deputies would be elected through regional electoral colleges, introducing a veneer of representation while retaining HTS control over the process. HTS also planned to strengthen the role of local councils in conjunction with local government and the Ministry of Municipalities. This move was framed as an effort to "bring the 2011 revolutionaries back into the game," according to a member of the committee tasked with drafting the new law for local councils.[20] These changes ostensibly aimed to address grievances but remained tightly controlled to ensure HTS's dominance.

The final key reform involved restructuring the security sector. The announcements appear promising—intelligence agencies would no longer have direct arrest powers. The General Security would be placed under the authority of the General Security Administration, which reports to the Ministry of the Interior, and mistreatment in detention would cease. But these changes would still remain under the oversight of Anas Khattab, the former head of General Security.

The revolutionaries were divided. On one side were the maximalist hardliners who rejected any compromise outright. On the other were those who take a more nuanced view, acknowledging—favorably—that part of the reform package aligns directly with the demands raised during the demonstrations. Their ambitions, however, remained modest:

> Of course, we know that HTS wants to retain power. But if we can simply force even a small degree of participation, that would already be a success. What we want is to take part in the political management of affairs, but not under the HTS umbrella. HTS seeks to co-opt us, but we are striving for a space for independent civil action, free from the control of any armed group—whether HTS or anyone else.[21]

HTS had taken consistent steps in terms of concessions, commitment to institutional reform and even a limited opening up of the political game. What was their calculation? For Ahmad al-Sharaa,

> We don't know who will be in the Shura Council and we risk having a very chaotic and polarised Shura Council with powers it didn't have before, such as withdrawing confidence from the government. But you can't delegate too much to a political

spectrum that's completely fragmented and incapable of playing the institutional game. There is an element of risk involved, but on the other hand, strategic patience and dialogue have helped calm the street. In fact, 90% of the demonstrators have now returned to their homes.[22]

One of his advisors also considered a degree of uncertainty the price to be paid for a return to calm:

> We don't know what will come out of these elections, and we're going to have to adapt to the new reality that has been created. The new Shura Council will be able to question ministers and withdraw its confidence in the government. Clearly, we run the risk of overloading the government with expectations, when it is nothing more than a crisis management government.[23]

Both agreed, however, that the Shura Council would ultimately have little authority over strategic issues, which would be discussed by a small appointed, non-elected committee: the Advisory Council. Clearly, the risk did not exceed a certain capacity for nuisance.

Bound to the revolution: HTS's lenient authoritarianism

The *hirak* lasted for about six months before becoming relatively marginal. But what did it reveal about HTS's authoritarianism and, more broadly, about the relationship between the loosening of religious radicalism and the relaxation of political authoritarianism? A former member of the Shura Council, now a critic of HTS, offers this view: "There has been genuine progress in terms of religious doctrine, but this hasn't translated into the political sphere. The old hierarchical mindset—*hala tandhimiyya*—persists, and the positive ideological developments have primarily served to reinforce the movement's appetite for power."[24] Is this a case of MBS redux? Perhaps not entirely. However, the former militant's observation raises an important question about the interplay between religious radicalism and political authoritarianism. While there is no direct causality between the reduction of radicalism and the intensity of political authoritarianism, to MBS's credit, there are notable correlations in Idlib that warrant closer examination.

The Islamist organisation, far from limiting itself to "strategic patience" or merely issuing reminders about red lines—such as the smooth operation of strategically significant ministries—took a more active approach. It employed targeted threats against the movement's leaders and occasionally resorted to physical violence against demonstrators.[25] These actions aimed to isolate the various fronts of the *hirak* and disrupt the dynamics of *fazaa*—the solidarity between towns. Checkpoints, established to hinder militant mobility, were often heavy-handed, intimidating would-be protesters and reinforcing a climate of fear. However, crowd control measures remained relatively restrained: over six months, only a few dozen arrests were recorded, most of whom were quickly released.[26] Incidents of injuries were minimal, and notably, there were no fatalities.

HTS's crowd management was not solely reliant on coercion—far from it. The Administration of the liberated areas, the body directly under Ahmad al-Sharaa and composed of Islamist technocrats tasked with managing and deconflicting local situations, actively engaged in dialogue with demonstrators. While protesters frequently criticised the management of the region for its inability to address broader political demands—issues that fell outside its mandate—these dialogues, often involving local notables aligned with HTS, frequently resulted in local agreements. These deals were most commonly related to resolving disputes around arrests.

HTS was also cautious to avoid rejecting the whole protest movement. While HTS often highlighted the influence of competing factions in its assessment of the *hirak*, it also demonstrated a nuanced approach in practice by distinguishing between the security and political manipulations of specific groups and the broader demands of the movement. These distinctions translated into differentiated treatment. For the wider movement, dialogue remained a consistent and multi-layered practice sustained over time. It involved various actors, from Ahmad al-Sharaa himself to local notables, as well as the Salvation Government, the HTS political bureau, and the Administration of the liberated areas.

The "police understanding"[27] as defined by the movement's leadership did not challenge the legitimacy of the protests, and HTS never defined the *hirak* as an enemy. On the contrary, the movement's leadership demonstrated a relatively clear-headed interpretation of the protests, viewing them as the result of widely acknowledged issues, such as the prevalence of torture. These protests emerged during a phase of consolidated truce, a period when the ruling authorities were increasingly accountable to a civilian population that had become more demanding than during wartime. The protesters often voiced legitimate grievances, and the leadership's responses were calibrated accordingly. On the other side, while maximalists existed, the majority avoided confrontation. This restraint stemmed from a shared understanding that no credible alternative to HTS domination was conceivable at the time.

Ultimately, HTS did not merely manage the protests but also proposed some reforms too. To demobilise the movement more structurally, its leadership partially or fully embraced some of the protesters' demands, such as the release of prisoners, the revitalisation of the local councils, and the adoption of elections for the Shura Council.

While it was too early to assess the full political impact of these commitments before the December 2024 victory, HTS accepted the principle of elections as a method for selecting parliamentary elites through an electoral law. Although the content of a law often holds less significance than its implementation, this law—framed as a response to a genuine crisis of legitimacy faced by the authorities—offers insight into how HTS envisioned political change and transition.

To better understand the new electoral law, it is important to separate the process of drafting the law from its content. Regarding the process, several points stood out. The main one is that the law was a concession by HTS to the *hirak*, which had called for a more representative and elected Shura Council. The agreement to form a committee tasked with drafting the electoral law was finalised during discussions in March between the HTS leadership and a group of leaders, technocrats, and other notable figures.

The composition of the High Elections Committee also reflected a pro-opposition stance without incorporating maximalist elements. The seven-member committee included three independent technocrats and four activists who identified as revolutionaries. Notably, no members or close associates of HTS were part of the committee.[28] According to the High Elections Committee president, Essam al-Khleif, "The authorities put the ball in our court and told us: unify your positions and come up with a law that addresses the issue of Shura Council representation. Truly, there was no real interference from the authorities."[29]

On the contentious question of HTS interference, Essam al-Khleif is mostly correct: HTS largely refrained from intervening in the High Elections Committee's work. However, one significant exception stood out. Initially, the High Elections Committee proposed limiting candidacy to "revolutionaries," defined as those who had resided in rebel-held territories before 1 January 2014. This criterion would have excluded a significant portion of Idlib city's population, which was retaken from the regime only in 2015. Consequently, it would have deprived the Shura Council of many technocrats currently active in HTS-controlled areas. Following discussions with individuals close to al-Sharaa, the High Elections Committee ultimately agreed to soften its stance. While HTS did interfere in this instance, the outcome was a broader inclusion of candidates, increasing the representativeness of the Shura Council.

Next comes the issue of women's participation. The law drafted by the High Elections Committee did not explicitly oppose women's involvement, but the topic remained contentious, even among revolutionaries. For some, like the president of the commission, while they do not actively encourage female candidates, they are not opposed to them either.[30] Others, however, express greater reservations. One High Elections Committee member argued, "Women can vote, the doors are open. But as candidates? No, because the job is already too challenging for men, so why involve women?"[31] The debate intensified when a photo of the discussions surfaced, showing a billboard in the background mentioning the possibility of women and minorities participating in the Shura Council. This sparked controversy, with conservative circles resorting to populist rhetoric. Some accused al-Sharaa of trying to appease the West,[32] using Shura Council reform to "promote feminism and undermine God's law,"[33] or even acting as an "agent of the democratisation of the revolution."[34] In response to the backlash, and following a request from the High Elections Committee, HTS had to provide protection for the committee members. Seeking a middle ground to defuse tensions and reassure hardliners, one committee member remarked, "to calm tempers and appease the hawks, we say that we're not going to push women to run, but if they want to, they can."[35]

After examining drafting the law, let us now turn to its content. Without spending too much time on the technical details, the law drew on a combination of traditional legal frameworks, partially influenced by Shariʻa principles, alongside previous legislation, which as a whole reflects a controlled approach to governance. The structure and provisions of the law revealed a dual dynamic: on the one hand, there were genuine efforts to introduce elements of openness; on the other, the framework remained rooted in a legal tradition where the legislative body assumed a largely consultative role. This approach is characteristic of systems transitioning from absolute rule to more representative forms of governance. The emphasis on supervision and qualifications within the law highlighted a deliberate effort to maintain control over political representation. Interestingly, HTS interference in the drafting process was minimal, with the sole intervention aimed at removing the criterion of commitment to the revolution—a move that ultimately broadened inclusivity.

These characteristics aligned the electoral law with the practices of semi-authoritarian regimes, where elections primarily legitimise the ruling authorities rather than facilitate genuine political competition. Key features—such as tightly controlled candidate selection, centralised oversight of the electoral process, restricted political pluralism, and state-managed conflict resolution—reflected an electoral system engineered to preserve the dominance of the ruling elite while offering a constrained avenue for public participation.

Political openness hence remained limited, although HTS agreed to make two concessions. First, it promoted the establishment of a consultative council to broaden the leadership involved in formalising strategic decisions, though this council lacked any real decision-making authority. Second, HTS accepted the principle of elections for a parliament. While this body did not wield power over strategic issues, HTS granted it the ability to influence the functioning of administrative and political institutions, such as withdrawing confidence from the government. In this context, HTS allowed for the introduction of a controlled degree of uncertainty—what its leader describes as the price of restoring calm.[36] Although the expansion of political participation was genuine, it stopped short of delegating real power. Instead, it represented a managed adaptation of authoritarianism, maintaining firm control while permitting marginal concessions to political inclusion.

Two key points are worth mentioning. First, the legacy of the Arab Spring persisted: HTS could not suppress popular movements outright without undermining its legitimacy rooted in revolutionary consciousness. Second, despite limited repression, HTS remained authoritarian by controlling security, stifling political space, and exhausting social movements through leader pressure, co-optation, and dialogue.

HTS's authoritarianism did not primarily rely on repression, as its main concern was internal divisions and potential coups rather than public protests. Interestingly, neither the security apparatus nor al-Sharaa himself exhibited paranoia toward the *hirak*. While al-Sharaa demonstrated strategic patience, HTS reacted disproportionately to suspected internal sedition. This prioritisation followed an authoritarian logic: power struggles were not centred on the population or political opposition but rather within HTS itself. The group feared internal coups far more than popular dissent. As a result, factional rivalries became the primary arena for power struggles, fuelling tensions within Idlib's leadership and leading to abuses, including alleged torture. HTS's authority depended more on controlling internal factions than on managing broader societal engagement. Its authoritarianism turned politics into a contest among elites, sidelining public participation, with repression deployed selectively when needed. Al-Sharaa's "strategic patience" thus reflected both a calculated revolutionary pragmatism and an effort to consolidate power within a tightly controlled inner circle.

The attenuation of authoritarianism: HTS and the village mayor syndrome

Confronted with unprecedented protests, HTS structured its response around two main strategies: sporadic instances of harsh enforcement, though without systemic violence, and a controlled political opening that allowed for the partial autonomy of a weak legislative body within a highly centralised decision-making framework. Six months after facing a highly unfavorable situation—where HTS, challenged by its own base, appeared to replicate the reflexes of the very regime it had once risen against—the movement managed the unrest with relative sophistication. By employing a broad spectrum of responses and significantly limiting the use of force, HTS effectively addressed a protest movement that was both substantial and, at times, radical in its demands.

Let us return to our original question: what is the relationship between the "silent revolution" that facilitated religious deradicalisation on one side, and the gradual erosion of political authoritarianism on the other? Is the erosion of political authoritarianism a continuation or consequence of religious deradicalisation, or is it, conversely, driven by an entirely separate dynamic?

Relocation shaped both religious deradicalisation and the erosion of political authoritarianism. In neither case did HTS unilaterally decide to alter these religious or political dynamics. Rather, these shifts emerged from evolving power dynamics between the group, the local population, and the protest movement in Idlib.

To understand how HTS's relocation operated, it is crucial to remember that its break with global jihad was not just about distancing but also about re-engagement. Severing ties with al-Qaeda led to a deliberate re-anchoring in local dynamics. This shift unfolded on multiple levels. Sociologically, HTS co-opted local religious, familial, and revolutionary elites. Religiously, it embraced the dominant Shafi'i school, reintegrated and institutionalised elements of Sufism, and showed greater tolerance for popular Islam. Politically, it re-appropriated revolutionary symbols and narratives as sources of legitimacy. This strategy reshaped HTS, moving it away from global jihadism and embedding it more deeply in Idlib's sociopolitical fabric.

This process of multi-faceted re-anchoring, which we refer to as relocalisation, sets in motion a logic of political dependency akin to what Jean-Noël Ferrié describes as the "village mayor syndrome": the closer a political actor is to their constituents, the less they can afford to ignore their expectations and the more they are compelled to engage with them—precisely what HTS demonstrated throughout the *hirak*.[37] By relocalising, a political actor simultaneously shifts the basis of its own legitimacy. The grandiose, Homeric legitimacy derived from global jihad and epic battles is no longer sufficient, giving way to a more grounded legitimacy rooted in governance. Governance thus becomes the new focal point for generating—or challenging—the consent necessary for both effective administration and the conduct of war. On one hand, this relocalisation deepens the dependency of power on the population, enabling feedback dynamics, or "social inertia," as discussed throughout these pages. On the other hand, it allows governance to be achieved at a lower political cost, a critical factor for HTS, which requires domestic social peace in order to sustain its war effort against the Assadist regime.

As a result, relocation fostered an effect of social and political proximity that created significant overlaps between the protest movement and HTS itself. Many of those arrested, tortured, and later released were middle-ranking members of HTS's military apparatus, deeply rooted in local society.[38] Similarly, the protest movement often included former members of the Salvation Government, aligned with HTS through a shared political framework of co-optation,[39] or veteran revolutionary figures from 2011 who, while not necessarily sympathetic to HTS, were nonetheless familiar to the organisation. This absence of alienation between HTS and the movement challenging it—facilitated by the group's socio-political and religious embeddedness, as well as the acknowledged legitimacy of many of the protesters' demands—created not only a "police understanding," as previously noted, but also a political one. This dynamic encouraged HTS to exercise restraint in its use of force, embodying what al-Sharaa referred to as "strategic patience."

More importantly, this strategic patience strengthened with HTS's willingness to delegate authority to institutions managing non-strategic affairs—specifically, civil rather than military matters—while maintaining minimal interest in broader questions of governance.[40] This inclination toward delegation, driven more by neoliberal pragmatism than democratic ideals, is nonetheless significant. It allowed for a calibrated political opening and a degree of responsiveness to the *hirak*'s demands for greater participation.

The attenuation of authoritarianism also resulted from a third by-product of relocation: not a power relation but a balance of weaknesses coupled with a relative convergence of views between the *hirak* and HTS. HTS, as a military-political organisation, recognised that social peace was essential for its war effort against an ever-threatening regime. This understanding led HTS to systematically avoid direct confrontation with the population, which motivated further concessions. On the other side, the *hirak* faced its own vulnerabilities in dealing with HTS. Its leadership was fragmented, its hierarchy weak, and its tactics often marked by significant internal disagreements. Most critically, the *hirak* lacked a viable political alternative to HTS's dominance; its position could only be either reformist or populist—and it was, to some extent, both. Paradoxically, this dynamic created an implicit convergence of views on fundamental issues, ensuring that a certain degree of alignment always existed between HTS and its challengers.

The decline of political authoritarianism was not a direct result of religious deradicalisation. Rather, the two evolved in tandem within a broader framework where religious deradicalisation, the loosening of authoritarian control, and socio-political realignment reinforced one another. This interplay did not emerge from an intrinsic link between these factors but from the deliberate and strategic political maneuvers of the involved parties.

Al-Sharaa's Islamist-populist critics could rest assured: any increase in political participation did not signal a shift toward democratisation. Power—defined as decision-making authority over strategic matters—remained firmly in the same hands. Likewise, while prison conditions may have improved compared to just a few months previously, no clear signs indicated a fundamental transformation. As for the management of political opposition, it remained constrained by the structural limitations outlined above, operating within the bounds of a restricted authoritarianism. This system continued to be shaped and constrained by the enduring balance of weaknesses between HTS and the population it governed before 2025.

In service of a new extreme centre: Deradicalisation as power politics

Ahmad al-Sharaa is not a replica of autocrats like Abdel Fattah al-Sisi or Bashar al-Assad. While he occasionally drew from the authoritarian playbook—utilising co-optation, applying security pressure, conducting arrests, and delegitimising certain opposition actors—he refrained from mass arrests and, more importantly, did not systematically demonise dissent, its leaders, causes, or demands. The legacy of the Arab Spring left its mark, and al-Sharaa remained constrained by the persistence of a revolutionary consciousness, which he actively sought to integrate into his claims to legitimacy.

Sceptics may argue that HTS's relatively restrained approach to the protests was not a sign of openness but rather an indication of authoritarian governance by an ideologue in a position of weakness—one who, if he possessed the necessary means, like the Taliban, the Iranian regime, or Islamic State, would not hesitate to employ significantly greater force. In other words, they argue that his true intentions will become apparent once he achieves *tamkin* (consolidation of power) and that this apparent moderation was merely a strategic form of *taqiyya*—a very controversial term to describe a calculated dissimulation supposedly characteristic of Islamist movements, perhaps even aided by Western communication coaching.[41]

To fully understand the political dynamics in Idlib—dynamics that are influenced by, but not confined to, the ideological changes explored in this study—we adopt a different perspective. We argue that using a comparative approach to revolutionary movements offers a clearer and more productive framework than the often overused and at times biased concepts drawn from classical Islamic studies, which often undermine understanding instead of promoting it.

HTS's ideological shift, along with its non-coercive management of protests, was neither about the concealment of a radical agenda, nor democracy. Instead, it reflected an extreme-centre regime, as described by Pierre Serna, historian of the French Revolution.[42] For Serna, the extreme centre refers to a political regime dominated by a proclaimed—or rediscovered—centrism, which, as part of a hegemonic strategy, positions itself as a moderate alternative to political extremes (such as left and right in France, or radical

Islamism and regime restoration in Syria), with the ultimate goal of rejecting any credible political alternative to the existing order.

HTS strategically combined de-radicalisation with "extreme centrism." HTS legitimised itself through a "neither... nor" approach—neither the regime nor radical jihadis—while simultaneously constraining autonomous democratic movements. Civil society remained under tight security surveillance. When faced with the dynamics of social movements, HTS refrained from outright repression but also failed to open up the political field. Instead, HTS relied on familiar authoritarian tactics: co-optation, threats, limited concessions, and refrained from expanding beyond institutions where there is little or no power, such as the Shura council. In reality, HTS consolidated a *fait accompli*, justifying it by the notion that there was no alternative to the group. The future of Idlib, in his view, was limited: if HTS were to leave, the only options would be extremism or the return of the regime.

Extreme centre regimes consistently aim to neutralise opposition by co-opting it, thereby preventing any viable alternation of power while eliminating the most radical elements. This strategy often serves the broader goal of consolidating control. As a result, it creates an illiberal society where the "common sense" is that no political alternative exists. Deradicalisation, as defined in the introduction, therefore constructs a new boundary of religious legitimacy. It is not merely an ideological shift but a political practice in its own right. It serves to legitimise the centre, delegitimise what lies outside, and sustain a dynamic of the extreme centre—where spaces for political alternatives are deliberately limited. This process is driven by an actor undergoing an ideological realignment.

What defined HTS authoritarianism, therefore, was not the use of coercion, but the establishment of a non-competitive political order in the name of a policy of double negation, and its ability to impose the idea that there was no alternative. A competitive model accepts the coexistence of radicals and non-radicals, forcing the former to form social and political coalitions in order to survive or win. In a model of extreme centrism such as Idlib, de-radicalisation made it possible to disqualify radicals while positioning oneself as the sole champion of centrism. The competition for power did not disappear; instead it moved out of the political and public arena to be played out behind closed doors in the factional warfare at the apex of the system. Hence, al-Sharaa was never particularly concerned by the *hirak* movement but reacted aggressively at the slightest hint of internal dissent, as seen in the "security cell" affair that ultimately triggered the entire protest movement.

The extreme centre represents the end of radicalism and the preservation of power by strategically leveraging soft majorities against radical fringes, often through a centralised and authoritarian approach. This is facilitated by the relatively unthreatening nature of the revolutionary centre. In Idlib, the political representation of the revolution had become increasingly fragmented, with various entities divided among undisciplined groups with limited mobilisation capacity, typically numbering only a few hundred individuals. While there was a desire for participation, it was hesitant, non-assertive, and tinged with apprehension, both among men and women. Participants aimed to protect their vested interests, avoid aligning with an authority labeled as terrorist internationally, or simply remembered the violence that endured before the movement began distancing itself from its past. As one leader from the "revolutionary blocs" (*kutal thawriyya*) put it,

> Our revolutionary blocs are like balloons, undermined by individual ambitions of members trying to join the Syrian opposition coalition abroad while constantly criticising it. The problem is that the revolution has not produced any political entities outside of armed groups. It hasn't institutionalised itself, and it's illusory to believe that revolutions can succeed without concrete forces. As a result, it ends up being co-opted by others.[43]

The extreme centre regime: A new Bonapartism

How should we conceptualise and characterise the 'authoritarianism of the extreme centre' in Idlib? Once again, the analytical framework of the political sociology of revolutions offers valuable insights, as both cases appear to involve a transition from a Thermidorian situation to the consolidation of a strongman regime, albeit moderated by reformist tendencies and constrained by limited resources.

As in post-1789 France, Idlib's Thermidorian moment marked the end of radical revolutionary governance and a retreat from doctrinal intransigence and terror. The ideal of a revolutionary *tabula rasa*—which, in Idlib's case, was rooted in Salafi-inspired efforts to erase former social norms—and was being gradually supplanted by social inertia and the reassertion of entrenched social structures, within a context marked by ideological disengagement and autocratic self-restraint.

Moreover, the takeover of Damascus was a decisive turning point in the trajectory of the Syrian revolution. Amid growing political and social fragmentation, the erosion of centralised authority and a deepening economic crisis, a broad demand for order and stability was emerging. The Thermidorian phase, crystallised in Idlib, undercut revolutionary extremes and fostered a yearning for ideological temperance, while simultaneously laying the groundwork for a concentration of power rooted in coercive institutions.

The shift from Idlib to Damascus signifies more than a mere geographic transition: it encapsulates a passage from Thermidor to some kind of Bonapartism, i.e. the establishment of a regime led by a charismatic figurehead, vested with expansive executive authority, invoking revolutionary legitimacy while asserting rigorous control over both the political apparatus and the religious but with limited use of physical coercion.[44]

10

RESPECT THE MARTYRS BUT DON'T KILL THE MARKET!

MORALISING A NASCENT PUBLIC SPHERE IN IDLIB

HTS significantly transformed between its emergence in 2017 and its victory over the regime in December 2024. The group clamped down on its more radical commanders, severed ties with global jihad, and largely suspended the application of Salafi principles in governance. Still, this transformation did not preclude occasional efforts to establish some forms of Islamic governance in Idlib. More surprisingly, we should not assume that HTS was directly behind all initiatives to make governance in northwest Syria more Islamic. HTS operated within a complex ecosystem where it delegated authority to a local government, the Salvation Government, which it influenced but did not micro-manage. Important local figures and Islamist actors unconnected to HTS—sometimes even very critical of the group—continued to pursue their own agendas, independently from HTS's strategic direction. These actors, in turn, responded to local economic and social factors, which inform their agendas. This is the context, in 2023 to 2024, in which the Salvation Government briefly attempted to introduce a morality police through a law that HTS subsequently froze.

The law on public morality is particularly intriguing for it highlights the complex dynamics at play in northwest Syria between a range of actors that HTS did not control. It illustrates HTS's positioning on the imposition of Islamic norms as it attempted to re-engage with society, the international community, and mitigate radicalism within the province and its own ranks. HTS was not, paradoxically, the source of the law, which resulted from a bottom-up dynamic fuelled from a growing trend towards moral and economic openness, which had gained momentum in the newly established public sphere created by the 4 March 2020 truce. The law mirrored a cultural clash between conflicting currents within Idlib's social fabric. HTS's approach to this law demonstrated a careful balancing act amid a divisive cultural dispute, which suggests that its leadership operated in a fundamentally transactional—and therefore political rather than doctrinal—manner, responding to demands for Islamic norms from conservative societal segments. This law finally highlighted the difficulties political Islam faces in navigating a transformed radicalism that evolved from its original jihadi legacy into a new conservative populist guise. HTS's religious challenges provide valuable insights into the limitations of the silent revolution initiated by the organisation in recent years.

The quest of religious norms: A bottom-up process relying on a loose moral coalition

At the end of 2023, the Shura Council ratified a public morality law (*qanun al-adab al-'ama*).[1] The law featured sections regulating different areas such as wedding halls, markets and malls, restaurants and cafés, public spaces and playgrounds. Prohibitions included the following: insults to the Prophet, criticism of Muslim rites or religious scholars (*ulama*), the practice of witchcraft, the practice of trade during Friday prayers, gender-confusing clothing, tattoos, homosexuality, prostitution, adultery, the consumption of alcohol and drugs, gambling and betting, insults, violence against animals, gender mixing in working spaces, smoking on public transport and in hospitals, mockery of the elderly or disabled. The law also established a new morality police directly under the authority of the High Council of the Judiciary to enforce these prohibitions. There were no penalties associated with the various offences mentioned in the law, which only specified disciplinary measures of up to 48 hours detention. It also called for treatment that preserves the dignity of individuals during their deprivation of liberty.

Shortly after its ratification by the Shura Council on 24 December 2023, a draft of the law leaked out and immediately caused a public controversy. Already wary of a zone described as "toxic", foreign representatives committed to humanitarian aid were up in arms, thinking of condemning it publicly, and consulting the UN bodies in charge of Syria on the best course of action.[2] Some pushed for disinvestment in Idlib, others called for a focus on less ideologically problematic areas such as regime zones of influence or the PYD-controlled northeast of Syria.[3] As for the diplomats in charge of Syria, they immediately saw this as a "radical setback" and raised the spectre of "Talibanisation",[4] pointing out—and rightly so—that this law effectively contradicted the mainstreaming of the movement and, far from reproducing them, hardened the codes of conservative social morality dominating Idlib.[5]

The law also provoked anger in Syrian opposition circles who took it as a sign of regression and proof of the dominance of the hardliners within the movement, pointing to its Iranian and Saudi precedents.[6] Even a well-known Islamist academic from Damascus, then based in the conservative town of Al-Bab who had a favourable view of the movement's evolution was taken aback:

> Here in Al-Bab, all the women wear the full veil [*niqab*], and ultra-rigorism is the order of the day. By contrast, the atmosphere in Idlib has always been more open, even with HTS. Then this law took us by surprise and reminded us of Saudi Arabia and its Agency for the Promotion of Virtue and the Pursuit of Vice.[7]

The supporters of the law insisted that it responded to the vacuum created by HTS's abandonment of religious policing. Since the establishment of the Salvation Government in 2017, HTS had relinquished its direct control over religious affairs. It abolished the former Preaching Bureaus (*al-makatib al-da'awiyya*) in 2017 and delegated religious policing (*hisba*) to the Salvation Government, a government that the HTS leadership systematically called to order and restraint.[8] HTS also abolished the Salvation Government Moral Apparatus (*jihaz al-hisba*) in 2017 and its successor body, the Arms of Good (*sawa'id al-Khayr*), which civilians criticised for being repressive. The last attempt at moral policing was the Centre of Devotional Prosperity (*markaz al-Falah*), under the Preaching Section of the Ministry of Affairs. Ahmad al-Sharaa himself dissolved the Centre at the end of 2021 because of the abuses committed by members of this institution and in anticipation of international criticism that risked blocking the adjustment of perceptions towards the organisation at a time when the delisting of HTS was a priority objective for the movement.

While parts of society eagerly embraced the newfound social freedoms made possible by the relative easing of previous moral constraints—resulting from the end of the war and the abolition of the morality police in 2021—others, more mobilised, were determined to reinstate regulatory control over public behaviour. Since 2023, the city's conservative circles led by certain notables of the old urban families, especially those who had been victims of harassment,[9] contended that HTS's abolition of the *hisba*, the former Islamic morality police, created a vacuum which had to be filled.[10] "The city's old urban families have considered for some time that the openness of recent years has been excessive and needed to be regulated," insisted a conservative notable from the city.[11] On the other end of the local ideological spectrum, a feminist activist made a similar assessment:

> With the end of the war, society is revitalised, and a certain relaxation of moral pressure is taking place. Idlib's corniche has become a place of gender mixing. Women drivers have multiplied since driving lessons have been authorised for them, make-up at Idlib University is becoming common, and women's clothing is increasingly colourful. Society was really changing. Mixed couples in cars increased, and guards at checkpoints were instructed not to check the nature of their relationship. The boom in malls over the past two years has amplified this openness, which, for notable segments of the population, is seen as uncontrolled.[12]

In the summer of 2023, the Idlib Family Council (*Majlis 'Awa'il Idlib*) took the initiative:

> It was summer. It was shopping event season, the situation had become messy, gender mixing was spreading. And the female students were also walking around freely. It was a big deal. So, as the Idlib Family Council, we decided to take the issue to the Shura Council to ask them to introduce a public morality law.[13]

A moral coalition initially made up of some of Idlib's old family dignitaries formed. They articulated a political demand to local authorities based on a pervasive sentiment among certain segments of society that, since 2020, Idlib has experienced "excessive openness leading to numerous abuses".[14] This sentiment was one opinion among many, and was not shared by all. But it was quickly relayed publicly by certain relatively influential clerics, most of them unaffiliated with HTS or evolving in its periphery. Among them, Ibrahim Shasho, the former Minister of Justice, a former Ahrar al-Sham judge who later joined the Salvation Government;[15] Abderazzaq al-Mahdi, a former Ahrar al-Sham affiliated cleric who spent a short time in the ranks of HTS before leaving the organisation due to his disavowal of the policy of confronting other factions; Melhem Khawam, better known as Abu al-Waqid al-Shami, a shaykh from the city of Hama known for his Salafi leanings, registered as a mosque imam with the Ministry of Religious Affairs but not affiliated to HTS, and Abu al-Fath al-Farghali, the impetuous Egyptian cleric—also formerly in Ahrar al-Sham—dismissed by HTS as part of an amicable divorce due to his difficulty in adjusting to the movement's new political line. According to an activist and early revolutionary,

> We are in a reactionary moment. The excessive openness of society, the gender mixing on the Corniche and in the malls, after the truce are seen by large sections of society as a problem. After HTS banned *hisba* in 2018, a sense is developing that it needs to be regulated. And while many people criticise the law, there is a consensus on the need for regulation.[16]

This moral coalition, a blend of Facebook activism, pious urban bourgeoisie bitterness, local and foreign critics of clerics, without necessarily being in the majority, succeeded in creating momentum: a trilateral committee composed of members of the Ministry of the Interior, clerics from the Fatwa council and members of the Office of Legal Affairs met and worked on the law. After three long sessions, the last of which lasted over three hours, the Shura Council finally ratified the law on 24 December 2023.

The political leadership of the movement—Ahmad al-Sharaa and his inner circle—was clearly not the driving force behind the law. At first, al-Sharaa paid little attention to its development, and when he eventually became aware of it, he was rather hesitant. But he was also reluctant to invest political capital in a sensitive issue that influential sections of society supported.[17] It was thus the staff of the clerical institutions of the Salvation Government, and not the leadership of HTS, who relayed the moral coalition's demands for regulation and channelled it within the existing governance institutions in Idlib. Thus, according to a close associate of al-Sharaa,

> After al-Sharaa's cancellation of the morality police [*hisba*], the Arms of Good, then the Centre of Devotional Prosperity, we faced an increase in cases of inappropriate individual behaviours [*tabaruj*] and pressure from conservative circles [*al-multazimeen*] became more insistent. HTS, having delegated the management of the religious field to the Salvation Government, did not intervene. The Salvation Government, on the other hand, is well aware of the void and has been thinking about a new morality police model for just over a year. It considers that the best response is a form of morality police, which needs a law to function. The law was mainly a local initiative of the Salvation Government and the religious shaykhs. The process took place below the radar of HTS's political leadership. Ahmad al-Sharaa knew about it, of course, but he didn't take much interest in it. Then it happened very quickly and we were taken by surprise: the Ministry of Religious Affairs formalised a draft law in cooperation with the Ministry of the Interior, the Fatwa Council approved it and the Shura Council ratified it.[18]

The law was thus the by-product of the activism of an ad hoc moral coalition formed in response to the openness enabled by the truce. It happened largely independently from HTS, although its proponents effectively leveraged channels within the institutional governance that HTS set up to articulate its demands. HTS's political leadership, while rather reticent, allowed it to happen. It was initially reluctant to engage political capital on an ideologically legitimate issue—the centrality of the Islamic norm in the public arena—that influential segments of society supported. The bill was established through a bottom-up trajectory stemming from society. It was partly achieved against the movement's leadership, not through a top-down autocratic-radical decision-making process.

RESPECT THE MARTYRS BUT DON'T KILL THE MARKET!

The birth of a consumerist public sphere

The public morality law was an effort to regulate the burgeoning consumerist and hedonistic public sphere in a society that remains divided on social and religious issues. This regulation aimed to prevent such an environment from becoming a source of societal discord.[19]

The emergence of new public spaces was a recent phenomenon in Idlib province. Prior to 2020, the tenuous security conditions forced society into a narrow, inward-looking routine, characterised by essential outings such as work, schooling for children when feasible, and taking part in armed militancy which frequently required family involvement for logistical support and care. Charitable and humanitarian efforts persisted in these challenging circumstances though leisure activities were virtually non-existent.[20] The dynamics shifted with the announcement of a truce, formalised by the Russian-Turkish agreement on 4 March 2020. As the grip of both war and COVID-related restrictions began to loosen, a new era of public life gradually unfolded, which offered a tentative resurgence of leisure for those with means. Initially, restaurants took the lead, followed by cafes in 2023, often outfitted with plasma screens broadcasting the European football championships. Soon after, zoological gardens paired with mini amusement parks emerged, alongside the reopening of the Idlib stadium. This revival of leisure pursuits marked a departure from the strict ethos of order and discipline advocated by political Islam, reflecting a shift in societal norms and aspirations.

The multiplication of commercial calls was the most visible stage in the formation of this public space. More risky and costly investments, malls began to appear in 2021, mainly in border towns spared from the regime's bombardments, especially between the two towns of Dana and Sarmada, and to a lesser extent in Idlib itself. Most of these establishments relied on small groups of investors and local capital from large families such as the Badawi or al-Shaykh families in Sarmada, or the al-Qash (who are the main shareholders in the al-Hamra mall) and al-Hajj Hamidi families in Dana, often backed up by businessmen from Aleppo who, having settled into a temporary situation that is now quasi-permanent, began to reinvest locally. A consumerist place emerged for what remains of the local elite—the families of local traders and employees of NGOs—for others they were a time for leisure. People went there to have a coffee and socialise. For the most disadvantaged, it was also a place to discover the most basic forms of the consumerist dream: elevators, escalators, all in a festive, musical atmosphere.[21]

The emergence of public leisure spaces was a novel and ideologically diverse phenomenon, which developed in partial cooperation with HTS. Within less than two years, nearly twenty-nine malls opened along the border strip and deeper into the territory, particularly in Idlib, Salqin, and Binish. Restaurants also proliferated, strategically dispersed across the area to minimise exposure, along with an even greater number of cafeterias, some offering shishas. This growth included four zoos, each accompanied by children's recreational playgrounds. The burgeoning public leisure space had thus become not only widespread but also highly lucrative. While this public space was ideologically diverse, it relied on global references and pop culture rather than on the play of a 'Muslim' identity card. While there were some explicit references to local culture—Beit al-Karam, for example, or the Rawaq restaurant in Dana—names with Western references dominated, far removed from the trappings of Islamist identity. In fact, there were countless names inspired by global pop culture, such as the giant "Charisma" café, the "Grand Arizona" in Sarmada, the "North Cafe" with its two branches in Dana and Hazano, "Wings", "Mister Black", "City Rose", "KFC" and "Green Parc". The development of public leisure spaces was frequently driven by consortia formed in collaboration with traders aligned with the ruling authorities, and thus, they operated with the tacit approval of HTS, which likely took a share of the profits.[22] The Disneyland restaurant exemplified this arrangement. Located adjacent to the new Idlib zoo—home to gazelles, parrots, and a recently acquired family of lions from Baghdad Zoo—Disneyland occupied a property that formerly belonged to the Committee of the Spoils of War (*lajna al-ghana'im*). Owned by traders connected to HTS, the restaurant accommodated mixed families but restricted gender mixing outside of familial groups and offered hookahs in its garden.[23]

RESPECT THE MARTYRS BUT DON'T KILL THE MARKET!

Paradoxically, there was no correlation between the degree of Islamic compliance—broadly defined by the proscription of gender mixing, shisha and music—and the presence of investors close to HTS. For instance, shishas were available at Disneyland, a venue that permits gender mixing in a controlled, conservative manner—allowing mixed families and women accompanied by a mahram, though HTS was the primary investor in this establishment. The Rawaq restaurant was conversely not open to gender mixing but had no capital tied to HTS. Café Charisma, a two-storey hookah café, set up with HTS capital, allowed gender mixing. The al-Hamra mall relied partly on HTS related traders and yet is mixed with music on every floor. This disconnect between Islamic norms and Islamist investments by HTS or its affiliates explained why some conservative criticism of the mall's celebrations on social media targeted the moral laxity permitted by the group. Critics denounced HTS's role in fostering this hedonistic sphere within a public space otherwise defined by revolutionary and Islamist austerity.[24] According to one of the mall's regulars, "people know that most of the investors are close to HTS, and they often point out the hypocrisy of HTS, which calls for *'iltizam'*, strict adherence to Muslim morality while opening the doors to corruption".[25]

A kulturkampf between market hedonism and war conservatism

The tipping point in favour of societal regulations came with the rapid proliferation of shopping malls, though the societal debates started earlier. The push for regulation initially stemmed from debates over the increasing instances of inappropriate individual behaviours (*tabaruj*) and the rise in gender mixing, particularly noticeable around the Idlib Corniche—a ring road that encircles the city and serves as a popular recreational area—and at Idlib University, where gender integration was at an all-time high, with women now forming the majority of the 25,000 students.[26] However, the rapid proliferation of shopping malls further spotlighted the ongoing divergence in opinions: some embraced the current trend toward liberalisation, while others strongly opposed it.

The celebration of al-Hamra Mall's second anniversary on 8 December 2023 in the small border town of Dana sparked controversy and attracted significant media attention.²⁷ Nine days of celebrations and sales, massive crowds of people, gender mixing and music set the standards on this day. It was not the first time this kind of event had taken place. But the co-occurrence of the celebrations in the mall on one side and, on the other side, the loss of martyrs in a failed infiltration operation on Aleppo's western front, 11 kilometres away, a few hours before the opening of the ceremonies, amplified criticisms and highlighted the polarisation of society.²⁸

A new hedonistic spirit, unknown for almost a decade, was evident in the atmosphere at the celebration of the mall's inauguration on 8 December 2023.²⁹ One of Idlib's media activists, Khaled al-Khatib, sarcastically noted the Salvation Government's attempts to "follow the trend" (in English in the Arabic text). On the other side, a few preachers from the Ministry of Religious Affairs felt the loneliness of a missionary in this consumerist desert, as they struggled to find an audience and attentive ears. In Idlib, as elsewhere in the world, people do not come to a mall to be preached at,³⁰ and the Ministry of Religious Affairs did not repeat its initiative.³¹ Some revolutionary activists, such as Mohand Najjar of Maarat al-Nu'man, also justified the hedonism present in the mall as an expression of the very gains that the revolution had succeeded in preserving and developing. Najjar challenged the definition of conservative public modesty put forward by Islamist moral entrepreneurs, and reminded us that this mall is de facto a market, an institution which in the time of early Islam was always a space for gender mixing.³²

However, the new hedonistic spirit, along with the unprecedented emergence of a public space centred around leisure in a territory long defined by the closed-door realities of war and revolution—further reinforced by an Islamist narrative—was almost certain to provoke hostile reactions. They did not take long to appear. The first salvo of criticism was mainly religious. Some Friday preachers and former HTS religious scholars, notably Abderazzaq al-Mahdi and the impetuous Egyptian scholar Abu al-Fath al-Farghali, considered such ceremonies to be "collaboration with the enemy".³³ Ibrahim Shasho, the former Minister of Justice, expressed his indignation from atop his minbar, voicing his grievances over the fact that "the death of thousands of people in Gaza and those a few kilometres away do not count for these blood merchants[34] who, despite this, provokes people with music and inappropriate scenes in order to facilitate the marketing of their goods".[35]

The second wave of criticism stemmed from a "war conservatism"[36] that denounced all forms of hedonism and advocated instead for an ascetic ethic shaped by the war's context, the hardships in the camps, and a revolution that appeared to be losing momentum. It called for social life to be brought into line with the armed operations that were still ongoing, sometimes via mosques, occasionally conveyed by Salafi shaykhs but also often by ordinary militants.[37] Local journalist and YouTuber Mohand al-Masri expressed his exasperation that the celebration took place when martyrs of the commando operation were killed:

> We see celebration and mixing, as if the question [of the martyrs] didn't concern them, as if they were in another world. These people are sacrificing themselves for us so that we can live here in peace [...] We're not against celebrations, but they have to be done within the framework of traditions and customs.[38]

The conservative backlash finally culminated when a group of masked men opened fire on the mall. After the attack and the following wave of criticism, the Salvation Government convened a meeting between the mall's management and local officials, and decided to continue with the mall events, albeit in a more restricted manner: only families were allowed to enter the mall, which was out of bounds to unaccompanied young men; gender mixing was forbidden, but only in the workplace; and stores were asked to reduce the volume of music and limit themselves to songs that are not contrary to Islamic norms. The Ministry of the Interior deployed patrols to protect the mall. Although the celebrations went ahead in spite of intense pressures, other malls, such as the Royal Mall, which were planning similar events, postponed them.

What we observed—structurally—was the uneasy coexistence of two distinct public spheres. The first was a political space shaped by wartime conservatism, which dictated prescriptive norms in the religious and media arenas. The second was a sociological, apolitical sphere characterised by consumerism, leisure, and a degree of hedonism. This latter space served as both a societal pressure valve and a source of financial accumulation for HTS. It stood as the moral inverse of the former, though it lacked a legitimising discourse of its own. Naturally, these two spheres clashed and placed HTS in a precarious balancing act: attempting to regulate without outright prohibiting this space, as it remained both socially indispensable and economically lucrative.

Managing a polarised public space: HTS's balancing act

The handling of the public morality bill in this polarised context demonstrated that it was not an attempt by HTS hardliners to enforce a radical interpretation of Islamic norms on a supposedly moderate society, as some analyses suggested in the case of the Taliban in Afghanistan. Instead, it highlighted a delicate balancing act by the movement's leadership on two fronts: first, navigating between two opposing public spheres, each deeply rooted locally and second, managing the interplay between internal dynamics and external pressures linked to Idlib's international engagement, particularly with an eye on donor countries' reactions regarding humanitarian aid.

HTS fostered the development of public spaces centred on leisure and a mild hedonism—evident in public expressions of joy, social mixing, the presence of shishas, and the blend of Western symbolism with Arab pop culture. This approach sought to harmonise adherence to Islamic norms with the prevailing trends of globalisation and consumerism.[39] However, HTS was also accountable to a political public sphere deeply influenced by wartime conservatism, which is both Islamic—sometimes Salafi in ideology—and anti-hedonistic in its invocation of a revolutionary austerity and respect for the martyrs.

As a result, the bill served to regulate the emerging public space not only through repression but also to safeguard a key sector of HTS investment. The law was a balancing act between the need to appease conservative circles with regulatory measures (hence the legislative push) and the necessity to protect this investment sector without diminishing its appeal to customers—namely, its public visibility. This leads to the peculiar outcome of a law enacted

RESPECT THE MARTYRS BUT DON'T KILL THE MARKET!

without an accompanying penalty regime that might otherwise deter patrons.

Another balancing act followed this first internal one. It was linked to the management of external pressures. Diplomats and donor states involved in Idlib saw this law through the prism of Talibanisation, consulted each other, communicated with the UN and Turkish Foreign Affairs and hesitated to condemn:

> Over time, we began to see the authorities in the northwest behaving better than those on the regime side. But this law is likely to be a major game-changer in our investment debate. Indeed, we have divergent voices, with some pushing for a focus on government-controlled areas, while left-wing parties tend to favour aid investments in Kurdish-controlled areas instead.[40]

Faced with the very real spectre of shrinking humanitarian aid budgets, the HTS leadership discreetly froze the implementation of the law to give itself time to gather criticism and comments on the law from both inside and outside Idlib, and then, possibly, return to the text of the law and adjust it on this basis. HTS hence navigated a complex transactional dynamic as it balanced the tangible reactions of local society with the anticipated responses of the international community. Confronted with societal demands for moral regulation and the risks associated with a legal response to these demands, HTS doesn't preach, it plays politics.

The dubious talibanisation of Idlib: HTS and its transactional morality management

To better understand the specific nature of the current dynamic, a comparison with the Taliban, invoked by HTS's critics, is useful. In the days of the Islamic republic established in the aftermath of the US intervention against the Taliban, as early as 2007, malls appeared in Kabul. Lifestyles were conservative, but gender mixing and music were tolerated, at least in the capital. Then, after 2021, this public space for leisure and consumption suffered from the Taliban's repressive policy: a ban on all music and mixing, even between married couples, in all public spaces, from zoos to public gardens and malls. Under the triple fire of the public moralisation undertaken by the Taliban, which imposed its new moral order without any resistance, American sanctions and the widespread impoverishment of the middle classes, the malls gradually either closed down or were re-traditionalised, like the Gulbahar mall, which had been converted into a jewellers' market. In a very short space of time, this public space, governed by consumerism and leisure, collapsed.[41]

In Idlib, the situation stands in stark contrast to that of the Taliban in Kabul. Unlike the Taliban, who imposed a rural moral order on an urban society, HTS is deeply embedded within the community it governs. Sociologically, Idlib lacks a village-urban divide, as HTS draws recruits from across the region. Ideologically, it embraced locally recognised political and religious traditions, unlike the PYD in the Arab areas of eastern Syria. Furthermore, HTS was not an outsider to the emerging public sphere; it actively shaped and contributed to its development through financial investments.

The malls could not survive in post-US Afghanistan's order because the Taliban were economically, morally and socially outside this sphere, and because the Taliban, like IS in Syria and Iraq in 2014–16, had the upper hand in a balance of power with society at large that enabled them to crush it without compromise. HTS, on the other hand, has always dealt transactionally with society in Idlib, in a context of war where social peace is a strategic imperative and, by extension, repression a potentially costly option.[42] But above all, faced with a society divided between two public spaces, one governed by an ethic of wartime austerity and the other by a practice of consumerism and leisure, HTS has never taken a side, investing in (and practising on the margins)[43] the latter, while having the majority of its members identify with the former's set of values.

While the Taliban enforce their vision of Islamic norms through outright prohibitions, HTS adopted a transactional approach: it sought to mediate the coexistence of two conflicting public spheres with opposing normative frameworks, while also accounting for the reactions of the international community. HTS rarely imposed outright bans, and when it did legislate, it typically reacted belatedly and in response to specific triggering events. For instance, it did not entirely prohibit gender mixing but placed restrictions on it: allowing mixed families and permitting it in public spaces while banning it in workplaces. Similarly, music was not outright banned but had to conform to Islamic principles and local customs. Shops did not have to close for daily prayers, only during Friday sermons. Although HTS enforced a range of prohibitions, it refrained from establishing a system of penalties tied to them, limiting sanctions to disciplinary measures that do not exceed 48 hours and avoiding physical punishments. The hijab was mandated as a reflection of the social consensus, but the niqab was not, as it remained a subject of debate. When the leadership recognised the potential international repercussions—such as redirected aid budgets or harsher perceptions of Idlib's situation—it froze the legislation and initiated a new round of consultations to amend the law, reflecting its pragmatic and adaptive approach.

HTS faced a classic dilemma similar to that of Sunni Arab conservative states. Al-Sharaa's approach to managing public morality mirrors the strategy employed by late Egyptian President Anwar al-Sadat in the late 1970s, when he faced pressure to adopt Islamic criminal law. Confronted with opposition from left-wing and nationalist factions, Sadat sought to strengthen his Islamic credentials by rehabilitating the Muslim Brotherhood and positioning himself as a "believing president". However, when Islamists and clerics produced drafts for the "codification of Islamic Shari'a" between 1978 and 1982 which they debated in the People's Assembly, Sadat was in a bind. While publicly embracing Islam, he also sought alignment with the West. He could neither outright reject the proposed penal codes nor fully endorse them. Instead, he quietly shelved them and avoided further debates.[44] Similarly, al-Sharaa could not openly oppose calls from a vocal minority for the implementation of Islamic precepts, given his role as a defender of religious values. Both leaders, navigating the tension between religious obligations and strategic external alliances, skillfully avoided committing to strict legal codification. This approach reflects their need to balance internal pressures, avoid alienating key constituencies, and manage the expectations of both domestic and international actors.

However, HTS also engaged in a cost-benefit calculation that led it to regulate without instituting a retribution regime and eventually to suspend the application of the law. The organisation aimed to uphold Shari'a as part of identity politics but avoided implementing the physical penalties, which, even for Islamists, can be very controversial. By freezing the law, HTS adopted a stance similar to that of Swiss Muslim thinker Tariq Ramadan, who, in 2005, publicly called for a "moratorium on corporal punishment, stoning, and the death penalty in the Muslim world."[45] HTS sought to balance openness with regulation and tried to reinterpret the management of religious norms within a modern state framework. According to somebody close to al-Sharaa, "this law represents a civil evolution of the hisba concept, where enforcement is managed by a civil government rather than religious authorities. It aligns with Syrian law derived from the 1951 constitution, which also provided for a morality police force."[46]

Ultimately, HTS's approach to codifying public morality through a faith-based bill of law did not emulate the models of the Taliban, Iranian clerical power, or Saudi Wahhabism. Instead, it mirrored the classical strategies that conservative Arab state leaders have historically employed when faced with populist religious demands. The novelty in Idlib lies not in HTS's policy itself, but in the emergence of this populist current. For a movement like HTS, which has only recently moved beyond traditional Salafi jihadi radicalism, the rise of such populism introduced new and complex challenges.

A post-Salafi radicalism recast in populist terms

A new form of radicalism very distinct from global jihad emerged in Idlib before the 2024 takeover of Damascus, which posed a unique challenge for HTS. Unlike the previous security-centric radicalism, this new problem was primarily political: the moral relaxation enabled by the ceasefire fueled a conservative backlash that exploited positive law to formalise and rigidify norms that were previously considered cultural givens.[47] The rise of a consumerist and hedonistic culture sparked demands for public space regulation, which left the HTS leadership with few solutions and presented both ideological and political dilemmas. Idlib's conservative families advocated for order, articulated in moral and religious terms, and successfully formulated political demands supported by clerics within and outside HTS.

Although the push for greater Islamic norms in the public sphere aligned with HTS's principles, the conservative demand for full Shari'a implementation along with strong support for the morality law placed the movement's leadership in a bind. This new development forced HTS to address an issue it considered secondary, which explained its initial disinterest during the early drafting stages of the law. It also forced HTS to take a definitive stand on a contentious issue, potentially dividing society and forcing the movement to choose sides. Internationally, this issue placed HTS at odds on the international stage, complicating its aspirations for normalisation with the West.

The call for societal regulations highlighted a clear distinction between clerics both within and outside HTS on the one hand, and HTS's own leadership on the other. This internal differentiation—where clerics are driven by religious considerations, while the leadership makes decisions based on primarily political factors—is a hallmark of political Islam.[48] In Idlib, the organisation's leadership perceived the clerics as an external influence, distinct and separate from its political agenda:

> We are facing a broader reality, a populist trend [*tawajuh shaabawi*] based on a clerical current [*tayyar al-mashiyakhi*] which is deeply rooted in society and in the mosques. And this current is now largely exterior to HTS. Inside the movement's structures, things are under control. But most of the Friday preachers are not members of the movement. And we have a real problem with this. Recently, Ahmad al-Sharaa met with several hundred of these shaykhs and he was shocked by the lack of political awareness of what was possible to do or not to do at the moment. During this meeting, one of them asked Ahmad al-Sharaa to give them 200 missiles to liberate Damascus, another urged him to crush the Sufi current.[49]

The question of radicalism was no longer framed in security terms—jihadi Salafism—but in "populist" terms.[50] Populism is the "publicisation" of a revolutionary conservatism in Islamic terms, which comes with religious and moral legal demands that often contradict HTS's strategic choices. Populism directly stemmed from the socio-economic openness that HTS supported. A researcher close to the HTS leadership considered that

> it is no longer HTS that constitutes the dynamo of Salafism in Idlib today. Religious excess and inflationist rhetoric now come from outside the movement, for the simple reason that those without positions of responsibility can easily engage in verbal inflation, unlike those having their hands in the fire.[51]

This populist trend therefore extended beyond the hardliners within HTS.[52] It was less the work of organised groups or factions, which HTS largely submitted to its political will. Nor did populism stem from internal factional rivalries, such as that between al-Sharaa's inner circle and the networks of Abu Maria al-Qahtani and Abu Ahmad Zakour that the previous chapter discussed.

This episode showed once again that the HTS leadership operated with a rationality that was more political than religious. The group sought compromise as it recognised existing divisions in society. In enforcing public morality legislation, HTS had to balance multiple objectives within a cohesive political and legal framework. It aimed to maintain social order while also preserving its economic interests and containing radical elements within its ranks. The group also had to navigate the influence of a powerful "moral coalition" while managing the coexistence of two public spheres with conflicting values. Additionally, HTS was mindful of the potential international repercussions of such legislation, including the risk of reduced aid. Ultimately, these efforts were also tied to its broader goals of being removed from the UN's list of armed groups associated with al-Qaeda and IS. Clearly, by enforcing religious norms in a transactional and reactive manner—unlike the proactive and uncompromising puritanism of the Taliban—HTS did not impose its will from above but instead navigated a polarised society divided by the previously described *kulturkampf*, while also contending with the constraints of its pursuit of international normalisation.

The shift from jihadi Salafi radicalism to populist social conservatism revealed a twofold process of normalisation. First, radicalism moved into the mainstream. It was no longer an exogenous force tied solely to global jihad; rather, it originated within society, intertwining with the revolutionary context and sometimes adopting Salafi concepts, thus becoming embedded in the social fabric. However, this mainstreaming did not diminish the radical nature of certain aspects of social conservatism. The demand for criminal and religious regulation of behaviours specified in the law remained radical in two ways: it insisted on the uncompromising application of religious norms, and if not moderated from above, particularly in severe cases like adultery or homosexuality, it led directly to calls for the implementation of Islamic penal punishments (*hudud*). Within HTS, this extreme approach even caused discomfort at the highest levels of the leadership due to its severity.

However, taking governance in Idlib away from the Sunni Muslim mainstream would mean reverting to a form of radicalism that the leadership wanted to avoid. This brings us to our second point: the normalisation of HTS's response. Faced with populism, al-Sharaa reacted with political pragmatism, similar to that of Sunni Arab conservative leaders like Anwar al-Sadat in the 1970s. He first accepted the principle of the law, then attempted to mitigate its effects by freezing its implementation, and engaged in cost-benefit analysis concerning potential international reactions.

A constraining "negative solidarity": The identity trap and the vulnerabilities of the silent revolution

The draft law on public morality and its management by HTS does not only reveal a fundamentally radical or Salafi political order in Idlib; it also reinforces our contention about how the movement prioritised its political strategy. This dominance of politics, however, is ambivalent—it serves as both an asset and a liability. On one hand, HTS's political pragmatism allowed its leadership to assert autonomy and distinguish itself from the clerical faction, both within and outside the movement. On the other hand, this strong emphasis on political considerations over religious doctrine created a significant vulnerability. By prioritising political calculations, the leadership inadvertently steered the movement toward a "silent revolution"—a shift that, while avoiding direct religious entrenchment, left it without a clear doctrinal alternative when confronted with a growing religious discourse that threatened its interests.

Lacking the conceptual framework to challenge a religious surge, HTS's leadership perceived direct doctrinal opposition as too costly. Faced with a law that it found problematic even from its own perspective, Ahmad al-Sharaa could only propose a covert suspension, akin to Tariq Ramadan's moratorium or Anwar al-Sadat's discreet freezes, without openly declaring it. This approach epitomises the movement's structural indecision—a hallmark of its ongoing transformation within the constraints of a "silent revolution".

HTS's management of the public morality law underscored its shift toward doctrinal centrism. The group sought to balance two competing priorities: addressing a populist conservative trend that remains embedded in the mainstream—similar to the dilemmas faced by European centre-right parties—while simultaneously promoting "social normalisation," a process that aligned with both societal demand and its own economic interests. Businesses such as malls and restaurants, which provided relatively gender-inclusive spaces by Idlib's standards, catered to a genuine need for social relief after years of conflict. This pragmatic approach challenges interpretations that frame HTS's stance as radical or akin to Talibanisation; instead, its position was a calculated political manoeuvre rooted in centrist pragmatism.

However, this same political primacy made it difficult for HTS to push back against conservative faith-based populist pressures from below. This exposes a fundamental weakness of its "silent revolution": without a coherent religious doctrine of its own, HTS lacks the ideological tools necessary to counter a grassroots conservative movement that operates in a gray zone. This movement reinforces entrenched social conservatism without veering into extremism (*ghulu*), which would justify HTS imposing security-based crackdowns. As a result, HTS is left navigating an ambiguous space, constrained by its own doctrinal limitations.

Faced with the rise of populist sentiments, the leadership of the movement found itself in a delicate position. It opposed the propositions of this populism, as evidenced by its rejection of the morality police law, which contradicted the movement's policy of abolishing the *hisba*, a stance reiterated by Ahmad al-Sharaa publicly since 2017. Despite certain aspects of the law clearly deviating from societal norms of conservatism—such as the prohibition of gender mixing in public spaces or workplaces, or the ban on music—the leadership hesitated to openly oppose it. This reluctance persisted despite the potential adverse effects of the law: internal resistance, decreased support from humanitarian aid donor states, and a dent in the credibility of HTS's inclusive "nationalist" discourse, which aims to appeal to all, including minorities, as part of a hegemonic strategy wherein the organisation positions itself as the embodiment of revolution and/or opposition.

The failure to repeal the morality law was not due to any inherent or exceptional radicalism within HTS's leadership. The same leadership had made far bolder moves in the past. Over the last eight years, its strategic decisions extended well beyond the potential repeal of this law: breaking away from and later confronting al-Qaeda, suppressing Islamic State, marginalising hardliners, reconciling with mainstream Islam, forging security and military agreements with a NATO member, and even opening channels to minorities and Western actors. Moreover, the leadership was either uninterested in or actively opposed to the morality law in the first place. Nor was this stagnation the result of an internal power struggle that prevented backtracking. Hardliners within HTS did not form a cohesive faction capable of overruling the movement's political leadership. In fact, the group previously accepted far more contentious policies—such as the deployment of joint Russian-Turkish patrols—without facing significant internal resistance. This suggests that the real obstacle laid elsewhere, beyond mere ideological rigidity or internal factionalism.

If HTS's reluctance to repeal the morality law did not stem from personal convictions or internal power struggles, what was the real reason? The answer lies in a paradox: the leadership viewed abandoning a public law as politically too costly, even though it had never strongly backed it in the first place. This hesitation was rooted in "negative solidarity"—a dynamic shaped by the hegemonic influence of religious references in Idlib's public sphere. Idlib's social fabric remained deeply marked by revolutionary asceticism, often framed in religious terms and upheld by powerful actors crucial to HTS's legitimacy, including prominent urban families and respected clerics. Negative solidarity does not imply full agreement but rather an implicit constraint: neither the leadership nor other influential factions could openly oppose the law without facing a backlash. While HTS's leadership maintained a subjective distance from its religious wing—commonly referred to as the "*mashaikh*" (the shaykhs) or "*shar'iyyeen*" (the legalists)—it cannot outright reject demands for stronger Islamic norms, even when privately sceptical of their content. This dilemma stemmed from the ideological hegemony of religious discourse, a force that even HTS's political dominance could not fully counterbalance.

Islamists think politically but they are also ontologically bound to Islam. As such, they cannot easily and freely manipulate the reference in order to address their cost-benefit calculations, because the reference comes with a set of constraints, as expressed by the King of Morocco, who, this time embarrassed by an overly liberal personal status law, recalled his own limits and set the perimeter of the reform, which cannot violate the formal texts of the Quran: "I cannot authorise what God has prohibited, nor forbid what the Highest has authorised".[53] HTS was caught in a similar "ontological trap": one cannot set oneself up as the protector of Islam and disavow Muslim principles that the majority does not contest and that an active minority defends. And when there is a tension between a politically rationality and the demand for religious norms, the response of an Islamist leader is always the same: dilute, ignore, freeze or impose a moratorium in order to postpone the application of the principle without questioning its foundations. In other words, one can now define an Islamist as a political driven actor who relies ontologically on a religious identity that can occasionally embarrass him.

Thus, the adoption of the law did not stem from top-down imposition or explicit support from the movement's political leadership. Nor did it reflect a social consensus, as the law extended beyond social conservatism and encountered pushback even within Idlib. Rather, it emerged from the collective difficulty in openly expressing dissent, regardless of the level of authoritarianism within the political leadership. Simply put, the inherently political nature of the movement's leadership, which had consistently deferred the need for doctrinal updates, left it vulnerable to the sway of "populist postures" that the leadership otherwise (albeit silently) disavowed. Consequently, despite the military and political defeat of radical factions, the emergence of populism recast within the framework of social conservatism suggests that significant gains in radicalism remain a possibility. While there is no inherent need for democrats in a democracy,[54] radicalism may also emerge in the absence of radicals.

11

HTS'S SILENT REVOLUTION

WHY DERADICALISATION DOES NOT NEED MODERATES AND WHY INTENTIONS DO NOT MATTER

The debate on deradicalisation frequently revolves around the question of the actors' true intentions. However, fixating on whether HTS is genuinely committed to its ideological shift risks overlooking a more crucial dynamic: the fact that initial intentions—whether strategic, tactical, or sincere—ultimately matter less than the transformations they set in motion. Once a movement embarks on a Thermidorian path of mainstreaming, it triggers shifts in internal power structures, often weakening hardliners and reinforcing more pragmatic elements. In this section, we will examine how this process unfolds and the mechanisms through which it reshapes the movement from within.

How tactical adjustments led to a strategic transformation

HTS's transformation stemmed from a series of tactical choices that gradually took on a strategic dimension. As HTS addressed the role of governing northwest Syria—amid the presence of other armed groups, a dynamic society, Turkey's influence, and certain expectations from parts of the international community—it had to make a series of decisions that shaped its evolution. It had to adapt, purge its own ranks, and impose a new direction from the top down. In the end, this process led to a transformation towards deradicalisation that was never part of its original plan.

HTS's transformation was driven more by practical necessity than by ideological revision. The group formed in 2017 with the aim of uniting the armed opposition, but this effort failed as many factions were unwilling to join a designated group they did not trust. Between 2017 and 2019, HTS had no well-defined political project; instead, it continuously adapted to emerging threats to ensure its survival. This explains why it chose to fight Ahrar al-Sham and its allies first, viewing them as a viable alternative that foreign states, including Turkey, might support. It then turned against al-Qaeda-aligned groups, which risked undermining its cohesion by rejecting its evolving tactical choices and potentially recruiting some of HTS's own commanders. But its immediate objectives remained unclear beyond mere survival.

What truly transformed HTS was territorialisation and, with it, relocalisation. After facilitating the creation of the Salvation Government and co-opting local elites who participated in a civilian administration that HTS never fully controlled, the group found itself shouldering far greater responsibilities than ever before. HTS's transformation through civilian governance occurred in multiple ways, from the group's growing dependence on its regional environment—in particular the necessity to make concessions to Turkey—to its evolving approach to governing civilians.

HTS's relationship with Turkey, as Idlib's de facto governor, forced it to make choices it had previously opposed. While Jabhat al-Nusra never waged an all-out war against Turkey or declared it an enemy like IS, it consistently rejected any association with Ankara. In its first communiqué, the group denounced Turkey and later opposed other armed groups that sought ties with it—especially those operating in northern Aleppo—as well as its own allies like Ahrar al-Sham, which pursued stronger relations with Turkey by 2016. However, after 2017, Idlib became increasingly dependent on Turkey. Turkish military outposts and Ankara's political negotiations with Russia became the province's ultimate safeguard. Neither HTS nor any other faction could have withstood a Russian-backed regime offensive without Turkish political and military support. As HTS assumed governance of Idlib and became directly responsible for its fate, it had to acknowledge the new reality. It engaged in a strategic rapprochement with Turkey, and while it occasionally resisted its neighbour—hesitating, for instance, to accept joint Russian-Turkish patrols on the M4 highway—it ultimately had little choice but to concede.

Dependence on Turkey transformed HTS. More radical voices, including al-Qaeda sympathisers and factions aligned with them, sought to turn HTS commanders against these new choices. The threat was not military but ideological and strategic—these factions challenged HTS's internal cohesion by undermining trust in its leadership, accusing them of betrayal. To counter this, HTS had to marginalise dissident voices in the short term while also readjusting its long-term approach. The group hence adjusted its internal training for new recruits, reducing ideological emphasis—including banning jihadi literature from ideologues previously taught in the training camps—and instead adopting a more localised religious frame of reference to socialise them in a way that was easier to control. This shift was facilitated by the integration of fighters who were less educated or ideologically driven, namely those primarily motivated by the desire to defend their villages or reclaim their homes from the regime.

The need to sideline internal radicalism and reassert control intersected with the practical demands of governance. Becoming the ruler of Idlib through the Salvation Government forced HTS to make new choices. In the past, it might have simply empowered judges to implement Islamic law, assuming this would be sufficient. This was also the Salafi approach to judicial ruling, often adverse to the tradition and established religious authority. However, this approach risked losing control over the judiciary, as rulings from more hardline judges could prove too radical, antagonise the international community, and undermine HTS's strategic position. To prevent this, HTS asserted greater control over judicial governance, maintaining an Islamic legal framework but ensuring that its interpretation remained in the hands of al-Sharaa's close associates. It also regulated the religious institutes that started to spread outside governmental control.

This was the context in which HTS reconciled with other religious communities. Christian and Druze communities continued to live in the province, despite the exile of many. As the governing authority, HTS had to engage with them—an unavoidable reality that also forced it to adapt. Initially, the group sought some form of reconciliation. Al-Sharaa's first major media appearance in June 2023 was a calculated move—part of a broader communications strategy to present the HTS leader as open to minorities. At the time, the movement was increasingly positioning itself as the nationalist leader of the Syrian opposition and the dominant force within opposition-held territory. However, this outreach to the media triggered backlash from HTS's mid-level ranks and unaffiliated armed groups. Some local commanders responded with direct threats against Druze notables, insults, and even physical assaults. This unrest ultimately compelled HTS to intervene.[1]

The fear of unchecked lower-ranking commanders and the Druze community's wariness meant that HTS had to be more proactive. According to a Druze notable, "we are afraid. If it is clear to us that HTS is trying to open up to us, it is no less clear that there are radical groups in our mountain who reject this opening up. It is now vital that al-Sharaa implements what he promised us in his speech".[2] Al-Sharaa's public assurances—promising security, "no coercion in religion," and openness toward the Druze community—faced resistance from within HTS's own ranks and provoked hostility, sometimes violent, from radical factions entrenched in the Samaq mountain, where the Druze villages are located. To counter the tensions, HTS tightened its security grip and cracked down on radical elements both within and outside its movement. In the Jisr al-Shughur district, local officials intensified mediation efforts, urging mosque shaykhs inclined toward inflammatory rhetoric to exercise restraint, while arresting or expelling some radicalised youth. At the request of Druze dignitaries, HTS established three new checkpoints and increased patrols in the mountain villages. Following unrest around the Qalb Loza mosque, HTS installed a permanent police presence. In a further bid to stabilise the situation, the head of TIP, seeking alignment with HTS's relocation policies, visited the village at HTS's request to deliver a message of conciliation.[3]

This cycle of ideological concessions, resistance, and the marginalisation of radical voices created a self-reinforcing dynamic. As HTS steadily sidelined its internal opponents, it found it easier to adopt more centrist positions—which, in turn, forced it to marginalise remaining dissenters. Over time, internal resistance dwindled, as those who remained increasingly aligned with the movement's new political direction. This is precisely how the movement's leadership perceives the situation. As one of al-Sharaa's advisors stated in August 2022: "We now have the opportunity to accelerate—the fewer opponents we face, the more freedom we have to advance. What works in our favor is the absence of any credible alternative for those who choose to leave."[4] By the end of this process, the balance of power within the organisation significantly and permanently changed. As one insider put it:

> Over time, resistance fades, and transformations become easier to implement. Al-Sharaa has now consolidated control over all internal opposition—there is no real force left to challenge him. This was not the case before. In 2017, when Turkey asked him to accept the observation posts, al-Sharaa agreed, but he still had to consult the movement's Shura Council, where resistance was strong and ideologically driven.[5]

HTS's transformation therefore differed significantly from that of other Islamists that had moderated their positions in the past since its shift was neither driven nor accompanied by formal ideological revisions. HTS did not follow the Egyptian and Libyan jihadi groups that, after failing to achieve their objectives and facing imprisonment, reassessed their ideology in prison and questioned the legitimacy of violence against Muslim regimes and al-Qaeda's strategy in a series of publications. It also differs from Islamist movements such as the Muslim Brotherhood in the 1970s, which had to respond to the radicalism of Sayyid Qutb by producing its own texts to refute his views. Instead, HTS evolved pragmatically, making decisions that contradicted its past positions, and even reversing its own harsh critiques of others for making similar decisions, all without clarifying the ideological implications of these shifts. Abu Maria al-Qahtani, a prominent HTS leader killed by an IS cell in 2024, proudly insisted that the group acted on its own, without pressure:

> The key difference between me and the Egyptian jihadis is that I made my revisions while still holding my weapon. I was the religious authority [mas'ul shar'i] for al-Qaeda in the Levant. I believe that al-Qaeda was wrong to attack the Pentagon. I refuted the ideological foundations of al-Qaeda by exposing the deviations

of [Abu Muhammad] al-Maqdisi and Sayyid Imam [an Egyptian jihadi ideologue]. I insisted that we should leave al-Qaeda, not because of weakness, but because it fights a war we do not believe in—the war against the West—while we are engaged in our own struggle against Iran. Most importantly, I made these revisions not from a prison cell, but as a free man, a leader, and from a position of strength.[6]

Crossing the point of no return

A series of tactical decisions have thus led to a strategic transformation (a new political orientation internally sustained by a favorable power balance)—one that has occurred without formal ideological revisions. Since HTS did not clearly articulate its core principles, one might argue that, had circumstances shifted, the group could have simply reversed course and reverted to its old ways. However, this perspective overlooks the lasting nature of these changes.

The first reason concerned both the global context and regional constraints. Before 2025, HTS sought to turn its fragile partnership with Turkey into a political alliance while aligning strategically with the West—primarily against Russia and Iran—to secure access to Western humanitarian aid and obtain the West's acquiescence to its de facto rule. Meanwhile, its radical opponents were unable to offer a compelling alternative. Marginalised within the movement and fragmented outside it, they no longer benefited from international jihadi support networks as in 2012–13. Private support for these groups in Idlib dried up; after more than three years of frozen conflict, Syria's jihad no longer attracted non-state sponsors, and state backers shifted priorities. With regional de-escalation underway, all major players scaled back support for Islamist militancy in any form.[7]

The second reason is that the movement's radicals lost their former influence due to deaths, desertions, marginalisation, and containment, which facilitated the leadership's push for further transformation despite the reluctance of some rank-and-file. HTS's internal composition hence shifted considerably. While the core leadership remained largely unchanged, the second tier had undergone a drastic transformation—foreign cadres and fighters largely disappeared, replaced by alliances with local elites who are Islamist or conservative but rarely Salafis let alone jihadis. Meanwhile, much of the rank-and-file consisted of new, locally recruited members with little ideological commitment.

This transformation reinforced a self-sustaining dynamic. Through gradual and tactical departures from its original Salafi worldview, the movement crossed a critical threshold of no return. For nearly four years, its implicit strategy was to rally the soft majority against the radical factions. And now, after five years of internal struggle against hardliners, a definitive break from al-Qaeda, significant ideological shifts, and efforts to reconnect with the tenets of the revolutionary legacies—even extending limited overtures to minorities—HTS found itself at a point of no return. A reversion to its original ultra-radical stance would not only be strategically and diplomatically counterproductive on both regional and international fronts but also deeply misaligned with the evolving mindset of its newer base of supporters. Moreover, such a reversal would inflict severe damage to its credibility, undermining the fragile political capital it has painstakingly built internally and externally through its repositioning efforts.

On the governance side, the need to maintain social peace sustained HTS's transformation. HTS embarked on its governance experiment from a position of weakness. Unlike Islamic State, which became more authoritarian as its governance structures solidified, HTS lacked both financial and human resources and was forced to govern while engaged in open warfare with the regime. As a result, it had to adapt to an environment it could not afford to antagonise. This explains its willingness to backtrack in response to public pressure, as seen in the 2021 protests against the olive oil tax and demands for detainee releases. This led to compromises and helped counterbalance the influence of radicals. In this power dynamic, governance provided tools to consolidate control over the movement's ideological and structural direction. Centralisation dismantled the micro-authorities once held by local Jabhat al-Nusra commanders. Institutional constraints limited the influence of radical shaykhs. Additionally, governance enabled the containment of other radical groups. Yet, these tools were effective only because there was genuine political will to de-radicalise—driven by the factors previously outlined. While the Idlib enclave was marked by authoritarianism, it was never an emirate.

Abu Maria al-Qahtani recognised the significant impact that governance and exchanges with external actors had on his group's evolution:

> Every Islamist movement emerges as a product of its people and reflects its behaviour. Over time, external influences—such as ideas and methodologies—alter its very structure, much like genetic mutations. Besides, the truth is that power is unforgiving, and governance is politics. Politics, in turn, requires engagement with the international system while preserving an Islamic identity—one that is religious and not jihadi.

Ultimately, the factors that once fuelled radicalism disappeared. The ideological uncertainty that marked the movement's early days has been resolved through a series of clarifications, even without ideological revisions. The movement's ties to global jihad ceased—both organisationally, through deliberate disengagement, and in terms of militant composition, as successive waves of desertions, schisms, confrontations, and de-radicalisation have reshaped its ranks. Meanwhile, theological radicalism gradually faded, driven by the self-reinforcing dynamics of thermidorian calculations, ideological differentiation and pragmatic adaptation.

A silent revolution took place, regardless of the leadership's initial intentions or sincerity. HTS leaders also changed through the very process they set in motion, even if they did not originally aim to move in this direction. Their sincerity is therefore paradoxically irrelevant—what matters is that they started to be propelled by the logic of the system and its constraints. This process has had genuinely transformative effects, not merely tactical adjustments but lasting, strategic shifts. In this game, there is no turning back.

What is particularly striking is that HTS's transformation was not only enduring but also influenced other factions. What is at play is a "field effect"—an *effet de champ*, as described by Pierre Bourdieu—where a dominant force within a given space establishes a new norm, compelling other players to adapt accordingly.[8] A clear example of this occurred on 24 August 2022, when an elderly Druze couple was murdered in their village of Keftine, west of

Idlib.⁹ While pressure on the Druze and other minorities was not new, this incident marked a shift. For the first time, Druze leaders received messages of sympathy from Islamist faction leaders, who condemned the attack and reiterated their view of the Druze as friends and allies. Notably, this response extended beyond HTS—other factions in Idlib followed suit.¹⁰ Even the Turkistan Islamic Party (TIP) publicly distanced itself from the murder, emphasising that its fighters were not present in the Druze mountain region. This reaction underscores how HTS's evolving stance is reshaping the broader militant landscape, compelling other actors to align with the emerging norms it has set.

The case of the Turkistan Islamic Party (TIP) is particularly revealing. Historically, the party, in search of military training, seized upon the Syrian civil war as an opportunity to establish itself.¹¹ Over eight years of conflict, it moved across multiple locations—including eastern Syria, Aleppo, and Jisr al-Shughur—while generally attempting to avoid direct confrontation, even with the Syrian regime. However, it was sometimes drawn into clashes, such as fighting the YPG in the east and ISIS in Aleppo. It ultimately settled in Jisr al-Shughur, where it led an offensive that strengthened its position and garnered significant resources, including tanks, wealth, and real estate. The group also expanded its economic activities and became a hub for Uyghur fighters in Turkey. In Istanbul, the Party competed with ISIS to gain the loyalty of Uyghur communities, which solidified its influence.

A similar dynamic of territorialisation and relocalisation influenced the TIP, much like HTS. The Party established a distinct territorial presence and then fought for years to secure its control, which strengthened its sense of belonging. This process of territorialisation consolidated with social integration, including mixed marriages—reportedly, three hundred Uyghur men married Syrian women. The Party prioritised community preservation by founding schools and emphasising language and religious instruction based on the Hanafi school of jurisprudence, which it positioned as an ideological counter to ISIS. While the TIP maintains symbolic ties to its leadership under Abdul-Haq in Afghanistan, it asserts autonomy in decision-making. Its emotional and familial connections to the cause of East Turkistan remain strong, with members frequently recounting stories of relatives imprisoned in China. Still, the Party has largely lost the capability to conduct operations within the China. Looking ahead, the group appears focused on replicating past settlement strategies, establishing itself in marginalised areas of Syria—previously in the northeast, now in the northwest—to deepen its social and territorial integration.

These developments stand in sharp contrast to the past, where radicalisation shaped the insurgency as a whole, impacting even non-jihadis. Many armed groups, including those within the Free Syrian Army (FSA), engaged in sectarian practices. The desecration of Christian tombs and churches, for example, was not exclusively carried out by jihadis but also by non-Islamist FSA brigades.[12] Similarly, militant anthems were often drawn from the Islamist repertoire, featuring songs by figures like Abu Rateb or Abu Dojana, while sectarian rhetoric in naming the enemy was commonplace.[13] This was not necessarily the result of deep ideological commitment but rather a "Salafisation of minds"—a process in which daily exposure to violence gradually shaped worldviews and behaviors. Three key factors drove this radicalisation: the presence of a powerful extremist pole—Islamic State—which pressured rival groups to escalate their rhetoric and actions; strong regional support for jihad, both private and state-sponsored; and the dynamics of open-ended conflict, which fuelled bottom-up radicalisation, making armed Salafism the prevailing ideological framework in everyday life.

In many ways, HTS set the new standards of conduct for other factions in Idlib before 2025 as the conditions that once drove extremism largely faded. Four key factors pushed forward this transformation simultaneously: the emergence of a new mainstream hegemon replacing Islamic State, which lost its territorial stronghold in 2019; the decline of bottom-up radicalisation, as the intense war-driven violence that once ignited extremism subsided with the freezing of the conflict in 2020; the waning appeal of the Syrian jihad on the regional stage, driven by geopolitical shifts such as Qatar's international normalisation (distancing itself from political and militant Islam), the growing rapprochement between Turkey and Qatar, and the broader de-escalation among states that once supported Islamist movements,[14] including Saudi Arabia; and finally, the slow ideological alignment of certain foreign fighter groups with HTS, particularly the TIP. In a context where jihadi Salafism lost momentum and HTS's new external reference points became the West and Turkey, governance and international aid became central issues. It is no coincidence that the first two major long-form profiles of Ahmad al-Sharaa were published by the Western media—one American,[15] the other French.[16]

A general reorganisation of the armed opposition was underway before 2025. The new geopolitical context redefined militant cultures in a way that mirrored—in opposition—the radicalisation of 2014–18. In the early years of the conflict, moderate groups often radicalised from below as they responded to battlefield pressures and the influence of more radical groups around IS. Since 2016, however, the reverse had become true: formerly radical groups de-radicalised their bases from above. This shift created tensions between different layers of HTS especially. On one hand, some in the militant rank and file socialised by the earlier era of jihadi momentum—when international networks mobilised radicalisation, war reinforced extremist tendencies, and a powerful ideological pole, such as Islamic State, attracted fighters. On the other hand, leadership circles adapted more quickly to the new strategic landscape, where jihadi Salafism lost traction, and governance, rather than jihad, became the central concern. This transformation is also marked by new avenues of engagement—with Turkey, Western think tanks, and UN agencies.

On a side note, it is noteworthy that trainers of HTS elite troops express concerns about maintaining fighting spirit in a context of prolonged ceasefire and ideological de-radicalisation. According to one of those trainers, fighters are now spending too much time with their families, and the overall quality of recruits started to decline. This shift was partly due to the increasing localisation of the force, with newer fighters being less educated and less ideologically driven than their predecessors.[17]

Reclaiming the roots: Deradicalisation, relocalisation, retraditionalisation

So to define precisely what HTS is, how can it be characterised? Before 2025, the group never explicitly defined what it stood for. Instead, its political practice silently transformed it over time. This transformation, which happened without ideological revisions, is what makes HTS unique—not only among jihadis but also in contrast to mainstream Islamist movements, including those linked to the Muslim Brotherhood or to Salafi Islam. The broader Islamist landscape is far from monolithic. Various dominant trends exist within it, and situating HTS in relation to other Islamists—whether violent or not—provides a clearer understanding of its distinct trajectory and singular evolution. Let us begin with the more straightforward aspect of these ontological considerations by identifying what HTS is not—or what it has ceased to be.

The first clear point is that HTS is no longer jihadi. The group rejected the core tenets of the jihadi trend—namely, opposition to Muslim regimes that do not implement Islamic law and hostility toward the West. This shift represents more than just an organisational rupture with ISIS in 2013 and al-Qaeda in 2016; it marks a fundamental ideological reorientation. HTS signaled its evolution through practice rather than legitimising this transformation through formal ideological statements or a new political programme defining what it stands for. Its engagement with states, including a de facto alliance with Turkey, and its abandonment of core jihadi principles—such as ceasing to promote divisive ideological concepts in religious training camps—demonstrate a clear departure from its past ideological leanings.

The second clear point is that HTS is also clearly distinct from the Muslim Brotherhood. Unlike the Brotherhood, whose ideology is rooted in a comprehensive (*shumulia*) approach—seeking to control and reform society at all levels, from the individual to the family to the state—HTS's origins in Jabhat al-Nusra are closer to avant-garde militant elitism than the Brotherhood's structured socio-political vision. While the Brotherhood integrates socialisation, grassroots activism, and participation in parliamentary elections to gradually establish an Islamic society—embodied in its famous slogan "Islam is the solution" (*al-Islam huwa al-hal*)—HTS never embraced a comprehensive approach to society. This fundamental difference also meant that HTS's transformation was more fluid. Unlike the Brotherhood, which embraces a specific ideological tradition and methodology, HTS lacks a rigid framework, which gave its leadership greater flexibility in adapting to changing political and strategic realities.

Third, even though HTS had not formalised a new ideological platform, there was a clear strategic effort to distance itself from Salafism in two ways. At the doctrinal level, the group gradually set aside fundamental Salafi tenets, albeit through this silent revolution we are now familiar with. The group has not explicitly rejected the fundamental tenets of Salafism; however, through its practices, it effectively *deprogrammed* them, preventing them from shaping its approach to politics and society, but without explicitly developing a new theological framework. As a result, while HTS does not reject its fundamental tenets, they are gradually being sidelined. For instance, the *Book of the Foundations of Faith* (*Kitab Usul al-Iman*) by Muhammad Ibn Abd al-Wahhab is still part of the curriculum at the Faculty of Shari'a. On the other side, in its engagement with society, the movement appears to be pursuing a form of inverted Salafism—one that selectively unravels its traditional outlook: rather than imposing its worldview on the population, HTS is increasingly shaped by societal pressures, inputs or tactical reliance on soft majorities. This shift—what François Furet might call "social inertia"—stands in stark contrast to classical Salafism, which seeks to transform society through doctrinal purity rather than adapt to it.

Then, once a movement—primarily for reasons of acceptability and social stability—abandons its proactive efforts to reshape society (as seen in the renunciation of *hisba*), it is society that begins to define religious norms. From that perspective HTS is at best a traditionalist movement, something that al-Sharaa implicitly acknowledged when he asserted, as noted earlier, that enforcement should be limited to matters that enjoy broad consensus among Muslims. In doing so, he concedes that religious authority is no longer imposed from above but increasingly shaped by societal expectations. This process of retraditionalisation by social inertia is evident in the revival of practices such as the *musaharati* in Idlib's old districts and renewed visits to tombs in cemeteries. Retraditionalisation is somehow the ideological dimension of HTS's political strategy of relying on "soft majorities". Retraditionalisation is a fully assumed choice that HTS consciously embraces and leverages.

HTS has become traditionalist in three ways: first, by taking tradition as a reference, as seen in its endorsement of Shafi'ism;

second, by valuing or tolerating tradition, with popular Islamic practices either accepted (such as shrine visits) or institutionalised (as seen in the continued presence of local clergy and official recognition of figures like the *musaharati*); and third, by using tradition as a source of legitimacy, a strategy that also helps sideline hardliners. Through this transformation, HTS has embraced a conservative identity that prioritises pragmatism and local adaptability over ideological intransigence. At its core, HTS leadership accepts almost anything within mainstream Sunni tradition, excluding only extreme Sufi affirmations and radical excesses (*ghulu*). Rather than imposing a rigid doctrine, they enforce only what enjoys broad consensus among Muslims.

Putting the cart before the horse: An Islamist view of pragmatism

If it is relatively straightforward to define what HTS is not—or no longer is—then the challenge lies in capturing the movement's identity at the culmination of its transformative trajectory. A useful starting point is to compare the group's own self-perception with the perspectives of its ideological companions and prominent jihadi thinkers like Abu Qatada in Jordan. A common thread emerges: HTS lacks a clearly defined identity beyond being a conservative Sunni revolutionary movement opposing the regime. Descriptions vary. Abd al-Rahim Atun refers to it as *Islam haraki*—"activist Islam." One of its advisors describes it as "conservative and revolutionary Islam," adding, "we are a revolutionary organisation breaking with jihadi Salafism. We are a civil project with still uncertain contours, and our problem is the absence of a foundational reference." A former member of the Shura Council echoes this critique, observing that "HTS is shifting from a clear identity—jihadi Salafism—to a floating identity." In his view,

> They have lost their ideological core. They are no longer jihadi Salafis, nor are they truly a part of political Islam. They are a former jihadi group now defining itself through practical experience. But they lack an ideological anchor. By moving away from traditional jihadi literature toward a mix of diverse references, they have diluted their political identity.

HTS'S SILENT REVOLUTION

This fluidity underscores HTS's ongoing transformation—a conscious break from its Salafi jihadi roots, yet without a clearly defined ideological framework to take its place. The group navigates between pragmatism and doctrine, adapting to political realities while remaining ideologically unanchored. A former fellow traveller, Abdullah al-Muhaysani, confirms that:

> Al-Sharaa is on the side of the victims of injustice and he remains an Islamist. But by not proactively adopting the fundamental pillars of contemporary jihadi thought, such as the rejection and anathema of non-Islamists [*ikhraj wa takfir al gheir al muwahideen*], or the notion of rejecting states [*takfir al-Duwal*], he cannot be called a jihadi.[18]

The longtime al-Qaeda leaning religious scholar, Abu Qatada al-Filistini, similarly views HTS as engaging in a bottom-up project—one that evolves through lived experience rather than imposing a predefined ideological framework onto the Idlib context:

> It is a mistake to try to see HTS from the point of view of ideas. Don't analyse them through the lens of ideology. Because HTS is a movement above all guided by practice. Indeed, Syria is a revolution more than a jihadi reality. What fundamentally distinguishes the Idlib experience is trial and error. The HTS experience is dictated by adaptation to the context more than by the application of a pre-conceived theory. They are both the products of a practice and the legatees of an Islamist experience. This creates vagueness and a lot of improvisation. HTS are like all Islamist groups that form or function as political parties. They are always in a way of thinking where politics prevail. It is politics above all other considerations that is guiding them. From this point of view, we are putting the cart before the horse, practice before ideology.[19]

When Abu Qatada argues that HTS is putting the cart before the horse—building political action first and only then seeking an ideological foundation—he captures the essence of pragmatism: the prioritisation of practice over a rigid, predefined ideological framework. In this model, local (and sometimes international) constraints dictate political action, which in turn shapes the group's evolving identity. Rather than adhering to a fixed ideological system, the group operates within a loosely defined framework of conformity to Islam, where the boundaries of acceptability have significantly expanded. Anything outside of *turuqiyya* (Sufi orders) and *khurafat* (superstitions) on one side, and *khawarij* (extremists) on the other, is broadly tolerated. HTS navigates pressures from its religious right while maintaining a flexible stance: the Friday sermons or *khutba* remain broad and non-binding, and the codification of Shari'a is more about compliance with Muslim conservatism than the creation of a new Islamic legal system. In practice, HTS tolerates or accommodates everything except what is perceived as extreme deviation—whether in the form of excessive Sufi practices (with shrine visits largely exempt) or extremism (*ghulu*)—and imposes nothing beyond what is commonly accepted among Muslims.

HTS has indeed severed certain ideological moorings but has not sought a new doctrinal anchor, which explains its reluctance to adopt a new founding document and its deeper ontological difficulty in defining itself. At best, we can discern what the movement no longer is—or at least no longer entirely. It retains from political Islam the idea of a political project rooted in religion but abandons *shumuliyya*, Hassan al-Banna's vision of controlling all social practices. Armed action, or jihad, becomes indistinguishable from the conception of non-Islamists, as self-defence against a violent regime. While remnants of Salafi doctrine persist in its teachings, HTS fundamentally inverts Salafism's relationship to society, incorporating certain of its concepts rather than seeking to reform radically its organising principles.

Instead, this transformation, shaped by the dual forces of societal resurgence and Thermidorian inertia—that is defines what we call retraditionnalisation, is best understood through the silent revolution traced throughout these pages unfolds without a fully articulated ideology, resisting confinement within specific categories from studies of other Islamist groups.

HTS's Thermidorian turn

Interlocutors in Idlib from across the whole ideological spectrum confirmed that the dynamic of change within HTS was genuine. They mainly disagreed about their criticism of al-Sharaa's opportunism, praise for his pragmatism or their fear of the risk of a "dilution" (*tami'a*) of the fundamentals (*thawabit*) of the jihadi movement.[20] The evolution of the group before the liberation of Damascus helps us articulate the strategic vision of the movement before it formed the new Syrian government. It also historicises these changes in order to re-think these transformations beyond the overused categories of "moderation" and "pragmatism."

Recent transformations before 2025 suggested that HTS was committed to the establishment of a Thermidorian situation, which captures an inversion in the revolutionary dynamic in which an actor who embodied a radical break is now more oriented toward power consolidation than imposing disruptive transformations on the social fabric.[21] The political context in Idlib before 2025 was Thermidorian in more than one way: disenchantment with the revolutionary utopia, postponement of armed struggle, renunciation of utopia in governance, reliance on external actors, rediscovery of social inertia and marginalisation of hardcore segments of the movement.

The disenchanted relationship of HTS's leadership with local power structures is the first illustration of the Thermidorian situation in Idlib. The Salvation Government was a "provisional reality"[22] qualified as a "government caretaker" by Ahmad al-Sharaa[23] or a "technocratic government" by its leading staff.[24] The disenchanted outlook on local governance should not be pejoratively described as an act of renunciation. It also opened up opportunities for the movement to regain the initiative by thinking in terms of previously unthinkable alliances, including a patronage relationship with Turkey and a search for normalisation with Western countries. For an informed local analyst, HTS was in an "opening" process as it became "a movement capable of realism." The objective was, before 2024, less about taking over Damascus than to stay in power and organise the rebel territories.

Second, Thermidor is the rediscovery of "social inertia", and the need for political negotiation in a context of "real society's revenge on ideology." The revenge of society was found at all levels of the political project. The theological relocalisation of the group was Thermidorian. So were the return to the schools of jurisprudence, the marginalisation of divisive concepts and the reliance on the lower clergy entail the recognition of the autonomy of society. In this process of rapprochement with the local population, society set the tone, irrigated public discourse and shaped the normative project. As the group's leader explained, "our policy derives from the conditions of the context. We do not follow any particular shaykh or a certain reference. Our reference is the surrounding reality—*al-waqi'a.*"[25] In other words, the focus on the local was also the end of the illusion of a potential *tabula rasa*. This marked a significant reversal. The movement had to adapt to society more than radically reform it. It was "transformed by the people".

The reopening of the game of alliance authorised by revolutionary disenchantment and the revenge of society imposed significant constraints on HTS. The population, Turkish demands and anticipation of Western expectations did not, *de facto*, authorise a safe haven or a radical emirate. The emirate idea was unacceptable to Turkey and the other factions with which HTS cooperated. Second, the choice to bring religion closer to the population meant that any proclaimed Islamic project becomes risky because, according to a local analyst close to HTS:

> Having an emirate presupposes the application of standards. From this point of view, renouncing the emirate is paradoxically a response to the radicals. The stake is there: proclaiming an emirate exposes the party taking the initiative to certain standards that HTS, for reasons of management of its social bases, prefers not to apply.[26]

The apolitical presentation of the Salvation Government followed the same logic: in order to neutralise radical criticisms that Idlib did not conform to their conception of an Islamic order, it depoliticised that very local political order in the absence of a capability or willingness to Islamise it.

This brings us to the third characteristic of a Thermidorian situation: the need to neutralise hardliners that refuse to abide by the conservative redirection of the revolutionary dynamic. Their belligerence had two rationales. First, war is self-justifying. It is a religious imperative, *fard 'ayn*, that defines both the means and the end. This is a common criticism of al-Qaeda, which groups like Ahrar al-Sham and HTS denounce for emphasising jihad as an end in itself. Second, war paid dividends. Foreign aid for jihad requires active fronts to enable cash flow and, later, spoils of war. War was therefore an existential necessity for them as much as a moral ideal. On the other hand, active conflict was counterproductive for HTS for three reasons. War set in motion an unfavourable balance of power. The movement could not hold out militarily against the regime and the Russians. Moreover, war could thwart the policy of sanctuary promoted by Turkey and, last, the Salvation Government's political economy (including the taxation of goods and expansion of projects) needed truces.

Three policies can be instituted with radicals: distancing, marginalisation and confrontation. HTS resorted to all of them. The movement distanced itself from al-Qaeda General Command. Severing ties with al-Qaeda in 2016 fits well in a Thermidorian logic since the umbilical cord with the original matrix was a hindrance at all levels. These ties prevented political reversals and the development of a new approach to resilience entailing the practical abandonment of active war fronts, which were replaced by the collective self-defence of the province for more than four years up to the December 2024 victory. Moreover, the allegiance impeded the theological relocalisation inherent in the rediscovery of the inertia of society. In July 2020, HTS unleashed a confrontation with Hurras al-Din, the last al-Qaeda franchise refusing sanctuary and its political (alliance with Turkey) or military (renouncing a logic of active war) constraints. Finally, HTS marginalised hard-core religious scholars that remained purists and unable to adapt to the inertia of society. Some were excluded from the movement, others were relegated to the administration of justice and other clerics were silenced through the institutionalisation of the production of religious norms by the movement. As a result, according to an HTS advisor, already in 2019:

> Ahmad al-Sharaa is now in a position of strength. There is no strong opposition from within anymore and he now feels secure. But he is also very keen to consult. He does not want to impose ideas on others and ask them to obey. He wants to convince them. In order to deal with it, political decisions are channelled into the religious leadership of the movement in order to ensure their support. This process of internal transformation is real. But it takes time.[27]

Ahmad al-Sharaa's strategic vision coalesced in this Thermidorian context. He acknowledged the prevailing balance of power on the ground without supporting a 'political solution' imposed from outside. He explained that "the convergence of interests will never work. The interests are too divergent. How can we imagine that Israel, Turkey, the US, Russia, Saudi Arabia, and Iran can find common ground? It is not possible."[28] Al-Sharaa was convinced that the conflict would be suspended rather than politically solved. He understood that the main objective was therefore to consolidate the ceasefire: "if we can no longer progress then at least stay where we are, protect the populations, and organise ourselves already here."[29] An informed analyst added in May 2019, when the last round of confrontations with the regime and Russia had only just begun, that HTS's leadership saw a "Syria divided into three zones and as many protectors. HTS's strategic objective is to preserve this territory because if it loses it, it would be the end of the revolution. And, for that, HTS must open up to the West."[30] Echoing those views, al-Sharaa explained that "the maintenance of Bashar al-Assad in power will lead to the partition of the country. Only regime change can maintain the unity of the country."[31] The only viable option was therefore to remain resilient while awaiting a transformation of the balance of power on the international scene and seeking to graft onto the geostrategic game. The two essential objectives of the movement stemmed from this assessment: to consolidate its social base internally and to work on its political acceptance externally.

The first objective unfolded through the suspension of the normative project and adaptation to the local context. "We don't have a ready-made project. Our point of reference is the context in which we are. We will also strengthen the acceptability of our project by taking it into account."[32] Nevertheless, the quest for social acceptance was not yet sought through a major revision of HTS's human rights record. The second objective, entering the geostrategic game, pushed the movement to actively support Turkey's strategy of sanctuarisation in the hope that, in the long term, cooperation on the ground would be transformed into a strategic relationship with its neighbour in the north playing the role of "protector." This would then allow HTS to seek alignment with the West on the basis of a sense of shared interests, such as opposition to the regime, Islamic State, and Iran, and the desire to organise the population locally and avoid a spill-over of refugees.

Al-Sharaa nevertheless had no clear vision of an endgame before the 2024 takeover, nor HTS's role in it.[33] This was for two reasons. First of all, al-Sharaa's vision was a survival strategy. A long-term strategic vision was inherently difficult to coalesce since HTS constantly adapted to short-term circumstances. But ambiguity also had its merits. The absence of a clearly articulated endgame vision allowed the group to manage its internal contradictions and to appease its more radical constituencies, avoiding the risk of alienating them through an ideological shift that might otherwise have been perceived as too abrupt and divisive. At the same time, a half-hearted ideological clarification carries the risk of backfiring at the international level, as state actors may interpret such gestures as insufficient and remain reluctant to engage.[34]

From this point of view, al-Sharaa's vision was indeed Thermidorian. The self-defined "revolutionary Islamist" leader no longer believed in salvation only through revolutionary action, but through support from external forces.[35] He adopted a posture of wait-and-see that reflected a principle of resilience and dependency on foreign forces that was inward-oriented, since it entailed a prioritisation of governance and the management of the territory more than the immediate takeover of Damascus.

12

IDEOLOGICAL RECENTRING IN AN AGE OF ILLIBERALISM

Though HTS's experience is unique, it offers a distinct perspective on what political Islam might become. Islamism itself remains politically undefined since it remains a loosely structured ideological framework that provides minimal direct political guidance beyond invoking Islam in governance and society.[1] This is comparable to socialism, which has given rise to vastly different movements, from European social democracy to violent regimes like the Khmer Rouge—the equivalent of Islamic State in Islamist terms. Operating within a diverse range of concrete power dynamics—many of which have little in common across different national contexts, the Islamist sphere encompasses a broad spectrum of actors, from IS to Turkey's AKP and Tunisia's Ennahda, each operating under vastly different conditions, from civil wars to semi-authoritarian states defined by fluctuating political opportunities and constraints.

HTS stands out as one of the few Sunni Islamist movements to have genuinely and sustainably established territorial control. The two other contemporary examples—both of which HTS is keenly aware of—are Hamas's governance of Gaza until 7 October 2023, and the Taliban's rule in Afghanistan, though HTS did not replicate Hamas' authoritarianism nor the Taliban's rigid religious edicts. While Turkey's AKP is a noteworthy example, it has largely distanced itself from Islamism over the past two decades. The Muslim Brotherhood's rule in Egypt from 2012 to 2013 was also both short-lived and limited, as the military retained ultimate control of the state. Similarly, while IS briefly held territory in Iraq and Syria, its so-called "provinces" elsewhere remain loosely organised, including

ISWAP in Nigeria, while the al-Qaeda franchise al-Shabaab in Somalia primarily operates in rural areas. This also makes HTS the only movement with roots in jihadi Salafism that has successfully exercised governance—though only after abandoning jihadism and hollowing out Salafism from its political and societal demands.

The limited number of enduring Islamist governance experiences leads us to expand the HTS comparison beyond strictly Islamist cases. More importantly, no Islamist movement has pursued a path of deradicalisation while operating from a position of strength. We discussed in Chapter 11 HTS within an "Islamist" framework—somewhere between the Muslim Brotherhood, Salafis, and jihadis, though we found that reality defies current classifications. These established categories allow us to define HTS only in negative terms: it is easier to identify what HTS no longer is—global jihadis, Salafis, or Muslim Brothers—or what it has not become, such as a new iteration of political Islam, than to precisely define what it is today. The only broad label that might apply is "traditionalist", however, this remains too vague to account for the transformations that have occurred within HTS and offers limited utility for capturing the movement's current reality.

Thus, while we discuss religious categories and analytical frameworks to analyse HTS, our approach does not rely on Islamic studies. Instead, through recurring references to the French Revolution we have sought to present HTS's history in a way that, perhaps ambitiously, strives for a degree of universality. This explains our frequent use of concepts and historical parallels from outside the Islamic world that provide valuable analytical insights into the group's trajectory. By doing so, we aim to move beyond an exclusive reliance on the well-established—though undoubtedly rich—findings of jihadi groups. We wish to conclude in the same spirit.

HTS's trajectory has revolved around two principal axes: an ideological realignment toward the centre, and a Thermidorian shift marked by the abandonment of aspirations in favor of an ideological tabula rasa and, instead, the endorsement of a strategic reliance on the silent majority. This shift was never openly acknowledged and did not stem from an outright rejection of the revolution itself. The movement's leadership consistently spoke of and aspired to

IDEOLOGICAL RECENTRING IN AN AGE OF ILLIBERALISM

a revolutionary breakthrough—the capture of Damascus—while maintaining its arsenal and continuing localised confrontations with the regime. However, from as early as 2017, and especially between 2017 and 2024, political calculations increasingly diverged from a strictly revolutionary agenda. The primary focus shifted toward consolidating control over acquired territories, developing a bureaucratic structure, positioning itself as the representative of the Syrian revolution, avoiding military overstretch, and securing opportunities for continued armed activity.[2] Since 2019, however, HTS's military engagements had largely targeted other opposition groups rather than the regime. In 2019, its primary objective was to consolidate control over Idlib at the expense of mainstream revolutionary factions, while in 2022–23, it sought to assert dominance over the Free Syrian Army's zones north of Aleppo. These actions reflected a hegemonic strategy within the revolutionary camp rather than a push for a grand revolutionary breakthrough against the regime. Thus, HTS's temporary departure from the revolution is best understood as an objective shift in political priorities rather than a strategic renunciation of revolutionary ideals.

Ideological realignment was closely linked to relocalisation and incorporated elements of deradicalisation. It unfolded through mechanisms explored throughout this book, including a hegemonic strategy—where, from the summer of 2020 onward, HTS shifted from a policy of containment to direct confrontation with radicals, including al-Qaeda, Islamic State, and their affiliates. Other key dynamics shaping this shift included the assertion of "social inertia," "societal revenge," the reinforcing effects of a "virtuous circle," and the establishment of thresholds of no return. These mechanisms collectively explain how the book's two central themes—the departure from the revolution and ideological realignment—materialised in practice.

The analytical framework offered by traditional Islamic studies provides limited conceptual tools for grasping the current trajectory of the movement. To more effectively understand its evolution, it is useful to draw comparisons with movements that have undergone analogous processes of centrist ideological realignment. In this regard, HTS's ideological repositioning bears greater resemblance to the trajectory of far-right political parties than to earlier jihadi experiences. Such parties have often adopted strategies aimed at distancing themselves from the political extremes, typically in contexts marked by relative strength, an ambition to attain power, and minimal engagement in doctrinal refinement.

A time of evanescent radicalism: The crosscurrents of the centre and extremes

As HTS's political and religious radicalism softened, the revolutionary centre has become a fertile ground for the resurgence of radicalism, extreme centre is not the radicalisation of the mainstream. It is a policy of deligitimisation of political competition in positioning itself as the center and disqualifiying all alternatives as radicals. Both the lobbying for the pro-morality law and the 2024 anti-HTS protests exemplified the emergence of a new form of radicalism—one that is not jihadi but rather populist-Islamist. This radicalism arose from Idlib's ideological centre, shaped by a blend of revolutionary and socially conservative elements, without needing to attribute it to a clandestine resurgence of al-Qaeda or Islamic State.

With the public morality law, "moral entrepreneurs" sought to impose Islamic norms in the public sphere—an initiative Ahmad al-Sharaa would have preferred to avoid.[3] This forced HTS's leader into a delicate balancing act: quietly freezing a law that was not particularly Islamist while being unable to openly reject it. After all, public morality and moral policing are standard tools of legitimation and control in contemporary Arab states. The anti-HTS protests from February to July 2024 marked another manifestation of radicalism emerging from the mainstream. During this period, the streets of Idlib and surrounding towns witnessed a renewed wave of revolutionary intransigence, with demands for al-Sharaa's ouster, the dissolution of General Security, the release of all prisoners, and, on the fringes, calls for the restoration of the caliphate, full implementation of Islamic law, and even the establishment of … a morality police.

HTS's response—sustaining street protests and deploying a show of force for nearly six months—underscores the consolidation of a low-intensity authoritarian regime. The strategy relied on self restraint, minimal arrests, the absence of violent suppression, repeated calls for dialogue, and significant concessions on issues such as taxation and detentions. Throughout the unrest, HTS engaged in continuous popular consultations, reinforcing its image as a regime willing to negotiate rather than outright repress. Ultimately, it considered elections as a principle for rotating authority but confined them strictly to non-sovereign civil institutions, excluding critical domains such as security, the military apparatus, and economic control.

As with the debate over the public morality law, the *hirak* protests marked another moment of reaffirmation of a radicalised mainstream, again manifesting through religious populism. Once more, HTS found itself outflanked on its right. Within the anti-authoritarian movement led by the *hirak*, Hizb al-Tahrir reiterated its demand for the establishment of a caliphate, while some clerics framed the implementation of Shari'a as the ultimate safeguard against torture. Meanwhile, HTS's proposed reforms—particularly its cautious political opening through elections—became a focal point for populist criticism. Debates over the potential inclusion of women and minorities in these reforms fuelled a backlash, with some social media voices branding Ahmad al-Sharaa a puppet of the West and an agent of democracy, effectively casting him into the camp of the "enemies of God."

We thus observe a dynamic of reversal: the mainstream, caught between rising revolutionary intransigence and Islamic populism, absorbs radicalism and reveals itself to be far less centrist—if it ever truly was. Meanwhile, HTS's own radicalism was scaled back, both in its religious dimension as it moved away from its early Salafi adherence and in its political approach when rigid authoritarianism gave way to a more strategic and measured management of dissent. In this dialectical shift between the centre and the extremes, ideological boundaries blurred, and positions became deterritorialised: radicalism was no longer confined to a specific faction or ideology, just as centrism could now emerge from what were once the peripheries of extremism.

Ultimately, the real challenge lies in the very notion of radicalism. As it evolves, radicalism becomes diffuse—shaped by the simultaneous deradicalisation of extremes on one side and the consolidation of an "extreme centre" on the other, as outlined in Chapters 6 and 8. Rather than vanishing, radicalism becomes elusive.

Nine lessons on centrist ideological realignments

Such blurring of ideological categories is hardly new, and history offers numerous examples of centric ideological realignment: a segment of the communist left 'social-democratised' in the early twentieth century, while far-right parties began to "de-demonise," to use the head of France's National Rally Marine Le Pen's term, at the start of the next.[4] From a broader perspective, what does the HTS experience reveal about the dynamics of ideological realignment?

1. Ideological realignments are never purely instrumental

No centrist ideological realignment is purely instrumental. It inevitably provokes a backlash, disrupts internal coherence, and generates significant internal tensions. In many cases, maintaining cohesion requires internal purges. HTS exemplifies this pattern: its realignment has been marked by splits, including the pro al-Qaeda Hurras al-Din, defections, marginalisations, amicable separations, and dismissals. In short, ideological realignments rarely occur without substantial internal friction, and it is the radical fringes that bear the brunt. Realignments, therefore, deradicalise 'in the negative': rather than fostering moderation, it expels the most intransigent members, forcing them into silence or exile. This, in turn, creates the conditions for a self-reinforcing cycle of transformation.

2. Ideological realignments also depend on the condition of the central actors

The centrist ideological realignment of radical movements depends on the strength of the centre—its ideological coherence, organisational capacity, popularity, and mobilisation power. The weaker the centre, the easier the realignment. With less competition, realigned former radicals can position themselves as viable alternatives. In Idlib, this dynamic was particularly evident: the revolutionary centre collapsed and left a void to be filled. This collapse manifested in several ways. First, militarily, the centre disintegrated—Free Syrian Army factions that once embodied it lost the war against radicals and forfeited its credibility with the population. Second, in governance, the revolutionary centre eroded—local councils were dismantled in 2017 and 2019 as the Syrian Salvation Government consolidated power, and their failure to institutionalise effectively further weakened their legitimacy. Third, the centre's political capacity fragmented—so-called revolutionary political bodies are inert, leaderless, and divided, unable to respond to the resurgence of protests in the spring of 2024. Finally, externally, no credible representation remained—the Opposition Coalition functions more as a symbolic entity than a legitimate representative, having lost influence both domestically and internationally.

3. No ideological realignment occurs without a transformation of the centre …

Ideological centrist realignments transform the 'centre' itself. Even if the centre no longer exists as an active force, it endures as a political culture, shaping the contours of an ideological mainstream. However, this mainstream is not static—it evolves in response to the dynamics of the 'extreme centre.' Just as France experienced the *lepénisation des esprits* for Pierre-André Taguieff, who described the gradual normalisation and mainstreaming of far-right ideas associated with Jean-Marie Le Pen, here we observe a diffuse, elusive influence that resurfaces unpredictably in the political arena when opportunities arise, such as Islamist populist lobbying for a public morality law or the instrumentalisation of the 2024 protest movements to advance religious agendas. In other words, realignment is not a one-way process in which only radical actors shift toward the centre; the centre itself is reshaped in the process. It is not a fixed ideological anchor but a fluid space that mutates by absorbing elements from its radical fringes. This occurs through two key mechanisms: the increasing disinhibition of grassroots militant culture and the radicalisation of right-wing policies on issues such as immigration and security.

4. ... nor any centrist ideological realignments without differentiation from the radical ecosystem

On the other side, no ideological realignment occurs without fierce confrontation—sometimes marked by violence and bloodshed, as in Idlib. HTS's attempt to negotiate a peaceful separation from al-Qaeda failed to some extent.[5] Large numbers of refuseniks broke away, took up arms, upheld the original organisational and ideological line, endured containment efforts, and, by the summer of 2020, engaged in open armed clashes with HTS. In short, ideological realignments are rarely a smooth transition. It almost inevitably leads to a sharp and often violent rupture between those shifting toward the centre and the 'ultras'—whether radical-right factions or jihadi Salafis refuse to abandon their original positions.

In this context, it is crucial to distinguish between the different dimensions of realignment and their respective criteria: external communication, policy programmes and public initiatives, partisan alliances, the militant ecosystem, and the doctrinal foundation.

The National Rally in France serves as a useful benchmark for ideological realignments, though its trajectory presents a mixed record. On one hand, its communication strategy is clear—exemplified by Marine Le Pen's 2018 push for 'de-demonisation' and now embodied by Jordan Bardella's carefully cultivated "ideal son-in-law" image. However, realignment extends beyond rhetoric. The party also signaled a break with its fascist legacies by relegating Jean-Marie Le Pen to the past, reinforcing its shift toward broader electoral legitimacy.

Partisan alliances have also undergone significant recalibration. The National Rally distanced itself from traditionalist Catholics while maintaining ambiguous ties with the most radical factions of the French far right, including neo-Nazi movements and hardline identitarian groups. At the same time, it made unsuccessful attempts to forge closer ties with the Republican right. Though these efforts did not yield lasting alliances, they helped blur the boundaries between the National Rally and mainstream right-wing parties. On the European stage, the National Rally played a key role in establishing the Identity and Democracy (ID) group in the European Parliament, uniting nationalist and Eurosceptic parties such as Matteo Salvini's Italian League and Geert Wilders's Party for Freedom in the Netherlands. However, it remained cautious about aligning with even more extreme or controversial parties like Greece's Golden Dawn or Hungary's Jobbik.

However, the National Rally's policy proposals remain largely anchored in the traditional repertoire of the radical right. While it has avoided endorsing overtly extreme measures—such as "remigration," the mass expulsion of foreigners in precarious or irregular situations, as advocated by Germany's AfD—it continues to maintain personal ties with far-right extremist groups like the GUD (*Groupe Union Défense*) and other ultranationalist factions. As a result, its affiliations and militant base continue to straddle the margins of mainstream politics.

In Idlib, the rupture appeared even more pronounced. The de-demonisation strategy was evident—marked by public disengagement from al-Qaeda, outreach to minorities, and engagement with Western media and think tanks. At the same time, the fragmentation of the radical Salafi jihadi ecosystem was both extensive and violent. Clashes and security crackdowns targeted factions aligned with al-Qaeda or IS cells, while radicals were expelled, subdued, or detained in an effort to consolidate control.

The movement's policies fully realigned. Normative projects were restrained—even under counter pressures from the base, as seen in Chapter 6 with the public morality law. Ideological sectors were delegated to external actors, such as Western NGOs for education and the local lower clergy for preaching, albeit without a specific ideological agenda. The movement also adhered to international commitments, including the ceasefire negotiated by Turkey with Russia. Meanwhile, HTS's alliance-building strategies—often designed to secure dominance—targeted the centre. This included co-opting former figures from the 2011 revolutionary movement, fostering clientelistic ties with Free Syrian Army factions, and making symbolic concessions to the "centre," such as participating in commemorations of the 2011 Syrian revolution.

Regarding its doctrinal framework, while HTS's revolution remained largely unarticulated in ideological revisions—likely for some time—it nonetheless fully realigned. This is evident in its endorsement of the dominant jurisprudential school in Idlib,

Shafi'ism, an implicit renunciation of Salafism in HTS-controlled religious schools and the Shari'a Faculty at Idlib University, and the introduction of deradicalisation courses for fighters. These steps were motivated not by a preference for a "moderate" approach to Islam but by the need to prevent splits and a drift towards more radical factions, similar to the militant exodus experienced by Jabhat al-Nusra in 2013 with the rise of IS.

Thus, while the de-demonisation strategy of the National Rally extends beyond communication efforts, and despite significant fractures, the continuity between the radical ideological ecosystem and the party remains strong, in contrast, HTS's radical ideological ecosystem has been deeply disrupted due to years of factional conflicts and multiple purges.

5. Ideological reorientation: More than just ideology

Ideological reorientation—and the resulting deradicalisation—often occurs more through practice than through formal ideological shifts. There is no *aggiornamento*, new theology, or *muraja'at* (revisions). The revolution remains silent. Political calculations and power struggles drive the shift in ideas, not doctrinal revolutions. In France, the National Rally's de-demonisation has primarily been a matter of style—embodied by the polished image of Jordan Bardella—and political communication, rather than a deep doctrinal transformation. As a result, the movement's political culture sometimes lags behind; mid-level leaders, when tweeting or preaching, often express xenophobic or sectarian views within both the RN and HTS ranks. These remarks are less about exposing the "true face" of the movement and more about the challenging adjustment of militant cultures to a new political direction that lacks a clear doctrinal framework. On the HTS side, the militant culture has consistently lagged behind the political shifts of the leadership. Lingering sectarian tendencies and the persistence of Salafi postures still permeate the ranks, partially explaining some of the abuses at the grassroots level, particularly during the sectarian violence of March 2025.

At first glance, the "silent revolution" may seem like a weakness, one that could be remedied by a later doctrinal "coming out"—but this is not necessarily the case! Rather than indicating a lack or void, the silent revolution is more akin to "heresthetic", as defined by William Riker. It should be understood as a fully political act. For Riker, "heresthetic" refers to the art of framing a political situation in such a way that a difficult decision is presented to the public without challenging their underlying preferences and principles—in other words, without directly contradicting their likely convictions. To argue against these convictions could reignite old disputes and spark dangerous controversy. The goal is to avoid getting bogged down in doctrinal revisions or *aggiornamento*, as seen in the debates within jihadi groups. A formal charter or clarifying founding document is therefore unlikely to emerge anytime soon.

6. Politics is only part of it: Ideological realignment is always an interaction with society

Ideological realignments are never purely political; they are deeply intertwined with society and shaped by phenomena such as Bayart's "revenge of society" and Furet's "inertia of the social". Just as HTS was compelled to reckon with the socio-religious realities of its local context, European far-right parliamentary parties too must engage with their own sociological realities—namely, the modern behaviour and practices shaped by cultural and sexual revolutions.[6] While HTS moved away from its Salafi past, rejecting an exclusive focus on prophetic revelation as its ideological lens, the dominant European far-right parties, though identitarian in many respects, no longer idealise a "Judeo-Christian" identity, regardless of how this concept is interpreted. Nor do they reject the liberal values that evolved from the May 1968 movements onwards.

Significant segments of today's parliamentary far-right have adapted to sociocultural shifts, including recognising homosexuality—some leaders, like Geert Wilders, even openly support it. These parties no longer advocate for a traditional family model; both Giorgia Meloni and Marine Le Pen are unmarried, and neither is homophobic. Le Pen, for example, did not oppose same-sex marriage during France's "marriage for all" debate in 2012–13. Additionally, anti-abortion stances have proven electorally unappealing. "In terms of society, values, and culture, a large portion of the far-right has shifted towards the centre, integrating the new parameters of sociological modernity that began to take shape in the 1960s."⁷ As a result, in terms of society, values, and culture, a substantial portion of the far-right has shifted toward the centre, integrating the new parameters of sociological modernity that emerged in the 1960s. The "revenge of society" thus applies equally to these realigned far-right movements.

7. Reversals are the exception

Ideological realignments are durable and rarely followed by reversals or "re-radicalisation" backlashes. The trajectory is generally consistent: shedding old legacies, such as former Waffen-SS members associated with Jean-Marie Le Pen or the global jihadis with HTS, distancing from the margins—whether neo-Nazis, fascist groups, or various Salafi jihadi factions—and gravitating toward the "centre". This centre can be defined politically as with the revolution in Idlib, religiously as with the broad Sunni consensus, or sociologically as a synthesis between revolutionary austerity and post-war openness. Striving for the centre imposes constraints that fundamentally reshape the nature of the actors undergoing realignment, even when this is viewed primarily as a tactical objective. The durability of this shift is supported by various mechanisms of deradicalisation, as outlined throughout this book: the ratchet effect, the logic of no return, and the virtuous cycle.

Reversals are rare. Iran is likely the only case of re-radicalisation among revolutionary actors following a Thermidorian phase, and this occurred because the regime remained divided between reformist Thermidorians and a deep state that was more rigidly attached to the original orthodoxy.⁸ The latter was never truly weakened by the rise of reformists. In Idlib, however, where the deep state itself—namely, al-Sharaa's inner circle—established the Thermidorian regime, a reversal would have been unlikely for the reasons evoked above.

8. Electoral calculations are not the only political rationale behind the reorientation

The shift toward the centre is not necessarily the exclusive product of electoral dynamics within an institutionalised and democratic political field. Generally speaking, it is the institutionalisation of these groups—through their insertion into the parliamentary process and electoral calculations—that drives such a transformation. However, in Idlib, the ideological reorientation does not stem from electoral rationality since there is no institutionalised political game in Syria; rather, it is driven by political calculations of a different nature.

Three factors played a particular role. First, the pursuit of social peace and efforts to ensure the movement's acceptability in Idlib. HTS operated in a context where it could not—or did not wish to—subjugate society through force, in contrast to the strategy adopted by Islamic State. Second, HTS bet on its international acceptability: as HTS took over responsibility for administering northwest Syria, it became crucial for the group to engage with the international community. HTS operated in a neoliberal mode, with limited resources, a minimal state, and a strong tendency to delegate service provision—including ideologically charged services like education—to civil society, specifically international actors such as NGOs and the UN. Consequently, HTS depended heavily on Western aid. Third, the ideological reorientation was motivated by the desire to represent the revolution and, simultaneously, provide an alternative to the regime. This explained the group's efforts to engage with minorities, among other considerations.

9. Ideological realignments and the issue of authoritarianism

Ideological realignments can shape the nature of authoritarianism, though there is no automatic correlation between the two. In Europe, the mainstreaming of far-right movements has at times coincided with an authoritarian drift within liberal democracies—seen in increasingly militarised crowd control tactics, restrictive immigration policies, censorship of discourse on Islam, and curbs on civil liberties through counterterrorism measures. In Idlib, the combination of ideological recalibration and the retreat from revolutionary ambitions not only led to a relaxation in the enforcement of religious norms, unlike the Taliban, which reaffirmed strict moral policing in 2024, but also to a relative reduction in political authoritarianism. Unlike Hamas in Gaza (2007–23) or the Thermidorian regime in post-revolutionary France, HTS distanced itself both from religious radicalism (by abandoning Salafi norms and global jihadi networks) and, to a lesser extent, from outright political repression. HTS incorporated revolutionary ideals and co-opted segments of the opposition; while dissent was occasionally met with force, and torture in detention centres remained a reality, there was growing resistance to such practices. In response to radical opposition, HTS even considered introducing limited electoral mechanisms in its governance.

HTS did not govern as the stereotypical "Oriental despot" in the mould of Abdel Fattah al-Sisi or Bashar al-Assad, nor did it allow genuine political pluralism. Similar to Morocco's political model, HTS made significant concessions to protesters to maintain social stability, granted limited oversight powers to parliament and the government, but ultimately kept the deep state unchanged and power tightly controlled. By shifting responsibility for day-to-day governance, social policy, and parts of the economy onto controlled political structures, HTS retained ultimate authority while mitigating direct opposition.

While ideological moderation often entails both a softening of religious strictures and a reduction in political repression, these two shifts are not causally linked. The latter is not an inevitable consequence of the former. Instead, both are byproducts of HTS's broader political strategy, driven by objectives such as social peace, national legitimacy—framing itself as a revolution for all Syrians, including engagement with Christians, Druze, and Kurds—and international recognition. Once again, political calculus—not ideological transformation—determined both the movement's stance on religious governance and its approach to authoritarianism.

Contrary to the beliefs of the former al-Qaeda mufti, Mahfouz Ould al-Walid, better known as Abu Hafs al-Mauritani,[9] HTS is not a model destined to be emulated in the region. Abu Hafs believed that jihadi groups in similar contexts might follow the Syrian organisation in its path of ideological recalibration. However, there are no comparable contexts: HTS's trajectory is too specific and is unlikely to find many emulators in the region. By extension, it cannot provide normative recipes for deradicalisation. We should understand HTS for what it is: a revealing case that sheds light on the broader issue of centric ideological realignments. It is more reflective of the "global zeitgeist"[10] than a solution to the persistent issue of global jihad. HTS's recent trajectory is intellectually compelling, yet it will have little global impact on the war on terror. At best, the West lost a former adversary and may have secured a strategic ally.

EPILOGUE

IN SEARCH OF ITSELF: THE AMBIGUOUS RISE OF SUNNI IDENTITY POLITICS

The Idlib matrix in power in Damascus

On 27 November 2024, the HTS-led alliance—previously organised around the Fath al-Mubin operations room, rebranded as the Administration of Military Operations—launched a new round of hostilities. Within days, what began as a localised offensive aimed at advancing the eastern frontlines of Idlib toward Aleppo successfully shattered regime defences. The coalition rapidly reached Aleppo before turning southward, advancing through Hama and Homs, and ultimately toward Damascus. HTS and its allies were soon joined by other factions, including groups affiliated with the Syrian National Army in the north, as well as a range of armed actors from southern Syria.

On 8 December HTS formally assumed control of the new government. Ahmad al-Sharaa, now using his real name, took the helm of the country and formed a caretaker administration. His political advisor, Asaad al-Shaibani, was appointed Minister of Foreign Affairs. HTS's military chief, Murhaf Abu Qasra, became Minister of Defence, while Anas Khatab, head of the group's intelligence apparatus, was named head of Syria's national intelligence before taking the position of Minister of Interior. Alongside Abd al-Rahim Atun, HTS's senior religious figure, and current religious advisor to the president, the core leadership that had guided the group's break from Islamic State and al-Qaeda—and charted its new strategic course—now held the reins of state power.

To conclude this book, our aim is not to provide an exhaustive account of a post-victory transition that remains fluid and largely shaped by the ad hoc decisions of the new government in response to shifting circumstances. Instead, we narrow our focus to the trajectory of ideological mainstreaming in Idlib and reflect on how this new revolutionary chapter sheds light on the central theme of our book: the dynamics of centrist ideological realignment and the corresponding transformation of radicalism.

A new Sunni pride rooted in the Umayyad legacy

On Friday, 21 February 2025, the Umayyad Mosque was preparing for a sermon by Shaykh Yassine Alloush. A prominent figure and former Dean of the Faculty of Shari'a in Idlib, Alloush is a native of Idlib and a key architect of the new dispensation's policy direction. He acted as a mediator on many occasions between Jabhat al-Nusra and other revolutionary factions in Idlib between 2014 and 2015, while maintaining a position that aligned with neither the Sufi nor Salafi approaches to Islam.

Just two days before the scheduled funeral of Hassan Nasrallah—the former leader of Hezbollah—the broader regional mood was one of acute polarisation. Inside the mosque, however, it was calm. Sufi devotional circles (*halaqat*) made up of shaykhs in traditional red and black garments engaged in mystical chants for nearly an hour as they awaited the Qur'anic recitations that traditionally precede the sermon.

With the traditional sword at his side—a symbol historically associated with Friday sermons since the era of Mu'awiya Ibn Abi Sufyan, the first Umayyad caliph and a figure often invoked by contemporary Sunnis as a model of political leadership—shaykh Yassin anchored his sermon firmly in contemporary events. He did not hesitate to condemn "Hizb al-Shaytan" (the 'Party of the Devil'), a pejorative term now entrenched in the lexicon of contemporary Sunni populism to disparage Hezbollah, the party of God. Yet, as observed by researcher and political sciences professor Mohamed-Ali Adraoui—whose detailed account informs the description above and who was present during the sermon—the shaykh maintained a stance of 'historical neutrality,' deliberately avoiding any engagement with the deep theological schism that has long divided Sunni and Shia traditions.

EPILOGUE

The scene effectively encapsulates the current reality of HTS, now the backbone of the new government in Syria: the consolidation of dominance over a clearly defined territorial base from Damascus; an opening toward the Sunni 'silent majority,' inclusive of historically established Sufi elements; and HTS's mobilising invocation of Umayyad heritage through the lens of 'Sunni pride' connected to its geo-strategic assertion against the Iranian axis, all the while consciously avoiding overtly anti Shia sectarian rhetoric. The sword placed beside Yassin Alloush harks back to the venerable Umayyad tradition and conveys a powerful message of Sunni reclamation of power, signalling their return to their historic position at the helm of the state.

The sword is but one element in a broader remobilisation of the Umayyad legacy. Just days before Shaykh Yassin's sermon, on 19 February Musa al-Omar—a prominent journalist supportive of the new government—posted a video on his X account showing Sharaa on horseback, set to a song that opened with the line: "*The Umayyads are of golden lineage; their name sent fear in Persian kings; books cannot praise them enough*".[1] And this phenomenon extends well beyond presidential propaganda. The white flags bearing the black *shahada* (the Muslim profession of faith)—sold by street vendors across the capital—and the frequent references to Banu Umayya (the Umayyad dynasty) on social media have become ubiquitous. These symbols function variously as expressions of Sunni pride, assertions of symbolic power, and, at times, instruments of intimidation aimed at perceived adversaries.

The presence of the white flag with the black *shahada* during the inaugural session of the interim government in December was swiftly seized upon by critics on social media as the ultimate proof of jihadi continuity among the new rulers in Damascus. In reality, the meaning of the flag itself is evolving. Once adopted by various armed groups as an Islamic symbol meant to counter the black flag with the white *shahada*—popularised by al-Qaeda—the white flag with black script emphasised state-building over perpetual warfare though it is also incidently the flag of the Taliban in Afghanistan. In the new Syria, the white Islamic flag is also the banner of the Umayyads, and today it projects a Syrian-centred Islamic identity. Its revival signals the embedding of a national framework within an Islamist aesthetic—offering a deliberate counter-symbol to the radical universalism of global jihad.

In terms of content, the Umayyad reference emblematically embodies the process of relocalisation, aligning closely with the core tenets of the political project first shaped in Idlib and now asserted in Damascus. Second, it evokes a historical era marked by relative tolerance toward the People of the Book—Jews and Christians—symbolising the delicate balance between Sunni hegemony and limited inclusiveness toward minorities. Third, on a geostrategic level, the Umayyad motif dovetails with HTS's post-2019 doctrine: zero tensions with neighbours and the broader international community, paired with a resolute ideological opposition to Iranian political Shiism and its regional ambitions. The Umayyads, after all, are remembered as the historical antithesis of the Safavids—a Persian dynasty that ruled Iran from the early sixteenth to the eighteenth century and established Twelver Shi'a Islam as the state religion—making the symbol a vehicle for both Western outreach and Arab reconnection.

This Umayyad-centred Sunni pride transcends symbolic discourse and broad political messaging; it is increasingly evident in concrete policy decisions in the realm of religious affairs at the leadership level, even as it simultaneously shapes grassroots identities and community dynamics that often diverge from, or stand in tension with, top-down trends.

Engineering Sunni pride: Thermidor continues with a soft hand on tamkin

It was during its initial seizure of power in Idlib that HTS undertook its 'Thermidorian turn,' moving away from the Salafi ideal of *tabula rasa*—the wholesale purification of creed and society—and instead, began to accommodate the inertia of the social. The group strategically shifted its focus toward the silent majority. Unsurprisingly, now that victory is defined not merely by territorial control but by the ability to govern an entire state, this wager on the silent majority continues to shape its policy.[2]

Religious governance in Damascus illustrates this approach to perfection. Much to the dismay of the shaykhs of global jihad—who have lambasted their former allies for failing to exploit this new phase of *tamkin* (consolidation of power) to implement Islamic law fully and establish an Islamic state—HTS has neither activated nor revived the salafi revolutionary ideal of *tabula rasa*. Instead, it has stayed the course of its Thermidorian centrism, doubling down on the strategy of reliance on the silent majority. In Idlib, this meant preserving the status quo of popular Islam; in Damascus, it translates now into a careful respect for the city's long-established religious equilibria, shaped by elite families and diverse Islamic traditions.

The signs of this respect have been clear. On 6 January 2025, at a condolence ceremony for the death of Saria al-Rifa'i, Ahmad al-Sharaa publicly kissed the head of Usama al-Rifa'i—a senior Damascene shaykh and vocal critic of HTS. The gesture marked not only deference to a prominent figure of traditional Damascus Islam but also an implicit triple recognition: of the Damascene Islamic heritage, of the 'ulama of the opposition, and of the Ash'ari theological tradition. A couple of months afterwards, al-Shara'a appointed Usama al-Rifa'i as Grand Mufti of the Republic, preferring him over HTS's own religious scholars.

This deliberate balancing act between revolutionary, Damascene, Salafi, Ash'ari, and sometimes Sufi elites has now become part of the new religious choreography in the capital.[3] On 19 April Abu al-Khayr Shukri—an Ash'ari-oriented preacher—delivered the Friday sermon at the al-Shafi'i Mosque. After the prayer, worshippers remained to listen to the Sufi chants of Mu'tasim al-Asli, a rising young reciter. Standing beside him was Abd al-Rahim Atun, the chief ideologue behind HTS's ideological realignment—composed and measured, yet unmoved by the religious fervor that envelops some of his fellow believers. The moment confirmed HTS's strategic anchoring in Damascene religious elites: a symbolic and tactical move sending a double message—both domestic and international—underlining the movement's centrist reorientation.

The formation of the new Fatwa Council underscores this break from doctrinal imposition and signals a clear intent to align state institutions with a mainstream Sunni orientation, one that demands a delicate doctrinal balance. The Council's new composition marks a deliberate tilt toward Ash'ari scholars associated with the Keftaro and Rifai circles. The appointment of Abu al-Khayr Shukri as Minister of Religious Affairs—a figure closely aligned with this current—

fits within the same logic, as does the integration of actors linked to the Jama'at Zayd, perceived as a conciliatory gesture between the two dominant religious schools of Damascus.

The newly established Fatwa Council, traditional in its orientation—neither modernist nor radical—is composed of roughly equal numbers of Ash'ari and Salafi scholars. At its core, the Council "seeks to address a fundamental challenge: controlling the production of religious norms to prevent the chaotic proliferation of competing fatwas."[4] If the full extent of its authority remains somewhat unclear, the Council's composition sends a clear message: a deliberate reliance on the major local doctrinal families, aiming to strike a balance between appeasement and institutional credibility.

Still, even the meanings of being Ash'ari or Salafi—traditionally tied to theological creeds that define how one understands God—are themselves evolving. In reality, a broad spectrum of religious scholars—ranging from senior figures in the Shari'a faculty at the University of Damascus to prominent clerics affiliated, or formerly affiliated, with factions such as Jaysh al-Islam and HTS—acknowledge that, in part due to the war, the very meaning of Salafism in Syria has fundamentally changed.[5] The traditional model of Salafism inspired by Saudi influence—often referred to as the Najdi da'wa that has influenced many jihadis—has largely faded and now represents a minority view. In the Council, there is only one Wahhabi Salafi figure: Kheir Allah Talib, a traditional Najdi Salafi who lived in Saudi Arabia. In contrast, many scholars and adherents speak of a return to what they call 'Shami Salafism', a more eclectic and locally rooted tradition that is markedly less sectarian. Shami Salafism retains its Salafi identity, though elements of it increasingly align with the Ash'ari theological school while, on the other hand, some Sufi shaykhs openly acknowledge being influenced by Salafism.

What matters most is perhaps not the balance between the various currents, but rather the fluidity of these categories today. As one Sufi shaykh from Jaysh al-Islam put it, there is an ongoing process of, in his terms, "Salafisation" among segments of the Sufi community and a growing openness of many Salafis to Ash'ari doctrines, particularly in the context of deradicalisation.[6] Ultimately, this is not a case of rigid coexistence between clearly defined and opposing currents, but rather one of fluidity—fluidity of classifications, of ideological identities, and of positions within a religious field that remains in flux and under construction. The Muslim Brotherhood are also part of this fluid religious landscape. If they are not organisationally represented in any of the current institutions, yet some of its members—especially shaykhs trained at Jama'at Zeid— closely align with them. Many of the new technocrats appointed to government ministries come from a younger generation of families once affiliated with the Muslim Brotherhood, but who broke ties with the movement long ago.

HTS has had to navigate the Damascene religious landscape—a sphere it had previously not engaged with—comprised largely of religious institutes organised around prominent preachers. Central to this complex religious-political reconfiguration was Abd al-Rahim Atun. He emphasised to us the principles guiding the formation of the new Council: member competence and representativeness, both territorial and doctrinal.[7] The Council draws figures from across the Syrian governorates, notably Aleppo, Damascus and Homs, including Na'im al-'Irqsusi, Isma'il al-Majzoub, and 'Ala' al-Din al-Qasir—the latter associated with a Sufi lineage. Institutional representation spans influential groups such as the Abu Nur Institute, the al-Fath Institute represented by the Mufti from Damascus 'Abd al-Fattah al-Bazam (he already held this position under Bashar and was kept in office), and Jama'at Zayd, a popular Damascene religious trend with Sufi roots. Yet HTS's intervention was not purely inclusive. It also involved purging elements of the Damascene religious field. This effort was driven less by theological concerns than by political calculations—specifically, the removal of preachers within prominent institutes who were deemed too close to the regime. For example, Husam al-Din Farfour of the al-Fath Institute and his associates were dismissed for their regime affiliations. Similarly, Sharif al-Sawar from the Abu Nur Institute, along with numerous others, was sidelined for past pro-regime activities. In this context, Ahmad al-Sharaa and his inner circle have carefully crafted a balancing act: positioning both Salafi and Sufi figures in parallel, while marginalising more radical elements. This strategy aims to anchor HTS's authority in a version of Damascene Islam that is seen as more institutionalised and broadly consensual.

This is not to suggest that Salafism has vanished from Syria. Within institutions, it remains one actor among others—no longer hegemonic, but still present. On the ground, local power dynamics prevail. Salafism's persistence today is shaped less by top-down directives than by deeply embedded local forces.

The presence of Salafism is entrenched in specific areas. In the Damascus district of Qadam, former combatants returned from Idlib after reconciliation agreements, having become markedly more Salafi. In Duma—long a bastion of Salafism since the 1970s and later reinforced during the war by groups like Jaysh al-Islam—Salafi identity remains strong. In al-Tal, a suburb of Damascus, the return of Abu Malik al-Tali, a key figure in Syrian Jihadi Salafism and a former senior member of Jabhat al-Nusra and HTS, has triggered attempts to take control of mosques and install loyalists. In contrast, in Damascus city, the new authorities have chosen to leave the religious field to the traditionalists. In post-Assad Latakia, Salafis' engagement has evolved from overt coercion—such as armed mosque takeovers—toward more subtle, gendered strategies. After state intervention curtailed direct confrontations, Salafis female preachers (*da'iyat*) have the lead in organising religious study circles (*halaqat*). This shift has marginalizsd rival groups like the Qubaysiyat by limiting their access to mosques and public religious roles. The new, feminised approach is paired with a rigid, sectarian discourse that condemns Shi'ism, Sufism, and Ash'arism as infidels.

Where Salafi actors hold local legitimacy, the new government tolerates their presence—on the condition they stay confined to the mosques. However, when they attempt to assert themselves through force or grassroots agitation, both religious and political authorities tend to coalesce to suppress them. Following the fall of Bashar al-Assad's regime, for instance, young Salafis infiltrated mosques across major cities, occasionally seizing control of the minbar by force, conducting lengthy, ideologically charged training sessions, and aggressively taking to the streets to proselytise—at times even adopting sectarian rhetoric or positioning themselves as moral vigilantes in the absence of a functioning state institution, as we discussed in Chapter 10. In Latakia, for example, a preacher recently arrived from Idlib, and originally from the surrounding countryside, used a mosque sermon to advocate for corporal punishments, full-body veils for women, and the legitimisation of taking female captives (*jawari*). In Damascus, several violent raids targeting nightclubs also took place in May 2025.

Facing such a reality, the ministry of Religious Affairs, sometimes backed by local representatives of the Political Affairs department and local religious scholars, had to intervene with one main objective: the maintenance of public order. And like in Idlib, institutionalisation became key to regulating this new wave of disruptive proselytism: all activities must be declared, supervised, and authorised. It did not always play out this way, but the political compass is now set.

In summary, the control of the religious field does not primarily seek to impose a singular, unified religious vision. Rather, it is strategically aimed at defusing tensions, mitigating doctrinal conflicts, and preventing provocative actions that could destabilise the political landscape. This careful balancing act highlights the broader tendency of the current regime to exercise religious authority not for doctrinal enforcement but as a means to reinforce its control and navigate the complex sectarian dynamics within Syria.

Once again political considerations prevail in the head of the new rulers in Damascus. There is no coherent or centralised logic underpinning HTS's management of the religious sphere. While the group permits a degree of religious competition, it intervenes when such competition spills into the public realm—particularly when proselytising activism is perceived as a security threat. The absence of a unified religious authority has produced a locally improvised and reactive form of governance. HTS's bet on the 'soft majority' translates less into ideological moderation than into fluid balances of power shaped by local conditions.

This centrist pragmatism is further reflected in the reorganisation of the Ministry of Religious Affairs, where a moderate and pragmatic approach now prevails. The new leadership reflects an intentional balance: Samir Biraktar, a Salafi and former Hajj coordinator for the opposition coalition, has been appointed to Damascus, alongside Abu al-Khayr Shukri, a traditional Ash'ari figure. This coexistence signals a policy of inclusion within the Sunni ideological landscape: all Islamic schools of thought—Salafism, Maturidism, Sufism, Ash'arism—are tolerated, provided they steer clear of divisive rhetoric.

Friday sermons are largely unregulated, aside from occasional directives—such as encouraging celebratory messaging following the 8 December victory. Controversial theological texts, including works by Ibn Taymiyyah or Muhammad ibn 'Abd al-Wahhab, are generally avoided. Likewise, overt Sufi rituals like public *hadra* (ecstatic group chanting and movement) are discouraged, preferring instead more discreet *majalis al-dhikr* (gatherings for the remembrance of God). According to the raw estimate of a few clerics, an estimate of 10% of Friday preachers—primarily those closely linked to the former Minister of Awqaf or Assad's intelligence services—were removed. The sole criterion for exclusion is political alignment with the former regime, rather than theological or ideological orientation.

HTS has been reshaped by the very society it governs. Its deradicalisation reflects a reversal of the Salafi approach and core tenets—absorbing more norms, values, and religious personnel than it imposes, while deliberately resisting a coherent ideological line. In Idlib, HTS acted transactionally, even in religious matters, avoiding clear ideological commitments and instead favouring what one of Ahmad al-Shara'a's advisors calls "constructive ambiguity." From this angle, there's undeniably an element of strategic concealment—*taqiyya*, as critics with an Orientalist leaning might say—at play in HTS's ambiguous approach. But what, exactly, is being concealed? Is it a still-smouldering radicalism, lying in wait for the moment when power is fully consolidated? Or is it, rather, an ideological pivot—a shift toward a revolutionary, Sunni, and conservative project that, while deradicalised, prefers to remain unnamed? A project crafted to ease the integration of a fragile political model into a conservative social fabric that still views it with suspicion? The real challenge facing this project now lies less in the movement's founding principles than in the evolving political and ideological currents within its own social base.

In the shadow of Mu'awiya's Sword: The sectarian recasting of radicalism

Radicalism persists, but its configuration has evolved. It now emerges less from within the ruling factions and more as a populist groundswell from outside them. In the early years of the Syrian

EPILOGUE

revolution, radicalism was largely synonymous with jihadism and with the organisations that openly embraced it—such as al-Qaeda (and later Hurras al-Din), Islamic State foreign fighters and, to a lesser extent, jihadi-leaning factions like Ahrar al-Sham. The threat then was identifiable, ideologically coherent, and organisationally structured. Today, however, the trajectory of HTS reveals a dual transformation. On one hand, the group led by al-Sharaa and his inner circle realigned ideologically, repositioning itself closer to the centre and integrating into the mainstream. On the other hand, a populist current has emerged from within the broader Sunni mainstream—demanding a more assertive expression of Islam at the grassroots level. This movement largely operates outside HTS's control, though it occasionally finds support among the group's more hardline elements.

This dynamic was evident in the push for the creation of a morality police, as explored in Chapter 10. By that point, radicalism had already begun to shift away from its original jihadi framework, increasingly disseminated by less identifiable actors—devout members of the provincial bourgeoisie, independent preachers, and social media influencers. This transformation reflects a populist dynamic driven by the grassroots intensification of Islamic fervor, less structured yet more socially embedded than previous waves of militant activism.

The capture of Damascus has further altered the landscape of radicalism along the same pattern. A new, diffuse radicalism has emerged, lacking clear ideological or organisational boundaries, yet mobilising around a radicalised sense of Sunni pride. Similar to the populist radicalisation in Idlib, this movement originates from society rather than from the centres of power. It taps into revanchist sentiments toward the former regime's support bases—particularly the Alawite community—while mobilising identity politics to challenge groups situated outside the new regime's core social base, which largely consists of provincial and lower and middle class Sunni constituencies.

This new wave of radicalism is fueled by the less ideologically driven segments of the new authorities' support base. It includes parts of the Syrian National Army consumed by passions of revenge and identitarianism. It encompasses armed factions from the North—often former Free Syrian Army units now integrated into the Syrian National Army—rural communities or rival neighborhoods entangled in long-standing wartime tensions with neighbouring Alawite populations, Bedouin tribes across various regions, and young Sunni opposition members seeking retribution for the loss of family members. These groups often mobilise using symbols associated with Jihadi culture, such as al-Qaeda or Umayyad flags, militant hymns, and religious headbands, not out of ideological commitment but as expressions of identity and revenge.

Salafi-jihadi cultural symbols have undergone a significant transformation, becoming increasingly detached from their original organisational and ideological matrix. Rather than operating solely within the doctrinal confines of jihadi groups such as al-Qaeda or Islamic State, these symbols have been reappropriated and commodified within a broader socio political milieu. They now function as performative expressions of a newly assertive Sunni identity that often manifests in exclusionary, and at times, supremacist modes.

This semiotic shift is particularly evident in the iconography embraced by mobilised publics. For instance, the predominance of so-called 'jihadi flags' over the traditional revolutionary banner in public demonstrations raises critical questions about the evolving political imaginary. The revolutionary flag, once a symbol of inclusive resistance and national unity, is increasingly viewed by segments of the population as emblematic of compromise and political moderation. In contrast, the black-and-white flags commonly associated with Salafi-jihadi movements now serve as potent icons of rupture, defiance, and sectarian positions—precisely the qualities valorised in a context where symbolic gestures of exclusion and confrontation are seen as more politically resonant than those of reconciliation. This was evident during the anti-Alawite mobilisations on 6 and 7 March 2025, which were fuelled by criticisms of the authorities' policies perceived as protective of Alawites. The government's security forces were overwhelmed by these events, with some of their members participating in abuses, while others were simply outnumbered.

This complex interplay between ideological shifts, populist pressures, and the commodification of radical symbols underscores

EPILOGUE

the current evolving nature of radicalism from jihadism to Sunni supremacism. It highlights the challenges faced by the new authorities in navigating a landscape where the former matrix of radicalism has been supplanted by more diffuse, sectarian and socially embedded forms of symbolic and physical violence.

The reversal of the radical question: Perils of a post-ideological zeitgeist

What is particularly counterintuitive about the current wave of radicalism in Syria is that it is led not by HTS—the former jihadis—but by a new revolutionary mainstream mobilising around identity-based grievances and demands for retribution. This reversal of roles is not without precedent; it echoes dynamics first seen in Idlib during the rise of Sunni populism around issues such as the morality police. Then, as now, HTS's leadership—having led the radical agenda from 2012 to 2017, from the early days of Jabhat al-Nusra to the formation of the Salvation Government—had shifted course. Since assuming power in December 2024, the new rulers have continued the ideological realignment, now reinforced by the imperatives of state governance, recasting itself as an agent of de-escalation. In contrast, parts of the revolutionary mainstream has become the main engine of unrest, channeling popular discontent through identity politics and a thirst for retributive justice.

This inversion plays out across multiple fronts. In response to the violence committed by fringe elements of the movement's social base, the core of the new power structure has paradoxically pushed for self-restraint. In the Coastal area in March 2025, General Security forces, without being immune to abuses, have played a role in restoring order. The leadership in Damascus has committed to investigating and punishing wrongdoers while engaging religious leaders to promote moderation. In the Alawite mountains, the presence of General Security forces is now generally seen as a guarantee against the more undisciplined and violent factions even though the line between the former and the latter often remains blurred.[8]

A month later, in the south of the country, where local populations face increasingly aggressive incursions by Israeli forces, the local discourse was combative against Israel, with growing calls for a "popular resistance." Some took up arms and sometimes died. At funerals for young men killed in clashes with the Israeli army, preachers delivered fiery sermons.[9] Yet, faced with this grassroots radicalisation, state representatives, cognisant of the risks posed by rash escalation, called for calm, urging "strategic patience", "self-restraint", and reliance on the diplomatic efforts led by Damascus and its new partners.

Sunni supremacism is no longer driven exclusively by revanchist grievances against communities historically associated with the Assad regime—most notably segments of the Alawite population. Rather, violent identity politics have increasingly targeted other minority groups, such as the Druze, who by late April and early May had themselves become targets of this expanding wave of hatred.

The immediate catalyst for this shift seems to have been a widely circulated audio clip on social media, controversially attributed to a Druze elder, and purportedly containing blasphemous content. In response, tensions rapidly escalated. On 28 April 2025, the campus in Homs and Damascus became the first site of mobilisation, where Druze students were physically assaulted and forced to flee. The situation deteriorated further on the night of 29 April, when armed factions initiated attacks on Jaramana, a neighbourhood southeast of Damascus closely identified with the Druze community. These clashes resulted in the deaths of at least thirty fighters.

Although General Security forces ultimately intervened, their response was delayed and failed to prevent the violence—which persisted over several days and ultimately claimed the lives of more than 100 individuals. More critically, their inaction contributed to a widespread perception among the Druze community that the events were part of a calculated provocation—a 'good cop, bad cop' scenario wherein General Security played the conciliatory role, while militant Sunni factions enacted the aggression though there is no evidence for this scenario.

This interpretation was further reinforced by the rapid escalation of sectarian discourse across Sunni social media platforms, which reached unprecedented levels. The virulent rhetoric contributed to a broader climate of polarisation, increasingly influencing rank-and-file personnel within General Security, whose leadership appeared

EPILOGUE

to struggle to maintain cohesion and control amid the growing sectarian fervor.

Ultimately, a deal was reached confirming what we previously described. What is taking shape is a new radicalism festering at the periphery of the regime's evolving social base, while temperance is becoming structurally embedded at the centre. Whether confronting Alawite revanchism, responding to Israeli military incursions in the south, or navigating rising sectarian tensions with the Druze, the pattern remains consistent: deradicalisation from the top, re-radicalisation from below.

The ideology now guiding the new leadership heading the country is unmistakably more conservative and Islamic than the revolutionary ethos of 2011–12. Shaped by the legacy of early-stage radicalism and the pressure of conservative lobbying, Islamist populism is exerting increasing influence over both the movement's middle cadres and its grassroots base. This has, at times, forced HTS leadership to recalibrate and restrain conservative impulses—whether it be shelving plans to Islamise school curricula in Damascus after a late-December directive from the political leadership, backtracking efforts to enforce moral policing in Idlib, or reining in identity-driven mobs targeting Alawites and Druze alike.

The result is a movement that has undergone top-down deradicalisation, triggering a persistent tension between the leadership and segments of its own social base. HTS's long-standing Thermidorian strategy—moderation through institutional consolidation and reliance on the silent majority while accepting social inertia in the religious domain—succeeded in Idlib, marginalising radical fringe actors. Yet the conquest of Damascus reversed that dynamic. While it brought the movement into contact with new actors and worldviews, it also catalysed a partially radicalised *Sunni pride*, affirming a deeper inversion: the former radicals have become advocated for de-escalation, while segments of the revolutionary mainstream drifts toward a volatile blend of identity politics, revanchist zeal, and the rising clamour of sectarian supremacism.

In the end, the course of the silent revolution begins to veer off track, pulled by the gravitational force of its own contradictions. Confronted by a growing and volatile Sunni pride—and with the unsettling prospect of Islamic State re-emerging as the only organised force capable of harnessing this socio-identitarian wave—the revolution, now in power, finds itself increasingly challenged to chart a stable course as it still lacks a clear ideological compass. In Idlib, when the objective was to balance soft majorities against hardliners, constructive ambiguity proved a strategic asset. Today, under the constraints of national governance, that same ambiguity is no longer a tool of prudence, but a threat to coherence and authority.

In an era marked by populist volatility and the rise of Sunni supremacism, the posture of being 'transformed by the people' and relying on silent majorities has become a liability—not only for the leadership but for the broader population as well. Now in control of Damascus, the silent revolution finds itself at a pivotal crossroads, poised to find its voice and secure its ideological anchor.

The government has begun to respond. Its religious scholars—whether those who previously led HTS's deradicalisation efforts in Idlib or newer allies based in Damascus—have sought to craft a more inclusive religious discourse. This emerging discourse acknowledges the pluralism within Islamic jurisprudence and religious creed, and aims to position itself within the mainstream of Islam to counter exclusionary radicalism. Efforts are also underway to regulate proselytism, particularly in less conservative regions and areas with religious minorities, or counter hate speeches. It is still unclear whether they will evolve into a genuinely inclusive religious narrative capable of resonating with broader audiences, shaping mass appeal, and fostering a shared religious identity beyond the confines of theological detail.

NOTES

INTRODUCTION

1. Drevon, J. (2022). *Institutionalizing violence: Strategies of jihad in Egypt*. Oxford University Press.
2. Jean-Francois Bayart, "Le concept de situation thermidorienne: régimes néo-révolutionnaires et libéralisation économique", *Centre d'Etudes et de Recherches Internationales, Questions de recherche*, no 24, March 2008.

1. THE FOUNDATIONAL MATRIX

1. See for instance: Charles R. Lister. *The Syrian Jihad: Al-Qaeda, the Islamic State and the Evolution of an Insurgency.* London: Hurst, 2016. Hamming, T., *Jihadi Politics: The global jihadi civil war, 2014–2019*, Hurst, 2022.
2. The group's full name was Jabhat al-Nusra li ahl al-Sham min mujahidin al-Sham fi sahat al-jihad, or the front of support for the people of the levant by the Mujahideen of the Levant in the fields of jihad.
3. https://www.youtube.com/watch?v=yaw3g9vMMlw
4. Interview, Idlib, 2020.
5. The letters were leaked on Telegram.
6. https://www.economist.com/1843/2025/03/05/the-great-pretender-how-ahmed-al-sharaa-won-syria
7. Interview, Antakia, 2022.
8. Interviews with Ahmad al-Sharaa, Idlib, 2020.
9. Interview, Idlib, 2020.
10. The letters were leaked on Telegram.
11. Interviews with Ahmad al-Sharaa, Idlib, 2020.
12. Interview, Antakia, 2022.
13. Interviews with a range of armed groups' leaders in Turkey and Syria, 2017–2022.
14. Interviews with prison leaders jailed in Saydnaya, 2018.
15. Interview, Turkey, 2022.
16. Interviews with a wide range of civilians between 2012 and 2015.
17. https://www.youtube.com/watch?v=LK3QCWTPz_4
18. Interview, Idlib, 2019.
19. Interviews with a range of European and Egyptian foreign fighters in Europe and Egypt, 2012–16.
20. Interviews with European fighters, 2018.
21. Theo Padnos. *Blindfold: A memoir of capture, torture, and enlightenment*, London: Simon and Schuster, 2021.

NOTES

22. Interview, Antakia, 2022.
23. The letter was published online at the time.
24. Al-'Uraydi, *'Aqidatna'*.
25. Interview, Antakia, 2022.
26. Interview, Idlib, 2021.
27. Communique of Ayman al-Zawahiri, 2013.
28. Interview, Idlib, 2020.
29. Interview, Ahrar al-Sham leaders, Turkey, 2017.
30. Interview, Amman, 2022.
31. Interview, Idlib, 2020.
32. Interview, 2023.
33. Interviews, several journalists and analysts, Turkey, 2015.
34. Interviews with a range of armed groups leaders, 2018.
35. Interview, Idlib, 2019.
36. Interview, Turkey, 2018.
37. https://www.aljazeera.net/opinions/2014/5/31/%D9%85%D9%8A%D8%AB%D8%A7%D9%82-%D8%A7%D9%84%D8%B4%D8%B1%D9%81-%D9%86%D9%82%D9%84%D8%A9-%D9%86%D9%88%D8%B9%D9%8A%D8%A9-%D9%81%D9%8A-%D9%85%D8%B3%D9%8A%D8%B1%D8%A9-%D8%A7%D9%84%D8%AA%D9%8A%D8%A7%D8%B1
38. Jabhat al-Nusra communique.
39. Interview with al-Qahtani, 2024.
40. Rhodes, B. *The World As It Is: A Memoir of the Obama White House*. Random House Trade Paperbacks, 2019.
41. Interview, Turkey, 2020.
42. Interview, Idlib, 2020.
43. Interview, Antakia, 2022.
44. https://www.aymennjawad.org/2015/08/archive-of-jabhat-al-nusra-service-documents
45. Interview, Turkey, 2022.
46. https://www.aymennjawad.org/2015/03/archive-of-jabhat-al-nusra-dar-al-qaa-documents
47. For more details, see Svensson, Isak, Daniel Finnbogason, Dino Krause, Luís Martínez Lorenzo, and Nanar Hawach. Confronting the Caliphate: Civil Resistance in Jihadist Proto-States. Oxford University Press, 2022.
48. Interview, Turkey, 2018.
49. Interview, Idlib, 2019.
50. Interview, Amman, 2022.
51. https://www.aymennjawad.org/2017/12/the-hayat-tahrir-al-sham-al-qaeda-dispute-primary

2. THE STRUGGLE FOR DOMINANCE

1. Drevon, J. *From Jihad to Politics: How Syrian Jihadis embraced politics*. Oxford University Press, 2024.
2. Abu Fath Al-Farghali's Telegram channel.

3. Interview, Turkey, 2017.
4. Ahmad Abazeid, "How did the Ahrar al-Sham Movement Collapse?" (in Arabic), *Syrianoor*, 9 August 2017.
5. Interviews, Ahrar al-Sham leaders, 2019.
6. Interview, Idlib, 2020.
7. Interviews with military leaders of HTS and Faylaq al Sham, 2020.
8. Interview, Idlib, 2020.
9. Interviews with HTS military and political leaders, Ahrar al-Sham leaders, Faylaq al-Sham leaders, Idlib and Istanbul, 2020.
10. Interview, Ankara, 2020.
11. Ibid.
12. Interview, HTS military commander, 2020.
13. Interview, several Ahrar al-Sham leaders, Istanbul, 2020–22.
14. Interviews, Hurras al-Din commanders, 2018.
15. Interview with a range of HTS officials and security analysts, 2019–2020.
16. HTS left no more than seven positions on the front lines to Hurras al-Din. In addition to its presence on the frontline, Hurras al-Din had sixteen military positions in the town of Jisr al-Shughur shortly before the summer 2020 escalation.
17. Interview, Idlib, 2020.
18. "General Declaration by HTS Leadership" (in Arabic), 2017, retrieved from a Telegram channel.
19. Interview, Ahmad al-Sharaa, 2020.
20. Interviews with senior HTS leaders, 2020.
21. Interviews with several HTS leaders, Idlib, 2019.
22. Interview with an analyst close to HTS, Idlib, July 2020. See also Aymeen Jawad Al-Tamimi, "Why Ansar al-Tawheed Ended its Alliance with Hurras al-Din," *Pundicity*, 10 June 2020, https://bit.ly/33Sikmr
23. Interview, Idlib, 2020.
24. Ibid.
25. Ibid.
26. Ibid.
27. Interview with Ahmad al-Sharaa, February 2022.
28. Tensions between Abu Malik al-Tally and HTS seem to owe as much to geostrategy—his refusal to align with Turkey—as to influencing games within the organisation, according to our interviews with HTS leaders.
29. They would subsequently be arrested during the first part of June 2020 for participating in the establishment of the Fa-Ithbitu operating room or—in the case of Abu Salah al-Uzbeki—for having joined one of the groups in the room in question.
30. Interview, Idlib, 2020.
31. WhatsApp call with an analyst close to HTS, 2020.
32. Interview, Idlib, July 2020.
33. HTS, "Ta'mim" 2020, retrieved from HTS's Telegram channel. On 18 June, various jihadi factions reaffirmed their support for HTS in a statement. The most prominent was the TIP, but other small groups included individuals from Uzbekistan, the Maldives, Albania, Iran, Tajikistan, the Arabian Peninsula and the Caucasus.

34. Interview, Idlib, 2020.
35. Ibid.
36. This does not mean that HTS was in full territorial control in 2020. As a Turkish researcher and academic explained, "HTS patrols are afraid when they cross Jisr al-Shughur. The city is still full of foreign jihadis. HTS did not fight against Hurras al-Din there. There are no flags and no headquarters anymore but Hurras al-Din is still there and no one is chasing them". (Interview, Ankara, November 2020.)
37. Interview, Idlib, 2020.
38. Adnan Ahmad, "Attack Against a Russian Base in Eastern Syria: Hurras al-Din Returns to the Confrontation" (in Arabic), Al-Arabi al-Jadid, 2 January 2021, https://bit.ly/2KVguek
39. Interview, Idlib, 2021
40. Interviews with HTS security officials, 2021–2024.
41. Interview, Idlib, 2022.
42. Interview with a researcher close to the Salvation Government, Idlib, October 2022.
43. Interview with a researcher close to HTS, February 2022.
44. Islamic State leaders moved frequently, according to the daughter of Qardash's assistant. Interview, Idlib, February 2022. Additionally, the "*murafiq*" is a sympathiser but not a member of ISIS. Leaders hide behind unaffiliated merchants. Relying on non-local merchants was precisely what Baghdadi had done as well. Interviews with neighbours of the residence where Qardash was hiding, February 2022.
45. Interviews with the neighbours of Qardash, February 2022.
46. Testimonies from the family of Qardash's guard, February 2022.
47. Interview, Idlib, February 2022.
48. Interview Abd al-Rahim Atun, February 2022.
49. Interview, Idlib, February 2022.
50. Ibid.
51. Interviews with a range of HTS leaders, Idlib, 2020–24.
52. Interview, HTS security official, 2022.
53. Interview with HTS security officials, Idlib, 2021–23
54. Interview, TIP commanders, Turkey, 2022–24
55. Interviews with HTS leaders and security officials, Idlib, 2021.
56. Interview, Idlib, 2022.
57. Interviews with HTS leaders and security officials, Idlib, 2021.
58. Interview, Idlib, 2022.
59. Interviews, Damascus, 2025.

3. DISMANTLING THE RADICAL PAST

1. Interviews with a range of actors involved in these negotiations, Turkey, 2020.
2. Interviews with tribal leaders, local businessmen, and members of the academics' initiative, Idlib, July 2019 and July 2020.
3. Interview with one of them, Idlib, 2020.
4. Interview with a delegation from the Idlib Chamber of Commerce, Idlib, July 2020.

5. Each time a court resumed, the families of detainees had one month to reevaluate the cases if they refused the renditions of the former judges. Interviews, Dana court, Idlib, July 2019.
6. Discussion with residents of Saraqib, July 2019.
7. WhatsApp Interview with two local activists from Maarat al-Nu'man, May 2020.
8. Interviews with local notables from Dana and Saraqib, September 2019 and March 2020. For an initial typology of relations between HTS and local councils in Idlib, see Ayman Aldassouky, "The Role of Jihadi Movements in Syrian Local Governance," *Omran Centre for Strategic Studies,* 14 July 2017, https://bit.ly/3n4JXk
9. Information collected during visits to the various ministries and social groups mentioned, Idlib, June 2019 and July 2020.
10. Interviews with several of them, Idlib, 2020.
11. Interview with representatives of several such groups, Idlib, 2020–22.
12. On the Kurdish movement, see Patrick Haenni and Arthur Quesnay, "Surviving the Aftermath of Islamic State: the Syrian Kurdish Movement's Resilience Strategy," *Research Project Report*. (Florence: European University Institute, Middle East Directions, Wartime and Post-Conflict in Syria, 2020), https://bit.ly/3mTSZQx
13. According to UN estimates. Interview with an OCHA employee, March 2020.
14. Interview with a former Salvation Government prime minister, Idlib, 2021.
15. While the use of tribes in the administration of law is not new (the Syrian regime itself widely practised it), this trend reflects a real inflection in Idlib since factions did justice directly before and the tribes were side-lined. Interviews with judges and lawyers, Dana court, Idlib, July 2019.
16. Interview, Berlin, 2020.
17. Despite the multiplicity of operators present in the field, the level of education in Idlib was declining significantly. A study conducted by eleven researchers commissioned by the minister of Education in the camps showed that levels of illiteracy reached up to 40% of the population in the camps at the end of 2020. Interviews with Salvation Government officials and NGO operators, Idlib, December 2020.
18. Syria Relief. "Syria Relief Announces 107 New Schools through Partnership with Chemonics" *Reliefweb*, 15 November 2019, https://bit.ly/2VMQTGf
19. Interview, Idlib, July 2020.
20. HTS tried twice to revive trade by opening crossing points in Maarat Hattat and Saraqib in April and May 2020 respectively. The population opposed it with the argument that the decision would entail the tacit acceptance of the loss of Saraqib and Maarat al-Nu'man and that it would increase the cost of living in Idlib.
21. Interview, Western capitals, 2020.
22. https://en.wikipedia.org/wiki/Turkish_military_operation_in_Idlib_Governorate#/media/File:Syria_Idlib_November_2020.svg
23. Al-Farghali's Telegram channel.
24. https://en.wikipedia.org/wiki/Syrian_civil_war#/media/File:Syrian_Civil_War_map_(November_24,_2023).svg
25. Interview, Ankara, April 2020.
26. Interviews with Russian and Turkish diplomats, Ankara, December 2020. According to the military commander in chief of HTS the southern security gap was filled by 2020 as there were now seven new Turkish positions in the southern

triangle of Idlib in areas such as Kafr Awid, Deir Simbel, Ghalioun and Waqfin. Interview, Idlib, December 2020.
27. Interview with a Turkish official, Ankara, 2020.
28. WhatsApp interview, April 2020.
29. Interview with local analysts and journalists, Idlib.
30. Interview, Ankara, 2020.
31. Interview with the head of HTS military, Idlib, July 2020.
32. Interview, Hatay, March 2020.
33. Interview, 2023.
34. Interview with international interlocutors involved in Idlib, 2020.
35. Interview, Idlib, 2020.
36. Interview with a Turkish official, December 2020.
37. Interview, Anas Ayrout, Idlib, April 2022.
38. Interview, Idlib, April 2022.
39. Interview, clerics favourable to HTS, April 2022. It is interesting to note that the margin of tolerance is defined in relation to the risks of radicalisation. The official endorsement of the Shafi'i school provides assurances of non-radicalisation and allows institutes to bypass the potential sanctions from the Salvation Governmnet and HTS. In this regard, it is indeed the security considerations, i.e. deradicalisation and the control it entails, that prevail.
40. WhatsApp exchange with a judge in Idlib, May 2020.
41. Interview, Idlib, 2021.
42. Interview, Idlib, July 2020.
43. Interview, local cleric, Idlib, July 2020.
44. Interviews, officials from the High Council of Fatwa and the Ministry of Religious Affairs, Idlib, July 2020. The institute of Imam al Nawawi was founded in 1962. Of Sufi-Ash'ari obedience, the institute followed the revolutionary movement in 2011. WhatsApp calls with institute professors and Sufi shaykhs, May–June 2020.
45. WhatsApp interview, May 2020.
46. Written exchange, November 2020.
47. WhatsApp interview, May 2020.
48. No principal or teacher contacted complained about overly intrusive supervisors. WhatsApp interviews, May and June 2020.
49. Discussions with professors, directors and current and former senior officials in the Ministry of Education carried out between June 2019 and May 2020.
50. Interview, Idlib, June 2019.
51. WhatsApp calls with four school teachers, April 2020.
52. According to a former Salvation Government official who is now critical of it, around twenty shaykhs were dismissed from their posts during the Salvation Government's first year of operation. Four preachers close to HTS were sent back to Harem for opposing the policy on Turkey. Several sources opposed to HTS claimed none were fired for religious reasons, only political ones. WhatsApp calls, May–June 2020.
53. Interview, Istanbul, August 2022.
54. Interview with an HTS leader, Idlib, October 2021.
55. Interview, Idlib, September 2022.
56 Interview, Istanbul, September 2022.

57. Interview with an HTS commander, Idlib, June 2023.
58. Interview with the leader of a faction allied to HTS, Istanbul, September 2022.
59. Ibid.
60. Ibid.
61. Interview with the leader of a faction allied to HTS, Istanbul, 2023.
62. Interview, HTS leader, February 2021.
63. Ibid.
64. Binder, Leonard, *In a Moment of Enthusiasm: Political power and the second stratum in Egypt*, University of Chicago Press, 1978.
65. Interview, HTS leader, February 2021.
66. The director of the Idlib city section came from Qamichli, the one from Jisr al-Shughur from Deraa; the leader of Harem is from Deir al-Zor.
67. For example, tensions arose over the Turkish position in Sarmada, where Turkish forces took houses by force. In response, the administration of the liberated areas stepped in to act as a mediator. Interview with a member of the administration, Idlib, February 2021.
68. In Idlib, one of the key issues was the street vendors that blocked traffic in the main squares. This phenomenon arose from increased poverty, and the massive influx of population (Idlib's population had risen to an estimated 600,000 people, up from only 165,000 people prior to 2011). The local council was incentivised to establish an alternative market, which was successfully implemented, allowing for the relocation of 430 street vendors. The Office of Relations convinced the vendors to move to the new location.

4. EXITING JIHADISM

1. Interview, Amman, 2022.
2. Ibid.
3. Ibid.
4. Ibid.
5. Ibid.
6. Interview, Idlib, 2020.
7. Ibid.
8. Interview, Idlib, July 2020.
9. Interview, member of the High Council of Shari'a, Idlib, July 2020.
10. Interview, Idlib, March 2020.
11. Interview, 2019.
12. Interview, Idlib, September 2022.
13. Interview, August 2022.
14. Ibid.
15. Interview with a leader of a faction allied with HTS, August 2022.
16. Ibid.
17. HTS communiqués.
18. Interview, HTS leader, Idlib, 2020.
19. Ibid.
20. Interview, 2023.

NOTES

21. Discussions with former commanders from Jabhat al-Nusra and current leaders of HTS, Turkey, August 2022.
22. Interview, former commander of Jabhat al-Nusra, Turkey, August 2022.
23. Interviews.
24. Interview, Abd al-Rahim Atun, Idlib, April 2022.
25. Interview, Abd al-Rahim Atun, Idlib, June 2023.
26. Ibid.
27. Interview, Idlib, September 2022.
28. WhatsApp call, May 2020.
29. WhatsApp call, May 2020. *Fiqh al-Nawazil wa al-Azamat* (jurisprudence of crises and calamities) focuses on adapting Islamic legal rulings to contemporary emergencies, political upheavals, and societal challenges, emphasising pragmatism and flexibility. In contrast, *Fiqh al-Jihad* is a branch of Islamic jurisprudence that deals specifically with the rules, ethics, and conditions of armed struggle. While *Fiqh al-Jihad* provides rigid doctrinal guidelines for warfare, *Fiqh al-Nawazil wa al-Azamat* allows for more contextual and strategic decision-making in times of crisis.
30. Interview, Idlib, December 2020.
31. WhatsApp interview, May 2020.
32. Ibid.
33. Interview, Idlib, 2020.
34. Interview, HTS leader, February 2021.
35. Interview, Idlib, 2022.

5. HOLLOWING OUT SALAFISM

1. Interview with a former student, Idlib, 2019.
2. Interview, deputy dean of the Shari'a Faculty of Idlib University, Idlib, December 2020.
3. Interview, Idlib, 2020.
4. Ibid.
5. Ibid.
6. HTS communiqué.
7. Ibid.
8. Ibid.
9. For examples of these sermons, see https://bit.ly/3pMtIsz. See also Mazhar al-Weis in a presentation to the "Asking People for a Reminder" programme on courage in Islam, in which jihad is an example of courage in the Quran without elaborating on the details. https://bit.ly/2MoyMF4
10. HTS propaganda video, 2019.
11. Testimonials from people who have experienced this training, WhatsApp call, May 2020.
12. Interview, member of the High Council of Shari'a, Idlib, July 2020.
13. Interview, Idlib, March 2020.
14. Former shaykh in the Ministry of Religious Affairs, WhatsApp interview, May 2020.
15. Interview, Idlib, July 2020.
16. Interview, Idlib, 2021.

17. Ibid.
18. Interview, Idlib, 2022.
19. Interview, HTS leader, Idlib, 2022.
20. Interview, 2022.
21. https://www.syria.tv/؟مؤتمر-تقنين-الشريعة-بإدلب-يُغضب-السلفيين-المناهضين-لـتحرير-الشام
22. Interview, Idlib, April 2022.
23. Interview Idlib.
24. Discussion between two members of the Fatwa Council, October 2021.
25. Interview, Minister of Awqaf of the Salvation Government.
26. Interview, Idlib, 2022.
27. Ibid.
28. Interview, Idlib, July 2020.
29. Written exchange with a cleric close to HTS, May 2020.
30. The limited nature of its public speaking does not mean that the High Council of Fatwa is inactive. In fact, much of its work is direct guidance to individuals or, more significantly, with the various ministries of the Salvation Government. All the laws enacted by the Salvation Government are also reviewed by the High Council of the fatwa. Interview, three members of the High Council in the presence of the Minister of Religious Affairs, July 2020.
31. The Higher Council of Fatwa, "On the Repetition of the Diffusion of Defamatory Pictures of the Prophet Muhammad," 2020, retrieved from The telegram channel of the Council.
32. Interview, Abd al-Rahim Atun, Idlib, April 2022.
33. البيعان بالخيار ما لم يتفرقا، فان صدقا وبيانا بورك لهما في بيعهما. وإن كتما وكذبا محقت بركة بيعهما
34. The production of laws by the Shura Council is relatively low, and not all of them have received recommendations from the Fatwa Council. Out of 50 laws promulgated until October 2022, 27 received recommendations from the Fatwa Council. The analysis that follows is based on a review conducted in April 2022 of the written recommendations submitted by the Ifta Council, which evaluated each of the various laws enacted by the Shura Council one by one.
35. Interview, members of the Fatwa Council, April 2021.
36. Interview, HTS leader, 2023.
37. Interview with Abd al-Rahim Atun, Idlib, February 2022.

6. THE THERMIDORIAN OPENING TO SUFISM

1. Interview, 2024.
2. Whatsapp call with Thomas Pierret, November 2024.
3. WhatsApp interviews, September–November 2024.
4. WhatsApp interview, November 2024.
5. WhatsApp interview, October 2024.
6. WhatsApp interview, November 2024.
7. WhatsApp interview, October 2024.
8. WhatsApp interview, November 2024.
9. Ibid.
10. Ibid.
11. Interview, Damascus, February 2025.

12. WhatsApp interview, October 2024.
13. Ibid.
14. WhatsApp interview, November 2024.
15. Interview, Damascus, January 2025.
16. WhatsApp interviews, October-November 2024.
17. According to two prominent Sufi clerics, WhatsApp calls, October 2024.
18. Interview, November 2024.
19. In some neighbourhoods, they may have returned somewhat earlier, at the same time as the Salvation Government was set up in 2017. Interviews with Syrian youths in Idlib, Idlib, June 2023.
20. Interview, a Misaharati from the old districts of Idlib, WhatsApp, May 2023.
21. Interview, a religious singer, Idlib, WhatsApp, May 2023.
22. Interviews, two heads of households, WhatsApp, May 2023.
23. Interview, a recording studio owner, Idlib, WhatsApp, May 2023.
24. WhatsApp interview, May 2023.
25. Interview, Damascus, February 2025.
26. WhatsApp interview, November 2024.
27. WhatsApp interview, October 2024.
28. WhatsApp interview, November 2024.
29. Ibid.
30. Ibid.

7. DHIMMIS NO MORE, CITIZENS NOT YET

1. In a 2023 interview, a Christian notable from the village of Qnieh reflected on his experiences, recalling a comparatively less negative perception of ISIS—whom he described as violent but disciplined, with agreements typically honored—than of FSA factions, which, despite being less ideologically rigid, were often marked by overt sectarianism and operational disorder.
2. Interview, October 2022.
3. Interview, June 2023.
4. Ibid.
5. Interview with local residents, Qalb Lozeh, 2020.
6. Interview, Idlib, 2020.
7. Interview, June 2023.
8. WhatsApp interview with a Druze professor, June 2022; see also: https://syriansg.org/18073/
9. Written correspondence with a Druze professor from Jebel al-Sammak, June 2022.
10. Estimations provided by the remaining clerical authorities during interviews in June 2023.
11. Interviews, September 2022.
12. Interview, June 2023.
13. Ibid.
14. Interview, Idlib, 2022.
15. Interviews with local residents and the HTS leadership, Idlib, 2022.
16. WhatsApp interviews with Druze dignitaries, August 2022.

17. Ibid.
18. HTS video.
19. Interviews, Druze and Christian dignitaries, Kaftin, Qniyya, February 2022. Interview, officials from the management of the liberated areas, September 2022.
20. Out of the three Christian villages of Qneiyya, Jdeida, and Yaqoubiyya, 180 complaints regarding House and Land Property (HLP) issues were filed. Eighty of these have been resolved, allowing the complainants to regain their rights. It should be noted that the majority of HLP-related cases are managed through arbitration.
21. All confiscated houses, with the exception of one, were returned to their respective owners (interviews with Christian dignitaries and clergy, September 2022).
22. On at least two occasions, hate speeches have resulted in the removal of individuals involved and, in one instance, the dismissal of an imam from the Ministry of Religious Affairs. Interview, Minister of Religious Affairs, Idlib, February 2022; interviews, Christian and Druze dignitaries, 2022. Interviews, officials from the management of the liberated areas, September 2022.
23. Once commitments were made by the management of the liberated areas to return their houses, families were encouraged by their relatives on-site to make the decision to return. The return process took time due to the costs associated with the journey back, which had to be conducted through smuggling routes, passing through Kurdish areas and then FSA-controlled zones before entering Idlib. The expenses amounted to $800–950 per family. Upon arriving in Idlib, HTS, in cooperation with the religious dignitaries of the respective villages, took care of their needs. Interviews, Christian dignitaries and local officials from the management of the liberated areas, February 2022, October 2022. One Christian clergyman mentioned, "Fifteen families returned last year from Aleppo, and we are preparing the return of three more families this year. There is a fear of returning, but the deteriorating economic situation is pushing them. They are all pleasantly surprised by the security they find upon returning. The decisive factor for their return is the recovery of their houses and land to cultivate. Being displaced in government-controlled areas is costly". Interview, October 2022.
24. Interview, Christian clergyman, Yaqubiyya, June 2023.
25. Interviews, Christian dignitaries and clerical figures, Qneiyya, June 2023.
26. Interview with a Druze dignitary, September 2022. In reality, the TIP is following HTS in its policy of normalisation with minority groups. The leadership facilitated the restitution of houses. For example, they instructed their militants to vacate twenty new houses in Jdeida in December 2022 that party members were occupying among Christians. The Druze community is also aware of the party's presence: "In our mountain, we know their cars, their flags. On several occasions during tensions, their emir comes to calm things down, but we don't get the impression that they control much". Interview, Druze dignitary, September 2022.
27. According to the Syrian Observatory for Human Rights, negotiations led to the departure of families of TIP militants who were occupying the church and the attached monastery (source: https://www.syriahr.com/-بعد-أيام-من-افتتاح-كنيسة-/اليعقوبية-وان/557703).
28. Interview, Christian notable, Darkouch, June 2022.
29. When Ahmad al-Sharaa reminded a Druze dignitary of their pride in being

Muslims with the Quranic statement "there is no compulsion in religion," he wasn't merely referencing a principle but outlining a policy towards them. Thus, one of his advisors elaborated on the political significance of the HTS leader's visit to the Druze community in Idlib: "When the massacre in Qalb Lozeh occurred in 2015, a death sentence was indeed issued by the religious cleric of Jabhat al-Nusra against the commander who ordered the execution. However, internal pressure was too great. The sentence was not carried out, and the commander ultimately fled before dying in a confrontation against us. What HTS wants today is to resolve this issue definitively and for history. Ahmad al-Sharaa, by emphasising that there is no compulsion in religion, aimed to reset the clock, forget the past and forced conversions, and accept the Druze in their original faith". Interview, Idlib, September 2022.

30. WhatsApp interview with a Druze intellectual, August 2022.
31. Interview with a Christian dignitary, Qneiyya, February 2022.
32. Correspondence, August 2022.
33. Interview with a Druze activist, September 2022.
34. WhatsApp interviews with Druze dignitaries from Jabal al-Samaq, August–October 2022.
35. WhatsApp interview with a Druze dignitary, August 2022.
36. Interview, Idlib, 2022.
37. According to Isabelle Rivoal, "Although the term has been attested in France since 1437, the notion of a minority as a juridico-political construction specifying certain groups within generally territorially defined structures was developed during the 18th and 19th centuries, in the context of the construction of European nation-states. Its emergence is closely linked to evolving concepts of sovereignty and the recognition of the people—rather than divinity—as the ultimate source of legitimacy." Isabelle Rivoal. "Minorité religieuse." R. Azria & D. Hervieu-Léger (dir.), Dictionnaire des faits religieux, Presses Universitaires de France, pp. 718–725, 2010, Quadrige.
38. Observations during meetings between local authorities and Christian dignitaries, Idlib, 2021–22. It is worth noting that the egalitarian discourse accompanying the opening to minorities also has its limits. While freedom of worship is assured, it is still confined to the private sphere, as making a public display of piety is considered a form of proselytism: "We need to differentiate between the practice of religious rituals and the public announcement of these religious rituals. We do not intervene in anything internal, but the public space is a Muslim space" (Abd al-Rahim Atun, February 2021). The bells of churches and monasteries in Christian villages no longer ring or have not yet started ringing. The reminder of "rights and duties" is more ambiguous.
39. Interview, Idlib, 2022.
40. Interview, Idlib, October 2021.
41. Ibid.

8. FLIRTING WITH THE SILENT MAJORITY

1. WhatsApp interview, Antakia, August 2022.
2. WhatsApp interview with participants, Antakia, August 2022.

3. Interviews.
4. Interview, former Salvation Government cadre who was close to the revolutionary milieu inside Idlib, Antakia, August 2022.
5. Starting in 2015, revolutionary elites made numerous attempts to create representative bodies for the revolution, such as Tajamua Suriya al-Thawra (2015), al-Hayat al-Siasiyya fi Muhafathat Idlib (2016), Tajamua al-Adala al-Suri (2018), and Tajamua Bina Suria. Some of them joined established groups abroad, like Michel Kilo's Itihad al Dimuqratieen al-Suriyiin. While some political bodies have endured—most notably the Political Commission (al-Hayat al-Siyasiya), which includes approximately 800 members—none have successfully institutionalised themselves. Rather than evolving into structured organisations, they have primarily served as forums for debate, lacking the cohesion and authority necessary to assert lasting political influence.
6. Interview, Raefa Sami'a, Antakia, November 2022.
7. Interview, Ahmed Bakro, WhatsApp interview, August 2022.
8. Interview, Ossman Badaw, 2024.
9. Interview, Yasser al Sayyed, 2024.
10. Interview, Raefa Sami'a, Geneva, November 2022. Shaykh Ayman Mohsen was a graduate Shari'a and served as an imam in a mosque before the revolution.
11. Interview, August 2022.
12. Interview, Raefa Sami'a, Antakia, August 2022.
13. A woman leads the teachers' union, and women are well-represented in the pharmacists' union and student unions. WhatsApp call, October 2022.
14. Interview, Raefa Sami'a, Antakia, August 2022.
15. WhatsApp interview, November 2022.
16. Discussion with a high school teacher, WhatsApp, November 2022.
17. WhatsApp interview, November 2022.
18. Interview, Antakia, August 2023.
19. Discussion with a high school teacher, WhatsApp, November 2022.
20. Interview, Abd al-Rahim Atun, October 2021.
21. WhatsApp interview, November 2022.
22. WhatsApp interview, December 2022.
23. Ibid.
24. From this perspective, HTS's trajectory diverges from that of Islamic State, which did the exact opposite: applying little pressure during consolidation and then shifting toward massive totalitarianism once hegemony was achieved. HTS's methods of managing internal opposition are more reminiscent of the PYD's approach. In eastern Syria, the PYD initially exerted strong pressure on its Kurdish political opponents and the Arab revolutionary milieu before significantly easing that pressure over time.
25. Bronislaw Baczko. *Comment sortir de la terreur. Thermidor et la révolution*. Collection NRF Essais. Gallimard, 1989.
26. Interview.
27. Interview.
28. Interview, Ahmed Bakro, WhatsApp interview, August 2022.
29. Interview with Youssef Qardouch, Antakia, August 2022.
30. WhatsApp interview, April 2022.

31. Interview, Ahmed Bakro, WhatsApp interview, August 2022.
32. Interview, Aly Hamade, Antakia, August 2022.
33. Interview, Raefa, August 2022.
34. WhatsApp interview, August 2022.
35. Hind, WhatsApp, October 2022; Interview, 2023.
36. Interview, Idlib, November 2022.
37. Interview, Turkish official, Ankara, August 2022.
38. Interviews, Turkish experts, Ankara, Istanbul, Rome, 2022.
39. Interviews with Western diplomats, Paris, London, Geneva, and Berlin from October 2022 to January 2023.
40. HTS executive, June 2023.
41. Interviews, commanders of armed groups, Antakia and Istanbul, and via WhatsApp, between August and October 2022.
42. Interview, a former cadre of the movement, Gaziantep, June 2023.
43. Interview, Turkish officials, Ankara, October 2022.
44. Interviews, Turkish officials and researchers, Ankara, October 2022.
45. Discussions with leaders of armed factions in Afrin, Azaz, and Turkish and Syrian experts, March–April 2023.
46. Interview via WhatsApp, November 2022.
47. Interview.
48. WhatsApp Interviews, Civil Society Activists from Azaz, November 2022.
49. Interviews, humanitarian workers and diplomats, London, Paris, Berlin, Washington, Brussels, 2021–23.
50. WhatsApp conversations with FSA commanders and Turkish officials.
51. Interview, Ankara, 2022.
52. Ibid.
53. Interview, Turkish official, November 2023.
54. WhatsApp interview with a Turkish official, February 2023.
55. Jean-Francois Bayart, "Le concept de situation thermidorienne: régimes néo-révolutionnaires et libéralisation économique", *Centre d'Etudes et de Recherches Internationales, Questions de recherche*, no 24, March 2008.
56. An expert from Turkey rightly pointed out that economic factors also played a role in the northern push. He emphasised that, "In addition to the political ambitions, economics is key: their problem from that perspective is the Hamran-Ghazawiyya trade line. There are too many intermediaries along the line, and Shamiyya is taking $750,000 per month just to allow oil from SDF areas to reach Idlib. Securing the supply lines is an important factor in al-Sharaa's desire to push north. For that, he needs fewer intermediaries and more 'cooperation,' as they say. They told us they want more 'cooperation' with the factions."
57. One of al-Sharaa's close associates said, "'The Alawites are the most ready community for the revolution. They placed all their bets on Bashar al-Assad, who gave them nothing,'" as reported in HTS executive in October 2022.
58. Interview, Idlib, 2022.
59. Communiqué dated April 29 and published on his Telegram account: https://t.me/c/1535549123/4267.

9. THE 2024 IDLIB ARAB SPRING

1. Figures from Turkish observers closely following the situation in Idlib. Interview, Istanbul, July 2024. The HTS security services had a team that kept accounts of the demonstrations. According to them, the largest demonstration mobilised 3,000 men (interviews, Idlib, June 2024). According to HTS, the peak was reached on March 15 during the celebration of the revolution, with 10,000 people throughout the area controlled by HTS. Interview with an HTS executive, Idlib, June 2024.
2. WhatsApp interviews with demonstrators, April 2024.
3. WhatsApp interview, April 2024.
4. Interviews, residents in informal camps, Idlib, June 2023.
5. Bronislaw Baczko. *Comment sortir de la Terreur. Thermidor et la révolution*, Paris, Gallimard, 1989.
6. Interview, Idlib, June 2024.
7. Whatsapp call with one of the leaders of the *hirak*, April 2024.
8. Interview, well-informed Turkish researcher, Ankara, February 2024.
9. WhatsApp interview with one of the leaders of *hirak*, May 2024.
10. Ibid.
11. Ibid.
12. Local community leaders, interview, Istanbul, May 2024.
13. Interview with one of Ahma al-Sharaa's advisors, Idlib, June 2024.
14. In mobilisation hotspots such as Binish and Jisr, HTS encircled the area to restrict access, prevented known militants from entering and avoided solidarity dynamics. HTS also pressured the protestors in the checkpoints, where occasional beatings took place.
15. HTS undertook to release detainees without clear charges (releases have taken place, with over 130 people arrested under the security cell released—HTS executive, June 2024), suspended investigators in proven cases of torture, and agreed in principle to visits to General Security detention centres by independent observers. Details of these commitments can be found in a press release from Abd al-Rahim Atun, available on Telegram: https://t.me/abomuhammad2022/1600.
16. Some taxes have been abolished, particularly those affecting investors. For example, in Dana, permit fees for constructing malls—which could reach up to $70,000—have been eliminated. Taxes on private residential construction have been reduced by 90%, along with many other taxes previously owed to local councils.
17. Interview, Idlib, June 2024.
18. Ibid.
19. Ibid.
20. Ibid.
21. Interview with one of the movement's cadres in Jisr al-Shughur, WhatsApp, June 2024.
22. Interview, Idlib, June 2024.
23. Ibid.
24. Interview, Istanbul, March 2024.
25. Notably on April 19, 2024, when clashes between security guards and

demonstrators in Idlib resulted in a few minor injuries (WhatsApp interviews with *hirak* activists, May 2024).

26. For example, seventeen arrests were made in Jisr al-Shughur, one of the hottest spots in the *hirak* and one of the most sensitive because of the presence of radical groups like Jund al-Aqsa in some of the demonstrations (interviews with Jisr al-Shughur activists, WhatsApp, June 2024).
27. We owe this term to Olivier Filleule who defines it as "a professional ethos as well as the worldviews that are associated with it" (WhatsApp exchange, 2024).
28. Interview, HCE, Idlib, June 2024; WhatsApp interviews with independent activists based in Turkey and Idlib, July 2024.
29. Interview, Idlib, June 2024.
30. Thus, he stated: "The law says all Syrians, men or women. Legally, we do not exclude anyone. Now, we leave it to society to decide who they want as candidates." Interview with Esam al-Khleif, Idlib, June 2024.
31. Interview with a member of the HCE, Idlib, June 2024.
32. https://t.me/fromidlib/32164
33. https://t.me/fromidlib/32187
34. https://t.me/c/1295115437/32201
35. Interview, Idlib, June 2024.
36. Interview with Ahmad al-Sharaa, Idlib, June 2024.
37. WhatsApp interview with Jean-Noel Ferrié, August 2024.
38. It is the mobilisation of the brothers and families of some of the tortured militants that will explain why towns like Binish will be hotspots of the *hirak*.
39. This did not prevent them from adopting maximalist positions, some of them refusing to enter into dialogue with the book's authors, who were considered too close to the movement's leadership. Interviews with relatives of former Salvation Government cadres who had gone into dissidence, Istanbul, March 2024.
40. Unlike the Autonomous Administration set up by the PYD in the Northeast, the Salvation Government has never been the site of any utopian projections for HTS leadership.
41. The Western mainstream media have thus internalised the notion of *taqiyya*, giving an Orientalist flavor to the old anthem of doublespeak in which Islamism is said to be a master. See, for example: https://youtu.be/uS2xFbSBPk4?feature=shared
42. Pierre Serna. L'extrême centre: un poison français. Éditions Champ Vallon, Paris, 2019.
43. Yasser al Sayyed, Reihanli, August 2022.
44. https://orientxxi.info/magazine/syrie-ahmed-al-charaa-un-jeu-d-equilibre-pour-le-pouvoir-d-un-seul-homme,8093.

10. RESPECT THE MARTYRS BUT DON'T KILL THE MARKET!

1. For a good summary in English, see: https://english.enabbaladi.net/archives/2024/01/enab-baladi-publishes-details-from-idlibs-public-morality-draft-law
2. Multiple interviews with international actors.
3. Interviews, European diplomats, Paris, Berlin, February 2024.
4. WhatsApp interviews and discussions, Paris, Geneva, Berlin, February 2024.
5. If the movement sees this law as the legal translation of cultural norms stemming

from social conservatism, it is significantly hardening these codes. While the imposition of the hijab, for example, is a matter of consensus, the ban on music or gender mixing in the workplace are socially contested values and cannot be considered a matter of consensus within society. HTS, like most Islamist movements, (deliberately) confuses Islamic norms (as they define them) with social conservatism. For more details on this last point, see: Jean-Noël Ferrié. *Le régime de la civilité en* Égypte. *Public et réislamisation*. Paris, Presses du CNRS, 2004.

6. WhatsApp interviews with activists, lawyers, journalists and local notables, January–February 2024.
7. WhatsApp interview, February 2024.
8. For an overview of the various experiments in the morality police: https://www.syria.tv/تحرير-الشام-تنهي-عمل-جهاز-الفلاح-في-إدلب-وتستحدث-شرطة-أخلاقية.
9. Testimony of the sister of a woman victim of harassment. WhatsApp interview, February 2024.
10. WhatsApp interviews with feminist activists, shopkeepers, Idlib urban notabilities, revolutionary activists, February 2024.
11. WhatsApp interview with a doctor in Idlib, February 2024.
12. WhatsApp interview with a female activist, Idlib, February 2024.
13. WhatsApp interview with one of Idlib's family council members, February 2024.
14. Problematic cases have reportedly occurred: harassment of female students leaving university, blackmail of young women for nude photos. Interviews with urban notables and former police officers, February 2024.
15. He lost his sight in 2021 after he was attacked by Islamic State.
16. WhatsApp interview with a female activist, February 2024.
17. Interview, HTS employee, Istanbul, February 2024.
18. Ibid.
19. We define public space here as a space that is not governed by family or peer group norms and control. It is a space of geographical and sometimes gendered diversity, and of social interaction potentially not governed by the inter-knowledge of the village or neighborhood. Third, it is a space for leisure.
20. Observations during the battle of Wadi Deif, Idlib province. 2012-2013.
21. WhatsApp interviews with users of these malls, February 2024.
22. WhatsApp interviews with local activists and businessmen, February 2024.
23. Personal observations, Idlib, June 2023.
24. For example, a lawyer opposed to HTS (he is currently in prison for belonging to Hizb al-Tahrir) but steeped in "wartime conservatism", inveighs against HTS for not coming to the aid of the commando who left five martyrs a few hours earlier and who celebrated the inauguration of the mall: https://x.com/ibrahem_maaz/status/1733543174172197145?s=46&t=bAIimr5HX1D9yp96T8WXpA
25. WhatsApp interview, February 2024.
26. Interview with the university dean, February 2023.
27. https://eofjustice.substack.com/p/brouhaha-at-the-mall-the-study-of.
28. https://syria.news/c96937a9-08122312_m.html
29. This can be seen in these videos of commercial jubilation: https://x.com/khaleedalkhteb/status/1733046700778938536?s=46&t=bAIimr5HX 1D9yp96T8WXpA; https://youtube.com/shorts/CFO-znVnsvo?si=UbP9_HN8Z9cRLDGX

30. https://x.com/khaleedalkhteb/status/1734583267641237695?t=7cKp7Uy0MEpQvjBn8ohRog&s=08
31. Interview with an HTS executive, Istanbul, February 2024.
32. https://x.com/md2020k/status/1733635089282547971?t=jZjLwcLM1p6psGQecROUKw&s=08
33. https://www.syria.tv/مول-تجاري-يشغل-الرأي-العام-في-إدلب-هجوم-مسلح-بزعم-الاختلاط-والموسيقا-فيديو.
34. The expression "merchants of blood", *tujjar al-damm*, is poorly chosen here by the blind preacher. It conjures up the idea of war profiteers enriching themselves through war. With the al-Hamra mall, however, exactly the opposite is true: local merchants who position themselves outside the space of war and the moral order that the conservatism of war seeks to associate with it.
35. https://www.syria.tv/مول-تجاري-يشغل-الرأي-العام-في-إدلب-هجوم-مسلح-بزعم-الاختلاط-والموسيقا-فيديو.
36. In a minor way, this "war conservatism" can also be found among the Kurds in northeast Syria where, in 2018, an attempt to set up a beauty contest aroused the ire of part of the movement's leadership, invoking respect for the memory of the martyrs to stop the ceremony (interviews, Qamichli, November 2021). The same wartime conservatism structured the polarisation, during the 2014–18 war, between soldiers at the front and those in the rear, with the former accusing the latter of cheating on them with their wives while alcohol flowed freely.
37. The preaching of shaykh Melhem Khawam, better known as Abu al-Waqid al'Shami, a shaykh from the city of Hama known for his Salafi leanings, registered as a mosque imam with the Ministry of Religious Affairs but not affiliated to HTS, aptly reflects this wartime conservatism in its Salafi version: https://x.com/D1MHMOF4KPr53P9/status/1733427005780115765?t=Pi7whoyOWYkrbvxA9KTzKQ&s=08
38. https://youtu.be/D15nKlyenCs?si=tW1w_FX8B0h-ACK1
39. On a broader approach on this balancing act in the Islamic world, see Patrick Haenni. *L'islam de marché. L'autre révolution conservatrice*. Paris, Le Seuil, 2005.
40. Interviews with European diplomats and UN officials, Geneva, Paris, Berlin, February 2024.
41. WhatsApp interviews with researchers and former mall visitors in Kabul, February 2024.
42. The way in which Ahmad al-Sharaa backtracked in February 2024, apologising for a wave of purges that was too massive in his eyes, is just one of many examples, such as the cancellation of the 2020 olive oil production tax. The reluctance to repress protest demonstrations in no way prevents human rights abuses in prisons, as the latest purges have also clearly shown.
43. The Disneyland restaurant and shisha park is regularly visited by some of the movement's executives (authors' observations, 2020–24).
44. For more details on this episode, see Bernard Botiveau's excellent analysis: « Islamiser le droit? L'exemple égyptien », *Monde Arabe*, 1989/4 (no 126), pp. 12–13.
45. https://tariqramadan.com/appel-international-a-un-moratoire-sur-les-chatiments-corporels-la-lapidation-et-la-peine-de-mort-dans-le-monde-musulman/
46. Interview, Istanbul, February 2024.

47. Olivier Roy. *Holy Ignorance: When Religion and Culture Part Ways*, London, Hurst, 2010.
48. On this point, see Olivier Roy's classic *L'échec de l'islam politique*, Paris: Seuil, 1994. There are a few Sunni Islamist movements led by clerics, such as the Taliban, but they are the exception rather than the rule.
49. Interview with a movement executive, Istanbul, February 2024.
50. The term is used by some of the movement's leaders to describe preachers and media operators prone to one-upmanship on issues of moral and religious conservatism. Interview with a group of the movement's religious leaders, Idlib, March 2021.
51. Interview, Istanbul, February 2024.
52. If by hardliners we mean the *sharaiyeen of* HTS, then we have to admit that, while they were ardent defenders, they were not the initiators of this law.
53. Aurélie Collas, "Au Maroc, la réforme annoncée du code de la famille suscite l'espoir des défenseurs des droits des femmes", *Le Monde,* 23 October 2023.
54. Ghassan Salame. *Democracy without Democrats?: Renewal of Politics in the Muslim World.* I. B. Tauris, 1994.

11. HTS'S SILENT REVOLUTION

1. Testimonies from Druze notables, WhatsApp interview, August 2022.
2. WhatsApp interview with a Druze leader from Jebel Samaq, July 2022.
3. Interviews with TIP leaders, June 2021, February 2022. WhatsApp interviews with Druze notables from various villages in Jebel al-Samaq, August–September 2022.
4. Interview, Idlib, August 2022.
5. Interviews, Istanbul, August 2022.
6. Interview.
7. Interviews with security sources, Idlib and European capitals, 2022.
8. Pierre Bourdieu, "Effet de champ et effet de corps", *Actes de la recherche en sciences sociales*. Vol. 59, September 1985, Stratégies de reproduction-2, p. 73.
9. For some background, see https://www.middleeasteye.net/news/syria-north-druze-murder-uyghur-militants-suspicion
10. Private correspondence exchanged via WhatsApp messages with a prominent Druze community leader, August 2022.
11. Interviews with several TIP commanders, 2020–24.
12. Field observations, Idlib, Aleppo, 2012–13.
13. Ibid.
14. It is worth noting that al-Jazeera, the first international media outlet to interview Ahmad al-Sharaa, has not done so for over six years.
15. This is PBS Frontline. Transcripts of the various interviews in the film, as well as the film itself, are available online: https://www.pbs.org/wgbh/frontline/interview-collection/the-Jihadi
16. https://www.france24.com/en/video/20230511-inside-idlib-syria-s-last-rebel-held-enclave
17. Interviews, Idlib, March 2021.
18. Interview, Istanbul, June 2023.

19. Interview with Abu Qatada al-Filistini, Amman, July 2022.
20. Interview, Idlib, January 2020.
21. Interviews with Salvation Government executives, January 2020.
22. Written exchange, April 2020.
23. François Furet. *Interpreting the French Revolution*. Cambridge University Press, 1981, pp. 116, 123–4.
24. Interview with Ahmad al-Sharaa, Idlib, January 2020.
25. Interview, Idlib, July 2020.
26. Interview, Idlib, December 2020.
27. Interview, Idlib, May 2019.
28. Interview, Idlib, July 2020.
29. Interview with Ahmad al-Sharaa, Idlib, January 2020.
30. He said, "How can we plan in the long term and when we don't know who will hold these territories in a few months from now?" Iinterview, January 2020.
31. This careful balance was explicit in Abd al-Rahim Atun's public communiqué after meeting us in January 2020: Aymeen Jawad Al-Tamimi, "Hay'at Tahrir al-Sham's Abd al-Rahim Atun on Meeting Western Analysts," *Pundicity*, 10 March 2020, https://bit.ly/2K4E5Z3
32. Interview, Idlib, January 2020.
33. Interview, Idlib, June 2019.
34. Video dated 29 April 2019. Available at: https://bit.ly/3926Tdx
35. Ahrar al-Sham played a leading role attempting to unite Islamist insurgents. Jabhat al-Nusra allies with the group through local governance structures, as in Aleppo, and military operations rooms like Jaysh al-Fath.

12. IDEOLOGICAL RECENTRING IN AN AGE OF ILLIBERALISM

1. For a more in-depth analysis of this point, see: Olivier Roy. *The Failure of Political Islam*. Translated by Carol Volk. Cambridge, MA: Harvard University Press, 1994.
2. Thus, this close associate of al-Sharaa insisted that: "HTS is, of course, driven by a strategic objective of liberation. But since 2020, the calculations have become more complex due to the responsibilities we bear in governing the population. This comes at a cost. We are not going to blindly launch into a new battle without considering the potential impact on the population." Interview, Idlib, June 2024.
3. Howard S. Becker. *Outsiders: Studies in the Sociology of Deviance*. New York: The Free Press, 1963.
4. It should be noted that the definition of the centre is, of course, deeply political, subject to change, and generally the product of a common sense developed through a consensus among cultural and media elites.
5. To this end, Ahmad al-Sharaa was keen to be accompanied, during his public announcement of delinking, by Al-Qaeda's envoy to Syria at the time, Abu Faraj al-Masri. Interview, al-Sharaa, Idlib, January 2021.
6. On this issue see Olivier Roy, "La montée des populismes n'est pas corrélée à une remontée des valeurs traditionnelles dans la société", *Le Monde*, 29 October 2023.
7. Olivier Roy, ibid.
8. Bayart, Adelkhah, & Roy. *Thermidor en Iran*. Paris: Éditions complexe, 1993.
9. Interview, Nouakchott, 2022.

10. Zaki Laïdi. *Le temps Mondial*. Paris, Les Presses de Sciences Po, 2000.

EPILOGUE

1. https://x.com/mousaalomar/status/1892321641549484361?s=48&t=bAIimr5HX1D9yp96T8WXpA, quoted in: Charles Lister, *The New Umayyads. Syria's leaders is turning nostalgia into strategy*. https://www.syriaintransition.com/thenewumayyads
2. See also Laila Alrefaai, Restructuring Faith: The Transformation of the Religious Domain in Postwar Syria in al-Jabassini, Abdullah & Daher, Joseph, Syria: State, Society and Economy in the Shadow of the War (forthcoming).
3. For more details, see the analysis by Thomas Pierret : "Le nouveau pouvoir syrien face au champ religieux, ou les limites d'une stratégie hégémonique". *Bulletin de l'Observatoire international du religieux* 5, April 2025.
4. Discussion with Abd al-Rahim Atun, Damascus, April 2025.
5. Interviews with a range of clerics affiliated to the University of Damascus, HTS, and other factions, Damascus, 2025.
6. Interview, Damascus, 2025.
7. Interview, Damascus, January 2025.
8. Fieldwork observations, Homs, Latakieh, Tartous, February, March, April 2025.
9. Fieldwork observations, Deraa, Suweida, April 2025.

INDEX

Abd al-Huzafa al-Shami Secondary School of Shariʿa, 86
Abd al-Wahhab, Muhammad bin, 116, 138, 255, 290
Abu al-Khayr Shukri, 285–6, 289
Abu Ghraib prison, 20
Abu Hamoud, Khalaf, 142
Abu Hamud, shaykh Khalaf, 144
Abu Hanifa, Imam, 134
Abu Mundhar, 54
Abu Nur Institute, 287
Abu Qasra, Murhaf, 1, 51, 53, 56, 57, 84, 281
Abu Sib (Abu Ali al-Anbari), 22–3
al-Adhari, Abu Hanifa, 66
Administration of Military Operations, 281
al-Adnani, Abu Muhammad, 21, 23
AfD, 273
Afghanistan war, 28
Afghanistan, 65, 117
Afrin, 189, 192
Ahl al-Dhimma, 170
Ahl al-Kitab (People of the Book), 170, 284
al-Ahmad, Bassam, 183
Ahrar al-Sham, 24, 25, 27, 33–4, 37, 38, 39, 40, 41, 42–3, 45, 46, 47, 108, 162, 190, 202, 244, 260, 291
    HTS and, confrontation between, 48–50
    military forces, transforming, 54
    neutralisation of, 56
Ahrar al-Sharqiyya, 192
AKP (Turkey), 265
Al Saud family, 116, 137
Alawis, 20, 25–6
Alawites, 118, 121, 158, 164, 291, 294
Al-Bab, 191, 221
al-Dana, 60
Aleppo, 25, 50, 60, 78, 143, 158, 251, 281
    as centre of Sufi brotherhoods, 142
    courts, 40
    demonstrations in the north, 198
    Druzes conversions to Islam, 159
    fall of, 1, 43
    foreign fighters, 69
al-ghulu, 111, 238
Al-Hamra Mall, 225, 227–8
al-Jabhat al-Shamiyya, 187–8, 189, 190–1, 195

INDEX

al-Jamiliyya camp, 64–5
al-Khasnawiyya School, 89
Alloush, Shaykh Yassine, 282, 283
al-Mu'tasim, 190
al-Qaeda, 3, 5, 17, 59, 99, 260–1, 266, 291
    Al-Adnani letter to, 21
    al-Baghdadi complaint, 22–3
    Arab uprisings, benefited from, 22
    establishment of, 117
    ideological ties, 97–100
    and Jabhat al-Nusra, 12, 17, 18, 34–5, 37, 39, 43–5, 46, 100
    and Jabhat al-Nusra ideological views, 28–30
al-Shabaab, 266
Ansar al-Islam, 68
Ansar al-Tawheed, 56, 67
anti-Alawite mobilisations (March 2025), 292
Arab Spring (2011), 19–20
Arab Spring (2024). *See* Idlib Arab Spring (2024)
Arab Unified Code, 37–8
Ariha, 152
Ash'arism, 146
al-Assad, Bashar, 143
Astana Process, 77
Atarib, 60
Atun, Abd al-Rahim, 26–7, 30, 36, 40, 43–4, 64, 86, 101, 103, 104, 110–11, 112, 113, 120, 139, 256, 281, 285, 287
    codification of Shari'a, 125, 127, 130, 131
    on HTS normative project, 122–3
    on protests (2024), 204
    on Qalb Lozeh massacre (2015), 160
    stance on women's representation, 181
authoritarianism, 13–14, 154–5, 173
    attenuation of, 211–14
    ideological realignments and, 277–9
    relaxation of, 186–9
Ayrout, Anas, 123, 125
Azaz, 60, 190–1
Azzam, Abdullah, 98, 117

Baab al-Hawa, 27
Baath Party (Syria), 20, 95
Bab al-Hawa, 76, 174–5
al-Baghdadi, Abu Bakr, 22, 23, 32, 33
Bakour, Muhammad, 72
al-Banna, Hassan, 258
Barakat, Shaykh Abdallah, 142–3, 145
Bayart, Jean-François, 7, 193
al-Bazam, 'Abd al-Fattah, 287
Beit al-Karam, 226
bin Laden, Osama, 117
bin Unais, Saraya Abdullah, 62
Binish, 201, 202, 226
Biraktar, Samir, 289
Book of Healing, 147
Book of the Foundations of Faith (al-Wahhab), 118, 138, 255
Bourdieu, Pierre, 250
Bucca prison, 20

INDEX

Café Charisma, 226, 227
Caliphate, 38
Centre of Devotional Prosperity, 221–2
Christians, 157, 161, 170, 172, 245
    HTS contact with, 165–6
    population, 157–8
    reopening of a church in Idlib, 167
    restitution of properties, 168
Civil Administration Initiative, 72
Coalition of Opposition Forces, 178
Consultative Council of the Mujahideen, 27
The Covenant of Honor, 38–9
COVID-19 pandemic, 147, 225

Damascus, takeover of (2024), 71, 122, 130, 218, 219, 267, 281–82
    Friday sermons, 290
    new Fatwa Council, 285–6
    religious governance, 284–90
al-Darazi, Muhammad Ibn Isma'il, 159
Dawar al-Mihrab, 175
de-demonisation strategy, 12, 270, 272, 273, 274
Deir Ezzor, 60
deradicalisation, 3–4, 5, 6, 12, 14, 173, 243, 254, 296
    HTS's relocation, 212–13
    ideological reorientation, 274–5
    ideological training, complete overhaul of, 109–13
    political authoritarianism, decline of, 214
    as power politics, 213–17
    Shari'a, codification of, 124–9
development bureau, 186
dhikr gatherings, 148
al-Din Farfour, Husam, 287
al-Din, shaykh Mohi, 151, 153
Disneyland (Idlib), 226, 227
Drugeon, David, 35
Druze, 157, 166, 169, 172, 197, 245, 246, 294
    conversions to Islam, 159–60, 162–3
    dialogue with HTS, 167
    Druze couple, murder of, 250–1
    emigration, 158
    population, 158
    al-Julani's visit to the mountain villages, 168
    Qalb Lozeh massacre (2015), 160
    religious legitimacy, 170
    sanctuary in Lebanon, 161
    al-Sharaa visit to the Druze community, 163–5
Dugheim, Hassan, 145, 150

earthquake (2023), 192
Egypt, 4, 19, 117, 265
electoral law, 208–11
Ennahda, 265
European Union, 43
Europeans, 27, 33
excommunication (*takfir*), 119, 120, 123

INDEX

Faculty of Shari'a, 86, 90, 113, 118, 119–20, 121, 125, 138, 255, 274
al-Fadhli, Muhsin, 35
Fa-Ithibitu, 58
Fares, Raed, 187
al-Farghali, Abu al-Fath, 48–9, 107, 223, 228
al-Farghali, Abu Yahiyya, 118
Fa-Staqim kama Umirat, 49
al-Fath al-Mubin, 52–4, 84–5, 281
Fatwas and shari'a politics, 129–37
Faylaq al-Sham, 38, 50, 74, 202
al-Filistini, Abu Qatada, 98, 99, 102, 256, 257–8
fiqh [jurisprudence], 109–12, 134
Firqat al-Ghuraba, 67
Firqat al-Hamzat, 190
Foreign Terrorist organisation (FTO), 43
France, 7, 183
    National Rally, 270, 272–3, 274
Free Syrian Army (FSA), 24–5, 27, 35, 36, 45–6, 49, 74, 95, 174, 189, 252, 267, 271
French Revolution, 7, 266
Furet, Francois, 185, 255

General Security, 62, 167, 197, 198, 200, 205, 268, 293, 294
global jihadism, 97–103
GUD (Groupe Union Défense), 273
Gulf War I (1990), 116

al-Habanaka, Muhammad Hassan, 138
Haji Bakr, 32–3
al-Halabi, Abu Humama, 202
Hama, 1, 144
Hamas, 265, 277
al-Hamawi, Saleh, 21, 23–4, 29, 30–1, 41
Harakat Sham al-Islam, 69
Harem, 73
Harid al-Mu'mineen, 56
Hassan Sufan, 54
Hassouns, 142
Hayat Tahrir al-Sham (HTS)
    Aleppo, capture of, 1, 43
    confrontation with IS, 121, 122
    creation of, 18, 46, 48
    dominance over Ahrar al-Sham and its allies, 50–3
    engagement with Sufis, 13
    foreign fighters, strict constraints on, 66–9
    and Hurras al-Din relationship, 55–8
    ideological shift, 2–4
    initial engagement, bias, 10
    "integrated" approach to the revolution, 101
    military engagements (2022–23), 267
    military institutionalisation, 53
    openness toward Christians and Druze, 154
    opponents of, 11
    post-2019 doctrine, 284
    Russian airstrikes on HTS prison (Idlib), 61
    Russian-Turkish truce (2020) acceptance, 55, 57, 225
    "second stratum", 95–6

INDEX

Shariʻa council, 108, 120
tactical adjustments, 243–8
targeting mainstream groups, 54–5
territorialisation, 71–7, 244
Thermidorian dynamics, 6–9, 13, 173–4, 193
Thermidorian turn, 258–63, 284–90
transformation as irrevocable, 5
transformation as oriented, 5
transformation as political action, 4–5
transformation as stable, 6
wave of protests against (2024), 13
West and Turkey, diplomatic positioning with, 191
See also HTS's revolutionary realignment
Hazm movement, 39–40
Hezbollah, 26
High Council of Fatwa, 118, 129–34, 136
High Council of the Judiciary, 220
High Elections Committee, 208–10
hirak, 198, 201–2, 203–6
Hizb al-Tahrir, 200, 202, 203, 269
Homs, 1, 25, 158, 281, 287, 294
HTS. *See* Hayat Tahrir al-Sham (HTS)
HTS's revolutionary realignment against factions of FSA, 189
contacts with the revolutionary milieu, 174, 175–7
HTS's relationship with Turkey, 191–3
northern expansion, 187–95
policy towards the revolutionary milieu, 183–4
recognition of the revolutionary symbols, 174, 177
relaxation of authoritarianism, 186–9
security pressure on the revolutionaries, 176–7
shifting attitudes towards the ideological centre, 182–7
warlordism, 187–95
women's empowerment, 177–82
young revolutionaries, 184–5
Human Rights Watch, 183
Hurras al-Din, 55, 56, 57–8, 62, 66, 98, 105, 121, 166, 261, 270
Hussein, Husam Hajj, 125

Ibn Taymiyya, 119, 161, 290
Identity and Democracy (ID) group, 272–3
ideological realignments, lessons on, 270–9
Idlib Arab Spring (2024), 197–218, 268, 272
authoritarianism, attenuation of, 211–14
consultative council, creation of, 204
electoral law, 208–11
extreme centre regime, 216–18

323

INDEX

factional interests, 202–3, 204
General Security detention centres, 200
HTS and the village mayor syndrome, 211–14
HTS's crackdown, 199–201
HTS's multilayered response to the *hirak*, 198, 201–2, 203–6
HTS's lenient authoritarianism, 214, 198–9, 206–11, 216
internal divisions and competing agendas, 202
legacy of, 211, 215
people's Thermidorian's fatigue and its instrumentalisations, 199–203
"police understanding", 207–8
"Reform Initiative", 203
and the return of the people, 197–9
revolutionary ranks, divided, 201
security sector, restructuring, 205
tribal revolts, 197–8
Idlib Book Fair, 151
Idlib Chamber of Commerce, 72, 73
Idlib Corniche, 227
Idlib Family Council, 222
Idlib, 3, 14–15, 60, 215
'authoritarianism of the extreme centre' in, 217–18
administration of the liberated areas, 94–6
census and house-numbering initiative, 63

elites of, 72
Jaysh al-Fath take-over of, 162
as the "Little Azhar", 142
local environment, 5, 6
military structure, 53
mosques, 88
policing morality in, 13
protest (Feb 2024), 198
religious minorities, 158
reopening of a church in, 167
Salafi teachings, 117–18
as a Thermidorian situation, 6–9
Turkey's military presence in, 55, 71, 77–85
See also public sphere
In the Shadow of the Tree of Jihad (Al-Shami), 30
inertia of the social, 5, 8, 51, 141, 275, 284
Institute of Imam al-Nawawi, 86, 89, 147–8
institutionalisation, 85–7
International Academy of Islamic Jurisprudence, 135
Iran, 2, 4, 20, 31, 44, 136, 248, 262, 263, 276, 284
Iraq war (2003), 20, 21, 22, 28
Islamic Creed, The, 138
Islamic Front, 38, 40, 60
Islamic Secondary School, 138
Islamic State (ISI/ISIS/IS), 3, 12, 17, 18–19, 21, 26, 32, 35–6, 98, 105, 145, 251, 265–6, 290–1
foreign fighters recruitment, 32–3
governance strategies, 41

324

INDEX

HTS and armed oppositions war against, 60–5
international threat by, 38
IS militants, expulsion, 61
Jabhat al-Nusra/al-Sharaa and, 20–4
leaders in Abu Ghraib and Bucca prisons, 20
Mosul, capture of, 1
recruitment strategy, 28
Strategic Plan, 22
in the Yaqubia village, 158
Israel, 2, 117, 262, 293–4
ISWAP, 265–6
Italian League, 273

Jabal al-Druze, 158
Jabal al-Sammaq, 160
Jabal al-Zawiya, 74
raids, 143
Jabhat al-Nusra, 1, 8, 9, 11, 17–46, 99, 149, 160, 249
accommodating strategy, 26, 36
Ahrar al-Sham support, 33–4
Ahrar al-Sham, competition between, 42
al-Qaeda and, 12, 17, 18, 39, 43–5, 46
Al-Qaeda support, 34–5, 37
al-Sharaa and ISI, 20–4
autonomy, 19, 32
Dar al-Qada (court), 41
as dominant force, 47
embraced jihadi Salafism, 17
founding moment, 19
Friday protests (2013), 26
as a "front of support", 36
governance competition with IS, 41
governance efforts, 40–1, 71
ideological training, 109
imposition of Islamic law, advocated, 26
individuals linked to al-Qaeda's leadership, 99
interactions with Islamic State in Iraq (ISI), 17, 18–19
internal diversity, 31–2
international community stance against, 39
international threat by ISIS, 38
joint operations, 40
lectures for the training camps, 30
local strategy, 30
locals views on, 25
modus operandi, 24, 25
operations in Iraq, 20, 21, 22, 25
recruitment, 24–5
religious and sectarian narrative, 25–6
Salafism, 117, 118
social services, 41–2
split with al-Qaeda, 43–4, 100
split with ISIS, 32–3
strategic and selective approach, 40
strategic differences with ISI, 23
Syrian conflict and foreign fighters, 27–8
teachings of the religious training camps, 30–1
transnationalism, 99

INDEX

United Nations sanctions, 39
  See also Hayat Tahrir al-Sham
    (HTS); al-Sharaa, Ahmad
Jabhat Fath al-Sham (JFS), 43, 44,
    47, 100
Jama'at Zayd, 286, 287
Jaramana, 294
al-Jarrah, Abu Ubaida ibn, 135
Jaysh al-Ahrar, 49, 171, 200–1
Jaysh al-Fath, 42, 162
Jaysh al-Islam, 40, 49, 188, 189,
    190, 191, 286, 288
Jaysh al-Muhajirin wal-Ansar, 69
Jaysh al-Mujahideen alliance, 60
Jebel al-Samaq, 158, 166–7,
    168–9
Jendiris, 187
Jeneid, Hamoud, 187
jihadism, 3, 12–13, 97–113
  administration of the liberated
    areas, 94–6
  deradicalisation policy, 3–4,
    5–6, 11, 12, 109–13
  global jihad, severing the
    ideological ties with,
    98–103
  internal hardliners,
    marginalising (HTS), 105–9
  local emirs and militant clerics
    (*shari'in*), replacing, 91–4
  relocalisation, 3, 5, 103–4
Jisr al-Shughur, 59, 61, 246, 251
Journal of Judicial Rulings, 126
Judicial Training Institute, 118
Jumblatt, Walid, 161, 162
Jund al-Aqsa, 60, 69
Jund Allah, 66
Junud al-Sham, 66

Kafr Takharim, 74
Kaftin, 162, 169
Katiba al-Tawhid wal-Jihad, 69
Katiba Imam al-Bukhari, 69
Kayali, Sarah, 183
Khatab, Anas, 2, 281
al-Khatib, Khaled, 228
Khawam, Melhem, 223
Khaznawiyya, 147
al-Khleif, Essam, 208–9
Khmer Rouge, 265
Khorasan group, 35
Kili village, 184
Kishkich, Farouq, 72
Kurds, 158, 192, 278
Kuwait, 116

labor union law, 133
Latakia, 158, 288
Le Pen, Jean-Marie, 271, 272, 276
League of Ulema, 152
al-Libi, Atiyah Abd al-Rahman, 28
Libya, 4, 19
Liwa Abu al-'Alamein, 144

Maarat al-Nu'man, 73–4, 87, 228
Maaret Ikhwan, 161
al-Mahdi, Abderazzaq, 223, 228
Makers of Change, 178–9
al-Maqdisi, Abu Muhammad,
    29, 33–4, 39, 44–5, 55–6,
    98–102, 109
al-Masri, Abu 'Abd al-Karim, 55
al-Masri, Abu Farraj, 31, 46, 99
al-Masri, Abu Shu'ib, 106, 120,
    202
al-Masri, Abu Yaqthan, 106, 120
al-Masri, Abul-Khayr, 31, 46, 99

INDEX

al-Masri, Mohand, 229
al-Mauritani, Abu Hafs, 98, 278
Meloni, Giorgia, 275
Ministry of Agriculture, 168, 181
Ministry of Awqaf, 127, 152–3
Ministry of Education, 76, 90, 118, 181, 200
Ministry of Justice, 73, 74, 125, 128
Ministry of Municipalities, 205
Ministry of Religious Affairs, 88–9, 152, 223, 228, 289
Ministry of the Economy, 73
Mithaq: An Introduction to the Jurisprudence of the Pillars of Faith (Al-Rukf), 110, 138
Moral Apparatus, 221
moral police (*hisba*), 14, 138, 182, 186, 221–2, 224, 234, 238–9, 268, 277, 291, 293, 295
Morsi, Muhammad, 29
Muhammad bin Salman (MBS), 173, 199
al-Muhaysani, Abdallah, 107–8
murids, 141, 143, 146
Muslim Brotherhood, 117, 143, 233, 247, 254, 265, 266, 287

Na'iss, Mujahid, 72
Najjar, Mohand, 228
al-Nasr, Sanafi, 35
Nasrallah, Hassan, 282
National Front for Liberation, 50
NGOs (non-governmental organisations), 42, 65, 76, 96, 133–4, 178, 179–80, 226, 273, 277
Nur al-Din al-Zinki, 49, 108

al-'Omar, Abu 'Ammar, 45
al-Omar, Musa, 283
Omsen, Omar, 67
Organisation of Islamic Cooperation, 135
Ottoman Empire, 126, 142

Padnos, Theo, 27
populism, 234, 235–6, 237, 269
Preaching Bureaus, 221
Progressive Socialist Party, 162
Prophet's birthday, celebration of, 143, 147
public sphere, 219–41
    consumerist public sphere, emergence of, 223–5
    demands for public space regulation, 234–7
    doctrinal centrism, 237–41
    hedonism, 227–9
    HTS and its transactional morality management, 231–34
    HTS's balancing act, 230–1
    moral coalition, 220–2
    moral police (*hisba*), 138, 182, 221, 222, 239
    morality law, failure to repeal, 239–40
    public morality bill, 228–9
    public morality law, 221–2, 266, 267
    public morality law, ratified, 220–1, 223
    religious policing, 219–20
    "war conservatism", 227–8
purification of doctrine, 138

INDEX

Qadam, 288
Qadiriyya-Naqshbandiyya, 143, 147
al-Qahtani, Abu Maria, 27, 29, 39, 83, 195, 200, 236, 247, 250
Qalb Lozeh massacre (2015), 160
Qalb Lozeh, 160, 161, 163, 165
Qardash, Abdullah, 63
Qasem, Osama, 108
Qassem, Abd al-Salam, 127–8
Qatar, 42, 252
quburiyyun, 145

"radical heretics" (*khawarij*), 119
Rahmoun, Omar, 144
Ramadan, 130, 138, 148, 149
Ramadan, Tariq, 234
Raqqa, 59, 60
religious creed (*'aqida*), 29, 86, 109–10, 115–16, 119
Religious Guidance Council, 148
religious minorities, 10, 13, 25, 157–72
    HTS relations with Christian and Druze, 157
    HTS's discourse and identity, 170–1
    HTS's secularisation stance, 170–2
    ISIS pressure and conversions, 158–9
    minority politics, 170–2
    mosque preachers, 169
    Qalb Lozeh massacre (2015), 163
    reopening of a church in Idlib, 167
    restitution of properties, 166, 168
    sectarian Sunni radicalism, 157–63
    al-Sharaa visit to the Druze community, 163–5
relocalisation, 3, 5, 103–5, 141–2, 155, 212–13, 244, 251, 253–4, 259, 261, 267, 284
retraditionalisation, 253–4, 255
revenge of society, 5, 8, 259, 260, 275, 276
Revival of the Religious Sciences (al-Ghazali), 147
Rhodes, Ben, 39
al-Rifa'i, Saria, 285
al-Rifa'I, Usama, 285
Rifa'iyya, 143, 147
Riker, William, 275
Al-Rukf, Abdullah Hamad, 110
Russia, 4, 16, 18, 48, 51, 248, 262
    airstrikes on HTS prison (Idlib), 61
Russian-Turkish agreement (2020), 55, 57, 81–2, 83–4, 225, 245

Sabunji, Shaykh Rabeh, 159
al-Sadat, Anwar, 233, 237
al-Sadiq, Saraya Abu Bakr, 62
Salafi-jihadi cultural symbols, 292
Salafism, 3, 13, 17, 29, 30, 115–39, 255, 256–7, 286–9
    core principles, taming, 117–22
    Fatwas and shari'a politics, 129–37
    HTS's break from, 137–9

INDEX

Islamisation of society, abandoning (HTS), 122–4
punishments, 137–8
Shari'a, codification of, 124–9
struggle for purity over tradition, 115–17
Salems, 142
Salvation Government
centralised structure under, 71–7
HTS approach to other religious institutions, 87–91
inclusion of the urban elite, 75–6
institutionalisation, as a containment of radicalism policy, 85–7
lifted pressure on public schools, 90
moral police (*hisba*), 138, 182, 221, 222, 239
Turkish strategic game, adjustment to, 77–85
Samaq, Taher, 72
Sami'a, Raefa, 180
al-Sandal, shaykh Muhammad, 143–4, 145, 146, 153
Sarayat al-Mujahideen, 20
Saudi Arabia, 40, 42, 116–17, 199, 252
schools of jurisprudence, 90, 103–4, 119, 128, 259–60
sectarian Sunni radicalism, 157–63
sectarianism, 23–4, 26
secularisation, 170–2
Serna, Pierre, 215

Shadhiliyya, 143
al-Shaibani, Asaad, 281
'Shami Salafism', 286
al-Shami, Abu Humam, 58, 59
al-Shami, Shaykh Nafia, 143
al-Sharaa, Ahmad, 1, 2, 7, 9, 18, 20, 28, 44, 45, 46, 57, 58, 64, 69, 79–80, 94, 120, 171, 187–8, 195, 198, 199, 209, 216–17, 258–9, 290–1
in Abu Ghraib and Bucca prisons, 20
al-Baghdadi's letters, 23–4
al-Jazeera interview, 26
Christian community visit, 165–6
on customs, 138
on dignity sit-in, 83
dismantling of the local blocs, 91–4
Druze community visit, 163–6
first major media appearance, 246
on foreign fighters, 67
HTS's crackdown, 200
inner circle, 10, 69, 85, 94, 111, 223, 236, 276
Iraqi insurgency, 20–1
Jabhat al-Nusra as the brainchild of, 20
letter from al-Adnani, 21
moral coalition, 223–4
moral policing, 221–2, 266
populism, 237
power in Damascus, 281
protests (2024), 202, 204–5, 207
public morality, 233, 234

INDEX

on Qardash, 63
revolutionary realignment, 174
split with ISIS, 31–2
strategic vision, 261–2, 263
his "Syria-first" policy, 34–5
See also Hayat Tahrir al-Sham (HTS); Jabhat al-Nusra
Shari'a Commission, 40
Shari'a politics, 119, 128–37
    codification of Shari'a, 124–9
Shasho, Ibrahim, 88, 223, 228–9
Shaykh Hussari Institute, 148
al-Shibani, As'ad, 2
al-Shishani, Abu Muslim, 66
al-Shishani, Abu Omar, 33
Shura Council, 131, 133, 175, 181, 205–6, 208–9, 220, 223
Sihiouni, Bassam, 72, 104
"Sit-in of Dignity", 82
Sochi Accords (2017), 77, 119
Spaces of Hope, 179
Specially Designated Global Terrorist (SDGT), 43
Student's Provision, The (al-Farghali), 118–19
Sufism Between the People of Hadith and the People of Fiqh, 151
Sufism, 3, 141–55
    'authoritarian normalisation', 155
    "excuse of ignorance'", 119
    as intuitive religiosity, 142–4
    HTS's local engagement, 141
    Jihadis, 144–5
    management of, 141, 155
    occultation of Sufism in Idlib, 144–6
    openness, 152–3
    resurgence of, 146–50
    return of Sufism and HTS's extreme centre, 154–5
    "Thermidorian bet", 141, 150–3
Sultan Murad, 190
Sultan Suleiman Shah Division, 190
Sunni populism, 282, 293
Sunni schools of jurisprudence, 103–4
Suqur al-Sham, 40, 49, 50, 74
al-Suri, Abu Firas, 31, 39, 42, 99
al-Suri, Abu Musab, 26
Suweida, 197
Syrian Democratic Forces (SDF), 80, 177
Syrian Islamic Council, 88
Syrian Liberation Front, 50
Syrian National Army, 80, 187, 291–2
Syrian Opposition Coalition, 11, 217
Syrian Revolutionaries Front (SRF), 39

Tajamu al-Shahba, 190
Tajamu' Ahrar al-Sufiyya, 144
al-Tali, Abu Malik, 288
Talib, Kheir Allah, 286
Taliban, 65, 230, 231–2, 236, 277, 283
Talibanisation, 221, 231
al-Tally, Abu Malik, 58
al-Tamimi, Aymenn Jawad, 45
Tanjara village assault, 57
"Tansiqiyyat al-Jihad", 58
Tha'irun, 190

INDEX

theological teaching circles, 88
Thermidorian dynamics, 6–9, 13, 173–4, 193
13th Division, 39
al-Tunisi, Abu Abd al-Rahman, 160
Tunisia, 19, 20
Turkey, 4, 27, 42, 45, 48, 109, 111, 187, 188, 244
    al-Fath al-Mubin, 52–4
    Russian-Turkish agreement (2020), 55, 57, 81–2, 83–4, 225, 245
    sanctuary strategy, 77–85
al-Turki, Abu Yusuf, 35
Turkish Ministry of Religious Affairs, 88
Turkistan Islamic Party (TIP), 50, 59, 65, 66, 168, 171, 251

Uighurs, 162, 166, 168
Umayyad-centred Sunni pride, 284
Union of Syrian Democrats, 185
United Nations (UN), 30, 39, 62, 111, 179, 221, 253, 277
United Nations Security Council, 47
United States (US), 18, 43, 80, 189
    intervention against the Taliban, 231
    invasion of Iraq (2003), 20
    Khorasan group, targeted, 35
University of Damascus, 90, 286
University of Idlib, 72, 90, 93, 110, 118, 123, 125
al-Uraydi, Sami, 29, 39, 45, 55, 59
al-Urduni, Abu al-Hussein, 69
al-Urduni, Abu Julaybib, 31, 99
al-Urduni, Abul-Qasam, 31, 99
Uyghur identity, 65
al-Uzbeki, Abu Salah, 58
Uzbeks, 66, 69, 162, 166, 168, 169

vanguardism, 96

"Wahhabism", 116
warlordism, 187–95
"Warning against Extremism", 103
White Helmets, 192
women's empowerment, 177–82

Yaqubia village, 158
Yazidi community, 21, 38

Zakat, 130
Zakour, Abu Ahmad, 236
al-Zawahiri, Ayman, 31, 32, 44, 45, 100, 108